THE POLISH CATHOLIC CHURCH UNDER GERMAN OCCUPATION

THE POLISH CATHOLIC CHURCH UNDER GERMAN OCCUPATION

The Reichsgau Wartheland, 1939–1945

Jonathan Huener

INDIANA UNIVERSITY PRESS

This book is a publication of

Indiana University Press
Office of Scholarly Publishing
Herman B Wells Library 350
1320 East 10th Street
Bloomington, Indiana 47405 USA

iupress.org

 The paper used in this publication meets the minimum requirements of the American National Standard for Information Sciences—Permanence of Paper for Printed Library Materials, ANSI Z39.48-1992.

Manufactured in the United States of America

Cataloging information is available from the Library of Congress.

ISBN 978-0-253-05402-9 (hardback)
ISBN 978-0-253-05404-3 (paperback)
ISBN 978-0-253-05403-6 (ebook)

First Printing 2021

CONTENTS

ACKNOWLEDGMENTS

THIS BOOK REFLECTS THE CONTRIBUTIONS AND EFFORTS OF many individuals and institutions in the United States, Poland, Germany, Israel, and the United Kingdom. Research over the years has been supported by two summer fellowships from the Deutsches Historisches Institut/Niemiecki Instytut Historyczny, Warsaw; by the College of Arts and Sciences Dean's Fund for Faculty Development at the University of Vermont; by a University of Vermont Department of History Nelson Grant; by the Humanities Center at the University of Vermont; and by a Career Enhancement Grant/Research Opportunities Grant from the Office of the Vice President for Research and Dean of Graduate Studies at the University of Vermont. The Carolyn and Leonard Miller Center for Holocaust Studies at the University of Vermont has also provided generous research support.

I am especially grateful to the many mentors, colleagues, students, and friends who have offered their support, critiques, and advice over the years. These include, at the University of Vermont, Adriana Borra and Andrew Buchanan; Anne Clark and Sean Field for their ongoing help with Latinisms, Latin, and church history; fellow historians and interlocutors Boğaç Ergene and Sean Stilwell for their encouragement, friendship, and willingness to discuss some of the most important things in life, and many unimportant things as well; and for his support and leadership of the University of Vermont's superb Department of History, Paul Deslandes. In that department, I have had the privilege of working with three outstanding historians of Nazi Germany and the Holocaust: Frank Nicosia, Susanna Schrafstetter, and Alan Steinweis. They have shaped this book and my thinking as a historian in countless ways, and I am honored to have them as colleagues.

A number of University of Vermont students—Sarah Doubleday, Raymond Huessey, Sara Krumminga, Ben Lindsay, and Kelly Morgan—have assisted in this project in a variety of ways. I am also grateful to Timber Wright for designing the maps in this book and to Kiara Day for her careful reading of the manuscript in its final stages.

I am indebted to many archivists, librarians, and colleagues in various research institutes, archives, libraries, and museums who have offered their service and assistance at various stages of this project. These include Father Michał Sołomieniuk of the Archiwum Archidiecezjalne w Gnieźnie; Stephan Lehnstaedt, Ruth Leiserowitz, Eduard Mühle, Miloš Řezník, and Grażyna Ślepowrońska at the Deutsches Historisches Institut/Niemiecki Instytut Historyczny, Warsaw; Giles Bennett and Andrea Löw at the Institut für Zeitgeschichte, Munich; Renata Szulc at the Instytut Pamięci Narodowej–Komisja Ścigania Zbrodni przeciwko Narodowi Polskiemu, Warsaw; Father Janusz Nowiński of the Instytut Historii Sztuki of the Uniwersytet Kardinała Stefana Wyszyńskiego, Warsaw; Tomasz Budnikowski, Iwona Bykowicz, Bogumił Rudawski, and Maria Rutowska at the Instytut Zachodni, Poznań; Anna Ziółkowska of the Muzeum Martyrologiczne w Żabikowie; Barbara Jarosz of the Muzeum Miasta Ostrowa Wielkopolskiego; Bartosz Stachowiak of the Muzeum Miasta Turku im. Józefa Mehoffera; Sebastian Pluta of the Muzeum Regionalne w Jarocinie; Krzysztof Stoliński of the Polish Underground Movement Study Trust, London; David Silberklang at Yad Vashem—the World Holocaust Remembrance Center, Jerusalem; Michlean Amir, Aleksandra Borecka, Kassandra LaPrade-Seuthe, Jürgen Matthäus, and Vincent Slatt at the United States Holocaust Memorial Museum; Albert Joy and Christina Krupp from the Acquisitions Department at the David W. Howe Memorial Library at the University of Vermont; Lisa Brooks, Barb Lamonda, and Sarah Paige from the Interlibrary Loan Office of the same; Father Zbigniew Łukasik and Aleksandra Szulczewska of the Włocławskie Muzeum Diecezjalne; Father Krzysztof Kamiński and Sister Bernadeta Żabierek of the Wyższe Seminarium Duchowne, Włocławek; Sister Laurencja Jędrzejczak and Sister Benigna Kopeć of the Zgromadzenia Sióstr Wspólnej Pracy od Niepokalanej Maryi, Włocławek; and Sister Rafała Kisiel of the Zgromadzenia Sióstr Służebniczek Niepokalanego Poczęcia Najświętszej Maryi Panny, Luboń.

This book has also benefited from the counsel, criticism, encouragement, and support of scholars and friends in North America and beyond, among them Natalia Aleksiun; Kevin Beilfuss; Doris Bergen; Suzanne Brown-Fleming; Hanna Budnikowska; Martina Cucchiara; John Delaney; Catherine Epstein; Michael Eversole; Peter Fritzsche; Jan Grabowski; Micki and Brian Hodous; Jerold Jacobsen; Karolina Kamińska; Dariusz Libionka; John Pawlikowski, OSM; Annelies Piening; Antony Polonsky; Father Kazimierz Śmigiel; Kevin P. Spicer, CSC; and Robert Ventresca. I am especially indebted to Agnieszka Łuczak, Bożena Szaynok, and Jakub Tyszkiewicz for their careful readings of the manuscript, constructive suggestions, and helpful comments at a 2019 symposium sponsored by the Fundacja Przestrzeni Obywatelskiej i Polityki Społecznej, and to the anonymous readers for Indiana University Press, whose input has improved this book in countless ways.

Brief selections from my article "Nazi *Kirchenpolitik* and Polish Catholicism in the Reichsgau Wartheland, 1939–1941," *Central European History* 47 (2014): 105–137 (© Central European History Society of the American Historical Association, 2014) appear in the introduction and chapters 1, 3, 9, 10, 11, and 14, and are reprinted with permission.

It has been a pleasure to work with the editorial and production staff at Indiana University Press, and I especially appreciate the enthusiasm and counsel of my editor, Jennika Baines, the professionalism of Sophia Hebert and project managers Darja Malcolm-Clarke and Megan Schindele, and the copyediting skills of Gregg Baptista.

Finally, I have enjoyed the support and understanding of my wife, Marilyn Lucas, who made this book possible in more ways than can be listed here. Research and writing result in many absences, both physical and emotional, and my daughters, Anna Cécile and Myriam Justine, have patiently put up with so many of these over the years. With admiration and love, I dedicate this book to them.

Burlington, Vermont
January 2020

LIST OF ABBREVIATIONS

AAG	Archiwum Archidiecezjalne w Gnieźnie (Archdiocesan Archive, Gniezno)
AAN	Archiwum Akt Nowych (Archive of New Documents, Warsaw)
AAP	Archiwum Archidiecezjalne w Poznaniu (Archdiocesan Archive, Poznań)
ADSS	*Actes et Documents du Saint-Siège Relatifs à la Seconde Guerre mondiale*
ADW	Archiwum Diecezjalne w Włocławku (Diocesan Archive, Włocławek)
APP	Archiwum Państwowe w Poznaniu (Poznań State Archive)
APŁ	Archiwum Państwowe w Łodzi (Łódź State Archive)
AZSS	Archiwum Zgromadzenia Sióstr Służebniczek Niepokalanego Poczęcia Najświętszej Maryi Panny, Luboń (Archive of the Congregation of the Sisters Servant of the Immaculate Conception of the Blessed Virgin Mary, Luboń)
AZW	Archiwum Zgromadzenia Sióstr Wspólnej Pracy od Niepokalanej Maryi, Włocławek (Archive of the Sisters of Common Labor of Mary Immaculate, Włocławek)
BAB	Bundesarchiv Berlin (German Federal Archive)
DVL	Deutsche Volksliste (German Ethnic Registry)
DWM	Deutsche Waffen- und Munitionsfabriken (German Weapons and Munitions Manufacturing)
GSV	Gauselbstverwaltung (Gau Self-Administration)
IfZ	Institut für Zeitgeschichte (Institute for Contemporary History, Munich)
IMT	International Military Tribunal, Nuremberg/Nürnberg
IPN	Instytut Pamięci Narodowej–Komisji Ścigania Zbrodni przeciwko Narodowi Polskiemu (Institute of National Remembrance–Commission for the Investigation of Crimes Against the Polish Nation, Warsaw)

IPNLd	Instytut Pamięci Narodowej–Komisji Ścigania Zbrodni przeciwko Narodowi Polskiemu, Łódź (Institute of National Remembrance–Commission for the Investigation of Crimes Against the Polish Nation, Łódź)
IZ	Instytut Zachodni, Poznań
KriPo	Kriminalpolizei (Criminal Police)
NAK	National Archives, Kew
ND	Narodowa Demokracja (National Democracy movement) or Stronnictwo Narodowo-Demokratyczne (National Democratic Party)
NSDAP	Nationalsozialistische Deutsche Arbeiterpartei (National Socialist German Workers Party/Nazi Party)
NSV	Nationalsozialistische Volkswohlfahrt (National Socialist People's Welfare)
OJN	Organizacja Jedności Narodowej (Organization of National Unity)
OKW	Oberkommando der Wehrmacht (High Command of the Armed Forces)
PGuAL	Polizeigefängnis der Sicherheitspolizei und Arbeitserziehungslager in Posen-Lenzingen (Police Prison of the Security Police and Corrective Labor Camp in Posen-Lenzingen)
PISM	Polish Institute and Sikorski Museum, London
PUMST	Polish Underground Movement Study Trust, London
RSHA	Reichssicherheitshauptamt (Reich Security Main Office)
SD	Sicherheitsdienst (Security Service)
SiPo	Sicherheitspolizei (Security Police)
SS	Schutzstaffel
USHMM	United States Holocaust Memorial Museum, Washington, D.C.
YV	Yad Vashem, World Holocaust Remembrance Center, Jerusalem

LIST OF GEOGRAPHIC TERMS

Polish	German
Bąblin	Bablin
Białotarsk	Weißenmarkt
Blizanów	Schrammhausen
Boguszyń	Buchenhof
Bojanowo	Schmückert
Bruczków	Bruckau
Buczek	Buscheck
Chełmno	Kulm
Chełmno nad Nerem	Kulmhof
Chludowo	Truppenfeld
Chocz	Chocz/Petersried
Chodzież	Kolmar
Czarnków	Scharnikau
Częstochowa	Tschechenstochau
Dobra	Doberbühl
Dziekanka	Tiegenhof
Gdańsk	Danzig
Gniezno	Gnesen
Górna Grupa	Obergruppa
Gostynin	Waldrode
Grabów	Grabow
Inowrocław	Hohensalza
Iwanowice	Feldenrode
Jarocin	Jarotschin
Kalisz	Kalisch
Katowice	Kattowitz
Kazimierz Biskupi	Bischofsfelden
Kępno	Kempen
Klecko	Kletzko, Klötzen
Koło	Kolo/Warthbrücken
Konorzewo	Konradsfeld
Koryta	Krippenfeld
Kościań	Kosten
Koźminek	Bornhag

Polish	German
Kraków	Krakau
Kruszewo	Kruschendorf
Ląd	Lond
Leszno	Lissa
Lisków	Schönort
Lubasz	Lubasch
Lubiń	Lubin
Luboń	Luban
Łąck	Lonsch
Łask	Lask
Łęczyca	Lentschütz
Łódź	Lodsch/Litzmannstadt
Michorzewo	Michenau
Miejska Górka	Görchen
Mikstat	Mixstadt
Mosina	Moschin
Namysłów	Namslau
Nieszawa	Nessau
Nowe Miasto nad Wartą	Neustadt an der Warthe
Oborniki	Obornik
Odolanów	Adelnau
Osieczna	Storchnest
Ostrów	Ostrowo
Ołobok	Ollebach
Pleszew	Pleschen
Pniewy	Pinne
Poznań	Posen
Puszczykówko	Puschkau
Płock	Schröttersburg
Radogoszcz	Radegast
Rakoniewice	Rakwitz
Rozdrażew	Albertshof/Brigidau
Sieradz	Schieratz
Śrem	Schrimm
Środa	Schroda
Suchary	Suchenheim
Szczeglin	Scheglin
Szubin	Schubin
Toruń	Thorn

Polish	German
Trzemeszno	Tremessen
Ujście	Usch
Wągrowiec	Eichenbrück
Warsaw	Warschau
Warta	Warthe
Wielichowo	Wiesenstadt
Wielki Buczek	Hohenbusch
Wieluń	Welun
Włocławek	Leslau
Wrocław	Breslau
Zaniemyśl	Santomichel
Zbiersk	Vorwalde
Zduny	Treustadt
Zdziechowa	Zechau
Zgierz	Görnau
Żnin	Dietfurt

GUIDE TO POLISH PRONUNCIATION

THE FOLLOWING KEY PROVIDES A GUIDE TO THE pronunciation of Polish words and names. This material is used by permission of Ohio University Press (www.ohioswallow.com).

a is pronounced as in *father*
c as ts in *cats*
ch like a guttural h
cz as hard ch in *church*
g always hard, as in *get*
i as ee
j as y in *yellow*
rz like French j in *jardin*
sz as sh in *ship*
szcz as shch, enunciating both sounds, as in *fresh cheese*
u as oo in *boot*
w as v
ć as soft ch
ś as sh
ż, ź both as zh, the latter higher in pitch than the former
ó as oo in boot
ą as French *on*
ę as French *en*
ł as w
ń changes the combinations -in to -ine, -en to -ene, and -on to -oyne

The accent in Polish words always falls on the penultimate syllable.

THE POLISH CATHOLIC CHURCH UNDER GERMAN OCCUPATION

Fig. 0.1. Poland's borders, 1939–1945. Map by Timber Wright.

INTRODUCTION

With the invasion of Poland on September 1, 1939, National Socialist Germany aimed to destroy the Polish nation and Polish national consciousness. The Nazi regime attempted to accomplish this in a variety of ways, including the destruction of the Polish state and Polish cultural institutions, forced resettlement, forced labor, random and systematic roundups of prisoners, incarceration in prisons and concentration camps, and mass killing. To the German authorities in occupied Poland, and to many Poles, it was obvious that the occupation would target the Catholic Church with vigor and brutality. Catholicism was the religion of approximately two-thirds of interwar Poland's population; it dominated religious life and held tremendous wealth and political power; and its clergy were widely respected as members of the intelligentsia. More importantly for the Germans, the Catholic Church was a locus and symbol of Polish national identity.

The Nazi regime's hostility to the Polish Catholic Church was revealed in discrimination and persecution, but Nazi policy, contrary to what many would assume, was not uniform across the Polish lands under German occupation. The church suffered considerably less in the General Government (Generalgouvernement)—the German colony established in central Poland—than in those regions annexed to the Third Reich, which included eastern Pomerania and the subsequent Reichsgau Danzig-Westpreußen, as well as the Regierungsbezirk Zichenau in the north, East Upper Silesia in the southwest, and in the west, the Reichsgau Wartheland or "Warthegau."[1] The Nazi agenda of economic, cultural, and racial Germanization was pursued most vigorously in these regions, and especially in the Warthegau, where persecution of the church was most aggressive.

Germanization was an ambitious project that set out to transform the Reichsgau Wartheland in all sorts of ways, from planting trees to expelling ethnic Poles, from renaming streets to killing Jews, from constructing new monuments to the Nazi state to persecuting the Roman Catholic Church. Beginning in 1941, Jews in the Warthegau were marked for total annihilation. For ethnic Poles, the occupation and annexation of the Warthegau meant nearly six years of discrimination, material deprivation, exploitation, and, for tens of thousands, death—whether by malnutrition, disease, deportation, incarceration, or execution.

This was the context in which the Nazi regime mounted its attack on the Catholic Church in the Reichsgau Wartheland. With an area of approximately forty-five thousand square kilometers and a population of more than 4.9 million, including approximately 4.2 million Poles, 400,000 Jews, and 325,000 Germans,[2] the Warthegau was also home to more than 3.8 million Catholics, rougly 90 percent of whom were ethnic Poles. They were spread across seven dioceses, the borders of which did not at all correspond to the political realignments of the Nazi occupation. Thus, the Reichsgau Wartheland contained nearly the entirety of the prewar archdioceses of Poznań (Posen) and Gniezno (Gnesen), nearly all of the Włocławek (Leslau) diocese, the majority of the Łódź (Lodsch/Litzmannstadt) diocese, and fractions of the Częstochowa (Tschechenstochau), Warsaw (Warschau), and Płock (Schröttersburg) dioceses. There were 1,023 parishes in the Warthegau, with 1,829 diocesan priests. In addition, there were 277 members of male religious orders and 2,666 women religious.[3]

The German occupation authorities' attack on the church in the Warthegau, which began in September 1939, was far-reaching and consequential. Over the course of the next five years, the regime confiscated the vast majority of the church's property; it closed between 1,200 and 1,300[4]—some 97 percent[5]—of the churches; it dissolved all Catholic organizations; and it imposed countless restrictions that prevented Catholics from publicly practicing their faith or gaining access to the ministries and services of the church. Seventy-two percent of the Warthegau clergy were arrested by the Nazis; more than half were incarcerated in concentration camps; and more than a third of the Catholic priests in the Warthegau died during the occupation.[6] In short, persecution of the church in the Reichsgau Wartheland was considerably more severe than in the General Government or other territories incorporated into the Reich, and with the exception of the Chełmno (Kulm) diocese in the Reichsgau Danzig-Westpreußen, losses among the clergy in the Warthegau were the highest in German-occupied Poland.[7]

Polish historians, church historians, and scholars of the occupation have examined the Nazi regime's *Kirchenpolitik*, or "church policy," in the Warthegau in various ways: as a manifestation of Nazi anti-Christian ideology, as an aspect of anti-Polish nationality policy in the Warthegau, or as a form of political and administrative restructuring in this newly annexed territory. German measures against the Polish church indeed functioned in all these ways, but they were also a constituent element of the broader ethno-racial struggle or *Volkstumskampf* in the region. As such, the motives for Warthegau Kirchenpolitik were simultaneously and inseparably political, economic, national, and even racial. This book acknowledges National Socialism's anti-Christian animus as fundamental to the regime's measures in the Warthegau, but at the same time, it emphasizes a Kirchenpolitik that is predominantly nationalist and anti-Polish. It describes in detail the ideological bases and the most important goals, characteristics, and manifestations of Nazi policy toward the church in the Warthegau, even as it stresses the inconsistencies, contradictions, and contingencies in that policy. This book also considers the claim, dominant in the literature, that Nazi Kirchenpolitik was clearly aimed at the church's destruction, and correspondingly it emphasizes Polish responses to the Nazi agenda and the significance of the church's survival. It tells a story largely unknown outside of Poland and is the first English-language investigation of German policy toward the Roman Catholic Church in the Reichsgau Wartheland and the variety of responses to that policy.

Since World War II, Polish historians have addressed the importance of the Reichsgau Wartheland among the regions of German-occupied Poland,[8] but its history has been largely neglected outside that country. More recent research, however, has begun to emphasize the centrality of the region in our understanding of Nazi goals and brutal methods in the 1939 invasion,[9] the Warthegau's role as a "laboratory of National Socialist racial policy"[10] with respect to the regime's Germanization policies as they were applied to ethnic Poles and Jews,[11] and the long-term goal of developing the Wartheland as a political, administrative, cultural, and racial *Mustergau*, or "model Gau," for the Reich of the future.[12]

Scholarship on the churches in the Warthegau is likewise limited. The English-language literature is largely confined to general studies on National Socialism and the churches or broader church histories, while the German- and Polish-language secondary literature is somewhat more extensive. Already in the 1950s, West German church historians Bernhard Stasiewski[13] and Paul Gürtler,[14] relying primarily on German sources, focused on the characteristics of Nazi policy toward the churches in the region but did not address in depth institutional or individual Polish responses to it. Their work was amplified by more synthetic studies in the following decades. In his expansive *Polityka III Rzeszy w okupowanej Polsce*[15] (The politics of the Third Reich in occupied Poland), Polish historian Czesław Madajczyk argued, for example, that Nazi policy toward the Warthegau church, politically and ideologically wedded to a broader Nazi nationality policy and aimed at the church's destruction, was to be understood as part of a larger plan for the destruction of the Polish nation as a whole.[16] In *Nationalsozialistische Polenpolitik 1939–1945*[17] (National Socialist Poland policy, 1939–1945), Martin Broszat, a pioneering political and social historian of the Nazi era, likewise placed Warthegau Kirchenpolitik in the context of the regime's broader anti-Polish nationality policy, emphasizing the uniqueness of Nazi *Sonder-Kirchenpolitik* there and arguing that although the situation of the Catholic Church in other German-controlled eastern territories began to normalize over the course of the war, treatment of the church in the Warthegau worsened.[18] Making use of documents of the German Foreign Office, Broszat also stressed the ways in which church affairs in the Wartheland strained the relationship between the Third Reich and the Vatican.[19] Moreover, Broszat argued that Nazi policy toward the churches was not merely anti-Polish but was also based in the regime's anti-Christian and anti-religious ideology: German measures grew out of an energetic *Volkstumspolitik* but pointed as well to the goal of establishing a National Socialist *Weltanschauungsstaat sui generis* in the Wartheland.[20] Also worthy of note in this context is the well-known study by church historian John S. Conway, *The Nazi Persecution of the Churches 1933–1945*, in which he argued that a centrally directed "final settlement" with the Christian churches in occupied territories reached its "apotheosis" in the Warthegau, where Nazi church policy included measures that would have been implemented elsewhere had Hitler had the opportunity.[21]

The most extensive analysis of the church in the Reichsgau Wartheland remains Kazimierz Śmigiel's 1979 study *Kościół Katolicki w tzw. Okręgu Warty 1939–1945*[22] (The Catholic Church in the so-called Warthegau, 1939–1945) in which the Polish church historian confronted not only the political, philosophical, and nationalist origins of Nazi policy but also the effects of such policies on the Polish church. Using a variety of German sources, published Vatican documents, and materials from Polish church archives, Śmigiel addressed a range of themes, including internal diocesan administration in the Warthegau, treatment of religious orders, the loss of religious art and cultural artifacts, participation of the Warthegau clergy in acts of resistance, clandestine religious instruction, and Polish Catholic religious life in general. A work of detail and precision, Śmigiel's study is, however, founded on sources that are, by current standards, limited.

Other Polish historians, both within and outside of the Polish Roman Catholic Church establishment, have investigated the fate of the church and its clergy under the Nazi occupation, although some of their studies have taken the form of chronicles and necrologies rather than interpretive histories and, as such, tend to fall under what one might designate a "martyrological" idiom of postwar Polish scholarship.[23] The Polish historiography also includes more politically focused studies,[24] as well as recent works by Polish scholars that have focused on the experience of individual Roman Catholic dioceses in the Reichsgau Wartheland.[25]

Over the last two decades, the Catholic Church in occupied Poland has come under further scrutiny as scholars have begun to examine more extensively and critically Nazi anti-Catholic measures in Poland, Catholic reactions to Nazi policy, the role of antisemitism in the Polish Church, and Catholic responses to the annihilation of Jews in occupied Poland.[26] Contributing to this emerging literature, based in diverse archival sources, and approaching the subject from a variety of thematic angles, this study illustrates that the history of Polish Catholicism in the Reichsgau Wartheland is a compelling history that demands analysis on a number of levels.

First, it is a compelling history because, unknown to most, treatment of the Catholic Church was more brutal in the Warthegau than anywhere else in German-occupied Poland or German-occupied Europe. An underresearched aspect of the history of the Warthegau, the Polish Catholic Church in this "model Gau" was where the severity of Nazi policy intersected with Polish national consciousness and tradition, where persecution, resistance, national identity, religious devotion, and the demands for compliance all met in complex and even contradictory ways. From the fall of 1939 until 1945, Nazi policy aimed, through both administrative measures and violence, to control the church, to undermine its power, and, according to many scholars, to destroy it. This book therefore addresses the motives for and forms of Nazi church policy in the Warthegau in these years; contextualizes these policies in the broader national, racial, and economic Volkstumspolitik pursued there; and considers German measures in light of the claim, common in the literature, that the destruction of the Polish church in the Wartheland was the ultimate goal.[27] Although destruction may have been the long-term aim, a key contribution of this study is its emphasis on the nonlinear aspects of Nazi policy through the fall of 1941—when persecution of the church reached its apex in the deportation of nearly all remaining Warthegau clergy to the Dachau concentration camp—and on the regime's consistency and, in some respects, restraint in moving forward with its antichurch agenda in the years that followed. If we understand Dachau as a metaphor for the persecution of the Warthegau clergy and church as a whole, then the "road to Dachau" was indeed a twisted one.[28]

Second, the Nazi assault on Polish Catholicism in the Reichsgau Wartheland reveals much about the regime's long-term Kirchenpolitik in the Reich and beyond. The Nazi elite in the state and party apparatus, and their Reichsstatthalter (Reich lieutenant or Reich deputy) and Gauleiter (Gau party leader) in Poznań, Arthur Greiser, viewed this "model Gau" as a testing ground for policies against the churches, both Catholic and Protestant, to be launched in the Reich after the successful completion of the war. This does not mean that the Nazi leadership was creating in the Warthegau an exact "blueprint" for church policy in the *Altreich*[29] after the war, but measures against the Warthegau church—whether silencing the church's clergymen, regulating the church's finances, confiscating the church's property, or restricting the church's ministries—do indeed illustrate the regime's vision for the future, and Nazi policymakers at times described such measures in such a way, that is, with a view to the postwar Reich.

At the same time, the measures taken against the Warthegau church suggest the importance of ideological considerations in the formulation of policy. While the following analysis recognizes the significance of what Broszat called the "ideological moment"[30] behind German measures, it is at the same time unwilling to claim the primacy of one single motive in the formulation of the regime's Kirchenpolitik. It privileges the Nazi regime's "national," anti-Polish motives but also emphasizes, to a greater extent than the literature, the inseparability of political, security, national, and racial interests in the formulation of policy. Thus, the prohibition against participating in public worship on weekdays was a security measure to prevent Poles from congregating and fomenting dissent or resistance, but it was also intended to undermine Poles' sense of national identity and community. The prohibition against Germans and Poles sharing the same worship space was founded in Nazi notions of racial superiority and inferiority. Confiscation of rectories, convents, monasteries, hospitals, and orphanages deprived Poles of the institutional and spiritual support they received from the Catholic Church even as it enriched the "German" economy and provided "living space" for ethnic German settlers.

Any of the countless measures implemented in order to limit Poles' access to their church and its ministries could be seen as based in the National Socialists' fundamental anti-Christian ideology. But how fundamental was their hostility to Christianity, and were Nazism and Christianity really incompatible? This book will not resolve the controversies associated with those questions, but it will, with a view to the Reichsgau Wartheland, address them briefly in chapter 3. Complicating the matter further was the regime's selective and inconsistent application of antichurch measures across regions, nationalities, and denominations, whether in the Reichsgau Wartheland, occupied Poland, or Nazi-controlled Europe at large. If, for example, the attack on the Polish church in the Reichsgau Wartheland were based in the Nazis' anti-Christian animus, then how does one account for the regime's much more lenient policies toward the Altreich, or in the Slovakian puppet state where a Catholic priest was installed as president? If, for example, the attack on the Warthegau church was understood as an attack against Polish national identity and sentiment, then how to explain the considerably less aggressive policies toward the churches in the General Government and German-occupied East Upper Silesia? The answers to these questions lie in the exceptional circumstances that the Reichsgau Wartheland provided, and in the tactically applied and therefore inconsistent and diverse policies toward the churches across Nazi-occupied Poland and Nazi-controlled Europe.

Third, this analysis ventures into areas of inquiry that remain largely uncharted in the historical literature, such as papal and Vatican responses to the persecution of the Warthegau church; relations between the Polish church (its hierarchy, clergy, and laity) and the Vatican; and the varied Polish responses to anti-Catholic measures, ranging from compliance to overt resistance. Moreover, it engages sources that reveal much about the history of the Warthegau church "from below." We know much about everyday life in the Altreich, and much less about everyday life in occupied and annexed territories in east-central and eastern Europe, where the impact of Nazi policy was so much more brutal. Addressing that lacuna, this book therefore includes chapters that address themes as yet unexplored in the English-language literature, such as Polish responses to Nazi policies at the parish level, the persecution of women religious in the Gau, and the experiences of Polish clergy in Nazi prisons and concentration camps.

While this analysis addresses the Catholic Church in the specific region of the Reichsgau Wartheland, it also recognizes the broader implications of the narrative it provides. In occupied Poland, persecution of the Christian churches was not limited to the persecution of Roman Catholicism, and Nazi persecution of the Catholic Church was not, of course, limited to Poland. Thus, the book intends to contribute to a wider, comparative, "European" historiography that examines the motives and experiences of German occupation in a variety of national, cultural, religious, and political contexts. In addition, it adds a new voice to the ongoing discussion about Catholicism and the activism, reticence, or silence of the papacy in the face of injustice and persecution in wartime Europe. Finally, this work encourages a more precise and nuanced analysis of the German occupation in various regions of Poland. As noted above, Nazi church policy was hardly uniform across the Polish lands, and a detailed analysis of the Catholic Church in the Warthegau invites further investigation of the churches in Danzig-Westpreußen, Upper Silesia, the General Government, or the eastern territories of prewar Poland initially under Soviet, and later German, control.

In part political history, in part an exercise in *Alltagsgeschichte*, or the "history of everyday life," and in part diplomatic history, this book is an aggregate of stories that emerge in the Polish-language (and to a lesser extent, German-language) secondary literature, in the memoir literature from the years of occupation, and especially in archival collections that are as thematically diverse as they are geographically scattered. State archives such as the Bundesarchiv Berlin (German Federal Archive), Warsaw's Instytut Pamięci Narodowej–Komisji Ścigania Zbrodni przeciwko Narodowi Polskiemu (Institute of National Remembrance–Commission for the Investigation of Crimes Against the Polish Nation), the United States Holocaust Memorial Museum in Washington, DC, and regional state archives in Poznań and Łódź are the main repositories of documents that relate to the motives for and implementation of Nazi Kirchenpolitik in the Warthegau. Research centers such as Munich's Institut für Zeitgeschichte (Institute for Contemporary History), Poznań's Instytut Zachodni (Western Institute), and Yad Vashem, the World Holocaust Remembrance Center in Jerusalem, are repositories that document not only Nazi measures against the church but also Polish responses to those measures. The collections of the Polish Institute and Sikorski Museum and Polish Underground Movement Study Trust, both in London, contain a wealth of documentation on conditions "on the ground" in occupied Poland as reported by members of the Polish resistance, as well as diplomatic reports and correspondence that illuminate relations between the Polish government-in-exile and the Vatican. Finally, this work has relied extensively on Polish church archives to document the wartime experiences of the Catholic laity, clergy, and hierarchy. Such collections include diocesan archives in Poznań, Gniezno, and Włocławek, as well as the archives of convents in Włocławek and Luboń.

Moving forward, the reader may find a few points of orientation useful. German, Polish, and Latin words that are used frequently in the book (e.g., *Einsatzgruppe*, *Kirchenpolitik*, *Reichsstatthalter*) are italicized only at the first occurance. German or Polish proper nouns (e.g., "Reichsgau Wartheland") are not italicized. With respect to geographic designations, if there exists for a place or geographic feature a common English word, then I have deferred to that convention (e.g., Warsaw and not Warszawa, Munich and not München). Otherwise, I have used the current, official Polish names for cities, towns, and villages in present-day Poland. The vast majority of Warthegau communities had or continue to have German-language names, and for that reason, at first use I have provided parenthetically the German name or spelling (e.g., Poznań [Posen], Włocławek [Leslau]).[31]

The reader will also note that the book's organization is rather unusual, in that it is divided into eighteen brief chapters. My goal in structuring the book in this way is to provide cogent, tightly organized chapters that offer the reader an informative and simultaneously energetic narrative. Each chapter carries an epigraph (a word or phrase that is descriptive of that chapter's focus or theme) in German, Polish, or in one case, Latin.

Chapter 1 is an initiation into the Nazi regime's violence against the Catholic Church and its clergy in the context of the fall 1939 invasion and the weeks that followed. Chapters 2 through 4 analyze the ideological bases of National Socialist policy against the Polish church, addressing the regime's general anti-Polish hostility, its hostility toward the Polish Catholic Church, and its goals for the Wartheland as a "model Gau." To that end, the narrative in these three chapters requires some chronological "back and forth," but it lays the ideological foundation for chapters 5 through 9, which explore the various ways in which policy toward the church was applied, such as the arrest, imprisonment, and deportation of clergy; radical restrictions on their ministries; restrictions on public worship practicies and traditions; the destruction and confiscation of church property, broadly defined; and the strict separation of Polish and German coreligionists in public worship and parish life.

The year 1941 marked the culmination of the regime's antichurch policies and measures. Chapter 10 therefore describes the dramatic revisions to the churches' financial and legal status in that year, while chapter 11 recounts the apex of Nazi violence against the Warthegau clergy: the October 1941 mass arrest and subsequent deportation to concentration camps of more than five hundred priests. The final destination for the vast majority of those clerics was the Dachau concentration camp, so chapter 12 accounts for their experiences there. Exploring German measures against women religious in the Reichsgau Wartheland, chapter 13 sheds light on the history of the little-known camp for nuns, the *Nonnenlager Schmückert*. Chapter 14 then considers German policy after the fall of 1941, a period characterized by a Kirchenpolitik that was largely consistent with the previous years but that in some respects exercised a degree of restraint in persecuting the Polish church. With the epigraphs "*Parafia*" and "*Konspiracja*," chapters 15 and 16 address the responses, whether devotional, ritual, or conspiratorial, of Polish Catholics in the Warthegau to the restrictive and at times brutal measures of the occupation regime. The Vatican's relationship to the Warthegau church and, more specifically, Pope Pius XII's responses to its situation and struggles, are the controversial issues addressed in chapter 17. It is worth noting that this chapter is grounded in the currently available secondary literature, in published documents, and in unpublished archival sources. Its provisional conclusions do not, however, take into account the documentation in Vatican archives that is now becoming accessible to scholars. Revision of my conclusions based on newly available sources would, of course, be a welcome contribution to the conversation surrounding these issues. Finally, chapter 18 addresses the changes in Warthegau Kirchenpolitik, as well as the consistencies, during the last months of the occupation, a period characterized by both concessions to the church with respect to some policies and, at the same time, rigorous enforcement of others.

As the above outline makes clear, the book's organization is neither strictly chronological nor thematic. Although this story begins in September 1939 and ends in the spring of 1945, its path, like Nazi Kirchenpolitik in the Reichsgau Wartheland, is not entirely direct or linear. The narrative therefore interrogates the ideological bases of the regime's policies; dwells at some length on the role of the Wartheland as "model Gau"; and takes detours to, for example, numerous prisons in the region, to Dachau, to a labor camp for nuns, to the halls of Vatican diplomacy, or, on a more prosaic level, to the halls and churches of Catholic parishes across the Warthegau. Throughout, the reader should bear in mind that this book seeks neither to condemn nor to valorize the Catholic Church in the Reichsgau Wartheland. Exercising both the objectivity and empathy incumbent on the historian, it aims to let the sources speak for themselves and, no less, to capture the reader's interest, regardless of whether that reader is hostile, indifferent, sympathetic, or devoted to the traditions and doctrines of Roman Catholicism.

Notes

1. The term Gau refers to a geographic district of the National Socialist German Workers Party. After German occupation of Polish territory in 1939, the Nazi government, in an attempt to streamline party and administrative control, established the Reichsgau Danzig-Westpreußen and the Reichsgau Posen (later renamed Reichsgau Wartheland) in which the office of Nazi Party leader (Gauleiter) and government administrator or Reich lieutenant (Reichsstatthalter) were combined. Arthur Greiser simultaneously held the posts of Gauleiter and Reichsstatthalter in the Reichsgau Wartheland. The region was also frequently referred to simply as the Warthegau, and its capital was Posen, or present-day Poznań. Zichenau received the designation *Regierungsbezirk*, or "administrative district," and was subsequently absorbed into the Provinz Ostpreußen (East Prussia Province), while East Upper Silesia became the Regierungsbezirk Kattowitz, part of Provinz Schlesien, or Silesia Province.

2. On the surface area and population figures, which varied significantly over the course of the occupation, see "Wstęp," in *Położenie ludności polskiej w tzw. Kraju Warty w okresie hitlerowskiej okupacji*, Documenta Occupationis, vol.13, ed. Marian Olszewski (Poznań: Instytut Zachodni, 1990), vii–viii; Martin Broszat, *Nationalsozialistische Polenpolitik 1939–1945* (Frankfurt am Main: Fischer-Bücherei, 1961), 38; Catherine Epstein, *Model Nazi: Arthur Greiser and the Occupation of Western Poland* (Oxford: Oxford University Press, 2010), 135; Czesław Madajczyk, *Die Okkupationspolitik Nazideutschlands in Polen 1939–1945* (Köln: Pahl-Rügenstein Verlag, 1988), 36.

3. Kazimierz Śmigiel, *Die katholische Kirche im Reichsgau Wartheland 1939–1945*, Veröffentlichung der Forschungsstelle Ostmitteleuropa an der Universität Dortmund, Series A, no. 40 (Dortmund: Forschungsstelle Ostmitteleuropa, 1984), 34.

4. Vermerk, Meyer-Eckhardt, December 22, 1944, Instytut Pamięci Narodowej–Komisja Ścigania Zbrodni przeciwko Narodowi Polskiemu, Warsaw (hereafter IPN), GK 196/19, 58. Meyer-Eckhardt based his estimate of 1,200–1,300 churches on statistics provided by the Gau Self-Administration, a Gau office responsible for the administration of Polish property and institutions taken over by the Germans. These were also the figures that appeared in the letter of indictment against Arthur Greiser in his postwar trial. See Akt oskarzenia Artura Greisera, June 10, 1946, IPN, GK 196/34, 14.

5. Jerzy Kłoczowski, Lidia Müllerowa, and Jan Skarbek, *Zarys dziejów Kościoła katolickiego w Polsce* (Kraków: Wydawnictwo Znak, 1986), 352.

6. Śmigiel, *Die katholische Kirche*, 186.

7. Kłoczowski, Müllerowa, and Skarbek, *Zarys*, 358.

8. See, for example, the extensive work of historians Czesław Łuczak, Jerzy Marczewski, Stanisław Nawrocki, and Edward Serwański, and the journal *Przegląd Zachodni*, published since 1945 by Poznań's Instytut Zachodni.

9. Alexander Rossino, *Hitler Strikes Poland: Blitzkrieg, Ideology, and Atrocity* (Lawrence: University Press of Kansas, 2003); Jochen Böhler, *Auftakt zum Vernichtungskrieg: die Wehrmacht in Polen 1939* (Frankfurt am Main: Fischer Taschenbuch Verlag, 2006); Dorothee Weitbrecht, "Ermächtigung zur Vernichtung: die Einsatzgruppen in Polen im Herbst 1939," in *Genesis des Genozids: Polen 1939–1941*, ed. Klaus-Michael Mallmann and Bogdan Musial (Darmstadt: Wissenschaftliche Buchgesellschaft, 2004), 57–70.

10. Michael Alberti, "'Exerzierplatz des Nationalsozialismus': Der Reichsgau Wartheland 1939–1941," in Mallmann and Musial, *Genesis des Genozids*, 113.

11. Phillip T. Rutherford, *Prelude to the Final Solution: The Nazi Program for Deporting Ethnic Poles, 1939–1941* (Lawrence: University Press of Kansas, 2007); Michael Alberti, *Die Verfolgung und Vernichtung der Juden im Reichsgau Wartheland 1939–1945* (Wiesbaden: Harrassowitz Verlag, 2006).

12. The Gau was described as such by Gauleiter Greiser as reported in the *Posener Tageblatt* of September 22, 1939: "Unser Fernziel, das wir jedoch von vornherein bei allen unseren Handlungen stets im Auge behalten werden, soll sein, ein Mustergau des Großdeutschen Reiches zu werden." Quoted in Madajczyk, *Okkupationspolitik*, 26. On the notion of the "Mustergau" see Epstein, *Model Nazi*, 124–59; Rutherford, *Prelude*, 68; and Alberti, "Exerzierplatz."

13. Bernhard Stasiewski, "Die Kirchenpolitik der Nationalsozialisten im Warthegau 1939–1945," *Vierteljahrshefte für Zeitgeschichte* 7, no. 1 (1959).

14. Paul Gürtler, *Nationalsozialismus und evangelische Kirchen im Warthegau: Trennung von Staat und Kirche im nationalsozialistischen Weltanschauungsstaat* (Göttingen: Vandenhoeck und Ruprecht, 1958).

15. Czesław Madajczyk, *Politika III Rzeszy w okupowanej Polsce*, 2 vols. (Warszawa: Państwowe Wydawnictwo Naukowe, 1970). In German translation: Madajczyk, *Okkupationspolitik*, 26.

16. Madajczyk, *Okkupationspolitik*, 360.

17. Broszat, *Nationalsozialistische*, 147–57.

18. Broszat, 148.

19. Broszat, 154–56.

20. Broszat, 152.

21. John S. Conway, *The Nazi Persecution of the Churches 1933–1945* (London: Weidenfeld and Nicholson, 1968), 292.

22. Kazimierz Śmigiel, *Kościół katolicki w tzw. Okręgu warty 1939–1945* (Lublin: Katolicki Uniwersytet Lubelski, 1979). German translation: Śmigiel, *Die katholische Kirche*, 186.

23. In addition to many articles appearing in local diocesan periodicals, prominent among works of this type are Wiktor Jacewicz and Jan Woś, eds., *Martyrologium polskiego duchowieństwa rzymskokatolickiego pod okupacją hitlerowską w latach 1939–1945*, 5 vols. (Warszawa: Akademia Teologii Katolickiej, 1977–1981); Jan Domagała, *Ci, którzy przeszli przez Dachau: duchowni w Dachau* (Warszawa: Pax, 1957); and essays in Zygmunt Zieliński, ed., *Życie religijne w Polsce pod okupacją hitlerowską 1939–1945* (Warszawa: Ośrodek Dokumentacji i Studiów Społecznych, 1982). On the "martyrological" idiom in Polish scholarship, see Dariusz Libionka, "Antisemitism, Anti-Judaism, and the Polish Catholic Clergy during the Second World War, 1939–1945," in *Antisemitism and its Opponents in Modern Poland*, ed. Robert Blobaum (Ithaca, NY: Cornell University Press, 2005), 234;

Jonathan Huener, *Auschwitz, Poland, and the Politics of Commemoration, 1945–1979* (Athens: Ohio University Press, 2003), especially 47–58.

24. See, for example, Jan Sziling, *Polityka okupanta hitlerowskiego wobec kościoła katolickiego 1939–1945: tzw. okręgi Rzeszy: Gdańsk-Prusy Zachodnie, kraj Warty i regencja Katowicka*, Badania nad okupacją niemiecką w Polsce, vol. 11 (Poznań: Instytut Zachodni, 1970); Zenon Fijałkowski, *Kościół katolicki na ziemiach polskich w latach okupacji hitlerowskiej* (Warszawa: Książka i Wiedza, 1983). The former highlights the uniqueness of church policy in the Warthegau as distinct from other areas of occupied Poland and emphasizes its role as a template for the Reich as a whole, while the latter remains within the Marxist historiographical framework prevailing in People's Poland in the early 1980s. See also the recent brief study by Kasper Sipowicz, *Prześladowania religijne w Kraju Warty: represje wobec Polaków i duchowieństwa polskiego a polityka wyznaniowa rządu III Rzeszy 1939–1945* (Łódź: Księży Młyn Dom Wydawniczy, 2016). Although the title of this work suggests its focus on the Wartheland, it is primarily devoted to Nazi ideology, relations between the Nazi state and the German churches, and the region's role as Mustergau.

25. See, for example, Łukasz Jastrząb's encyclopedic *Archidiecezja Poznańska w latach okupacji hitlerowskiej 1939–1945*, Uniwersytet im. Adama Mickiewicza w Poznaniu, Wydział Teologiczny, Studia i Materiały, no. 153 (Poznań: Wydział Teologiczny Uniwersytetu im. Adama Mickiewicza w Poznaniu, 2012); Wojciech Frątczak, *Diecezja włocławskiej w okresie II wojny światowej* (Włocławek: Wydawnictwo Duszpasterstwa Rolników, 2013); Marek Budziarek, "Zarząd i organizacja diecezji Łódzkiej 1939–1945," in *Kościół katolicki na ziemiach Polski w czasie II Wojny Światowej: Materiały i Studia*, vol. 7, no. 3, ed. Franciszek Stopniak (Warszawa: Akademia Teologii Katolickiej, 1978); Marek Budziarek, "Geneza, przebieg i następstwa masowych aresztowań duchownych katolickich 5–7 października 1941 roku (ze szczególnym uwzględnieniem diecezji łódzkiej)," in *Martyrologia duchowieństwa polskiego 1939–1956*, ed. Bohdan Bejze and Antoni Galiński (Lódź: Archidiecezjalne Wydawnictwo Łódzkie, 1993); and Marek Budziarek, *Katedra przy Adolf Hitlerstrasse: z dziejów Kościoła katolickiego w Łodzi 1939–1945* (Warszawa: Instytut Wydawniczy Pax, 1984). For a collection of essays on German policies in the various dioceses in the Warthegau, see Antoni Galiński and Marek Budziarek, eds., *Akcje okupanta hitlerowskiego wobec Kościoła katolickiego w Kraju Warty* (Łódź: Okregowa Komisja Badania Zbrodni Przeciwko Narodowi Polskiemu w Łodzi–Instytut Pamięci Narodowej/Muzeum Historii Miasta Łodzi, 1997).

26. See, for example, Jonathan Huener, "Nazi *Kirchenpolitik* and Polish Catholicism in the Reichsgau Wartheland, 1939–1941," *Central European History* 47 (2014); Jonathan Huener, "Polityka Niemiec wobec Kościoła i polskiego Kościoła katolickiego w diecezji Kraju Warty i łódzkiej," in *Łódź pod okupacją 1939–1945: Studia i szkice*, ed. Tomasz Toborek and Michał Trębacz, Biblioteka Oddziału Instytutu Pamięci Narodowej w Łodzi, vol. 45 (Łódź: Instytut Pamięci Narodowej, 2018); Klaus-Peter Friedrich, "Collaboration in a 'Land without a Quisling': Patterns of Cooperation with the Nazi German Occupation Regime in Poland during World War II," *Slavic Review* 64, no. 4 (winter 2005); Viktoria Pollmann, *Untermieter im christlichen Haus: die Kirche und die 'jüdische Frage' in Polen anhand der Bistumspresse der Metropolie Krakau 1926–1939* (Wiesbaden: Harrassowitz Verlag, 2001); Ronald Modras, *The Catholic Church and Antisemitism: Poland, 1933–1939* (Amsterdam: Harwood Academic Publishers, 2000); Szymon Rudnicki, "Anti-Jewish Legislation in Interwar Poland," in Blobaum, *Antisemitism*; Konrad Sadkowski, "Clerical Nationalism

and Antisemitism: Catholic Priests, Jews, and Orthodox Christians in the Lublin Region, 1918–1939" in Blobaum, *Antisemitism*; Dariusz Libionka, "Die Kirche in Polen und der Mord an den Juden im Licht der polnischen Publizistik und Historiographie nach 1945," *Zeitschrift für Ostmitteleuropa-Forschung* 51, no. 2 (2002); Dariusz Libionka, "The Catholic Church in Poland and the Holocaust, 1939–1945," in *The Holocaust in the Christian World: Reflections on the Past, Challenges for the Future*, ed. Carol Rittner et al. (New York: Continuum, 2000); Dariusz Libionka, "Duchowieństwo diecezji łomżyńskiej wobec antysemityzmu i zagłady Żydów," in *Wokół Jedwabnego*, ed. Paweł Machcewicz and Krzysztof Persak, vol. 1; and Dariusz Libionka, "Antisemitism." Of special significance in this regard is volume 5 (2009) of the journal published by Warsaw's Centrum Badań nad Zagładą Żydów, *Zagłada Żydów–Studia i Materiały*, which contains articles on the Roman Catholic Church, its hierarchy, the Vatican, and their responses to the annihilation of Jews in the Polish lands.

27. On this claim see, for example, Broszat, *Nationalsozialistische*, 154; Jerzy Kłoczowski, *A History of Polish Christianity* (Cambridge: Cambridge University Press, 2000), 298; Kazimierz Śmigiel, "Die apostolischen Administratoren Walenty Dymek und Hilarius Breitinger," in *Katholische Kirche unter nationalsozialistischer und kommunistischer Diktatur: Deutschland und Polen 1939–1989*, ed. Hans-Jürgen Karp und Joachim Köhler (Köln: Böhlau Verlag, 2001), 259; and Stasiewski, "Kirchenpolitik," 74. The claim that the German authorities aimed at the Polish church's destruction was, not surprisingly, also put forth by wartime and early postwar documentation provided by the Polish underground, as well as Catholic parishes and clergy in the Warthegau. See "Raport Sytuacyjny okupacji niemieckiej za czas od 1.I. do 1.VII.1941 r." in Sprawozdanie sytuacyjne z kraju 1939–1941, tom I, 49, Polish Underground Movement Study Trust, London (hereafter PUMST). Similarly, a postwar June 1946 accounting of human and material losses under Greiser's regime in the Poznań archdiocese states, "From the commencement of the Hitlerite invasion of Poland it was evident that German party authorities aimed at the total destruction of the Catholic Church, its property, and its activities." "Wykaz szkód wyrządzonych Archidiecezji Poznańskiej przez okupację niemiecką za rządów namiestnika Greisera 1939–1945," IPN, GK 196/19, 139.

28. The reference is to Karl Schleunes' pioneering study *The Twisted Road to Auschwitz: Nazi Policy toward German Jews, 1933–1939* (Urbana: University of Illinois Press, 1979).

29. Altreich (literally, "Old Reich") was the term used by the Nazis to refer to that portion of the Third Reich within its borders prior to the March 1938 annexation of Austria.

30. Martin Broszat, "Verfolgung polnischer katholischer Geistlicher 1939–1945," Gutachten des Instituts für Zeitgeschichte, München (hereafter IfZ), unpublished manuscript, 1959, 87. Broszat's use of the German "Moment" is to be understood in the sense of "import" or "significance."

31. Unless otherwise noted, Polish and German names of villages, towns, and cities are taken from "Anordnung über Ortsnamenänderung im Reichsgau Wartheland vom 18. Mai 1943," May 18, 1943, *Verordnungsblatt des Reichsstatthalters im Warthegau*, no. 12 (May 18, 1943), 85–111.

1

TANNENBERG

The Einsatzgruppen *and the Polish Clergy, Fall 1939*

Mateusz Zabłocki was a Roman Catholic priest in Gniezno, a medium-sized city in western Poland that was the seat of an archdiocese and one of the most important centers of Polish Catholicism. As head of Holy Trinity Parish, Father Zabłocki was asked to take on the role of the city's mayor in the chaos of the first days of the German invasion. On September 4, 1939, he received instructions from Polish military authorities to organize a citizens' militia to defend the city against German forces. He did so, but only a few days later, on September 10, he decided to approach the German military authorities in order to surrender the city, fearing that any continuation of fighting would lead them to destroy it. Wearing clerical dress, Zabłocki made his way that afternoon to nearby German headquarters and was injured by a hand grenade on the way. Late that evening he returned and reported that the Germans had accepted his offer of surrender. They entered the city the following morning.

The cleric's troubles were far from over. He was hospitalized in Gniezno, subjected to brutal interrogation by the Gestapo, and then arrested in the night of September 12–13. Wearing only a dressing gown, he was taken to the town of Inowrocław (Hohensalza), about fifty kilometers northeast of Gniezno, and imprisoned. There a German judge issued two death sentences against him. The first was for his participation in the Greater Poland (Wielkopolska) Uprising of 1918–1919, an anti-German insurrection after the conclusion of World War I, and the second for his role in organizing civilian resistance to the Germans in the first weeks of September 1939. Zabłocki was executed in the courtyard of the Inowrocław prison on October 14.[1]

Figs. 1.1, 1.2, and 1.3. Photographs taken at the trial and just prior to the execution of Father Mateusz Zabłocki, Inowrocław, October 1939. United States Holocaust Memorial Museum, courtesy of Instytut Pamięci Narodowej, USHMM, WS 51222, WS 51223, WS 74704A.

Fig. 1.2

Fig. 1.3

The Nazi attack against the Polish clergy in the fall of 1939 was not limited to the Gniezno diocese but extended across the entire territory of German-occupied Poland, including what would become the Reichsgau Posen, or what would later be named the Reichsgau Wartheland. Polish, German, and Vatican sources point to the incarceration and execution of dozens of priests throughout the region in "pacification measures" after the outbreak of the war.[2] With the arrival of German forces, Józef Sarniewicz, dean of the Trzemeszno (Tremessen) parish some twenty kilometers northeast of Gniezno, was imprisoned, forced to participate in the demolition of the local synagogue, released, placed under house arrest, and then held as a hostage at German police headquarters. He was then sent to the penal camp in nearby Szczeglin (Scheglin).[3] After two weeks of abuse there, he was returned, barely alive, to Trzemeszno.[4]

Within weeks of the invasion, at least fifteen parish priests were killed in the Gniezno archdiocese alone,[5] among them Kazimierz Nowicki, shot in a forest north of the city,[6] and Canon Maksymilian Koncewicz, head of the nearby Klecko (Kletzko, Klötzen) parish, shot in a mass execution of hostages in the Dalki district of Gniezno.[7] At times, clergy were the specific targets of executions; on other occasions, they were massacred among other

Poles, who were often members of the intelligentsia or leaders in society. For example, on September 24, forty-nine Poles were shot in the village of Świerkowiec, near Molgino. Among them were three village priests in the area: Zenon Nieziołkiewicz, Władysław Nowicki, and Michał Rólski.[8] On November 12, forty-five Poles were massacred in Paterek, a village in the far north of the diocese, and among them were thirteen diocesan priests.[9] On October 20, in the town of Śrem (Schrimm), nineteen Poles were lined up to be shot. Antoni Rzadki, a priest on the faculty of the local high school, offered to give his life in place of one of the condemned, a man with a family. The Germans agreed, and Rzadki knelt in prayer. Because he was kneeling, the first round of bullets missed him, so the German commanding officer shot him in the head.[10]

In the small town of Chocz (Chocz/Petersried), near Kalisz (Kalisch), German troops occupied the home of the seventy-year-old priest Roman Pawłowski, where they allegedly found an empty cartridge. Beaten until his shirt was soaked with blood, Pawłowski was brought to Poznań, where he was sentenced to death. He was then taken to Kalisz for a public execution

Figs. 1.4, 1.5, 1.6, 1.7, 1.8, and 1.9. The execution of Father Roman Pawłowski, Kalisz, October 1939. United States Holocaust Memorial Museum, courtesy of Instytut Pamięci Narodowej, USHMM, WS 50269, WS 50480, WS 50477, WS 50271, WS 50474, WS 50471.

Fig. 1.5

and shot on October 20, 1939.[11] According to a report filed by another clergyman, local Jews were forced to kiss the feet of the corpse, untie it, and then bury it in the Jewish cemetery.[12]

Mieczysław Posmyk, a vicar from Chodzież (Kolmar) north of Poznań, was spared execution but experienced an odyssey of flight, persecution, and incarceration that was typical of the experience of many priests in the region. When the German forces invaded, he fled Chodzież and, after more than two weeks on the run, returned to his hometown. Arrested on September 20, Posmyk was imprisoned in Chodzież for more than a month and released on October 28, only to be apprehended again as a hostage. Released once more, he was arrested at the end of November on suspicion

Fig. 1.6

Fig. 1.7

of distributing anti-German leaflets. Freed after a day of interrogation, Posmyk served as a substitute priest in Chodzież until June 1940, when he was arrested a final time and subsequently imprisoned in the nearby city of Toruń (Thorn). Later transferred to the Alexanderplatz police prison in Berlin, he was subsequently sent to the nearby Sachsenhausen concentration camp, and finally to the Dachau concentration camp, where he was liberated in 1945.[13]

The larger concentration camps across the Third Reich, as well as local prisons and camps, were the destinations of hundreds of Warthegau priests

Fig. 1.8

Fig. 1.9

in the early months of the occupation. Of the six other clerics in Zabłocki's Gniezno parish, two—Franciszek Dahlke and Henryk Fiszbach—died in Dachau. Augustyn Gałęzewski and Bronisław Pluciński were deported in August 1940 to Sachsenhausen and subsequently to Dachau in 1941, which they survived. Wawrzyniec Wnuk and Bogdan Bolz were deported in 1939 to the General Government; Wnuk was then deported in 1943 to Auschwitz and later to Buchenwald, where he was liberated in April 1945.[14]

Early in the occupation, the German authorities also established numerous camps and prisons across the Reichsgau Wartheland especially designed for the incarceration of the clergy: in the Salesian cloister in Ląd (Lond);[15] in Chludowo (Truppenfeld) and Obra; in the Franciscan friary in Miejska Górka (Görchen); and in the cloister of the Missionaries of the

Holy Family in Kazimierz Biskupi (Bischofsfelden), where priests faced the choice of paying four złoty per day for their upkeep or doing hard labor.[16] In early November 1939, twenty-six Poznań clerics were interned there.[17] To prevent escapes, three were imprisoned as hostages in nearby Konin.[18]

Imprisonment, execution, and deportation to makeshift camps in the region and to concentration camps in the Reich were all characteristic of the Nazi attack on the Polish Catholic clergy during and following the German invasion. The treatment of individual clerics may have been random in some cases, but generally, early German measures against Polish clerics and their church were undertaken broadly and systematically by seven *Einsatzgruppen* (Operational Groups) during the September campaign and the first phase of the occupation. Referred to in an August 1939 document as "Operational Groups of the Security Police," these units were divided into sixteen "Operational Commandos" of between 120 and 150 men, for a total of some 2,700 men drawn from the Security Police, Security Service (Sicherheitsdienst, or SD), Criminal Police (Kriminalpolizei, or Kripo), and Secret State Police (Geheime Staatspolizei, or Gestapo).[19] Officially under the authority of the army but de facto receiving orders from the head of the SS and German police, Heinrich Himmler,[20] they were charged with "combating all elements hostile to the Reich and German people in foreign territory behind the fighting troops."[21] Their deployment bore the code name Operation Tannenberg,[22] and the "elements hostile to the Reich and German people" included the Polish elite: members of the intelligentsia, former nobility, political and military leadership, and, not least, the clergy.[23] Incarceration and killing of elites, along with the destruction of their organizations and institutions, were intended to neutralize both resistance to German authority and the Polish nationalism that allegedly inspired it.

On August 25, 1939, Reinhard Heydrich, head of the Security Police (Sicherheitspolizei, or SiPo) and later chief of the Reich Security Main Office (Reichssicherheitshauptamt, or RSHA), established a *Sonderreferat*, or special administrative section of the Security Police, which was charged with coordinating and supervising the future activities of the Einsatzgruppen.[24] The office rapidly issued *Sonderfahndungslisten*, or lists of individuals labled and targeted as "anti-German." There were some sixty thousand Polish citizens on these lists,[25] and among them were not only clergy but also thousands of Catholics active in lay organizations. For the German authorities, the inclusion of the Catholic leadership among those targeted was self-evident, given their prominence among members of the intelligentsia and reputation as nationalist agitators. A September 30 memorandum of the Security Police attached to Einsatzgruppe III stated, "The stance of the Catholic clergy with regard to the German authorities and the German population can only be described as fundamentally anti-German."[26]

Priests and lay leaders were arrested, were often held as hostages along with other elites as a means of preventing attacks by Polish insurgents or hastening their capture,[27] or were simply shot with other prominent civilians as a means of intimidating and demoralizing the population. In early November 1939, the Security Police in Poznań were able to report to their Berlin office that a number of leaders and fuctionaries of the lay organization Catholic Action had been shot in "executions that had to be carried out as expiation for the murder of *Volksdeutsche*"[28]—that is, ethnic Germans living beyond the borders of the Reich. A September 1939 massacre likewise illustrates both the German goal of decimating the country's leadership and the inclusion of the clergy as targets among the elite. In a forest outside the village of Łąck (Lonsch), Gestapo officers and local Volksdeutsche shot twenty-one Poles and three Jews from the nearby town of Gostynin (Waldrode), eighteen of whom were identified by their professions. They included four teachers, the mayor and deputy mayor, two artisans, the chief of police, a bookkeeper, a surgeon, an attorney, the president of the local bank, the owner of a mill, the local delegate to the Polish parliament, and three priests. After the massacre, the victims, their wrists bound in wire, were thrown into a pit and buried. Some were still alive.[29]

It is significant that these killings were carried out by police associated with the Einsatzgruppen instead of the German army, which Hitler considered a potentially unreliable executor of such measures. According to Field Marshal Fedor von Bock, commander of Germany's Army Group North, Hitler had stated in an August 22, 1939, meeting with military leaders that he "did not wish to burden the army with the necessary liquidation [of] the Polish upper class, especially the Polish clergy."[30] Some military leaders were, in fact, uncomfortable with the killings. As a November 1939 report issued by German Army Command stated, "SS-formations" embedded with "ethnic-political special assignments" (*volkspolitische Sonderaufträge*) had hampered the work of transforming the region. "Public shootings have taken place," the report continued, "in nearly all of the larger municipalities. The choice [of victims] has been entirely random and often incomprehensible; the executions in many respects dishonorable."[31] This should not suggest, however, that the Wehrmacht remained on the sidelines of executions and other atrocities during the Polish campaign. As historians Jochen Böhler and Alexander Rossino have convincingly demonstrated, during the fall of 1939, the Wehrmacht played a particularly important role in Nazi Germany's transition to a form of warfare that included mass murder and genocide—a transition that scholars had traditionally identified with the invasion of the Soviet Union in 1941.[32]

If some in the Wehrmacht had concerns about shooting civilians, it soon became clear that they would have to accept the roles of the SS, Gestapo, and other civilian authorities in carrying out the "ethnic extermination" (*volkstümliche Ausrottung*) in occupied Polish territory.[33] Initial actions against the clergy and intelligentsia were curbed because of Wehrmacht protests,[34] but Heydrich remained impatient. "The little people," he is reported to have demanded, "we want to spare, but the nobility, clergy,[35] and Jews must be killed. After we enter Warsaw, I will reach an agreement with the army on how we will do away with these wretches."[36] The Einsatzgruppen may not have done away with all Polish clergymen, but their reach in the fall of 1939 was broad and deep. By the end of the year, the so-called ethno-political reallotment (*volkstumspolitische Flurbereinigung*) in the Reichsgau Posen had claimed at least ten thousand victims,[37] and it is estimated that by the spring of 1940 some sixty thousand Polish civilians had fallen victim to the Einsatzgruppen and the SS and police units who succeeded them.[38]

Two transitions in leadership and authority helped to ensure the long-term effectiveness of German police terror. First, the Einsatzgruppen were officially disbanded on November 20, 1939, but already on October 17, the *Sonderreferat* charged with their supervision had been transformed into a bureau for Polish affairs in Section (Amt) IV of the RSHA. This helped provide continuity between the military invasion of the first weeks and the occupation in the years that followed.[39] Second, on October 26, 1939, administration of the Reichsgau Posen was transferred from the German military to German civilian authorities, which then took on the "main and direct responsibility" for crimes against the Polish civilian population.[40] In what may appear counterintuitive to those unfamiliar with the character of the occupation, German civilian rule in the Warthegau was generally more brutal for Poles than was life under the authority of the German military. Although, as noted above, initial actions against the Polish intelligentsia may have been limited because of protests on the part of the Wehrmacht, after the end of military administration, the SS and police units resumed the incarceration and killing of Polish elites with renewed vigor, although perhaps in more covert ways.[41]

The subsequent treatment of Catholic clergy and laity, who of course counted among those elites, was consistent with an order of November 12, 1939, that required, for the purpose of "cleansing and securing" the Warthegau, the removal of "the entire intelligentsia as well as all political and criminal elements." This included Poles who were members of "Polish national organizations, political parties of all orientations, and the politically Catholic clergy and lay organizations."[42] According to a memorandum of the head of the Poznań State Police Office (Staatspolizeistelle), Helmut Bischoff, this initial attack on the clergy was concluded by the following summer,[43] but the arrest, incarceration, and deportation of priests was not always undertaken in such a selective manner.

Persecution of the clergy was, for example, particularly aggressive in the subdistrict or *Kreis*[44] of Inowrocław, where German authorities regarded the majority of priests as "directly or indirectly active as political leaders of Polishness."[45] Accordingly, all Polish priests there were either shot or arrested. Many of the incarcerated priests were eventually released, with the result, according to one German official, that their return to former parishes was leading to renewed anti-German behavior and a resuscitation of Polish national sentiment.[46] Such a situation, however, proved intolerable to the Nazi authorities, and arrests of priests consequently continued in the months ahead, so that by mid-1940 some 80 percent of the secular clergy in, for example, the Poznań *Regierungsbezirk* had been interned in cloisters. When these makeshift prisons were liquidated later in the summer of that year, the priests were deported to concentration camps in the Altreich.[47]

Persecution of the Polish Catholic Church was a constituent element of Nazi occupation policy in the Warthegau, and the incarceration and killing of priests was but one aspect of a broader agenda for the church. Returning to Gniezno, we can see how Mateusz Zabłocki's parish—one of more than a thousand parishes in the Reichsgau Wartheland[48]—illustrates how the Catholic Church would suffer in many other ways. The Church of the Holy Trinity remained officially in use until October 1941, but for the first two years of the occupation, worship services were allowed only on

Sunday mornings and were open only to ethnic Poles. Parishioners attending Sunday Mass there would sometimes be subject to police roundups at the church's exit, and those who did not have proof of employment were deported to the Reich interior for forced labor. The German authorities plundered the church, robbing it of its bells, paraments, and communionware, while the filial church in the nearby village of Zdziechowa (Zechau)—part of the same parish—was closed and turned into a storehouse for grain. The parish cemetery was likewise plundered and severely damaged, as the Nazi administration required the removal of all gravestone inscriptions in Polish. Roadside statues and shrines in the parish were destroyed. The German authorities also closed the nearby convent and hospital run by the Sisters of Charity of St. Vincent de Paul, requisitioned the hospital for other uses, and dispersed the nuns who worked there. Barred to Poles in October 1941, Gniezno's Church of the Holy Trinity would be made available to German Catholics in 1942. Any Poles who subsequently tried to attend Masses there were asked to leave by the German priest, who placed a sign at the church's entrance reading "Entry Prohibited to Poles."[49]

Fig. 1.10. Church of the Holy Trinity, Gniezno. Photo by the author.

These German measures against the Gniezno parish may, at first glance, appear random and spontaneous. They were, however, based on an ideology formulated in the months prior to the invasion, were applied systematically over the several years of the occupation, and were illustrative of the broader Nazi antichurch agenda in the Warthegau—an agenda that targeted not only the church's leadership but also its property, its administrative structure, and especially its relationship to Polish society and Polish national identity. The two chapters that follow consider the origins and early manifestations of Nazi hostility toward the Polish church: first, in terms of Nazism's fundamental animus toward ethnic Poles and the Polish nation, and second, in terms of Nazism's hostility toward Polish Catholicism, its proponents and adherents, clergy and laity.

Notes

1. "Zapiski z przesłuchania Księdza Prokuratura Bolza," March 28, 1947, Instytut Zachodni, Poznań (hereafter, IZ), document III-27, 14–16. Bolz stated that Zabłocki was executed on October 17, 1939. See also Instytut Zachodni (Pospieszalski, Wojciechowski) to Rada Państwa w Warszawie, April 3, 1947, IZ, document III-27, 17–18; "Sprawozdanie sytuacyjne z kraju 1939–1941," vol. 1, 107, PUMST; Befehlshaber der Sicherheitspolizei und des SD in Posen to Chef der Sicherheitspolizei Berlin, November 9, 1939, United States Holocaust Memorial Museum, Washington, DC (hereafter USHMM), RG 15.007M, reel 38, 466, 2–14. On Zabłocki's biography, arrest, and execution (which the authors date October 14, 1939) see also Wiktor Jacewicz and Jan Woś, *Martyrologium polskiego duchowieństwa rzymskokatolickiego pod okupacją hitlerowską w latach 1939–1945*, Kościół katolicki na ziemiach Polski w czasie II Wojny Światowej, vol. 2, no. 1, "Straty osobowe" (Warszawa: Akademia Teologii Katolickiej, 1977), 19–20; Agnieszka Łuczak and Aleksandra Pietrowicz, *Polityczne oczyszczanie gruntu: zagłada polskich elit w Wielkopolsce (1939–1941). Politische Flurbereinigung: die Vernichtung der polnischen Eliten in Großpolen (1939–1941)* (Poznań: Instytut Pamięci Narodowej, 2009), 14, 30.

2. August Hlond, "First Report of Cardinal Hlond, Primate of Poland, to Pope Pius XII," January 6, 1940, in *The Persecution of the Catholic Church in German-Occupied Poland. Reports Presented by H. E. Cardinal Hlond, Vatican Broadcasts and Other Reliable Evidence*, by August Hlond (New York: Longmans, Green, 1941), 1–24; Cardinal Luigi Maglione to Ribbentrop, March 2, 1934, document 480, in Secrétairerie D'État de Sa Sainteté, *Actes et Documents du Saint-Siège Relatifs à la Seconde Guerre Mondiale* (hereafter ADSS), vol. 3, no. 2 (Città del Vaticano: Librera Editrice Vaticana, 1967), 744; Der Befehlshaber der Sicherheitspolizei und des SD in Posen to Chef der Sicherheitspolizei Berlin, November 9, 1939, USHMM, RG-15.007M, reel 38, 466, 2–14; "Aufstellung Priester und Kirchen in der Erzdiözese Posen," October 10, 1941, Bundesarchiv Berlin (hereafter BAB), R 5101/22437, 13; Harry Siegmund, *Rückblick: Erinnerungen eines Staatsdieners in bewegter Zeit* (Raisdorf: Ostsee Verlag, 1999), 245; Sprawozdanie sytuacyjne z kraju 1939–1941, vol. 1, 105–11, PUMST;

"A Note of His Eminence the Cardinal Secretary of State to the Foreign Minister of the Reich about the Religious Situation in the 'Warthegau' and in the Other Polish Provinces Subject to Germany," March 2, 1943, document 3264-PS, in International Military Tribunal, *Trial of the Major War Criminals before the International Military Tribunal. Nuremberg 14 November 1945–1 October 1946* (hereafter IMT), vol. 32 (Nuremberg: International Military Tribunal, 1945–1947), 93–105; "Wiadomość o prześladowaniu koscioła katolickiego przez okupanta niemieckiego na terenie parafii Farnej w Gnieznie," July 10, 1945, IPN, GK 196/19, 182; Kuria Metropolitalna w Gnieźnie, "Statystyka. Szkód wojennych osobowych i kościelnych w Archidiecezji Gnieźnieńskiej," IPN, GK 196/19, 163; "Spis księży zamordowanych przez Niemców poza obozami koncentracyjnymi," Archiwum Archidiecezjalne w Poznaniu (hereafter AAP), zespół 133, syg. OK 121.

3. Główna Komisja Badania Zbrodni Hitlerowskich w Polsce—Rada Ochrony Pomników Walki i Męczeństwa, *Obozy hitlerowskie na ziemiach polskich 1939–1945—Informator encyklopedyczny*, ed. Czesław Pilichowski et al. (Warszawa: Państwowe Wydawnictwo Naukowe, 1979), 643.

4. Świadectwo Ks. Józefa Sarniewicza, n.d., IPN, GK 196/19, 168.

5. Hlond, *Persecution*, 4.

6. Biography of Ks. Kazimierz Nowicki, Vikariusz w Miasteczku, n.d. IPN, GK 196/19, 164.

7. "Zapiski z przesłuchania Księdza Prokuratura Bolza," March 28, 1947, IZ, document III-27, 16; Łuczak and Pietrowicz, *Polityczne*, 32.

8. Maria Wardzyńska, *Był rok 1939: operacja niemieckiej policji bezpieczeństwa w Polsce. Intelligenzaktion* (Warszawa: Instytut Pamięci Narodowej-Komisja Ścigania Zbrodni Przeciwko Narodowi Polskiemu, 2009), 92; Jacewicz and Woś, *Martyrologium*, vol. 2, no. 1, 121–22.

9. Jacewicz and Woś, *Martyrologium*, vol. 2, no. 1, 74.

10. Nikodem Kowalski to Dyrektor Archiwum Archidiecezjalnego w Poznaniu, August 30, 1990, AAP, zespół 133, syg. OK 237; "Sprawozdanie sytuacyjne z kraju 1939–1941," vol. 1, 107, PUMST; Zeznanie Ks. Dr. Józefa Nowackiego, June 24, 1946. Najwyższy Trubunał Narodowy, Akta w sprawie Arthura Greisera, tom V, IPN, GK 196/38/CD1, 58; Jastrąb, *Archidiecezja*, 594, note 1451; Jacewicz and Woś, *Martyrologium*, vol. 2, no. 1, 20.

11. Bekanntmachung, October 18, 1939, Instytut Pamięci Narodowej-Komisja Ścigania Zbrodni przeciwko Narodowi Polskiemu, Łódź (hereafter IPN Ld) 9/104, 19; "Bericht verfaßt von einer dem höheren Klerus Polens angehörenden Persönlichkeit, dem Papst vorgelegt vor seiner Zusammenkunf [*sic*] mit Ribbentrop," April 15, 1940, BAB, R58/7470, 46; Frątczak, *Diecezja*, 153–55.

12. "The Murder of Father Roman Pawlowski of Chocz, Report of November, 1939," in Hlond, *Persecution*, 105–6.

13. Mieczysław Posmyk, ankiet, May 17, 1974, AAP, zespół 133, OK 224, 450/74.

14. "Wiadomość o prześladowaniu koscioła katolickiego przez okupanta niemieckiego na terenie parafii Farnej w Gnieznie," July 10, 1945, IPN, GK 196/19, 182–83. On Wnuk, see also Jan Walkusz, "Kontakty polonijnego duszpasterza ks. Wawrzyńca Wnuka z Polską," *Roczniki Historii Kościoła* 1, no. 3 (58) (2011), 134.

15. "Ląd - niemiecki obóz przejściowy dla duchowieństwa," *Kronika diecezji włocławskiej* 50, no. 6–10 (June–October 1967), 235–36; Jarosław Wąsowicz, *Lądzcy męczennicy: obóz dla*

duchowieństwa w Lądzie n/Wartą styczeń 1940-październik 1941 (Ląd: WSD Towarzystwa Salezjańskiego w Lądzie, 2013), 8–9.

16. "Sprawozdanie sytuacyne z kraju 1939–1941," vol. 1, 106. PUMST; Hlond, *Persecution*, 5.

17. Befehlshaber der Sicherheitspolizei und des SD in Posen to Chef der Sicherheitspolizei Berlin, November 9, 1939. USHMM, RG 15.007M, reel 38, 466, 4.

18. Jan Krajewski, ankiet, AAP, zespół 133, syg. 220, 516/74.

19. On the organization, activities, and significance of the Einsatzgruppen in Poland, see Stephan Lehnstaedt and Jochen Böhler, "Einführung," in *Die Berichte der Einsatzgruppen in Polen 1939*, ed. Stephan Lehnstaedt and Jochen Böhler (Berlin: Metropol Verlag, 2013); chaps. 1 and 2 of Rossino, *Hitler*, 1–57; Klaus-Michael Mallmann, Jochen Böhler, and Jürgen Matthäus, eds., *Einsatzgruppen in Polen: Darstellung und Dokumentation* (Darmstadt: Wissenschaftliche Buchgesellschaft, 2008), 11–108; Helmut Krausnick and Hans-Heinrich Wilhelm, *Die Truppe des Weltanschauungskrieges: Die Einsatzgruppen der Sicherheitspolizei und des SD 1938–1942*, Quellen und Darstellungen zur Zeitgeschichte, vol. 22 (Stuttgart: Deutsche Verlags-Anstalt, 1981), 32–106; and Kazimierz Leszczyński, "Działalność Einsatzgruppen Policji Bezpieczeństwa na Ziemiach Polskich w 1939r. w świetle Dokumentów," *Biuletyn Głównej Komisji Badania Zbrodni Hitlerowskich w Polsce* 22 (1971), 7–290.

20. Klaus-Jürgen Müller, *Das Heer und Hitler: Armee und nationalsozialistisches Regime 1933–1940* (Stuttgart: Deutsche Verlags-Anstalt, 1969), 426; Lehnstaedt and Böhler, "Einführung," 7.

21. "Richtlinien für den auswärtigen Einsatz der Sicherheitspolizei und des SD," n.d. (August 1939), document 2, in Mallmann, Böhler, and Matthäus, *Einsatzgruppen*, 117; Lehnstaedt and Böhler, "Einführung," 7.

22. The designation Tannenberg was intended to recall two battles: the fifteenth-century defeat of the Teutonic Knights by Polish-Lithuanian forces and the August 1914 victory of the German army over Russian forces. On the larger significance of the code name, see Daniel Brewing, *Im Schatten von Auschwitz: deutsche Massaker an polnischen Zivilisten 1939–1945*, Veröffentlichungen der Forschungsstelle Ludwigsburg der Universität Stuttgart, vol. 29 (Darmstadt: Wissenschaftliche Buchgesellschaft, 2016), 158–59.

23. On the treatment of elites, see Agnieszka Łuczak, "Eksterminacja elit narodu polskiego w Wielkopolsce w 1939r.," in *Konferencja: "Od Westerplatte do Norymbergi. Druga wojna światowa we współczesnej historiografii, muzealnictwie i edukacji" w Muzeum Stutthof (2–5 września 2009 r.)*, ed. Piotr Chruścielski and Marcin Owsiński (Sztutowo: Muzeum Stutthof, 2009), 57–65.

24. Rossino, *Hitler*, 14, 29–30.

25. Maria Rutowska, "NS-Verfolgungsmaßnahmen in den eingegliderten Gebieten," in *Polen unter deutscher und sowjetischer Besatzung 1939–1945*, ed. Jacek Andrzej Młynarczyk, Einzelveröffentlichungen des Deutschen Historischen Instituts Warschau, vol. 20 (Osnabrück: Fibre Verlag, 2009), 201.

26. Der Chef der Sicherheitspolizei, Sonderreferent "Unternehmen Tannenberg," Tagesbericht für die Zeit vom 29.9.39, 12:00 Uhr bis 30.9.39, 12:00 Uhr, September 30, 1939, in Leszczyński, "Działalność," 143.

27. Rossino, *Hitler*, 65, 133–34.

28. Befehlshaber der Sicherheitspolizei und des SD in Posen to Chef der Sicherheitspolizei Berlin, November 9, 1939, USHMM, RG 15.007M, reel 38, 466, 4.

29. Edward Serwański, "Materiały do sprawy eksterminacji w tzw. Kraju Warty, Powiaty: Wieluń—woj. Łódzkie, Gostynin—woj. Warszawskie," *Przegląd Zachodni* 11, no. 7–8 (July–August 1955), 621.

30. Quoted in Rossino, *Hitler*, 10.

31. Bericht des Wehrkreiskommandos XXI, Posen, November 23, 1939, document D 141, in *Macht ohne Moral: eine Dokumentation über die SS*, ed. Reimund Schnabel (Frankfurt am Main: Röderbergverlag, 1957), 395–96.

32. See Rossino, *Hitler*, 10, and Böhler, *Auftakt*.

33. "Aktenvermerk des Oberstleutnants von Lahousen über die Besprechung im Führerzug am 12.9.1939 in Ilnau," September 14, 1939, in Helmuth Groscurth, *Tagebücher eines Abwehroffiziers 1938–1940. Mit weiteren Dokumenten zur Militäropposition gegen Hitler*, ed. Helmut Krausnick, Harold C. Deutsch, and Hildegard von Kotze, Quellen und Darstellungen zur Zeitgeschichte, vol. 19 (Stuttgart: Deutsche Verlags-Anstalt, 1970), 558.

34. Alberti, "'Exerzierplatz," 113.

35. For the clergy Heydrich uses the word *Popen*, a derisive term with no precise translation in English.

36. Entry of September 8, 1939, in Groscurth, *Tagebücher*, 201.

37. Mallmann et al., *Einsatzgruppen*, 87–88. The figure of ten thousand by year's end appears conservative, as Łuczak claims the same number of dead had been reached by October 26, 1939. See Czesław Łuczak, *Pod Niemieckim Jarzmem (Kraj Warty 1939–1945)* (Poznań: Pracownia Serwisu Oprogramowania, 1996), 18–19, and also Czesław Łuczak, "Das deutsche Okkupationssystem im unterworfenen Polen während des zweiten Weltkrieges," *Studia Historiae Oeconomicae* 22 (1997), 43. The German term *Flurbereinigung* refers to an integration and redistribution of parcels of agricultural land and is used here metaphorically.

38. Lehnstaedt and Böhler, "Einführung," 7.

39. Lehnstaedt and Böhler, "Einführung," 10.

40. Szymon Datner, *Crimes Committed by the Wehrmacht during the September Campaign and the Period of Military Government* (Poznań: Instytut Zachodni, 1962), 24.

41. Alberti, "Exerzierplatz," 113–14.

42. Anordnung, Der Höhere SS- und Polizeiführer, Posen (Rapp), November 12, 1939, IPN, GK 196/28, 151.

43. Bischoff, Geheime Staatspolizei Posen, June 4, 1940, Abschrift, Yad Vashem—The World Holocaust Remembrance Center, International Institute for Holocaust Research (hereafter YV), TR.17, 72.

44. The designation *Kreis* referred to an administrative subdistrict that was part of one of the Warthegau's large administrative districts or *Regierungsbezirke*, of which there were three: Posen, Hohensalza (Inowrocław), and Kalisch (Kalisz), which was redesignated in April 1940 as Regierungsbezirk Litzmannstadt (Łódź).

45. "Bericht über die Entwicklung der kirchlichen Lage im Reichsgau Wartheland (Abschnittsbereich Hohensalza)," n.d., BAB R 58/7581, 26. Although the report is not dated, its content makes clear that it postdates June 1940.

46. "Bericht über die Entwicklung der kirchlichen Lage im Reichsgau Wartheland (Abschnittsbereich Hohensalza)," n.d., BAB R 58/7581, 29.

47. Heydrich to Reichsminister für die Kirchlichen Angelegenheiten, February 13, 1940, BAB, R 5101/22185, 111–12; Sprawozdanie sytuacyjne z kraju 1939–1941, vol. 1, 105–11, PUMST; Sicherheitsdienst des Reichsführers-SS, SD-Leitabschnitt Posen, to Reichssicherheitshauptamt - Amt II B/32, Berlin, 10 December 1940, USHMM, RG-15.007M, reel 15, 216, 22.

48. Fijałkowski, *Kościół*, 217.

49. "Wiadomość o prześladowaniu koscioła katolickiego przez okupanta niemieckiego na terenie parafii Farnej w Gnieznie," July 10, 1945, IPN, GK 196/19, 182–85.

Fig. 2.1. Poland under German occupation. Map by Timber Wright.

2

GRÖßTE HÄRTE

The Invasion of Poland: Ideology and Execution

When German forces invaded Poland on September 1, 1939, the Third Reich initiated a drive for territorial expansion, economic exploitation, and Germanization. Control over the Polish lands would regain territory lost in the Treaty of Versailles, would avenge some of the national humiliation associated with that settlement, and would be an important step toward accomplishing the goal of establishing a Nazi empire in the east. Linked to these more conventional political-military objectives were, however, the imperatives of what Nazi ideology understood as an ethno-racial struggle, or Volkstumskampf, that was to begin on conquered Polish territory. The path that struggle was to take had not yet been fully charted in 1939, but German plans for the invasion reveal much about how Nazi ideology would direct its course in the years ahead. A people, a nation, and a race could not, according to this ideology, survive without expanding territory at the expense of other peoples and states. The target for expansion was that part of Europe east of Germany's borders, and the primary objective was Poland. In targeting Poland, the German forces would have to exercise, in Adolf Hitler's words, *Größte Härte*, or the "greatest severity."[1]

Territorial gain was inextricably linked to the goal of racial prosperity. As Hitler reportedly stated at a meeting of government ministers and military leaders in November 1937, "The goal of German policy is the securing and maintenance of the *Volksmasse* and its proliferation," and this objective could not be separated from *Lebensraum*, or "living space."[2] Expansion would mean occupation, domination, exploitation, Germanization broadly conceived, and eventually the removal of those populations regarded as a racial threat or hindrance to Germany's political, economic, and military plans. The German drive to the east at Poland's expense therefore saw the convergence of more traditional military initiatives with the racial goals of Nazi ideology, and assumed their interdependence. The former could not succeed without the motivation of the latter, just as long-term racial objectives were dependent on the rapid and consequential fulfillment of military objectives.

Both the racial-ideological and the military objectives were a project in the making, and Poland's place in the broader plans of the Third Reich remained unspecified until early 1939, when Hitler decided that the conquest of Poland was the necessary first step toward the goal of German dominance in eastern Europe.[3] The ferocity of the September 1939 invasion and subsequent occupation of Poland have led many to assume that the German anti-Polish animus had been a constituent element of Nazi ideology since, or even before, the assumption of power in 1933. The Nazis did, of course, have a firm commitment to revising the territorial losses of World War I, and they were eager to support Poland's German minority. German opinion across the political spectrum tended to regard Poland as a *Saisonstaat* (a temporary, seasonal state), and the derisive phrase *polnische Wirtschaft* (literally, "Polish economy") was broadly used to describe a chaotic situation,[4] but Hitler had relatively little to say about Poland before the war, and his attitudes were unclear. From 1934, when Germany signed a nonaggression treaty with Poland, until early 1939, the National Socialist government officially regarded Poland as a potentially friendly state,[5] and in January 1939, Hitler even considered the possibility of invading the Soviet Union in alliance with the Poles. In short, before September 1939, plans for Poland and its inhabitants were vague and undeveloped.[6]

It was in the spring and summer of that year when Poland became for Hitler the crucial first step in the fulfillment of German imperial ambition, and when the ideological imperatives driving that ambition coalesced.[7] Anti-Jewish ideology was, of course, fundamental to the National Socialist movement since its origins, although the implementation of antisemitic policy would be marked by improvisation and would take what has become known as a "twisted road to Auschwitz."[8] By contrast, the articulation of Nazi anti-Polish ideology and the formation of policy emerging from it were telescoped into a comparatively short period beginning in 1939. The brevity of that period emerges as all the more remarkable in light of the ferocity of the invasion and the brutality of the German occupation that followed.

Polish resolve in the face of Nazi foreign-policy objectives grew in the last months of 1938 and early 1939, as German diplomacy used a combination of threats and promises in an effort to win Polish concessions. The Poles, however, rejected German demands that they adhere to the Anti-Comintern Pact, as well as German proposals for an extraterritorial thoroughfare through the so-called Polish Corridor between West and East Prussia and for the incorporation of Gdańsk (Danzig) into the Reich.[9] Following the German occupation of Czechoslovakia, British Prime Minister Neville Chamberlain made a declaration of British support for Poland on March 31, followed by a formal communiqué guaranteeing mutual assistance on April 6. France, on April 13, likewise reiterated the validity of its 1923 alliance with Poland. Hitler then proceeded to repudiate the Polish-German nonaggression pact of 1934, for by that time, plans for an invasion of Poland were already underway.

On April 3, 1939, the High Command of the Armed Forces (Oberkommando der Wehrmacht, or OKW) had submitted to Hitler a "Directive for the Unified Preparation of the Wehrmacht for War 1939/1940," which Hitler approved, stating that the army must be ready to attack by September 1 at the latest.[10] On May 23, addressing the commanders-in-chief of the armed forces, Hitler made his intentions regarding Poland clear. Poland, he stated, was no "secondary enemy," but a state "always on the side of our enemies." The object of German policy was not, he continued, simply resolution of the struggle over the future of the free city of Gdańsk but also "the extension of *Lebensraum* in the east and the seizure of foodstuffs [*Sicherstellung der Ernährung*]."[11]

In a meeting with his military commanders only days before the invasion, Hitler emphasized the urgency of the Polish campaign and set further guidelines for conduct of the war. Germany's relationship with Poland had become "unbearable," he stated, and now was the time to strike against Poland "or be destroyed with certainty sooner or later."[12] That strike, Hitler continued, would be undertaken in agreement with the Soviet Union after the imminent conclusion of a nonaggression pact. "Now," he concluded, "Poland is in the position in which I wanted her."[13] Hitler also left no doubt that this was to be an unconventional campaign, the goal of which was, according to notes recorded by the head of German military intelligence (Abwehr) Admiral Canaris, "not the arrival at a certain line," but the "elimination of living forces." "Have no pity," Hitler reportedly urged his generals. "Brutal attitude. Eighty million people shall get what is their right. Their existence has to be secured. The strongest has the right. Greatest severity [*Größte Härte*]."[14] The magnitude of Hitler's plans was echoed in the diary of General Franz Halder, whose notes claimed that Hitler had in fact called for the "annihilation of Poland" and the need to "steel ourselves against humanitarian impulses."[15]

Such were the outlines of the broader goals and tactics for treatment of Poland's civilian population, and they were put into practice during the military campaign in the weeks that followed. In a conversation with Abwehr officer Helmuth Groscurth on September 9, Halder reported that "the slaughter of Poles behind the front was increasing so much that soon drastic measures would have to be taken." It was, Halder claimed, "the intent of Hitler and [Hermann] Göring to annihilate and exterminate the Polish people." The remainder of Halder's comments could not, according to Groscurth, be put into writing.[16]

Even if one allows for the hyperbole of Hitler's rhetoric and references to "annihilation" and "extermination," the fact remains that the Polish campaign was a turning point in military conduct, and marked, in the words of Alexander Rossino, "a critical place in the history of Nazi Germany's descent into mass murder and genocide."[17] German effectiveness on the battlefield was complemented and bolstered by an ideological imperative, hastily formulated as it was, that was manifested in the massacre of civilians, the razing of villages, the terror bombing of civilian targets, the taking of hostages, and the actions of the Einsatzgruppen discussed in the previous chapter. "In its combination of military and ideological dimensions," Rossino writes, "the invasion of Poland heralded a fundamental shift in the way that Germany waged war in Eastern Europe. Both the civilian population and the Polish army were enemies in this new war, and mass murder was employed on the battlefield as an instrument of state policy."[18]

The ideological bases of such policy can be found in a variety of documentary sources from before, during, and after the campaign, but in analyzing these sources, it is important to remember that German policy was neither clearly linear, as if directed at some predetermined goal, nor entirely consistent. Early on, some in the National Socialist leadership were even eager to pursue the possibility of a Polish puppet government led by German-friendly political and cultural elites. It quickly became clear, however, that the "new order" in Poland would be accomplished not by political means and collaborative arrangements but by police methods and severe occupation regimes.[19] Nazi ideology required the eradication of the

Polish state, the Germanization of its territory, the complete subjugation of the allegedly racially inferior Polish *Untermensch* (subhuman), and the destruction or neutralization of all Polish cultural institutions.

Behind this rapidly developing ideology were, in many cases, high-level academics and scholars of reputation. In early October 1939, for example, a working group of the North- and East-German Research Collective (Nord- und Ostdeutsche Forschungsgemeinschaft, or NOFG) met in Wrocław (Breslau). Established in 1933, the NOFG was a research institute that, in the words of historian Ingo Haar, "became the institutional link between ethnographic research and state policymaking."[20] The working group was charged with developing recommendations for the "ethnopolitical reallotment" to be executed in occupied Polish territory, and emerging from its meeting was a lengthy memorandum, authored by the historian Theodor Schieder, on "settlement and ethno-racial questions [*Volkstumsfragen*] in the reclaimed eastern provinces [of Poland]." The memorandum called for the deportations of Jews and Poles from the western annexed areas, justifying such measures on the basis of the "unprecedented destruction and displacement of German *Volkstum*" that had taken place in the region after the formation of the post–World War I Polish state. It also demanded a clear distinction between German and Polish ethno-racial characteristics, referring to the "dangers of ethnic and racial mixing and infiltration." Nazi population policy in the annexed territories was to be advanced in part through the "intensification of agriculture" and the "removal of Jews from the large Polish cities,"[21] reflecting the document's preoccupation with the Germanization of not only the region's population but also its land—its cities and villages, urban and rural enterprises, farms and forests. This "spatial" aspect of Germanization policy would hold particular significance for the Catholic Church in the Reichsgau Wartheland in the months and years ahead, as the Nazi authorities would go to great lengths to efface Polish Catholicism's physical structures (churches), symbols (shrines, statues, and gravestones), and supporters (clergy, laity) from the Warthegau's landscape.

According to Nazi racial principles, Poles' racial inferiority was axiomatic. Echoing the Schieder memorandum of the previous month, a November 1939 memorandum of the Office of Racial Policy of the NSDAP (Rassenpolitisches Amt der NSDAP) on "The Question of the Treatment of the Population of the Former Polish Regions according to Racial-Political Considerations," authored by Dr. Erhard Wetzel and Dr. Gerhard Hecht, stipulated that there were considerable racial differences between the Polish and German populations. Any racial similarities, the document stated, arose from German and Nordic racial elements in the Polish blood, while Poles' racial deficiencies were the result of their mixing over the centuries with east Baltic, oriental, and Asiatic populations, as well as the "high-level contamination of the Polish people by Jewish blood."[22]

As a self-styled expert on racial theory and praxis, Heinrich Himmler issued in May 1940 his own brief treatise on the treatment of non-German populations in the occupied eastern territories, in which he argued that non-Germans should attend only four years of school with the goal of teaching them simple arithmetic and the writing of one's own name. They should, he argued, also learn to be obedient toward Germans, honest, diligent, and well behaved.[23] From a distance of many decades, the rhetoric of what Martin Broszat referred to as the Nazi leadership's "ethno-political alchemy" appears to belong to the realm of senseless fantasy. Yet, as in the case of Hitler's vocabulary of invasion, the rhetoric of Nazi racial policy—terms such as "decomposition," "encystment," " cleansing," "restructuring," "skimming," and "leaching"—corresponded all too literally to its implementation.[24]

Motivated by Nazism's racial imperatives, Germanization of Poland's annexed western territories meant the removal of Poles and Jews, and for those Poles who remained, the erasure of any vestiges of their state and cultural institutions. As Reinhard Heydrich outlined to the division chiefs of the Reich Security Main Office (RSHA) and commanders of the newly formed Einsatzgruppen in a September 21, 1939, meeting, the annexed territories were to become German "Gaus," while an adjacent Gau (the later Generalgouvernement, or General Government), with Kraków (Krakau) as its capital, would be a dumping ground for the "foreign-language population" (that is, Poles and Jews). The annexed territories in the west of the prewar Polish state (that is, that portion of Polish territory incorporated into Silesia, the subsequent Reichsgau Danzig-Westpreußen, and the subsequent Reichsgau Wartheland) were to function as the Third Reich's "eastern wall" (*Ostwall*), a bulwark against racial and ideological threats from the east.[25] Achieving this goal meant cleansing the region of Poles and Jews and securing it, both racially and politically, for future generations. In the words of historian Phillip Rutherford, "three political paths—*Judenpolitik*, *Polenpolitik*, and *Sicherheitspolitik* (security policy)—had merged into one sweeping policy of destructive Germanization."[26]

Thus, in the long term, the Pole was to be the German's slave, servant, or, at best, a seasonal and itinerant worker who would eventually be concentrated in the General Government. According to Heydrich, what remained of Poland's political leadership class was to be rendered harmless and sent to concentration camps, while other Polish elites, including military officers, teachers, members of the nobility, and clergy, were to be arrested and deported to the General Government as well. The spiritual needs of Poles were to be tended to by priests "from the west" who would be prohibited from speaking Polish.[27] Thus, Heydrich's reference to Polish Catholics and their clergy at the September 21 meeting was not at all arbitrary, but points to the perception, axiomatic among Nazi leaders and officials in the Reichsgau Wartheland, of Catholicism as a bastion of Polish nationalism and threat to German interests and security in the occupied Polish lands.

Notes

1. "Second Speech by the Fuehrer on 22 August 1939," translation of Document 1014-PS, Prosecution Exhibit 1102, in Nuernberg Military Tribunals, *Trials of War Criminals before the Nuernberg Military Tribunals under Control Council Law No. 10. Nuernberg, October 1946–April 1949* (hereafter NMT), vol. 10 (Washington, DC: United States Government Printing Office, 1951), 703.

2. Memorandum, Hossbach, November 10, 1937, on conference held on November 5, 1937 at the Reich Chancellery, document 386-PS, IMT, vol. 25, 403.

3. Rossino, *Hitler*, 4–5.

4. Gerhard L. Weinberg, *Germany, Hitler, and World War II: Essays in Modern German and World History* (Cambridge: Cambridge University Press), 1996, 42.

5. Hans-Jürgen Bömelburg and Bogdan Musial, "Die deutsche Besatzungspolitik in Polen 1939–1945," in *Deutsch-polnische Beziehungen 1939–1945–1949: eine Einführung*, Einzelveröffentlichungen des Deutschen Historischen Instituts Warschau, vol. 5., ed. Włodzimierz Borodziej and Klaus Ziemer (Osnabrück: Fibre Verlag, 2000), 44. On the treaty and German-Polish relations in general during the first six years of Nazi rule see Anna M. Cienciała, "The Foreign Policy of Józef Piłsudski and Józef Beck: Misconceptions and Misinterpretations," *The Polish Review* 56, nos. 1–2 (2011).

6. Rutherford, *Prelude*, 36. See also Richard Evans, *The Third Reich at War* (New York: Penguin, 2009), 10. On the place of Poland in National Socialist propaganda and indoctrination practices from the 1920s through the end of the regime, see "Ignorancja i nienawiść. Obraz Polski i Polaków w nazistowskich środkach masowego przekazu," chap. 8 in Eugeniusz Cezary Król, *Propaganda i indoktrynacja narodowego socjalizmu w Niemczech 1919–1945: Studium organizacji, treści, metod i technik masowego oddziaływania* (Warszawa: Oficyna Wydawnicza Rytm, 1999), 511–643.

7. On the formation of German objectives and policy prior to the invasion see Klaus Hildebrandt, *The Foreign Policy of the Third Reich*, trans. Anthony Fothergill (Berkeley: University of California Press, 1973), 74–90; Broszat, *Nationalsozialistische*, 11–15.

8. See Schleunes, *Twisted Road.*

9. Gerhard L. Weinberg, *A World at Arms: A Global History of World War II* (Cambridge: Cambridge University Press, 1995), 32. I am also grateful to Jakub Tyszkiewicz for his observations on Polish-German relations in the months prior to the war.

10. Rossino, *Hitler*, 8.

11. Memorandum, Schmundt, May 23, 1939, document 079-L, in IMT, vol. 37, 548.

12. "The Fuehrer's speech to Commanders in Chief on 22 August 1939," translation of Document 798-PS, Prosecution Exhibit 1101, in NMT, vol. 10, 700.

13. "The Fuehrer's speech to Commanders in Chief on 22 August 1939," translation of Document 798-PS, Prosecution Exhibit 1101, in NMT, vol. 10, 701–2.

14. "Second Speech by the Fuehrer on 22 August 1939," translation of Document 1014-PS, Prosecution Exhibit 1102, in NMT, vol. 10, 703.

15. Entry of August 22, 1939, in Franz Halder, *The Halder War Diary, 1939–1942*, ed. Charles Burdick and Hans-Adolf Jacobsen (Novato, CA: Presidio, 1988), 31.

16. Entry of 9 September 1939, in Groscurth, *Tagebücher*, 201–2.

17. Rossino, *Hitler*, xv.

18. Rossino, *Hitler*, 1–2.

19. Broszat, *Nationalsozialistische*, 18–19; see also Halik Kochanski, *The Eagle Unbowed: Poland and the Poles in the Second World War* (Cambridge: Harvard University Press, 2012), 97–98.

20. Ingo Haar, "German *Ostforschung* and Anti-Semitism," in *German Scholars and Ethnic Cleansing 1919–1945*, ed. Ingo Haar and Michael Fahlbusch (New York: Berghahn, 2005), 8.

21. "Aufzeichnung über Siedlungs- und Volkstumsfragen in den wiedergewonnenen Ostprovinzen: Erster Entwurf von Theodor Schieder," Appendix no. 4 to Angelika Ebbingshaus and Karl Heinz Roth, "Vorläufer des Generalplans Ost. Eine Dokumentation über Theodor Schieders Polendenkschrift vom 7. Oktober 1939," *Zeitschrift für Sozialgeschichte des 20. und 21. Jahrhunderts* 7, no. 1 (1999): 84–91. The same article provides the most thorough analysis of the Schieder memorandum. See also Ingo Haar, *Historiker im Nationalsozialismus: Deutsche Geschichtswissenschaft und der 'Volkstumskampf' im Osten*, Kritische Studien zur Geschichtswissenschaft, vol. 143 (Göttingen: Vandenhoeck und Ruprecht, 2000), 330–31.

22. E. Wetzel and G. Hecht, "Die Frage der Behandlung der Bevölkerung der ehemaligen polnischen Gebiete nach rassenpolitischen Gesichtspunkten," November 25, 1939. The document is reprinted in its entirety in Karol Marian Pospieszalski, ed., *Hitlerowskie "Prawo" Okupacyjne w Polsce*, Documenta Occupationis, vol. 5, no. 1 (Poznań: Instytut Zachodni, 1952), 7–8. See also Broszat, *Nationalsozialistische*, 26; Epstein, *Model Nazi*, 197–98; Alberti, *Verfolgung*, 88.

23. Helmut Krausnick, "Denkschrift Himmlers über die Behandlung der Fremdvölkischen im Osten (Mai 1940)," *Vierteljahrshefte für Zeitgeschichte* 5, no. 2 (April 1957): 197.

24. Broszat, *Nationalsozialistische*, 25.

25. Walter Rauff, Aktennotiz über eine von Reinhard Heydrich geleitete Besprechung der Amtschefs und der Führer der Einsatzgruppen der Sipo am 21. September 1939, September 27, 1939, document 12, in Werner Röhr and Elke Heckert, eds., *Die faschistische Okkupationspolitik in Polen (1939–1945)* (Köln: Pahl-Rugenstein, 1989), 119.

26. English: "Jewish policy, Polish policy, and security policy." Rutherford, *Prelude*, 48.

27. Rauff, Aktennotiz über eine von Reinhard Heydrich geleitete Besprechung der Amtschefs und der Führer der Einsatzgruppen der Sipo am 21 September 1939, September 27, 1939, document 12 in Röhr and Heckert, *Die faschistische Okkupationspolitik*, 119. See also Broszat, *Nationalsozialistische*, 21.

3

HETZKAPLAN

The Polish Church and the "Agitator Priest" in Nazi Ideology

Nazi hostility toward Poles and Poland may not have been based on a coherent ideological foundation in the years leading up to the war, but in developing the *Feindbild*—that is, the enemy image of the Poles necessary for the prosecution of the war and occupation of Polish lands—Nazi propagandists could draw on stereotypes and enmities common among Germans for generations. Likewise, Nazi hostility toward Polish Catholicism did not arise *ex nihilo*, but was founded on a legacy of Prussian and German animosity and mistrust since the partitions of Poland in the late eighteenth century. The German occupation of Poland during World War II saw the convergence of multiple strands of anti-Catholic and anti-Polish sentiment that had emerged over the course of many generations, and the result in the Reichsgau Wartheland was persecution of the church and a murderous campaign against the so-called *Hetzkaplan*, or "agitator-priest," who was allegedly a champion of the Polish-national cause. This chapter investigates the ideological bases of Nazism's hostility toward Polish Catholicism.

Protestantism had dominated religious life in Prussia, with Reformed and Lutheran Christians combined in a united Protestant (in German, *evangelisch*, or "evangelical") church in the early nineteenth century. After a brief period (1815–1830) characterized by a spirit of relative tolerance and reform, Prussia embarked on a policy of greater hostility toward the Catholic Church in its eastern lands, and toward its Polish clergy, whom the governor of Posen Province at the time, Eduard Heinrich Flottwell, criticized for their "hypocrisy," "benightedness," "coarseness," and "egotism."[1] The infamous anti-Catholic *Kulturkampf* (or, literally, "culture struggle") in the newly united Germany of the 1870s was intended primarily to curb German rather than Polish Catholic influence in the new empire, but its effects were far-reaching in predominantly Polish-speaking regions. Otto von Bismarck's government banned the Jesuit order, required civil marriage in addition to church ceremonies, placed restrictions on use of the Polish language, and undertook a broad effort to Germanize education there. German became the compulsory language in state schools, Polish was permitted only as a language of religious instruction, priests had to relinquish their supervision of elementary schools to laymen, and all graduating candidates for the priesthood were required to pass an examination on German culture, history, and literature. Hundreds of Polish (and German) priests refused to comply with the new restrictions, and ninety Polish priests, including the primate of Poland, Archbishop Mieczysław Ledóchowski, were imprisoned.[2]

Not only did such measures increase the mistrust and animosity of Polish Catholics vis-à-vis the German state in the eastern provinces; they also reinforced the simplistic and misleading, yet increasingly automatic, association of Poles with Catholicism and Germans with Protestantism. Even as the Kulturkampf failed miserably in its effort to undermine Catholic resolve and solidarity in the empire as a whole, so too did its measures, along with Bismarck's aggressive Polenpolitik, encourage rather than diminish the growth of Polish nationalism.[3] In addition, the unity it forged helped to expand the Polish national movement geographically and socially, beyond the clergy and aristocracy to the Polish peasantry and urban workers.[4] Many Poles therefore reacted aggressively against the dictates emanating from Berlin, and local parishioners at times even resorted to violence in defending their Polish priests and barring new "official" (i.e., German) priests from entering churches, or they simply boycotted their services and ministrations.[5] This was but one illustration of how the Polish church not only could stand as a defense against the modernizing ideologies of liberalism and socialism but also could serve the Polish national project as a defense against Germanization—a role that would help it emerge as an institution of social prominence with significant moral and cultural capital in a post–World War I independent Poland.

The church would maintain that prominence, but it would not go unchallenged in the two decades ahead. Many assume, based on the common and durable notion of a *Polak-Katolik* nexus in Polish society and culture, that the Roman Catholic Church enjoyed an immediate and undisputed position of power in the newly independent postwar Poland (often referred to as the Second Republic or Polish Republic). To be sure, the church was unrivaled among religious institutions in interwar Poland: its membership included roughly two-thirds of the population; Catholic devotion was common and transcended social class; the church possessed tremendous wealth, property, and influence in the education of Poland's youth; and the clergy were, in relation to the majority of the population, generally well educated and revered. Not least, with the signing of the concordat between the Vatican and the Polish government in 1925, the church was able to gain significant autonomy from state control. The agreement granted important privileges to the clergy, who were henceforth freed from military service, prosecution in the courts, and taxation of their incomes. In addition, religious instruction was deemed mandatory for Catholic children in public schools and was to be taught by church-approved instructors. The concordat also included provisions that benefitted the state: newly appointed bishops were required to take an oath of loyalty to the state, clergy were required to pray for government leaders, and diocesan boundaries were reorganized according to Poland's new postwar frontiers, insuring that no Catholics within Poland's borders would be under the jurisdiction of a foreign bishop, and thus offering also a degree of recognition to the Second Republic.[6]

These gains notwithstanding, the church faced increasing secularization, struggled against anticlericalism on the part of much of the Polish ruling elite, and had to compete with other Christian denominations that were usually identified with minorities in the multiethnic, multireligious, multilingual heterogeneity of the interwar republic.[7] As historian Neal Pease writes, "Confessional affiliation in reconstituted Poland closely followed lines of ethnicity, and dissent from the Roman Catholic religious norm qualified as one of the most reliable indicators of national minority status."[8] There were, of course, exceptions to this: patriotic members of Poland's Evangelical Augsburg (i.e., Lutheran) Church may have struggled against the association of their faith with German national identity, even as German Catholics of the Latin rite frequently worshipped in common with their Polish coreligionists. The fact remained, however, that 98 percent of Roman Catholics in Poland were ethnic Poles, and all but 9 percent of ethnic Poles declared themselves Roman Catholic.[9]

Given this religious demography and the legacy of discrimination against Polish Catholics in the era of the partitions, it is not surprising that in the interwar years the church functioned as a vector of Polish nationalism, and that its hierarchs and clergy were often supporters of the nationalist right in Polish politics, a great many of whom gravitated toward the National Democracy ("ND" or "Endecja") movement. The Endecja was socially conservative, was generally antisemitic, was hostile toward minorities, and advocated the Polonization of the German minority in Poland. Its geographic stronghold was, significantly, in the west of the Polish Republic, roughly in the area that was to become the central and western Reichsgau Wartheland under Nazi occupation.[10] Relations between the Endecja and the Catholic Church were initially hostile, but a reconciliation between the two began during the First World War,[11] and eventually, the National Democratic movement was able to garner the support of most of the Catholic clergy and the vast majority of Catholic periodicals.[12] It is not surprising that the Endecja drew consistent support from the regions of postwar Poland that were under Prussian and German control during the partitions, and where the Polish Catholic clergy had suffered under the Kulturkampf.

Over the course of the interwar period, according to historian Brian Porter-Szűcs, Catholicism and the National Democratic movement were brought together by the shared notion of a Poland under siege from conspiratorial enemies, foremost among them Freemasons and Jews. "Reinforced by a shared vocabulary of struggle," Porter-Szűcs writes, "Catholicism became more national and nationalism became more Catholic."[13] Accordingly, the church commonly confronted perceived external and internal threats—whether modernism, socialism, secularism, Jews, or Freemasonry—by assuming what Robert Alvis has referred to as its traditional "defensive crouch."[14] The Catholic Church was, to be sure, a vehicle of Polish national sentiment, and at the parish level at times even a motor of nationalist agitation, but it would be an oversimplification to regard relations between the church and the interwar Polish state, or relations between the church and the nebula of "nation" in the Second Republic, as fixed or clearly defined. Its role in society ambiguous, Catholicism, according to Pease, "acted as a salient indicator of Polish identity, but not as an element of great political significance or priority in statecraft."[15]

The role of Catholicism in the Polish national project and the church's relationship to the interwar state remain open to further analysis, but at issue here is how Nazi ideology understood Polish Catholicism and how

Nazi praxis responded to the church's alleged role in Polish society and culture. Or, to frame the issue as a question in reference to the previous chapter: Why would Heydrich single out the Polish Catholic Church and its clergy at the September 21, 1939, meeting with the Einsatzgruppen commanders, and what were the ideological and political bases for the breadth and brutality of Nazi anti-Catholic measures in the months and years that followed?

Broadly speaking, National Socialism's assault on the church in the Reichsgau Wartheland was motivated by its fundamentally anti-Christian ideology, by its view of Polish Catholicism as a locus of Polish-national identity and agitation, and by political expediency specific to local conditions and German occupation goals. Yet none of these three motors of Nazi policy—what some scholars have referred to as the "ideological," "national," and "political"[16]—emerged as a single overriding factor in the formulation of church policy in the Warthegau. They were linked, and they are best understood as constituent elements of a Nazi Kirchenpolitik that was but one aspect of a broader Volkstumskampf the Nazis were waging in the Warthegau.

Nazism's hostility to Christianity is well known. The faith and its traditions were considered weak, otherworldly, insufficiently masculine, and incompatible with the national and racial exclusivity that Hitler and his followers espoused. "Forgiveness was not for resentful haters," Michael Burleigh writes, "nor compassion of much use to people who wanted to stamp the weak into the ground. In a word, Christianity was a 'soul malady.'"[17] Scholarship in the first decades after World War II tended to emphasize this incompatibility, stressing at the same time the numerous ways in which the German churches suffered under Nazism, as well as the role of the churches and clergy in resistance against the regime and its policies.[18] More recent research has, however, been both more nuanced and more critical in its assessment of the German churches, as scholars have emphasized, to varying degrees, the clergy and churches' compatibility, accommodation, or collusion with the regime,[19] while others have focused on the churches' responses and relationships to Nazi crimes.[20] Debates over the questions "How Christian were the Nazis?" and "How Nazi were Christians in Nazi Germany?" continue,[21] but these are mostly restricted to consideration of the churches in Germany. The Polish churches—their clergy, laity, and institutions—have remained outside this conversation, but their experiences during the occupation illustrate two important points.

First, the regime's Kirchenpolitik, whether in the Altreich, occupied Poland, or elsewhere in Nazi-controlled Europe, was neither ideologically coherent nor consistently applied. It varied according to a given region's racial, ethnic, and religious characteristics, and according to the regime's political, economic, and ethno-racial priorities for that region. Hence, the Catholic Church was not significantly persecuted in the puppet state of Slovakia but was violently persecuted in neighboring occupied Poland. The National Socialists did not set out to destroy Catholic institutions in the Altreich and France in the same way as they did in Poland. Polish Catholics in the General Government were subject to far fewer restrictions than their coreligionists in the Reichsgau Wartheland. *Reichsdeutsche*[22] and Volksdeutsche German Catholics in the Reichsgau Wartheland were restricted in the public practice of their faith, but far less than Polish Catholics. In the Katowice District,[23] the vast majority of Catholic priests were permitted to remain in office, while in the Wartheland, only a tiny minority of priests remained after 1941. Thus, persecution of the Catholic Church in the Wartheland did not emerge solely or primarily out of the regime's hostility to Christianity or the Catholic Church per se, and the variety of responses to Catholicism in Nazi-controlled Europe attest to this.[24]

Second, National Socialism's treatment of the churches in the Warthegau reveals much about Nazi plans for the churches in the future. A postwar Reich would no longer require the tactical accommodation and compromise with the churches that characterized the war years, and the Warthegau was Greiser's experimental field for establishing a domain free of church power and influence. The persecution and murder of the clergy, legal disenfranchisement of the churches, confiscation of church property, and dramatic restrictions on public expression of one's faith in the "model Gau"—all to be discussed in the chapters to follow—pointed to the goals of persecuting, marginalizing, and even eradicating the churches more broadly in the future.

The issue of whether or not National Socialism and Christianity were compatible remains open to debate; the measures enacted in the Reichsgau Wartheland strongly suggest that, in the long term, they were not. Were it not for the Wartheland's "Mustergau" status, one could perhaps argue that Nazi persecution of the church there was simply a tactical, regional policy targeted against a Polish-national institution. "German" Protestant bodies and German Catholics in the Gau were, however, also persecuted, although to a lesser extent. Moreover, the fact that the Gau was to serve as a model for

Kirchenpolitik in the future Reich as a whole, where there would presumably be no danger of Polish-national resistance, suggests that a basic anti-Christian and anti-Catholic animus was also at work.

With respect to the Roman Catholic Church in particular, the Nazi regime always saw the confessional division in Germany as undermining its goal of national unity, which was intended to bridge regional, class, and religious boundaries. Roughly one-third of Germans in the Altreich were Roman Catholic, and this was an obstacle to achieving a strong and resilient *Volksgemeinschaft*, or "people's community." The Catholic Church was an international body that demanded external allegiances, and as such, it undermined the power and integrity of the German nation and its leader. Beyond Hitler, many at the highest level of the Nazi state, such as Heinrich Himmler, his subordinate Reinhard Heydrich, Alfred Rosenberg, and Martin Bormann, were openly hostile toward Catholicism, but the regime initially proceeded slowly with measures against the Catholic Church. Himmler had ordered in 1933 that no anti-Catholic policies be enacted without his approval, but after the death of President Paul von Hindenburg in August 1934 and the failure to establish a national Protestant church via the "German Christian" movement, anti-Catholic measures increased.[25]

In the years that followed, the regime issued countless restrictions against the church in Germany, from censorship of the Catholic press to limitations on the activities of Catholic organizations, from elimination of state subsidies for church-provided social services to the confiscation of monasteries, from monitoring of services and sermons to the removal of crucifixes in public buildings. As radical as these measures may seem, historian John S. Conway has argued that the Nazi campaign against the Catholic Church in the 1930s was characterized by its restraint. "Such restraint . . . ," Conway contends, "was only tactical. As events in Poland after September 1939 were to show, the Nazis had no compunction about launching a campaign of total persecution against the Churches when it suited their political ends."[26] A rather "intentionalist" view of the trajectory of the regime's antichurch policy, Conway's assertion points nonetheless to the centrality of Poland and the Reichsgau Wartheland in Nazi Kirchenpolitik as a whole. National Socialism's persecution of the church would reach its apex in the Warthegau, where the regime's basic anti-Christian worldview (the "ideological") was merged with the anti-Polish prejudice and racist imperatives (the "national") that the ethno-racial struggle demanded.

The Volkstumskampf required, for example, that Poles and Germans be strictly segregated, whether in the workplace, schools, recreational activities, or churches. Christian tradition and official doctrine held that the church would, ideally, function as a great equalizer and reconciler among classes, nationalities, and races. Modern nationalism and its many proponents among the German and Polish clergy had, of course, radically undermined this role, yet the churches in Germany and Poland still, officially at least, held to the notion that the church could unite rather than divide. By contrast, Nazi ideology and propaganda posited that "the Polish church is always in the service of Polish hatred."[27] It was understood as a bearer of Polish national tradition during the long nineteenth century of the partitions; as a vector of anti-German agitation during the years of the second Polish Republic; and, in the words of an official from the Reich Ministry for Church Affairs, as a "reservoir of anti-German hostility" that posed a grave danger to Nazi plans for occupied Polish territory.[28] According to Arthur Greiser's cousin and personal advisor Harry Siegmund, the Polish church was regarded as the "main pillar of aggressive and chauvinistic Polishness."[29] Or, as one German historian noted in a 1940 position paper titled "The Polish Religion," "For the Poles, it was under the mantle of Catholicism that were, and are, concealed radical nationalist passions and desires, and the great majority of Polish Catholic clergy are nationalist ringleaders. Germany's goal is merely to eliminate these excesses in order to render impossible any renewed surge in religious-nationalist hatred among the Poles."[30]

The Nazi perception of the Polish priest as *Hetzkaplan* was, of course, a stereotype, but it was a stereotype based to some extent in clerical activism for the Polish-national cause. Many Polish clergymen had resisted Prussian and later German anti-Polish measures during the period of the Partitions, especially at the time of the Kulturkampf. Following the reestablishment of the Polish state, many Polish clergymen became active in a wide variety of organizations advocating, to varying degrees, the Polish-national cause, such as the Union of Polish Scouts (Związek Harcerstwa Polskiego), Catholic Action, the National Democratic movement, the Polish army, or the aggressively anti-German Union for the Defense of the Western Provinces (Związek Obrony Kresów Zachodnich), later renamed the Polish Western Union (Polski Związek Zachodni).[31] Mateusz Zabłocki, introduced at the outset of this study, was an officer in the Greater Poland Uprising of 1918–1919 and represented the National Democrats in the Gniezno City

Council.[32] Walenty Dymek, the auxiliary bishop of Poznań, served on the executive board of the People's Council during the Greater Poland Uprising, and was later allegedly a member of the Polish Western Union.[33] Stanisław Adamski, bishop of the Katowice (Kattowitz) diocese as of 1930 and also a member of the Polish Western Union, had been instrumental in establishing state authority in western Poland after the post–World War I peace settlement and Greater Poland Uprising, had been a delegate to the Polish parliament (*Sejm*), and had served in the Senate from 1922–1927.[34]

Such affiliations and allegations aside, the Nazi authorities would, beginning in September 1939, cast their nets broadly in attempting to control, silence, or apprehend the Polish clergy. As the German military was making preparations for the invasion, the Army High Command had, already in July 1939, issued instructions declaring that "the Catholic clergy is primarily responsible for nationalistic rabble-rousing," while numerous military directives and reports in the weeks to follow pointed to teachers and the clergy as hostile elements in Polish society.[35] On August 1, 1939, one month before Nazi Germany launched its invasion, the German ambassador to Poland, Hans-Adolf von Moltke, issued to the Berlin Foreign Office a report on conditions in Poland during the diplomatic crisis preceding the outbreak of the war. In his report, von Moltke wrote specifically of the Polish Catholic Church, stating, "The Polish clergy deserve special attention, for their influence on an already highly religious population is enormous. The clergy has made itself personally responsible for influencing the population in the spirit of anti-German propaganda. . . . It preaches to the people that they are about to embark on a holy war. Its chauvinism is unmatched."[36] Von Moltke's observations were neither particularly original nor a comprehensive prescription for policy, but they do illustrate some of the ideological assumptions behind German policy. If, for the Nazis, the church was a bastion of Polish national identity, then its clergy were among Polish nationalism's most numerous and ardent defenders. Consistent with this view was the Nazi assumption that Polish Catholic teaching, tradition, and, of course, clergy would therefore inspire the population to clandestine resistance or even overt rebellion in defense of the Polish nation.

Already in September 1939, such views were echoed by the German official overseeing church affairs in West Prussia and the northern part of the region that would become the Reichsgau Wartheland. In a report to the Reich Ministry for Church Affairs, Dr. Leo Hawranke emphasized the urgent need to "break the influence of the Polish clergy" in the dioceses of

Chełmno, Poznań, and Gniezno. "The longer it takes to tackle this task, the more difficult it will be, for the Poles will have recovered from the first shock and will engage in resistance. Such resistance," Hawranke continued, "will be difficult to counter with force, because a considerable portion of the power of the Catholic Church stands behind the Polish clergy." It was also necessary to close seminaries, he argued, for "every Polish clergyman is a Polish agitator. It would be suicide to allow here for Polish agitators to be ordained as priests."[37]

The perception of the Polish priest as nationalist agitator served as justification for the arrests and incarcerations in the fall of 1939 at the hands of the Einsatzgruppen,[38] as well as subsequent restrictions on the Catholic clergy's ministries. In the first weeks following the invasion, Polish priests were labeled the "intellectual and actual ringleaders" of insurgency, who, according to Hermann Goering, should no longer be offered the opportunity to engage in their demagoguery.[39] Accordingly, and in conjunction with Heydrich's instructions of September 21, 1939, Arthur Greiser, still in his capacity as head of civilian administration (to eventually supplant the military authorities once hostilities had ceased) in Posen Province, ordered that secret lists of *Polenführer*—that is, influential members of the intelligentsia—be drawn up, with clergymen at the fore.[40]

The mantra of priest as dangerous agitator was no passing phenomenon. Several months later, a memorandum issued by the Reich Ministry for Church Affairs stated that "the higher and lower clergy in these [eastern] territories was, is, and remains a danger to the Reich and Germandom; the elimination of its influence will be one of the main tasks of the Reich Commissar for the Consolidation of German Nationhood in the east."[41] As Reichsstatthalter, Arthur Greiser would remain consistent in his views regarding the Polish clergy. Some two years later, in a June 1942 speech, he made clear why his administration in the Warthegau had undertaken such an ambitious program to neutralize the "bearers of the greatest Volkstumskampf against the German people." Whereas the nineteenth-century Prussian authorities had committed the "deadly sin" of allowing Polish Catholicism to prosper, his Gau administration had, by contrast, taken steps necessary "to eliminate [the clergy] from political life." Such steps were, according to Greiser, ultimately defensive and just: roadside crucifixes and statues had been uncovered as hiding places for weapons, while the confiscation of church property had eliminated economic resources central for the political struggle against the German people.[42] Accordingly, incarceration of members of the clergy would neutralize the most important vector of anti-German, nationalist agitation and resistance. As subsequent chapters will show, Greiser appears not to have wavered in his conviction that the Polish clergy continued to exert a dangerous, even mystical hold on the Polish population. "It is not for nothing," he claimed in a March 1943 speech, "that the Catholic clergy have a certain power over the broad masses in the Polish Volkstumskampf"—a power that, according to the Gauleiter, relied on the "glitz and hocus-pocus" of "altar, church, crucifix, and shrines."[43]

For Greiser and the Nazi administration of the Warthegau, neutralizing the Polish *Hetzkaplan* would remain a priority for the duration of the occupation, yet this was but one aspect of the goal of neutralizing the Polish church as a whole. The goal was consonant with the regime's broader anticlerical agenda for the Altreich and occupied territories combined, and beginning in 1939, the Reichsgau Wartheland would serve as the prime arena for putting that agenda to the test.

Notes

1. William W. Hagen, *Germans, Poles, and Jews: The Nationality Conflict in the Prussian East, 1772–1914* (Chicago: University of Chicago Press, 1980), 87–88. On the Catholic Church in Poznań and the Posen province in the early nineteenth century, see also Robert E. Alvis, *Religion and the Rise of Nationalism: A Profile of an East-Central European City* (Syracuse, NY: Syracuse University Press, 2005).

2. Hagen, *Germans*, 128; Kłoczowski, *History*, 232; Rutherford, *Prelude*, 18–21.

3. Norman Davies, *God's Playground: A History of Poland. Volume II: 1795 to the Present* (New York: Columbia University Press, 1982), 117, 126–31; Rutherford, *Prelude*, 18–21. It is worth noting in this context that Davies also makes the important point that German enforcement of anti-Polish measures in the years after 1871 were consonant with the efforts of European states to suppress the rights and cultures of national, linguistic, and ethnic minorities, and were, to that extent, not uniquely German or Prussian.

4. Rutherford, *Prelude*, 20.

5. Hagen, *Germans*, 147.

6. Neil Pease, *Rome's Most Faithful Daughter: The Catholic Church and Independent Poland, 1914–1939* (Athens: Ohio University Press, 2009), 69; Davies, *God's Playground*, 419–20; Robert Alvis, *White Eagle, Black Madonna: One Thousand Years of the Polish Catholic Tradition* (New York: Fordham University Press, 2016), 194.

7. According to the Polish government census of 1921, ethnic Poles constituted nearly 70 percent of the population, Ukrainians a bit more than 14 percent, Jews nearly 8 percent, and Belarusians and Germans each about 4 percent. The census also revealed that, in terms of religious composition, about 64 percent of the population was Roman Catholic, slightly more than 11 percent was Ukrainian Greek Catholic or "Uniate," while Orthodox Christians

and Jews each made up nearly 11 percent of the population. On these figures see M. B. Biskupski, *The History of Poland* (Westport: Greenwood Press, 2000), 83, and Pease, *Rome's*, 21–22.

8. Pease, *Rome's*, 22.

9. Pease, 22–23.

10. See Kłoczowski, *History*, 269.

11. Brian Porter-Szűcs, *Faith and Fatherland: Catholicism, Modernity, and Poland* (New York: Oxford University Press, 2011), 179–81; Sabrina P. Ramet, *The Catholic Church in Polish History: From 966 to the Present* (New York: Palgrave Macmillan, 2017), 112–13.

12. Porter-Szücs, *Faith*, 240.

13. Porter-Szücs, 328.

14. Alvis, *White Eagle*, 206. On the notion of the Catholic Church in Poland as "under siege," see Ramet, *Catholic Church*, 132–33, and especially Porter-Szücs, *Faith*, chaps. 7–9.

15. Pease, *Rome's*, 5. By contrast, Martin Conway has argued that the Polish Catholic hierarchy was indeed politically active, and that such activism was one reason that there was not a mass, Catholic-oriented political party in the interwar republic. See Martin Conway, *Catholic Politics in Europe 1918–1945* (New York: Routledge, 1997), 32.

16. See, for example, Madajczyk, *Okkupationspolitik*, 356; Jan Sziling, "Die Kirchen im Generalgouvernement," *Miscellanea Historiae Ecclesiasticae* 9 (1984); Martin Broszat, "Verfolgung polnischer katholischer Geistlicher 1939–1945," Gutachten des Instituts für Zeitgeschichte, September 1959, IfZ, 6–7; Fijałkowski, *Kościół*, 269–70.

17. Michael Burleigh, *The Third Reich: A New History* (New York: Hill and Wang, 2001), 255–56.

18. Richard Evans, "Nazism, Christianity and Political Religion: A Debate," *Journal of Contemporary History* 42, no. 1 (2007): 5.

19. Among the abundant studies to have emerged over the past decades see, for example, Doris L. Bergen, *Twisted Cross: The German Christian Movement in the Third Reich* (Chapel Hill: University of North Carolina Press, 1996); Robert P. Ericksen, *Complicity in the Holocaust: Churches and Universities in Nazi Germany* (Cambridge: Cambridge University Press, 2012), especially chaps. 2 and 4; Robert P. Ericksen, *Theologians under Hitler* (New Haven, CT: Yale University Press, 1985); Manfred Gailus, *Protestantismus und Nationalsozialismus: Studien zur nationalsozialistischen Durchdringung des protestantischen Sozialmilieus in Berlin* (Köln: Böhlau-Verlag, 2001); Susannah Heschel, *The Aryan Jesus: Christian Theologians and the Bible in Nazi Germany* (Princeton, NJ: Princeton University Press, 2008); Ernst Klee, *Die SA Jesu Christi: Die Kirchen im Banne Hitlers* (Frankfurt-am-Main: Fischer Taschenbuch Verlag, 1989); Kevin P. Spicer, *Hitler's Priests: Catholic Clergy and National Socialism* (DeKalb: Northern Illinois University Press, 2008); and Richard Steigmann-Gall, *The Holy Reich: Nazi Conceptions of Christianity, 1919–1945* (Cambridge: Cambridge University Press, 2003).

20. See, for example, the collected essays in Robert P. Ericksen and Susannah Heschel, eds., *Betrayal: German Churches and the Holocaust* (Minneapolis, MN: Fortress Press, 1999), and more recently, essays in Thomas Brechenmacher and Harry Oelke, eds., *Die Kirchen und die Verbrechen im nationalsozialistischen Staat*, Dachauer Symposien zur Zeitgeschichte, vol. 11 (Göttingen: Wallstein Verlag, 2011).

21. The stakes and terms of these and other related debates are effectively outlined in the "Discussion Forum—Richard Steigmann-Gall's *The Holy Reich*," appearing in the *Journal of*

Contemporary History 42, no. 1 (January 2007): 5–78, as well as in Steigmann-Gall's response: "Christianity and the Nazi Movement: A Response," *Journal of Contemporary History* 42, no. 2 (April 2007), 185–211.

22. That is, ethnic German from the Altreich, as opposed to those who were from the occupied Polish territories or elsewhere.

23. "Regierungsbezirk Kattowitz," in eastern Upper Silesia, annexed by Nazi Germany in 1939, part of Silesia Province until 1941, and thereafter part of Upper Silesia Province.

24. On the limitations of the "ideological" factor in explaining Nazi church policy, see Sziling, "Die Kirchen," 277–78.

25. Richard Evans, *The Third Reich in Power* (New York: Penguin, 2005), 237–38.

26. Conway, *Nazi Persecution*, 175.

27. Brochure, "Deutscher aus den luftgefährdeten Gebieten," n.d., NSDAP Gauleitung Wartheland, Gauamt für Volkstumsfragen, n.d., IPN, GK 196/12/CD, 69.

28. Reichsministerium für die Kirchlichen Angelegenheiten (Roth) to Oberkommando der Wehrmacht, Abteilung Inneres, September 23, 1939, BAB, R 5101/22185, 8.

29. Siegmund, *Rückblick*, 245.

30. Gotthold Rhode, "'Die Polnische Religion': der Missbrauch der katholischen Religion für polnische nationale Ziele," BAB, R 5101/24038, 84–128; here, 127–28. Rhode, the son of an ethnic German Protestant theologian, was employed by the Osteuropa-Institut Breslau (Eastern European Institute, Breslau/Wrocław) and was commissioned to write this position paper by the German Foreign Office. After the war, Rhode went on to a long and productive career as a historian of Poland—a career that culminated in his positions as chair for East-European history and as director of the Institute for East-European Studies (Institut für Osteuropakunde) at the Johannes-Gutenberg-Universität Mainz. See Eike Eckert, "Gotthold Rhode," in *Handbuch der völkischen Wissenschaften: Personen, Institutionen, Forschungsprogramme, Stiftungen*, ed. Ingo Haar and Michael Fahlbusch (München: K.G. Saur, 2008), 589–92.

31. Georg W. Strobel, "Die Kirche Polens, das gesellschaftliche Deutschensyndrom und beider Rolle bei der Sowjetisierung Polens," in *Katholische Kirche unter nationalsozialistischer und kommunistischer Diktatur: Deutschland und Polen 1939–1989*, ed. Hans-Jürgen Karp and Joachim Köhler (Köln: Böhlau Verlag, 2001), 111; Richard Blanke, *Orphans of Versailles: The Germans in Western Poland 1918–1939* (Lexington: University Press of Kentucky, 1993), 93, 159, 200–201.

32. Józef Glemp, "Zabłocki Mateusz," in *Wielkopolski Słownik Biograficzny*, ed. Antoni Gąsiorowski and Jerzy Topolski (Poznań: Państwowe Wydawnictwo Naukowe, 1981), 855.

33. Jerzy Pietrzak, "Dymek Walenty," in Gąsiorowski and Topolski, *Wielkopolski Słownik Biograficzny*, 165–66; Reichsministerium für die Kirchlichen Angelegenheiten to Reichsführer SS, Reichskommissar zur Festigung des Deutschen Volkstums, February 3, 1940, BAB, R 5101/22185, 101–2. Dymek's membership in the Polish Western Union, alleged in this document, remains unconfirmed.

34. Strobel, "Die Kirche Polens," 111; Krzysztof Dembski, "Adamski Stanisław," in Gąsiorowski and Topolski, *Wielkopolski Słownik Biograficzny*, 20.

35. Rossino, *Hitler*, 24, 132–34.

36. "Der deutsche Botschafter in Warschau an das Auswärtige Amt, Bericht vom 1. August 1939," document no. 444, in Germany, Auswärtiges Amt, *Dokumente zur Vorgeschichte des*

Krieges, 1939, no. 2 (Berlin: Reichsdruckerei, 1939), 20; Sprawozdanie sytuacyjne z kraju 1939–1941, vol 1, 105–11, PUMST.

37. Hawranke, "Bericht zur kirchen-politischen Lage," September 22, 1939, BAB, R 5101/22185, 15–16. The German occupation authorities did, in fact, proceed with vigor and brutality against the clergy in the Chełmno diocese, where 46 percent of the priests died during the occupation, the overwhelming majority of whom (224) were shot. See Fijałkowski, *Kościół*, 302. According to a later memorandum of the RSHA, Hawranke was so "shaken" by the German measures (that he was in part responsible for instigating) in Pelplin, a town south of Gdańsk (Danzig) in the Chełmno diocese, that he resigned as chargé d'affaires for church matters. Vermerk, RSHA Amt II B 3, n.d. USHMM, RG 15.007, reel 38, 465, 23. The memorandum is undated, but its content makes clear that it was authored after February 1, 1940, and before February 5, 1940.

38. Wardzyńska, *Był rok*, 189.

39. Brief, Generalbevollmächtigter für die Reichsverwaltung, Der Stabsleiter (Stuckart) an den RfKA, September 22, 1939, BAB, R 5101/22185, 117.

40. Der Chef der Zivilverwaltung beim Militärbefehlshaber in Posen (Greiser), "Richtlinien für den Verwaltungsaufbau in den Kreisen und Städten der Provinz Posen," September 29, 1939, Abschrift. IPN, GK 196/11/CD.

41. Reichsministerium für die Kirchlichen Angelegenheiten to Reichsführer SS, Reichskommissar zur Festigung des Deutschen Volkstums, February 3, 1940, BAB, R 5101/22185, 101. Himmler was appointed Reich Commissar for the Consolidation of German Nationhood (Reichskommisar zur Festigung des Deutschen Volkstums) in October 1939.

42. Arthur Greiser, speech, June 10, 1942, in Arthur Greiser, *Der Aufbau im Osten* (Jena: Verlag von Gustav Fischer, 1942), 10.

43. Bericht, Arbeitstagung des Gauamtes für Volkstumspolitik am 20. u. 21.3.1943 in Posen, IPN, GK 196/37, 106.

Fig. 4. 1. Reichsgau Wartheland, 1943. Map by Timber Wright.

Fig. 4.2. Dioceses in the Reichsgau Wartheland. Map by Timber Wright.

4

MUSTERGAU

The Reichsgau Wartheland as "Model Gau"

Among the various *Reichsgaue* established among territories annexed to Nazi Germany beginning in 1938,[1] the Reichsgau Wartheland was notable for its size, the demographic composition of its population, and the role it was to play in the Third Reich both during and after the war. According to a decree issued by Adolf Hitler on October 8, 1939, the western and northern portions of German-occupied Polish territory—part of what was more broadly understood under the Nazi regime as the "German East"[2]—were to be annexed to the Reich, establishing the Reichsgau Westpreußen and Reichsgau Posen. At the head of each of these stood a Reichsstatthalter. In the case of the Reichsgau Posen, this was Arthur Greiser, a native of the region and president of the Gdańsk Senate prior to the war.

The Reichsgau Posen was divided into three large administrative districts or Regierungsbezirke: Regierunsbezirk Posen (Poznań District), Regierungsbezirk Hohensalza (Inowrocław District), and Regierungsbezirk Kalisch (Kalisz District).[3] These were subdivided into thirty-nine Kreise, or subdistricts. On January 29, 1940, it was named the Reichsgau Wartheland,[4] after the Warta (Warthe) river that coursed through the region. It had an area of approximately forty-five thousand square kilometers—roughly the size of Vermont and New Hampshire combined—representing nearly half of the Polish territory annexed by the Reich in 1939, and making the Warthegau, in terms of geographic area, the second-largest Gau in all of Nazi Germany. With respect to population, the Warthegau was also the second-largest in the Reich, surpassed only by Saxony. In 1939, it had a population of approximately 4.9 million, including 4,189,000 Poles (85 percent),

325,000 Germans (less than 7 percent), 400,000 Jews (8 percent), and 23,000 of other nationalities.[5] Of the 4,557,000 inhabitants of the Gau in early 1941, nearly 1.3 million were in Poznań District, roughly 1.2 million in Inowrocław District, and nearly 2.1 million in Łódź District (the former Kalisz District had been renamed Regierungsbezirk Litzmannstadt, or Łódź District in January 1940).[6] In terms of ecclesiastical organization, the Warthegau comprised nearly the entirety of the Roman Catholic dioceses of Poznań, Gniezno, and Włocławek; the majority of the Łódź diocese; and small portions of the dioceses of Płock, Warsaw, and Częstochowa. All of these dioceses were administered by Polish bishops. It is also worth noting that for Poles, the west-central region of the Reichsgau Wartheland was considered the "cradle" of the Polish state established in the tenth century and therefore had tremendous importance for Poland's national and ecclesiastical history.

All this suggests that although the Warthegau was formally annexed to the Reich as one of the "Incorporated Eastern Territories" (Eingegliederte Ostgebiete), its ethnic and historical links to Germany were not nearly as strong as the Nazis claimed: while the western part of the Gau was indeed part of Prussia prior to World War I, half of the Inowrocław District and all of the Łódź District had been part of the Russian Empire. This also meant that the economic and cultural differences among the districts were significant. For example, industrial production was largely limited to the cities of Łódź and Poznań and was nearly absent from Inowrocław District. Residents of the Poznań district, entirely in the formerly Prussian part of the Gau, enjoyed a standard of living much higher than that of their counterparts in Łódź District. Far more Jews lived in Łódź District than in the other two districts combined.[7] In terms of economic policy, all the Warthegau's newly annexed Polish territory became part of the Reich's economic zone, and the German *Mark* replaced the Polish *Złota* as the valid currency. But on the urging of Reichsführer-SS and Chief of the German Police Heinrich Himmler, the *Polizeigrenze* ("police frontier") remained at the former German-Polish border. Passage to and from the Wartheland was therefore possible only with official permission and the requisite documents, making the Gau, at least in this respect, a foreign territory. This was intended to restrict and control the flow of people—whether Germans, Jews, or Poles—between the Gau and the Altreich and to shield the regime's ethno-racial population policies from the Altreich's view.[8]

This ethno-racial project was at the center of the radical changes that the Nazi leadership would initiate in the Gau—changes that called for the

Germanization of the region's government, administration, economy, culture, and racial character. The racial transformation was to rid the Gau of Jews and Poles, even as the Nazi authorities worked to undermine or destroy state institutions, cultural institutions such as the church, and Polish social networks. An edict of Hitler's from October 7, 1939, formally initiated this process and placed it under the authority of Reichsführer-SS Heinrich Himmler. Hitler's order called for the return to the Reich of all ethnic Germans living abroad, for creation of special areas of settlement for them, and, of special significance for the Wartheland, for the "elimination of the harmful influences of alien sections of the population that represent a danger for the Reich and the German people's community [*Volksgemeinschaft*]."[9]

"Harmful influences" could, of course, refer to many things—Jews and Poles, films and concerts, textbooks and hymnals, schools and churches—and Himmler and his subordinates were allowed considerable latitude in executing Hitler's orders. They therefore instituted countless measures to restrict, control, and burden the activities and lives of Poles in the Warthegau. Use of the Polish language in public and in schools was prohibited. Poznań's university was closed. Professors, teachers, artists, and leaders in politics, culture, and business were arrested, imprisoned, deported, and murdered. Polish subjects of the Reich were apprehended in random roundups and sent into forced labor. Theaters, cinemas, radio stations, and concert halls were closed and transformed into German institutions. Polish newspapers were forbidden. Poles were not permitted to own cameras or phonographs. Museums were closed and their collections confiscated, rendered inaccessible, or destroyed. For Polish subjects of the Reich who illegally crossed borders; listened to foreign radio broadcasts; had intimate relations with Germans; helped escaped prisoners, partisans, Roma, or Jews; or were found guilty of price gouging, the death sentence awaited.[10] Arthur Greiser ordered the Hitler Youth to confiscate books from libraries and burn them. And not least, the Nazi administration initiated a massive attack on the Catholic Church.[11] As Greiser's biographer Catherine Epstein has noted, "While Arthur Greiser is arguably best known for his role in the Holocaust, his anti-Polish policies are what most distinguished him from other Nazi leaders. To Greiser, anti-Polish measures were just as crucial for his Germanization program as the persecution and murder of Jews. The Warthegau thus saw the most severe anti-Polish policies in Nazi-occupied Europe."[12]

All was part of the broader Volkstumskampf, and these tasks were especially urgent in the new "Mustergau Wartheland"[13] or "model Gau

Wartheland"—a "virgin territory" that, under Greiser's ambitious leadership, was intended as a "parade ground"[14] for the rigors of Nazi policy. The notion of Mustergau is critical to understanding the region's role in the history of the Third Reich and the German occupation of Polish lands. As a system, structure, or pattern, a model is an example to be imitated, and Arthur Greiser was intent on making his Gau worthy of that distinction. According to Michael Alberti, the Warthegau was "far and away the most important and, with respect to territory, the largest experimental field of National Socialist racial policy."[15] There was considerable urgency attached to the experiment, as both Greiser and his counterpart in Danzig-Westpreußen, Albert Forster, had direct orders from Hitler to transform their Gaus into *Lebensraum*—"living space"—with a pure German population within ten years. Ever competitive with one another, both men approached this task with vigor and aggressive measures against the Polish and Jewish populations under their authority, whether in the form of discriminatory policies, forced expulsion, or annihilation.[16]

In Greiser's Gau especially, the task required enormous energy and commitment because 85 percent of the Wartheland's population was Polish. In the words of one of Greiser's deputies, "The Reichsgau Wartheland is not to be compared with other Gaus, for here the Poles do not live in a German Gau with a German population; rather, here there are few Germans in the midst of a purely Polish environment."[17] The region surrounding Poznań—what had traditionally been referred to in Polish as Wielkopolska, and in Latin as Polonia Maior (or "Greater Poland")—also had for Poles tremendous symbolic value, not only as the tenth-century "cradle" of both Polish Catholicism and the Polish state but also more recently as a battleground of Polish national identity in the nineteenth and early twentieth centuries. Nazi claims notwithstanding, for most of the past millennium the region had been controlled by the Polish state and—to the extent that one can even apply such modern categories—the ethnic German population was always outnumbered by the ethnic Poles. As Catherine Epstein has argued, the Warthegau's demographic situation demanded severe measures, for "the Warthegau could only become a 'virgin territory' if draconian methods were deployed to remove the Polish and Jewish populations. Precisely because it was so far from the Nazi ideal, Greiser's Gau did become a model—a model of Nazi brutality."[18]

The Warthegau may have demanded brutality, but it is significant that its special status as a somewhat separate experimental field offered tremendous opportunity as well. As Greiser stated in an October 1941 speech, "In this virginal developing territory of the German East, there is, for the first time, the opportunity for a new state order that conforms to National Socialist principles in all aspects of public life."[19] Moreover, whether in racial policy, policing, educational policy, or Kirchenpolitik, it was possible to enact in the Warthegau draconian measures that would perhaps have been impractical or unacceptable elsewhere. According to Greiser's deputy August Jäger, the Volkstumskampf in the Gau had to be pursued with zeal and precision, and in a manner distinct from that of the Altreich. "The Warthegau," Jäger claimed, "is the kernel of Poland, and it is here that the fate of the Polish people is determined. Here we are accomplishing both construction and destruction. We must therefore be different from Berlin."[20]

Not only was the Warthegau different from Berlin; the Nazi Party and SS generally held greater authority there than in the Gaus of the Altreich, and relative to other Gaus, it could function more independently from the strictures of the law, the meddling of various ministries and, in Greiser's words, become "a land free of traditional bureaucratic restraints."[21] Already in December 1939, Greiser referred to the situation of the churches in the Warthegau as "entirely free of legal constraint," for "all heretofore laws and regulations," he stated, "have become superfluous."[22] Moreover, because the offices of Reichsstatthalter and Gauleiter were combined, and given that these local chiefs were to be directly responsible to Hitler, political authority was streamlined, and the application of party ideology was, at least in theory, more efficient. In effect, as historian Dieter Pohl has argued, the Warthegau was characterized by a "decoupling" of the administration from ministerial control, a merger of party and state authority, and a symbiotic relationship between the administration and police organs, all of which enhanced Greiser's personal control and facilitated more radical measures in the service of the Gau's Germanization.[23] This was true with respect to the Warthegau's pioneering and increasingly aggressive racial policies toward Jews and Poles, but it likewise applied to policies toward the churches, which were also part of the broader Germanization project.

Martin Bormann, chief of staff in the Office of the Deputy Führer,[24] emphasized the interdependence of racial and ecclesiastical priorities in December 1939, stating in a letter to Forster, "There exists for me no doubt that in the new eastern Gaus the Volkstumskampf cannot be separated from ecclesiastical/political [*kirchenpolitische*] questions." Moreover, according to Bormann, the Gauleiter and Reichsstatthalter in these areas, who "had been accorded special powers by the Führer," should not be hindered by conventional ministerial control in exercising their authority over religious organizations in their territories.[25] In other words, while it may have been difficult or impossible for the Nazi leadership to violate traditional government policy toward the churches or conventional legal ties between the state and the churches in the Altreich, the newly annexed areas of formerly Polish territory, in the words of one historian, "offered the opportunity to pursue National Socialist church policy in all its brutality," so that the experimental field that was the Warthegau could be an exemplar for church policy in the Reich of the future.[26]

It is also worth noting that, because of the oppressive character of the occupation, the Catholic Church in the Warthegau was a much less formidable opponent than the church in the Altreich. In the words of one scholar, "What the Nazi powers were still unable to do in Germany, where they faced a very solid ecclesiastical structure, they felt they were powerful enough to bring about in a country now in the hands of its army and police."[27] In sum, the Warthegau as "virgin territory" offered the freedom and flexibility to undertake revolutionary change, whether with respect to Volkstumspolitik in general or Kirchenpolitik specifically. Neither was intended as a temporary regional experiment; both were rapidly evolving long-term projects.[28]

This invites further consideration of the Wartheland's status among the various Gaus in National Socialist Germany. Undoubtedly, many Gauleiters sought to uphold their territories as "models," hoping that their Gaus would be examples to others.[29] Southwest of the Warthegau, Nazi officials in Oberschlesien (Upper Silesia) aimed to develop an exemplary administrative, economic, and nationality structure that would attract German settlers with the slogan "Upper Silesia—the new Ruhr Valley."[30] In annexed Austrian territory, the Reichsgau Steiermark (Styria) likewise aspired to a leading role, and the resident Gauleiter, Dr. Siegfried Uiberreither, took particularly aggressive measures against the Christian churches, although not nearly on the level of the Reichsgau Wartheland.[31] Karl Kaufmann in Hamburg and Konrad Henlein in the Sudetenland also aspired to a "model" status in the Third Reich.[32] These multiple claims and aspirations perhaps suggest that the term Mustergau is of limited value,[33] for clearly, no single Gau emerged as a template for the Reich as a whole, or for all other Gaus.

It nonetheless remains appropriate to analyze the Wartheland in terms of its status as a "model." Like the other *Reichsgaue*, the Wartheland was largely free of ministerial control and saw an intertwining of SS, police organs, and Gau administration. A number of characteristics, however, distinguished it from other Gaus. For example, the use of terror against the civilian population in the Warthegau was unprecedented and set it apart from that applied elsewhere in occupied Poland. In the words of Michael Alberti, terror in the Warthegau reached a "new dimension" and continued in a state of "permanent expansion."[34] Most significant among the Warthegau's unique characteristics was, however, the Volkstumskampf waged there, which was rigorous, consequential, and exceptionally violent. Compared to Danzig-Westpreußen and Upper Silesia, for example, the Warthegau was especially strict in limiting access of formerly Polish citizens to the Deutsche Volksliste (German Ethnic Registry, or DVL)—that is, a registry for those in occupied Poland having allegedly ethnic German characteristics that would potentially gain them German citizenship and other privileges.[35] The Warthegau essentially had to import its Germans, and by 1944, only some 13 percent of its residents were German, in contrast to Danzig-Westpreußen, where Germans made up 58 percent of the population[36]—this despite an aggressive program, discussed in the following chapter, that dispossessed and expelled ethnic Poles by the tens of thousands. Moreover, the separation of Germans and Poles in public and private life was "more severe and brutal" than in any other province of the Third Reich.[37]

The ethno-racial battle as applied to the Jewish population in the region was not only effective, destroying all but some 10,000–15,000 of the 435,000 Jews living in the Wartheland in September 1939, but also innovative. At the forefront of the "final solution to the Jewish question," the Warthegau was where the first ghettos were established, where the first systematic deployment of ghetto Jews for labor occurred (in Łódź and other ghettos), where the largest network of slave labor camps was established, and where the first extermination center (Chełmno nad Nerem / Kulmhof) began operation in December 1941.[38]

Finally, it is worth noting that the term Mustergau was not invented and deployed by postwar historians but was used by the Wartheland's Nazi leadership, which was forever intent on upholding the Gau's unique and pioneering status. Arthur Greiser used the term publicly in a programmatic speech given in Poznań only days after the occupation began,[39] continued to refer to the "Mustergau" in the years to follow, and referred to it as such during his 1946 trial in Poznań.[40] Dieter Pohl has suggested that use of the term during the occupation reflected the "self-understanding" of the

German occupiers, and that the Warthegau was to function less as a model for the Altreich, and more as a model for additional areas to be Germanized in the east.[41] That may well have been the case with respect to some aspects of the Gau's party and state authority and administration, which was in many ways chaotic, redundant, and inefficient, but with respect to areas as diverse as agricultural production, labor exploitation, Volkstumspolitik and Kirchenpolitik, the Wartheland did indeed function as a testing ground for policies to be implemented in a victorious Reich after the war.

All this conferred on the Mustergau Wartheland a status and significance that were frequently described in terms of metaphor. The speeches, public pronouncements, and propaganda of the German leadership in the Wartheland were rife with metaphorical language—often hyperbolic and eschatological—to describe, explain, publicize, or even abbreviate Nazi Germany's revolutionary initiatives. Thus, through the use of visual imagery, the metaphor could render abstract ideas more tangible and lend those ideas more emotional immediacy. Metaphors deployed by the Nazi leadership in the Gau, and especially Arthur Greiser, also looked to the future—a future that would transform space into territory, backwardness into modernity, chaos into order, spiritual into secular, Poland into Germany.

A 1941 publication by Arthur Greiser is illustrative. Appearing in *Der Schulungsbrief*, the official organ of the educational section of the Nazi Party and German Labor Front, the article emphasized the Warthegau's agricultural and economic importance as a future "breadbasket" or "granary" (*Kornkammer*) of the Greater German Reich. Moreover, as a Gau on the frontier, the Wartheland would also function as a "rampart" (*Schutzwall*) and "eastern wall" (*Ostwall*) of the Reich. Military metaphors such as these suggested not only the defensive role of the Warthegau as a bulwark against the political and racial threats posed by the allegedly Slavic, Jewish, and Bolshevik east; they also highlighted its role as a salient of Germandom projecting into the very same hostile territory. Continuing in this military vein, Greiser referred to the Warthegau as the "parade ground" (*Exerzierplatz*) of National Socialism. As such, the region would be an arena for both the evaluation and demonstration of Nazi policy. Finally, underscoring the Gau's significance as a racial testing ground, Greiser also stated that it would serve not only as the *Kornkammer* of the Reich but simultaneously as the Reich's *Kinderkammer* (nursery or, literally, "children's chamber"), bolstering the German population that would replace Poles and Jews who had been removed from the Gau or murdered. The new eastern province,

Greiser summarized, was to be "a living and strong organ, with its own pulse, of the greater German body. Therefore, it is in this way that the greater German destiny is fulfilled in the Wartheland, and it is only natural that all events in the Wartheland take on a significance that transcends the local and is always directed at the Reich in its entirety."[42]

Other metaphors abounded in the Nazi rhetoric used to describe the Wartheland's importance. In a June 1942 speech, Greiser described it as the "core territory" or "heartland" (*Kernraum*) of the Reich, even as it functioned as part of the "gateway to the East" formed by the Incorporated Territories as a whole.[43] In an October 1940 article, Greiser referred to the Warthegau as a "melting pot" (*Schmelztiegel*) of various Germanic tribes that, following the resettlement in the Gau of hundreds of thousands of ethnic Germans from various other eastern regions, would be refined to form a "unified German body" (*Volkskörper*) that was to endure for the ages. "We no longer stand in the Warthegau as a temporary presence," Greiser stated, "but to remain for all time as the standard-bearers of a new European future."[44] Striking an even more eschatological chord, Joseph Goebbels, Reich minister for public enlightenment and propaganda, referred to the German East as the "land of destiny" (*Schicksalsraum*), where generations of German colonizers had served as "pioneers" and "heralds," anchoring the German *Volk*, race, and culture over the centuries. According to Goebbels, that process did not end with the consolidation of National Socialist power in the region but would have to continue with urgency and speed in order to overcome the East's "cultural deficit" as quickly as possible.[45]

In the Warthegau this was a daunting task, and it presented a paradox. On the one hand, the region lacked the strong German ethnic and cultural presence that other Incorporated Eastern Territories could offer, and relative to other Gaus, it was economically and culturally underdeveloped. On the other hand, it was to be a model for the Reich of the future, with both its leadership and rank and file serving as, to echo Arthur Greiser's words, the "standard-bearers of a new European future." As Gauleiter and Reichsstatthalter, Greiser was chosen to lead the effort to reconcile these contradictions, and with Nazi state structures, administrative machinery, military, and police at his disposal, he would confront this challenge with vigor and ruthlessness.

Born in 1887 in Środa (Schroda), a small town in Prussia's Posen Province, Arthur Greiser was a native son of the Wartheland for whom the appointment as Gauleiter in 1939 marked a homecoming of sorts. Greiser's efforts to develop Germany's "model Gau" paralleled his personal career ambition, as he worked consistently to demonstrate his credentials as a "model Nazi," the eponym of Epstein's biography of the Gauleiter.[46] From a staunchly anti-Polish family, he attended a *Gymnasium* in Inowrocław where approximately half the students were Poles.[47] He never completed his studies there, however, but volunteered for the navy in 1914 and was decorated as an airman. According to historian Ian Kershaw, Greiser exhibited a classic "authoritarian personality," as he was eagerly submissive to his superiors, especially Hitler, and tyrannical toward his underlings.[48]

Too great a focus on Greiser's biography and his role as an executor of German policy runs the risk of excessively personalizing events in the Warthegau, but the Gauleiter nonetheless has a central place in this book, as he was of decisive importance to the formulation and implementation of church policy for several reasons. First, he consistently revealed a deep commitment to Nazi *völkisch* and racial ideals as they related to the Germanization process in the East. Although opportunistic and career obsessed, Greiser also remained remarkably consistent over the years in his commitment to Nazi population policy in the Warthegau and the necessity of undermining the power of the Polish church.

Second, as Ian Kershaw notes, Greiser's behavior illustrates how his ideological principles could result in increasingly radical measures. A "fanatical protagonist" of Nazi racial policy, Greiser was endowed by Hitler with far-reaching powers and responsibilities that he used as an "initiator and author of barbarian measures," rather than a mere executor of dictates from above.[49] Polish scholar Renata Wełniak ascribes to Greiser a similar role, referring to him as both an *initiator* and *realizator* of Nazi policy toward the Warthegau church.[50] In this respect, Greiser emerges as typical of many upper- and middle-level Nazis who authored and implemented measures that contributed to what some historians have described as the "cumulative radicalization"[51] of German policy.

Third, Greiser's aggression toward the Polish Church reveals the complex interplay, or even contradictions, between ideology and opportunism in his policies. Consistently anti-Polish and exhibiting a "missionary zeal"[52] in his quest for the Germanization of his Gau, Greiser also showed a more conciliatory approach to some Poles over the course of the war and occupation. Although infamous for his ruthless antichurch policies, especially with respect to the Polish Catholic Church, Greiser was not raised in a particularly antichurch household, his first wife was the daughter of a pastor, he did not appear to exhibit a rigorously atheistic worldview, his children were confirmed, and not until 1937, after years in the Nazi Party, did he cease to list himself as "Protestant" on official documents.[53] Greiser correctly understood the Polish church as a bastion of Polish national identity, and as the executor of the broader Germanization policies in the Warthegau, he was committed to undermining the church's power and influence. At the same time, however, Greiser also struck out against *German* Catholics and Protestants, who had often been advocates of German interests and German *Volkstum* during the twenty-one years of the Polish Republic. Greiser's treatment of what he would eventually designate "German" churches was not as dramatic or aggressive as his policies toward the Polish churches,[54] but the discriminatory measures taken against them do reveal an important aspect of National Socialist Kirchenpolitik in the Warthegau: it was not merely "national"—that is, directed against a Polish institution—but was also more broadly directed against the churches and Christians in general, whether Polish or German.

Fourth, Greiser remained consistent in his allegiance to the Mustergau concept, which not only enabled but also required him and those under his authority charged with church affairs to pursue an especially aggressive and radical Kirchenpolitik. It would not be appropriate to regard measures against the churches in the Wartheland as a "blueprint" for policy in the postwar Reich, but there is broad agreement among historians that the regime was using the Wartheland as a testing ground for future measures aimed at the disempowerment of the churches and secularization of society. As subsequent chapters will note, at various points in time and under various circumstances, members of the party elite as well as local authorities referred to measures in the Gau as paving the way for a Reich-wide Kirchenpolitik in the future. Such was the case, for example, with respect to the financing of churches and the "contribution law" issued in 1940, with respect to the goal of transforming religious denominations into private associations, as in the September 1941 decree to be discussed in chapter 10, with respect to what Kurt Krüger, a senior advisor for church affairs at NSDAP headquarters in Munich, called a "Reich-wide transformation [of the legal status of the churches] after the war,"[55] or with respect to the broader goal of, as Greiser stated during his 1946 trial, "spreading across the entire Reich the separation of church and state."[56]

Fig. 4.3. Arthur Greiser (*front, center*) reviewing troops on the occasion of his installation as Reichsstatthalter, Poznań, November 1939. Courtesy of Instytut Zachodni, IZ, Dział IV, 123-A.

Arthur Greiser was appointed chief of civilian administration (Chef der Zivilverwaltung) for the Poznań area on September 14, 1939, and was named Gauleiter of the province on October 21. Five days later, the Reichsgau Posen was formally annexed to Nazi Germany, marking the full transfer of power from the German military to German civilian authority. On November 3 Greiser was installed, with ceremony and pomp, as Reichsstatthalter.[57] The fall of 1939 was, according to Epstein, "a time of exuberant hope" for Greiser, who had already embarked on the Germanization of his Gau through the settlement of ethnic Germans, persecution of Jews, anti-Polish policies, and measures against the church. The speed with which Greiser undertook these measures is also remarkable and, as Epstein notes, made it possible to "telescope" the implementation of policies that would have taken years in the Altreich into weeks or months in the Warthegau.[58]

This was certainly true with respect to Kirchenpolitik. When, for example, one looks at the trajectory of antichurch measures in Nazi Germany prior to the war, it becomes clear that the regime felt the need to

Fig. 4.4. Arthur Greiser at his desk. Photo by Heinrich Hoffmann. United States Holocaust Memorial Museum, courtesy of National Archives and Records Administration, College Park, Maryland, USHMM, WS 20379.

proceed slowly. From the concordat between the Vatican and Nazi Germany concluded in 1933, to measures against Catholic lay institutions in the mid-1930s, to harassment of clerics, to the outright banning of Catholic organizations, to the dissolution of monasteries and confiscation of their assets late in the decade, "the power and influence of the Catholic Church in Germany," in the words of Richard Evans, "had been severely dented by 1939."[59] Standing in sharp contrast to the deliberate pace of antichurch policies in the Altreich was the rapid course of such measures in the Warthegau. As the chapters to follow will make clear, the Nazi occupation authorities in the Reichsgau Wartheland were able to accomplish far more with respect to the churches in far less time, as the measures they implemented, ranging from discriminatory policies to wanton brutality, were telescoped into a matter of months. And whereas the power and influence of the church in the Altreich had been, to use Evans's word, "dented," the power and influence of the Catholic Church in the Warthegau was, in short order, nearly destroyed.

Notes

1. These included the *Reichsgaue* formed from territory of annexed Austria, the Reichsgau Sudentenland formed from annexed Czechoslovakian territory, the Reichsgau Flandern and Reichsgau Wallonien, formed in 1944 from annexed Belgian territory, and in occupied Poland, the Reichsgau Danzig-Westpreußen and the Reichsgau Wartheland. A *Gau* was an administrative district of the Nazi Party, while a *Reichsgau*, according to Epstein, "was a territorial unit in which the Gau and local state borders were identical." Epstein, *Model Nazi*, 147.

2. On the uses and possible definitions of such notions as the "German East" or "German eastern territories" or "the East" in Nazi ideology and terminology, see Elizabeth Harvey, *Women and the Nazi East: Agents and Witnesses of Germanization* (New Haven, CT: Yale University Press, 2003), 20.

3. "Erlaß des Führers und Reichskanzlers über Gliederung und Verwaltung der Ostgebiete vom 8. Oktober 1939," in Pospieszalski, *Hitlerowskie "Prawo,"* 84.

4. "Zweiter Erlaß des Führers und Reichskanzlers zur Änderung des Erlasses über Gliederung und Verwaltung der Ostgebiete vom 29. Januar 1940," Germany, *Reichsgesetzblatt* I (Berlin: Reichsverlagsamt, 1940), 251.

5. Epstein, *Model Nazi*, 135–36. As of November 25, 1939, the surface area of the Reichsgau Posen was 40,309 square kilometers. See E. Wetzel and G. Hecht, "Die Frage der Behandlung der Bevölkerung der ehemaligen polnischen Gebiete nach rassenpolitischen Gesichtspunkten," November 25, 1939, in Pospieszalski, *Hitlerowskie "Prawo,"* 8. According to an article in the *Ostdeutscher Beobachter*, the NSDAP's organ in the Wartheland, the Gau had a surface area of 43,905 square kilometers. See "Die Gaugebiete des Reiches: Fläche und Bevölkerungsziffer des Reichsgaues Wartheland," *Ostdeutscher Beobachter*, March 23, 41, 4. For the population figures, see Epstein, *Model Nazi*, 135. Epstein relies on those provided in Łuczak, *Pod niemieckim jarzmem*, 83. The percentages correspond to those offered in Wetzel and Hecht, "Die Frage der Behandlung . . ." See also Wiesław Porzycki, *Posłudzni aż do śmierci (niemieccy urzędnicy w Kraju Warty 1939–1945)*, Dzieje Gospodarcze Wielkopolski, vol. 3 (Poznań: PSO, 1997), 11. On ethnic distribution of populations in individual subdistricts (Polish: *powiaty*; German: *Landkreise* or *Kreise*) in western Poland prior to World War II, see Appendix B, "German Population of Western Poland by Province and County," in Blanke, *Orphans*, 244–45.

6. "Statistische Angaben zur Bevölkerung im Gau," January 17, 1941, IPN, GK 62/19, 10. The numbers here for the Hohensalza and Litzmannstadt Regierungsbezirke are based on a Polish census from the year 1931, while the population of the Posen Regierungsbezirk is based on a census conducted by German authorities in 1939. The transfer of the seat of the Kalisch Regierungsbezirk to Łódź took effect on January 4, 1940. See Alberti, *Verfolgung*, 50, fn. 75. Population figures certainly varied. According to the Reich Office of Statistics (Statistisches Reichsamt), the Warthegau had 4.7 million inhabitants. See *Ostdeutscher Beobachter*, "Die Gaugebiete des Reiches," 4.

7. On economic, cultural, and demographic differences among the three districts, see Siegmund, *Rückblick*, 205; Dorota Siepracka, "Die Einstellung der Christlichen Polen gegenüber der jüdischen Bevölkerung im Wartheland," in *Der Judenmord in den eingegliederten polnischen Gebieten 1939–1945*, ed. Jacek Andrzej Młynarczyk und Jochen

Böhler, Einzelveröffentlichungen des Deutschen Historischen Instituts Warschau, vol. 21 (Osnabrück: Fibre Verlag, 2010), 345–46.

8. Broszat, *Nationalsozialistische*, 41. See also Epstein, *Model Nazi*, 140.

9. "Erlaß des Führers und Reichskanzlers zur Festigung deutschen Volkstums vom 7. October 1939," document 686 PS, in IMT, vol. 26, 255.

10. Łuczak, "Das deutsche Okkupationssystem," 43–44.

11. Ian Kershaw, "Arthur Greiser–ein Motor der 'Endlösung,'" in *Die Braune Elite II. 21 weitere biographische Skizzen*, ed. Ronald M. Smelser and Rainer Zitelmann (Darmstadt: Wissenschaftliche Buchgesellschaft, 1993), 122; Evans, *Third Reich at War*, 33.

12. Epstein, *Model Nazi*, 193.

13. On the notion of the "Mustergau" as applied to the Reichsgau Wartheland, see Epstein, *Model Nazi*, 124–59; Rutherford, *Prelude*, 68; Alberti, "'Exerzierplatz," 111–26; Werner Röhr, "'Reichsgau Wartheland' 1939–1945: vom 'Exerzierplatz des praktischen Nationalsozialismus' zum 'Mustergau'?," *Bulletin für Faschismus- und Weltkriegsforschung* 18 (2002).

14. German: "jungfräuliches Land" and "Exerzierplatz," described by Greiser as such in a September 14, 1941, speech to the Posen Gauschulungsamt, IPN, GK 196/37, 87–98, here 95, 97. See also Arthur Greiser, "Der Aufbau im Warthegau," *Der Schulungsbrief* 8, nos. 5/6 (1941): 71; Alberti, *Verfolgung*, 85. Greiser appears to have been remarkably consistent over time in his view of the Warthegau as "parade ground," using this reference as late as November 1944 in his article "Gedanken zur nationalsozialistischen Volkstumspolitik," YV, TR.17, file 12309, item 4068282.

15. Alberti, "Exerzierplatz," 111.

16. Siegmund, *Rückblick*, 216; see also Alberti, "Exerzierplatz," 113.

17. "Bericht über die Tagung der Reichstreuhänder der Arbeit der Ostgebiete in Posen," October 9, 1941, IPN, GK 196/37, 41–50, here 45. The quotation is not direct but is from the conference protocol and is provided in German indirect discourse.

18. Epstein, *Model Nazi*, 7.

19. Greiser speech on October 25, 1941, *Ostdeutscher Beobachter*, October 26, 1941, 4.

20. "Bericht über die Tagung der Reichstreuhänder der Arbeit der Ostgebiete in Posen," October 9, 1941, IPN, GK 196/37, 41–50, here 46. The quotation is not direct but is from the conference protocol and is provided in German indirect discourse. On the unique role of the Reichsgau Wartheland, see also Germany, Gauamt für Volkstumsfragen, *Wir und die Polen: Was jeder Einheitenführer vom Zusammenleben der Deutschen und Polen aus der Geschichte unseres Gaues wissen muß* (Posen: Führerdienst Gebiet Wartheland, 1943), 2.

21. Greiser speech, October 25, 1941, *Ostdeutscher Beobachter*, October 26, 1941.

22. Reichsstatthalter (Jäger?) to Reichsinnenminister, December 28, 1939, document 323.I., in Gertraud Grünzinger, ed., *Dokumente zur Kirchenpolitik des Dritten Reiches: die Kirchenpolitik in den ein- und angegliederten Gebieten (März 1938–März 1945)*, vol. 6, no. 2, 1938–1945 (Gütersloh: Gütersloher Verlagshaus, 2017), 775.

23. See Dieter Pohl, "Die Reichsgaue Danzig-Westpreußen und Wartheland: Koloniale Verwaltung oder Modell für die zukünftige Gauverwaltung?," in *Die NS-Gaue: regionale Mittelinstanzen im zentralistischen "Führerstaat,"* ed. Jürgen John, Horst Möller, and Thomas Schaarschmidt (München: R. Oldenbourg, 2007), 401–2, 404.

24. Often referred to as "Stab Heß" or the "Hess Staff," the office was renamed the Party Chancellery in May 1941, with Martin Bormann at its head.

25. Bormann to Forster, December 29, 1939, USHMM, RG 15.007M, reel 38, 465, 4–5.

26. Friedrich Zipfel, *Kirchenkampf in Deutschland 1933–1945: Religionsverfolgung und Selbstbehauptung der Kirchen in der nationalsozialistischen Zeit*, Veröffentlichungen der Historischen Kommission zu Berlin beim Friedrich-Meinecke-Institut der Freien Universität Berlin, vol. 11, Publikationen der Forschungsgruppe Berliner Widerstand beim Senator für Inneres von Berlin, no. 1 (Berlin: Walter de Gruyter, 1965), 257.

27. Pierre Blét, *Pius XII and the Second World War According to the Archives of the Vatican*, trans. L. J. Johnson (New York: Paulist, 1999), 70.

28. Sziling, *Polityka*, 273. See also Alberti, "Exerzierplatz," 113; Broszat, "Verfolgung," 30–31.

29. Epstein, *Model Nazi*, 7.

30. Ryszard Kaczmarek, "Zwischen Altreich und Grenzgebiet: der Gau Oberschlesien 1939/41–1945," in John, Möller, and Schaarschmidt, *Die NS-Gaue*, 352–53.

31. Martin Moll, "Der Reichsgau Steiermark 1938–1945," in John, Möller, and Schaarschmidt, *Die NS-Gaue*, 367–68, 372.

32. Röhr, "Reichsgau Wartheland," 29–31.

33. Historian Frank Bajohr has even argued that the term Mustergau is "heuristically useless and empirically nonexistent." See Frank Bajohr, "Gauleiter in Hamburg: Zur Person und Tätigkeit Karl Kaufmanns," *Vierteljahrshefte für Zeitgeschichte* 43, no. 2 (April 1995): 269, note 8.

34. Alberti, "Exerzierplatz," 114, 122.

35. For a brief and clear description of the terms and categories of the Deutsche Volksliste, see Birthe Kundrus, "Regime der Differenz: Volkstumspolitische Inklusionen und Exklusionen im Warthegau und im Generalgouvernement 1939–1944," in *Volksgemeinschaft: Neue Forschungen zur Gesellschaft des Nationalsozialismus*, ed. Frank Bajohr and Michael Wildt (Frankfurt am Main: Fischer Taschenbuch Verlag, 2009), 114–15. See also Epstein, *Model Nazi*, 195–97, 208–15. For the law establishing the Volksliste, see "Verordnung über die Deutsche Volksliste und die deutsche Staatsangehörigkeit in den eingegliederten Ostgebieten. Vom 4. März 1941," *Reichsgesetzblatt*, pt. 1, no. 25, 1941, 118–20. On the Volksliste in the Wartheland as compared to other Incorporated Territories, see Pohl, "Die Reichsgaue," 403, Mark Mazower, *Hitler's Empire: How the Nazis Ruled Europe* (New York: Penguin, 2008), 195–98, and Rutowska, "NS-Verfolgungsmaßnahmen," 209–11. On the broader efforts to Germanize Poles in the Incorporated Eastern Territories see Madajczyk, *Okkupationspolitik*, chap. 24, 479–519.

36. Pohl, "Die Reichsgaue," 403; Harvey, *Women*, 79.

37. Kershaw, "Arthur Greiser," 121–22.

38. Alberti, *Verfolgung*, 3.

39. *Posener Tageblatt*, September 22, 1939, 3.

40. Najwyższy Trubunał Narodowy, Akta w sprawie Arthura Greisera, tom V, IPN, GK 196/38/CD1, 109.

41. Pohl, "Die Reichsgaue," 404.

42. Greiser, "Aufbau im Warthegau," 68–71, passim.

43. Greiser, *Aufbau im Osten*, 4.

44. Arthur Greiser, "Schmelztiegel Warthegau: Wege der Neubesiedlung im Osten," *Das Reich* 22 (October 20, 1940), 10.

45. Joseph Goebbels, "Der kulturelle Aufbau im Osten wird vom Gesamtreich getragen–Ansprache zur Eröffnung der Reichsgautheater Posen, gehalten im Großen Haus

am 18. März 1941," *Wartheland: Zeitschrift für Aufbau und Kultur im deutschen Osten* 1, no. 4 (April 1941): 1–3.

46. In her biography, the most extensive and balanced treatment of Greiser to date, Epstein writes, "Greiser as Gauleiter tried to act as a super Nazi by promoting the most extreme Nazi solutions to alleged problems. Indeed, while he explicitly aimed to make the Warthegau a 'model Gau,' he also tried to fashion himself into a 'model Nazi' . . . [and] expended much psychic and other energy to turn himself into what he believed his movement demanded." Epstein, *Model Nazi*, 8. On Grieser's biography see also Czesław Łuczak, *Arthur Greiser: hitlerowski władza w Wolnym Mieście Gdańsku i w Kraju Warty* (Poznań: PSO, 1997); Edward Serwański, *Wielkopolska w cieniu swastiki* (Warszawa: Instytut Wydawniczy "Pax," 1970), 67–68; Zdzisław Romanowski, "Poprzez Gdańsk do Poznania," *Nurt: miesięcznik społeczno-kulturalny* 5, no. 13 (May 1966): 8–11; Albin Wietrzykowski, *Powrót Arthura Greisera* (Poznań: "Pomóc," 1946), 5–8.

47. Serwański, *Wielkopolska*, 68; Romanowski, "Poprzez," 8.

48. Kershaw, "Arthur Greiser," 120.

49. Kershaw, 117, 121.

50. Renata Wełniak, *Duchowieństwo w obozie żabikowskim (1943–1945)* (Żabikowo: Muzeum Martyrologiczne w Żabikowie, 2010), 6.

51. Developed most prominently by historian Hans Mommsen, the concept is summarized effectively in his essay "Der Nationalsozialismus: kumulative Radikalisierung und Selbstzerstörung des Regimes," in *Meyers Enzyklopädisches Lexikon*, vol. 16 (Mannheim: Bibliographisches Institut, 1976), 785–90, and in Hans Mommsen, "The Realization of the Unthinkable: The 'Final Solution of the Jewish question' in the Third Reich," in *The Policies of Genocide: Jews and Soviet Prisoners of War in Nazi Germany*, ed. Gerhard Hirschfeld (London: Allen and Unwin, 1986), 97–144.

52. Kershaw, "Arthur Greiser," 116.

53. Epstein, *Model Nazi*, 221–22.

54. In comparing Nazi policy toward the German Catholics in the Warthegau to policy against the Polish churches, Śmigiel states that the former were "subject to coercive measures," while the latter faced "violence and repression." The authorities intended for the German clergy, only numbering thirty in the Warthegau, to "die a natural death," but marked the Polish clergy, he states, for biological extermination. See Śmigiel, *Die katholische Kirche*, 313.

55. Krüger to Hartl, June 17, 1940, BAB, R58/7581, 55–56.

56. Greiser, testimony of June 27, 1946, Najwyższy Trybunał Narodowy, Akta w sprawie Artura Greisera, IPN, GK 196/38/CD1, tom V, 109.

57. Epstein, *Model Nazi*, 134–35.

58. Epstein, 157.

59. Evans, *Third Reich in Power*, 247.

5

DOMINSELAKTION

The "Cathedral Island Action"

Located on the Ostrów Tumski island between the Warta and Cybina rivers, Poznań's imposing gothic cathedral is part of a larger "campus" of church structures that include the bishop's palace, the diocesan seminary, a diocesan archive and library, and numerous administrative offices. At 5:00 a.m. on October 3, 1939, members of the Gestapo and other police units from Einsatzgruppe VI—known among the Einsatzgruppen for its rigor in persecuting the clergy[1]—raided the island in what became known as the *Dominselaktion*, or "Cathedral Island Action."[2] The pretext for the raid was a weapons search. The goal was to secure archival documents that could reveal potentially dangerous clergy and church institutions. The result was disastrous for the Catholic Church and Poznań diocese. According to a report of the Poznań Sicherheitspolizei, the search did, in fact, uncover small amounts of gunpowder and munitions,[3] but the German authorities also determined that the most important documents had, on orders of the Polish primate August Hlond, been transferred to a monastery near Lublin. Frustrated in their efforts, members of the Einsatzgruppe closed the bishop's palace, consistory, diocesan museum and archive, and arrested, "on suspicion of direct anti-German activity" (they were either unable or unwilling to reveal the whereabouts of archival documents), four members of the cathedral chapter: Canon Henryk Zborowski, head of the archdiocesan chancellery; Dr. Edmund Nowicki of the ecclesiastical court; Kazimierz Schmelzer, notary of the ecclesiastical court; and Marian Magnuszewski, a cathedral vicar. They then placed the suffragan (i.e., auxiliary) bishop Walenty Dymek, who had been appointed vicar general[4] of the diocese by the Polish primate August Hlond prior to Hlond's departure from Poznań on September 3,[5] under house arrest.

The October 3 Dominselaktion began a wave of new actions against the church across the entire Warthegau in the fall of 1939, marking a turning point in Nazi church policy there. The September invasion had been accompanied by arrests and executions of individual clergy as an application of Nazi terror. Once hostilities had ended, however, the German occupation authorities shifted to a strategy of attacking the church's hierarchy, structure, organizations, and practices. This persecution of the church took two main forms. First, and most significantly, the occupiers incarcerated and deported allegedly conspiratorial and dangerous clergy, not only as a means of neutralizing potential anti-German sentiment and resistance but also as part of the demographic transformation of the Warthegau. To some extent, the arrest, persecution, and deportation of the clergy—the theme of chapters 6, 11, and 12—was a continuation of the terror actions in the first weeks of the occupation, but it was also linked to the anti-Polish population policy associated with the Volkstumskampf in the Warthegau.

Second, the Nazis enacted policies and issued restrictions intended to limit access to the church and its institutions and to undermine its activities. Removal of the clergy could, of course, go a long way toward accomplishing these goals, but persecution of the church was not necessarily synonymous with the persecution of the clergy. Indeed, the life of the church was also much connected to its physical structures (such as churches, statues, and shrines), organizations (such as hospitals, charitable groups, and schools), and rituals (such as diverse forms of public and private worship, devotion, and education)—all of which could exist for Catholic believers, and perhaps even prosper, outside the traditional forum of the Sunday Mass, and all of which stood in opposition to the broader Nazi plans to make the Gau German or, in the cant of Nazi propaganda, return the region to its allegedly organic German origins. This relates to what chapter 2 described briefly as a "spatial aspect" of Germanization in the Gau, and according to its logic, there was little place in the landscape of a "German" Gau for "Polish" (i.e., Catholic) shrines, churches, organizations, public religiosity, or vectors and ministers of that religiosity (the clergy). In the words of Ian Kershaw, "In posing their total claim on society, the Nazis were not willing to grant any institutional or organizational space which they themselves did not control."[6]

The Dominselaktion and aggressive measures that followed undoubtedly came as a shock to Polish Catholics, for as the region fell under German control in September 1939, members of the church hierarchy had sought, and received, assurances that the work of the church could continue. Already in the first week of Poznań's occupation, one of the cathedral canons there, an ethnic German named Joseph Paech, met with Greiser's aide Viktor Böttcher, who was responsible for church affairs in the areas already under Wehrmacht control.[7] Paech received assurances that the occupation authorities would not interfere with Catholic services on Sundays or weekdays and conveyed these guarantees to the suffragan bishop and vicar general Walenty Dymek.[8] Dymek and Paech then met with the German military commander of the city, General Max von Schenkendorff, on September 16 and submitted to him a declaration to be read in churches the following Sunday. The declaration admonished Catholics to attend to their spiritual needs, be charitable, remain calm, exercise prudence, comply with the orders of the authorities, and avoid any actions that could place the population at risk or result in any punitive sanctions.[9] Von Schenkendorff was reportedly pleased with the declaration and assured the bishop that Poles would be treated fairly. Paech then specifically requested that the occupation forces refrain from interfering in the ministry and affairs of the church, lest the Catholic population become embittered toward the authorities. Von Schenkendorff offered such assurances, and Dymek was apparently satisfied with the meeting.[10]

Later in September, Paech, who by that time was functioning as an intermediary between the church hierarchy and occupation authorities,[11] met with Hans Frank, chief of civilian administration for occupied Poland as a whole (he would soon be named head of the General Government). Frank assured Paech that Catholics in the region would not be hindered in their religious practices and duties.[12] In turn, Bishop Dymek then urged his clergy to communicate to the Catholic faithful their duty to work, remain calm, and cooperate with "the orders of the secular authorities."[13]

On September 25, the bishop issued to clergy in his diocese a memorandum outlining instructions and procedures "*imperata pro re gravi tempore belli*" ("ordered in a serious time of war"). Although Dymek made clear that the ministries of the church—education, distribution of the sacraments, care for those in physical and spiritual need—were to continue as ever, the memorandum also included instructions that reflected the difficult circumstances of the moment. The bishop thus called on his clergy to care for the poor and to maintain social peace, and also to comply with the orders of the authorities. Loosening conventional restrictions, he issued dispensations for priests to celebrate, if necessary, Mass in locations other than churches, and to celebrate more than one Mass per day (according to Canon Law, a practice permissible only in extenuating circumstances). Aware that the Germans saw the Polish church as politicized, patriotic, and potentially conspiratorial, he also issued directives to limit hymns to those with a purely religious (as opposed to national or political) character, to keep homilies purely "catechetical," and to limit conversations in the confessional to matters of faith and salvation only.[14] The bishop's desire to cooperate with the Germans and avoid provoking their aggression should not, however, be seen as expression of sympathy or eager compliance. Rather, he was simply attempting to ensure that Polish Catholics would continue to have access to "word and sacrament" and, more broadly, the ministries that the church provided.

Any hopes he may have had that the clergy would resume their normal work would, however, be severely disappointed, and the course that German policy would take became all too clear in the weeks ahead. On September 29, Greiser, in his capacity as chief of civilian administration of the region, issued a set of guidelines for the administration of the province. These included a call for giving each community a "German imprint," restrictions against Poles loitering, a prohibition against Poles "standing around with their hands in their pockets" as German military vehicles passed, the demand that military and police authorities undertake searches for weapons, and the compilation of lists of "Polish leaders and members of the Polish intelligentsia," including priests.[15]

The latter two demands directly affected the Catholic Church. They may well have been the impetus behind the Dominselaktion of October 3 and the actions that followed, for in the days ahead, the attack on the church was expanded, both in Poznań and in other cities in the region. On October 6 the German authorities closed the seminary of the Poznań diocese,[16] and two days later, the cathedral.[17] They undertook searches of twenty religious houses (e.g., monasteries, cloisters, and convents) in the city (where they reportedly discovered "incriminating" material),[18] and raided the archives of nine separate Catholic organizations, including those of the lay organization Catholic Action.[19] On October 4 and 5, the Security Police of Einsatzgruppe III took control of sixteen parishes in Łódź, designating in the process the leading clergy in each of the city's districts who would be listed as potentially dangerous to the Reich and appropriate for deportation.[20] In Gniezno, members of the diocesan curia were the target. According to a report of Einsatzgruppe VI, the fact that secret church archival materials had, as in Poznań, been removed to another location was clear evidence of the Gniezno curia's "burdened conscience."[21] It remains unclear what, specifically, the German authorities saw as potentially incriminating among the documents, but in any case, the Security Police went on to close the diocesan consistory, prohibit all instruction in the Gniezno seminary, and imprison three influential priests: Franciszek Marlewski, director of Catholic Action; Paweł Steinmetz, who had served as a chaplain during the Greater Poland Uprising of 1918–1919; and Jan Krajewski, director of the charitable organization "Caritas."[22] The Gestapo also issued an order prohibiting, "under the pain of the most severe penalties," priests from leaving the city, and thirty-five local priests were required to consent to the order with their signatures.[23] In addition, Greiser's office issued to the Gniezno diocese's vicar general, Eduard van Blericq,[24] strict regulations regarding corporate worship and public expressions of Catholic devotion: public worship services were limited to Sundays between 9:00 a.m. and 11:00 a.m., priests were required to limit the content of services to purely religious matters, and demonstrations of religiosity ("kneeling, gathering, or other gestures") were prohibited outside of churches.[25] In conveying these orders to the Catholic faithful, van Blericq also urged them to be diligent in their duty to attend Mass; despite the restrictions imposed, he maintained, the Gniezno cathedral could accommodate many worshippers. "Now," he added, "it will be revealed who is a Catholic."[26]

Whether van Blericq's words are to be understood as counsel, admonition, warning, or even a call to resistance against the authorities is not clear. They do, however, point to the urgency of the situation and serve as a reminder of how the Germans' demands must have been experienced by Polish Catholics as a gross violation of their traditions and practices. From the more secular perspective of more than eighty years, it is worth noting that among Catholics in Poland in the 1930s, kneeling in prayer and genuflecting at public shrines and crucifixes were common. Parish churches typically offered services at least once and often several times per day, and were generally open and accessible throughout the week for private prayer and devotion. In cities and towns, Masses were typically celebrated throughout the day on Sundays, so restricting services to two hours on Sunday mornings made it often impossible for Catholics to participate in worship. With this in mind, the vicar general's call to public piety and worship was both a reminder for Gniezno Catholics to fulfill their Christian duty and, in a sense, to "stand up and be counted." From the perspective of the German occupiers, who were eager for Polish Catholics to neglect their religious duties, a gathering of hundreds or thousands of Poles in and around churches was cause for concern, and in the months ahead they would target such gatherings for roundups and mass incarcerations.

Measures against the church continued on various fronts in the weeks ahead, as German officials continued to shut down church institutions and destroy roadside religious shrines and monuments.[27] On October 28, Greiser's office issued an order to all *Landräte* (subdistrict commissioners, or prefects) that expanded the worship restrictions in Gniezno to the entire Gau: all public weekday Masses were prohibited,[28] and public worship was limited to Sundays between 9:00 a.m. and 11:00 a.m.[29] On Wednesday, November 1—All Saints' Day in the Catholic liturgical calendar—Poznań's priests were ordered to appear at 7:00 a.m. in the offices of Helmut Bischoff, head of the city's Staatspolizei, or state police. There they were informed of the terms of the October 28 order, and were given further restrictions on their activities: no public Masses would be permitted on All Saints' Day; the traditional commemoration of the dead in cemeteries would likewise be prohibited; celebration of any weekday Masses would forthwith be permitted only behind closed doors, with no parishioners present; priests were to be allowed to hear confessions, but their parishioners were prohibited from participating in Holy Communion.[30] In the days ahead, local authorities stipulated that Sunday Masses were to be celebrated in German only, likely to enable surveillance at these gatherings, as the German police began to monitor attendance at these services, as well as their content.[31]

In December, Greiser and his staff also began to initiate, in cooperation with the Office of the Deputy Führer in Munich, a radical transformation of the legal status of the Warthegau's churches. At a meeting with Gerhard Klopfer, assistant to Martin Bormann, chief of staff in the Office of the Deputy Führer, the Gauleiter articulated his long-term goal of "a total separation of church and state" which, as noted in the previous chapter, would remain for years to come a broad objective for the Reich as a whole. Steps in the process would include reducing the status of churches from public corporations to "private associations," restricting churches from collecting contributions from parishioners, closing all church-run schools, and incorporating the church's charitable institutions into the National Socialist People's Welfare (Nationalsozialistische Volkswohlfahrt, or NSV).[32] The discussions also emphasized that the 1925 concordat between the Vatican and Polish Republic was no longer in effect, meaning that the Catholic Church in the Warthegau was no longer in a position to make any demands or claims vis-à-vis the German state on the basis of that agreement.[33]

Both Greiser and the Nazi Party's leadership would continue their efforts to transform the ecclesiastical landscape over the course of 1940 and 1941, but the genesis of ambitious plans such as these indicated that already by late 1939, policy toward the Polish Catholic Church had moved beyond the *Einzelaktionen* against locals priests in the first weeks and months of the occupation toward the broader and sustained objectives of a telescoped secularization and radical ecclesiastical "new order" for the future—a new order that would not only neutralize the Polish-nationalist threat that the church allegedly posed but also hasten the broader Germanization process underway.

In October 1940, a year after the Poznań Dominselaktion, Vicar General Walenty Dymek lamented in a report to a German colleague that prior to the invasion he "was administrating a thriving diocese, of which only shards remain." In the report, he related the dire situation in his diocese: churches were closed, rectories and parish houses had been confiscated by the Germans, roadside chapels and shrines had been destroyed, and the majority of diocesan clergy were either dead or deported to the General Government or concentration camps.[34] What had, in the course of a year, transpired? Beginning in the fall of 1939, Greiser's administration had charted three paths toward the "new order" for the Polish Catholic Church that are described in greater detail in the chapters to follow. First, the German authorities incarcerated and deported hundreds of priests; second, they enacted policies that restricted Poles' access to the church—its physical structures and spaces, its clergy and educators, and its traditions and rituals; third, they undertook economic and legal measures to undermine the unity, integrity, and structure of the Polish church as an institution.

Notes

1. Krausnick and Wilhelm, *Die Truppe*, 43.
2. The *Aktion* is described firsthand in "Der Chef der Zivilverwaltung beim Militärbefehlshaber Posen Nr. 54, S. 55. Aus einem geheimen Bericht der Sicherheitspolizei Posen vom 3.10.1939. Aktennr. R/Schr. B 99/39," in Czesław Łuczak, ed., *Dyskryminacja*

Polaków w Wielkopolsce w okresie okupacji hitlerowskiej: wybór źródeł (Poznań: Wydawnictwo Poznańskie, 1966), 100–101; in Der Befehlshaber der Sicherheitspolizei und des SD in Posen to Chef der Sicherheitspolizei Berlin, November 9, 1939, USHMM, RG 15.007M, reel 38, 466, 3; and in the 1946 testimony of the seminary professor and archivist Józef Nowacki: Zeznanie Ks. Dr. Józefa Nowackiego, June 11, 1946, IPN, GK 196/30, tom IV, 22–23.

3. Walenty Dymek, suffragan bishop of the Posen diocese, who was present at the raid, disputed this claim. Dymek to Reichsminister Hans Frank, Abschrift, October 6, 1939, BAB, R 5101/22185, 46.

4. A priest who is appointed as a bishop's deputy and holds executive power in the diocese.

5. Śmigiel, *Die katholische Kirche*, 129. The departure of the primate Hlond and the papal nuncio to Poland, Filippo Cortesi, at the request of the Polish government, was not uncontroversial. In the words of Neal Pease, "The decisions of Hlond and Cortesi to vacate their posts in this critical hour, depriving the wartime Church in the occupied country of its two most visible figures of leadership, were received badly in Poland and, it is said, in the Vatican as well, as a violation of the principle that the shepherd should not abandon his endangered flock." Pease, *Rome's*, 208.

6. Ian Kershaw, *The Nazi Dictatorship: Problems and Perspectives of Interpretation* (New York: Oxford University Press, 2000), 196.

7. Böttcher was a highly influential figure in the German administration and would subsequently be named *Regierungspräsident* (District President) of the Posen administrative district, or Regierungsbezirk.

8. Dymek to Reichsminister Hans Frank, Abschrift, October 6, 1939, BAB, R 5101/22185, 46.

9. Walenty Dymek, Wikariusz Generalny, to Wielebnych Księży proboszczów miasta, September 14, 1939, AAP, zespół 133, syg. OK 3.

10. Hilarius Breitinger, *Als Deutschenseelsorger in Posen und im Warthegau 1934–1945: Erinnerungen*, Veröffentlichung der Kommission für Zeitgeschichte, series A, vol. 36 (Mainz: Matthias-Grünewald-Verlag, 1984), 39. On von Schenkendorff and the Wehrmacht crimes committed under his command, see Rossino, *Hitler*, 126–29, 132.

11. Tagesbericht, Einsatzgruppe VI, September 27, 1939, document 57, in Lehnstaedt and Böhler, *Berichte der Einsatzgruppen*, 259.

12. Schreiben des Domherrn Dr. Paech an SS-Hauptsturmführer Grün, addendum to Befehlshaber der Sicherheitspolizei und des SD in Posen to Chef der Sicherheitspolizei Berlin, November 9, 1939. USHMM, RG 15.007M, reel 38, 466, 5–12, here 6.

13. Dymek to Reichsminister Hans Frank, Abschrift, October 6, 1939, BAB, R 5101/22185, 46.

14. Wikariusz Generalny (Dymek), Memorandum 12241/39, September 25, 1939, AAP, zespół 133, syg. OK 3.

15. "Richtlinien für den Verwaltungsaufbau in den Kreisen und Städten der Provinz Posen," September 29, 1939, Abschrift, IPN, GK 196/11/CD; Siegmund, 190.

16. "Aus einem geheimen Bericht der Sicherheitspolizeistelle Poznań vom 6.10.1939" in Łuczak, *Dyskryminacja Polaków*, 338; Dymek to Reichsminister Hans Frank, Abschrift, October 6, 1939, BAB, R 5101/22185, 46; Der Befehlshaber der Sicherheitspolizei und des SD in Posen to Chef der Sicherheitspolizei Berlin, November 9, 1939, USHMM, RG 15.007M, reel 38, 466, 4.

17. Breitinger, *Als Deutschenseelsorger*, 63.

18. Der Chef der Sicherheitspolizei, Tagesbericht der Einsatzgruppe VI, October 5, 1939, document 81, in Lehnstaedt and Böhler, *Berichte der Einsatzgruppen*, 334.

19. Tagesbericht der Einsatzgruppe VI, October 14, 1939, document 95, in Lehnstaedt and Böhler, *Berichte der Einsatzgruppen*, 375.

20. Der Chef der Sicherheitspolizei, Sonderreferent "Unternehmen Tannenberg," Tagesbericht für die Zeit vom 4.10.39, 12:00 Uhr bis 5.10.39, 12:00 Uhr, October 5, 1939, in Leszczyński, "Działalność Einsatzgruppen," 154; Śmigiel, *Die katholische Kirche*, 183. Poland's second-largest city, Łódź/Lodsch/Litzmannstadt would be added to the Warthegau the following month.

21. Der Chef der Sicherheitspolizei, Tagesbericht der Einsatzgruppe VI, October 5, 1939, document 81, in Lehnstaedt and Böhler, *Berichte der Einsatzgruppen*, 334.

22. Der Befehlshaber der Sicherheitspolizei und des SD in Posen to Chef der Sicherheitspolizei Berlin, November 9, 1939, USHMM, RG 15.007M, reel 38, 466, 4–5.

23. Kurenda, Eduard van Blericq, Wikariusz Generalny, October 5, 1939, Archiwum Archidiecezjalne w Gnieźnie (hereafter AAG), zespół 0131, AKM I, syg. 2178, 37.

24. Van Blericq had, like the Posen suffragan bishop Walenty Dymek, been named vicar general of the Gnesen diocese by the primate August Hlond prior to his departure from Posen on September 3.

25. Verordnung, Chef der Zivilverwaltung, Posen, October 6, 1939. Abschrift. AAG, zespół 0131, AKM I, syg. 2178, 39; Zarządzenie Wikariusza Generalnego Gniezno, October 6, 1939, AAG, zespół 0131, AKM I, syg. 2178, 40.

26. Zarządzenie Wikariusza Generalnego Gniezno, October 6, 1939, AAG, zespół 0131, AKM I, syg. 2178, 40.

27. Lagebericht des Landrats des Kreises Mogilno, October 23, 1939, in Łuczak, *Dyskryminacja Polaków*, 236; Regierungspräsident Posen (Böttcher) to Herrn Stadtkommissar in Posen, Herrn Polizeipräsident in Posen, Herren Landkommissare des Bezirks, December 21, 1939, IPN, GK 196/13/CD, 7.

28. Zarządzenie Wikariusz Generalnego Gniezno, November 4, 1939, AAG, zespół 0131, AKM I, syg. 2177, 2.

29. Der Befehlshaber der Sicherheitspolizei und des SD in Posen to Chef der Sicherheitspolizei Berlin, November 9, 1939, USHMM, RG 15.007M, reel 38, 466, 5.

30. Bericht des Domherrn Dr. Paech an SS-Hauptsturmführer Grün, November 4, 1939, addendum to Der Befehlshaber der Sicherheitspolizei und des SD in Posen to Chef der Sicherheitspolizei Berlin, November 9, 1939, USHMM, RG 15.007M, reel 38, 466, 5–12, here 7.

31. Kreis Kalisch, Lagebericht vom 1.-15. November 1939, November 15, 1939, Archiwum Państwowe w Poznaniu (hereafter APP), zespół 299/0/1.39/1832, microfilm no. O-60674, 12. The order likely refers to the homily and any other parts of the worship service not in Latin, the traditional language of the Catholic liturgy. Regarding surveillance of services, see Situationsbericht des Befehlshabers der Schutzpolizei in Ostrów, November 24, 1939, in Łuczak, *Dyskryminacja Polaków*, 81.

32. "Bericht über die Dienstreise nach Posen am 12.12.39," December 12, 1939, BAB, R 58/7578, 30–32; Epstein, *Model Nazi*, 222–23.

33. "Bericht über die Besprechung am 13.12.29, an den Höheren Polizei- und SS-Führer in Posen, n.d., USHMM RG 15.007, reel 47, 578, 50–51. This document, although

clearly describing the December 12 meeting, states that the meeting took place on December 13, 1939.

34. Dymek to Heinrich Wienken, October 14, 1940, document 19, in Ludwig Volk, ed., *Akten deutscher Bischöfe über die Lage der Kirche 1933–1945*, vol. 5, 1940–1942, Veröffentlichungen der Kommission für Zeitgeschichte, series A: Quellen, no. 34 (Mainz: Matthias-Grünewald-Verlag, 1983), 1010–12.

6

DEPORTACJA

The Deportation and Incarceration of the Clergy

THE PERSECUTION OF THE POLISH CATHOLIC CHURCH IN the Warthegau began during the German invasion and intensified in the aftermath of the Poznań Dominselaktion. The first step in establishing a "new order" for the church was the removal of the vast majority of its clergy. This was a natural step, because eliminating the clergy from the religious landscape deprived the church of its local leadership, severely challenged Catholics' ability to adhere to the traditions and requirements of their faith, and struck a grave psychological blow to Poles who looked to the clergy as symbols of the enduring power of the Catholic Church and defenders of Polish national identity.

As discussed in chapter 1, executions of Polish priests were not uncommon during the first weeks of the war and occupation, and they increased throughout the fall of 1939. Fifty-three priests were shot in September, 164 in October, and 165 in November.[1] With the establishment of civilian rule in the Warthegau, however, the German authorities turned to arrest, incarceration, and deportation as the most effective means of neutralizing the Polish clergy. This occurred in four main stages: (1) in the immediate aftermath of the fall 1939 invasion; (2) during the first three months of 1940, when the German authorities targeted priests mainly from the Gniezno and Poznań archdioceses; (3) in August 1940, when some two hundred priests were arrested and deported to the Sachsenhausen and Buchenwald concentration camps; and (4) in the mass *Aktion* of early October 1941, when more than five hundred Warthegau priests were arrested (the theme of chapter 11).[2]

In the first stage, the German military and police in the Warthegau targeted clergy who were allegedly active in Polish politics and cultural life.[3]

In October and November 1939, for example, eleven priests from the Szubin (Schubin) Subdistrict were imprisoned; on October 21, fifteen priests from Nieszawa (Nessau) and five Salesians were arrested and subsequently interned in a cloister in Górna Grupa (Obergruppa). Three weeks later, thirteen of them were shot, while the rest were deported to the Stutthof concentration camp near Gdańsk. On October 24, fourteen additional clergymen from Nieszawa Subdistrict were imprisoned, and a week later all but one were executed.[4] In Inowrocław, all thirty-nine priests in the city were arrested on November 5,[5] and two days later, fifty priests from Włocławek, including the suffragan bishop Michał Kozal, were incarcerated in a local prison, where they would remain until they were transferred in January 1940 to the Salesian monastery in Ląd.[6] For his part, the Włocławek ordinary, Bishop Karol Radoński, was prohibited from returning to his diocese[7] and would spend the remainder of the occupation in exile.

On December 13, 1939, the city commissioner (*Stadtkommissar*) in Włocławek reported as follows: "The entire clergy here, numbering about fifty, remain detained in the local prison along with the suffragan bishop. For police-security reasons, I request that these people be transported out for internment in either a concentration camp or cloister. There is no doubt that without exception, these clergymen have behaved in a manner hostile to Germany, and because of this, any return of these priests to their former duties is out of the question."[8]

It is worth considering briefly what the Włocławek official had in mind when he insisted that the clergy had "behaved in a manner hostile toward Germany." Some priests had likely been involved in Polish nationalist politics or organizations; others had perhaps preached patriotic sermons during the invasion or put up resistance against German measures and policies in the first months of the occupation. It remains unlikely, however, that all fifty clergymen had been documented demonstrating anti-German hostility in these ways. More probable was that the majority of priests were simply carrying out their duties: hearing confessions and offering absolution, celebrating Mass, teaching children to the extent possible—all activities that involved speaking Polish to public gatherings of Poles which, in the Reichsgau Wartheland, was considered inherently subversive behavior.

In Poznań, a similar mass arrest had taken place on November 9, and by the end of 1939, forty-two priests from that city had been incarcerated in the cloister of the Missionaries of the Holy Family in Kazimierz Biskupi, near Konin.[9] In the Łódź diocese, more than fifty priests, including the suffragan bishop Kazimierz Tomczak, were included in a mass arrest of some 1,500 people on November 9 and 10 and imprisoned in a new detention camp north of the Łódź city center in Radogoszcz (Radegast).[10]

The number of arrests, incarcerations, and deportations increased in the months ahead, as the persecution of the clergy converged with ambitious plans for the removal of tens of thousands of Poles from the Warthegau. Part of the broader Germanization effort discussed in the previous chapter, the program to deport hundreds of thousands of Poles and Jews from the territories annexed to the Reich was not the result of long-term prewar planning. Rather, it emerged during the early days of Operation Tannenberg and quickly developed a racial-ideological dynamic of its own. According to Phillip Rutherford, "Though Tannenberg was still in full swing and many executions were yet to come, the elimination of the Polish leadership, initially dictated primarily by questions of state security, was now considered but one component, albeit an integral component, of a larger project directed at the entire non-German population of western Poland. Evacuations, moreover, would soon displace physical liquidation as the primary means of neutralizing opposition to German rule."[11]

From September 1939 until March 1941, the Nazi regime deported nearly three hundred thousand people, the vast majority of them ethnic Poles, from the Reichsgau Wartheland to the General Government.[12] Removal of Jews and Poles was, however, to be only one step in this ethno-demographic project, which also called for the Germanization of those portions of the population deemed racially, culturally, and politically suitable, as well as the settlement of hundreds of thousands of Volksdeutsche from eastern and southeastern Europe—a program that required extensive cooperation with the Soviet Union.[13] All this made the Wartheland the arena for the most massive expulsion and resettlement action in annexed Polish territory, setting Greiser's Gau apart from the neighboring regions. Unlike in, for example, Danzig-Westpreußen to the north or Upper Silesia to the south, the Nazi authorities in the Warthegau were little interested in Germanizing Poles via the Deutsche Volksliste. Instead, they removed or destroyed them.[14]

On October 26, 1939, the day the Reichsgau Wartheland was formally established, Reich Minister for Church Affairs Hanns Kerrl wrote to Greiser and strongly emphasized the need to undertake a fundamental restructuring of church affairs in the new Gau. "The importance of this task probably

Fig. 6.1. Deportation of members of the intelligentsia, including clergy, from the Reichsgau Wartheland, October–November 1939. United States Holocaust Memorial Museum, courtesy of Archiwum Dokumentacji Mechanicznej, USHMM, WS 06003.

does not need to be justified," Kerrl stated. "One need only refer to the fact that the Catholic Church in Poland is the most dangerous and significant opponent of Germandom, that Posen is the seat of the Polish primate and headquarters of Catholic Action, and that there are no fewer than four bishoprics (Posen, Gnesen, Wloclawek, Lodz) in the Gau."[15] Kerrl also noted to Greiser the importance of church matters in relation to the ethno-political agenda that the Nazis were developing for the region—that is, plans for massive population shifts, which included the deportation of not only all Jews from annexed Polish territories but also "a yet to be determined number of especially hostile Poles."[16] This would require the movement or destruction of bishoprics and religious orders, as well as the removal of members of the Polish clergy.[17]

Greiser likely neither wanted nor needed instructions on church affairs in his Gau, and especially not from Kerrl, a minister with minimal status and waning influence in the hierarchy of Nazi power.[18] Kerrl's letter points, however, to a reflexive hostility to the Polish Catholic clergy and, at the same time, to the relationship between German plans for the clergy and the broader population policy under development at the time. That relationship would become clearer in the weeks ahead. On November 12,

Heinrich Himmler, in his capacity as Reich commissioner for the consolidation of German nationhood (Reichskommissar für die Festigung des Deutschen Volkstums), issued orders that all Poles belonging to the intelligentsia or who, because of their nationalist views, could pose a danger to the German nation, be deported from the annexed territories. The purpose of this order was twofold: to "cleanse and secure" these newly annexed areas and to provide homes and work for Volksdeutsche settlers. Himmler's ambitious plans called for the removal of 200,000 Poles and 100,000 Jews from the Wartheland over the course of only three and a half months, including, from the cities, 35,000 Poles and all Jews to be deported from Poznań, 30,000 Poles and 30,000 Jews from Łódź, 2,300 Poles and all Jews from Gniezno, and 2,300 Poles and all Jews from Inowrocław. The order especially marked "politically dangerous" Poles, a broad category that included members of "Polish-national organizations, Polish political parties of all types, as well as members of politically Catholic clergy and lay circles."[19]

In line with these broad plans, police in various communities in the Gau undertook investigations of local clergy, incarcerated many of them, and marked others for deportation to the General Government. In Kępno (Kempen) Subdistrict, the gendarmerie (subdistrict or county military police) determined that among the thirty-four clergy there, four were loyal to Germandom, twenty-three were relatively apolitical, and seven were politically dangerous. One priest had, for example, allegedly "acted in an anti-German manner," another had held leadership roles in various Catholic organizations, another was characterized as "a hater of Germans and great agitator," while yet another was accused of using the bell tower of his church for military observation.[20] Authorities in Poznań District completed similar lists in late 1939, and in Inowrocław District, in early 1940.[21] Meanwhile, on November 16, Albert Rapp, from the Higher SS and Police offices in Poznań, issued orders to refrain temporarily from the forced evacuation of clergy. He called instead for the internment of all priests, male members of religious orders, and nuns in the Warthegau in a single monastery so that they could be deported *en masse*.[22]

Such a plan would, however, have been both logistically impossible and politically dangerous, and so on December 13, the Poznań Gestapo issued a more realistic, if still ambitious plan to rid the Gau of its Polish clergy. According to this stratagem, the clergy were to be deported separately from Jews and other ethnic Poles. Although the clergy would be selected for evacuation on the basis of the "political danger" that they allegedly posed, the goal was to remove up to 80 percent of them from the Warthegau. According to this logic, then, it seems that the Polish clergy were, simply by virtue of their status, calling, and ministries, subversive, thus necessitating their removal from the Gau. In other words, four out of five priests were regarded as politically dangerous.

At the same time, the order revealed a concern over the social and political implications of a mass evacuation of the Polish clergy, noting that "a necessary level of spiritual care" was to be maintained, and that those priests to be deported should not be housed in the "standard transit camps" for Poles awaiting deportation, on account of the "possible international resonance." Instead, the directive called for them to be interned temporarily in monasteries where measures should be taken for their adequate care and provision.[23] On the one hand, the regime showed resolve and ambition in its plans for the deportation of the clergy, but this order also points to the limitations of Nazi Kirchenpolitik in the Wartheland. Removal of all priests from the Gau and their internment in camps were not feasible options, whether because of the social unrest among Poles or the criticism from abroad that such measures might generate.

By mid-December 1939, the Nazi authorities had succeeded in deporting more than eighty thousand Jews and Poles from the Wartheland to the General Government, among them thousands of Poles who were deported for their political activism or membership in the intelligentsia. The rapid and systematic removal and incarceration of the clergy—stage two in the deportation process—did not, however, begin until the following year. From January through March 1940, there were five mass arrests that resulted in the internment of 284 clergy in monasteries in Bruczków (Bruckau), Chludowo, Miejska Górka, Ląd, Lubiń (Lubin), and Puszczkówko (Puschkau). Of these, 206 were deported later in the year—not to the General Government but to the Buchenwald and Dachau concentration camps.[24] In total, from the fall of 1939 until next great wave of arrests in October 1941, 760 Warthegau clergy were arrested, 199 were released, and 561, or approximately 74 percent, were interned in prisons, monasteries, collection camps (*Sammellager*), transit camps (*Durchgangslager*), and concentration camps.[25] Beginning in May 1940, the German authorities began to send Warthegau priests to camps in the Altreich, such as Dachau, Oranienburg, Mauthausen, Gusen, and Buchenwald. By the end of 1941, the vast majority had been imprisoned in Dachau.[26]

There were, however, also numerous lesser-known sites across the Reichsgau Wartheland for the incarceration of the Polish clergy—sites that were diverse in terms of size, function, and the conditions under which the inmates lived and died. In the early months of the occupation, it was not uncommon to imprison clergy in cloisters, monasteries, and friaries, which were generally large, self-contained institutions that were relatively easy to guard. One of the first such "camps" reserved exclusively for clergy was in the cloister of the Missionaries of the Holy Family in Kazimierz Biskupi. Beginning in November 1939, members of the Poznań cathedral chapter were incarcerated there, as were clergy who worked for Catholic organizations.[27] As of November 9, there were twenty-six priests in the camp, and by the end of the year, forty-two.[28] To prevent escapes, the authorities held three priests in the nearby Konin prison as hostages. Were a priest to escape, the hostages would be shot.[29] According to a report issued by the exiled Polish primate August Hlond, prisoners in Kazimierz Biskupi were required to pay four *Złoty* per day for their upkeep; if they could not, they were forced to do hard labor.[30] Despite these conditions, the priests were apparently treated relatively well, were permitted to celebrate Mass, and could leave the camp temporarily for medical visits. The superior of the Poznań Franciscans, interned there in the fall of 1939, even expressed the hope that he and his brethren would be able to remain there until the end of the war.[31] Five months later, however, a number of the priests were transferred to the General Government, and the remainder were deported to Dachau.[32]

Warthegau clergy were also interned in the Salesian cloister in Ląd, a village about seventy kilometers east of Poznań. Beginning in January 1940, the German authorities imprisoned eighty-two priests and religious there, including Bishop Michał Kozal, the suffragan of the Włocławek diocese.[33] Like the cloister in Kazimierz Biskupi, Ląd offered rather mild conditions and relative freedom: the priests were generally allowed to move about freely on the cloister grounds, were housed in the cloister's living quarters, were permitted to celebrate Mass and participate in worship, and were supervised by one of their own, Father Franciszek Miśka, to whom the inmates referred, apparently in a spirit of ironic affection, as "Komendant." In general, they were not abused, and mistreatment at the hands the SS seems to have been limited to intoxicated guards shooting off their revolvers at night, or mocking the priests by dressing up in their liturgical vestments and pretending to celebrate Mass.[34]

Fig. 6.2. Priests outside the Salesian Cloister in Ląd, spring or summer 1940. Courtesy of Archiwum Towarzystwa Salezjańskiego, Piła/Janusz Nowiński.

In August of 1940, when the German authorities initiated another wave of clergy deportations in the Warthegau, the majority of inmates in Ląd, including nearly all Salesians and nearly all priests from the Włocławek diocese, were shipped to Poznań's Fort VII camp, and subsequently the concentration camps Buchenwald and Dachau.[35] The German army then assumed control of the cloister until a "second phase" for the Ląd camp began in October 1941, when seventy priests were deported there as part of the mass Aktion against Warthegau clergy. At the end of that month, thirty-five clergy were expelled to the General Government, 117 were deported to Dachau,[36] the camp was shut down, and the Ląd cloister was turned over to the Hitler Youth.[37]

Conditions in the "internment cloisters" may have been relatively benign, but such was not the case at other prisons and camps where Warthegau clergy were held. As noted above, in the Łódź suburb of Radogoszcz, the police hastily organized a temporary camp where some 1,500 people were imprisoned after the mass arrest on November 9–10, 1939. Among those arrested were more than fifty priests, including the Łódź suffragan bishop Kazimierz Tomczak.[38] The priests in the camp were forced to clean latrines and haul excrement,[39] beaten, left without food for days, and subjected to a variety of insults and humiliations.[40] Bishop Tomczak was released after only ten days and placed under house arrest, but the other clergy remained in Radogoszcz until January 1940, when they were released with orders to leave the territory of the Reich.[41] This may well have saved their lives, as the camp, expanded to another nearby factory and functioning as a prison as well in the years ahead, was characterized by insufficient food provisions, unsanitary conditions, and a high mortality rate throughout the years of the occupation.[42]

Most notorious among the destinations for Warthegau clergy was Fort VII, a Prussian stronghold built in the late nineteenth century on the western outskirts of Poznań. The first concentration camp designated as such in occupied Poland, it was opened in October 1939 and underwent numerous transformations in the years that followed. Until November 1939 it carried the official name "Sicherheitspolizei—Chef der Einsatzgruppe VI—Konzentrationslager-Posen." After the camp was taken over by the Gestapo, it was designated a transit camp and thus renamed "Geheime Staatspolizei-Staatspolizeileitstelle Posen—Übergangslager-Fort VII." From the middle of 1941 until it closed in the spring of 1944, Fort VII functioned primarily as a prison, known officially as "Polizeigefängnis der Sicherheitspolizei und Arbeitserziehungslager (Fort VII)."[43] The facility was intended to hold approximately 1,200 prisoners[44] but could accommodate as many as 1,500. Estimates on the total number of prisoners vary widely—between 10,000 and 15,000[45]—but it is clear that throughout its existence, Fort VII served as a central site for the incarceration of Polish clergy. Among members of the intelligentsia who died there, clergy constituted the largest group.[46]

Conditions at Fort VII were appalling. Surrounded by a moat, the fortress consisted of multiple levels. The underground cells, which held dozens of prisoners at a time, were windowless, unheated, damp, and foul smelling. In such conditions disease was rampant and the mortality rate high. Clergymen in the camp were often designated for specific and, for the guards, especially entertaining forms of abuse. Priests were, for example, ordered to conduct worship services and sing hymns, accompanied by the taunts and jeers of the guards, and were at times required to sing funeral hymns while one of their own was tortured.[47]

Torture, beatings, and executions were common at Fort VII, and were often directed at the clergymen among the inmates. Describing his interrogation on arrival at Fort VII, the Poznań priest Florian Deresiński recalled,

> From the very first day, I was subjected to interrogation and taken from my cell to the Gestapo headquarters, where every time, in order to extract a confession, I was laid on a table. Two Gestapo officials held me down by the legs and hands, and two beat me with rubber truncheon and a stick until I was unconscious. Every day, the interrogations lasted from 9:00 a.m. until 6:00 p.m.
>
> After a week, a different method was used, which consisted of twisting my legs. It was done in such a way that one of the Gestapo officers grabbed me by the foot while two others held me down on the table. He then twisted it to its limits. During one of these procedures I felt a pop in my knee and lost consciousness. After regaining consciousness I determined that my left knee was broken. Every time I lost consciousness, I was revived by pouring cold water on the back of my neck. During the interrogations, I was beaten many times.[48]

Stanisław Małecki, provost in Święciechów, a village near Łódź, was arrested for his alleged assistance to the Polish army during the September invasion. First imprisoned in Leszno (Lissa), Małecki was later transferred to Fort VII. According to one of his cellmates, Małecki, as a priest, was frequently singled out for abuse. One night, a group of SS men forced their way into the cell and beat several prisoners, among them Małecki. After fifteen blows Małecki fainted. Revived with water, he was subjected to ten more blows, after which he again fainted. Reviving him again, the SS inflicted five more blows. Małecki was then taken from his cell and shot, along with fellow priest Marian Poprawski and the Lutheran pastor Gustaw Manitius.[49]

The priest Ludwik Mzyk, head of Poland's branch of the Society of the Divine Word, a Catholic missionary congregation, was arrested on January 25, 1940, and taken to Fort VII. According to the testimony of a fellow priest, Mzyk was regarded by the SS as an "indomitable enemy," and therefore marked for especially harsh treatment. On March 20, 1940—payday for the camp guards—members of the SS, as part of their drunken celebration, began to torment the prisoners. Raging, ranting, and beating prisoners along the way, the SS men staggered toward cell 60 and screamed, "Now it's time for the priests." As Mzyk's colleague recalled,

> The door to our cell was opened. We all stood, according to regulations, at attention. "Out!" they screamed into the cell. Outside in the corridor we formed a line. The brutes permitted the old and blind Father Olejniczak to return to the cell. The rest of us were ordered: "March, and quickly!" We then ran through an adjacent corridor, at the end of which was a flight of stairs that opened outside. Fr. Mzyk wanted to climb the stairs, but SS-*Oberscharführer* Dybus ran after him and began to beat him, with the justification that he was attempting to escape. The other priests were ordered back into their cells—only Fr. Mzyk and I were ordered to stay. As we ran down the hall, Fr. Mzyk asked

> me for a general absolution, which I granted him. As soon as the others were in their cells, Dybus forced Fr. Mzyk against the wall and mistreated him in an inhuman manner. All that took place behind my back, and I heard the screams of pain coming from Fr. Mzyk. Dybus then went to the officer who stood by me, demanded two bullets, and then returned to Fr. Mzyk. With a shot to the back of the head he killed his victim, and then fired a second shot at the corpse lying on the ground. Fr. Mzyk suffered. I thought only that, for me as well, my last minutes were approaching. But it turned out otherwise: the murderers ordered me back into my cell. Shortly thereafter, we heard the steps of those who came to remove Fr. Mzyk's corpse.[50]

A register compiled by the Fort VII Gestapo listed the official causes of death of many clergymen between October 1939 and May 1940, including those mentioned above: Stanisław Małecki, weak blood pressure; Marian Poprawski, apoplexy; Gustaw Manitius, weak blood pressure; Ludwik Mzyk, pneumonia.[51]

The torture and murder of prisoners in camps such as Radogoszcz and Fort VII invites consideration of the forces motivating the Germans who executed Warthegau Kirchenpolitik in all its varied forms. Not surprisingly, those responsible—especially those responsible for criminal activity—did not leave a record of their motives. Were they bound to Nazi ideology? Aggressively anti-Polish? Aggressively anti-Catholic? Simply sadistic? Simply following the dictates of their superiors? Seeking career advancement? Subsequent research may provide clear answers, but for the moment, it is worth considering the extent to which the executors of Nazi policy were exhibiting a behavior common among upper, middle, and lower-level Nazi officials, a behavior that Ian Kershaw has described as "working towards the Führer." Referring to a speech given by a minor Nazi official in 1934, Kershaw's metaphor suggests that "anticipation of Hitler's presumed wishes and intentions as 'guidelines for action' in the certainty of approval and confirmation for actions which accorded with those wishes and intentions." According to Kershaw, "working towards the Führer" "offered endless scope for barbarous initiatives" on the part of the SS, but the notion can, he argues, be understood "in a more indirect sense where ideological motivation was secondary, or perhaps even absent altogether, but where the objective function of the actions was nevertheless to further the potential for implementation of the goals which Hitler embodied." "There was never any shortage," Kershaw claims, "of willing helpers, far from being confined to party activists, ready to 'work towards the Führer' to put the mandate into operation. Once the war—intrinsic to Nazism and Hitler's vision—had begun, the barbarism inspired by that 'vision' and now unchecked by any remnants of legal constraint or concern for public sensitivities plumbed unimaginable depths." Physicians, technocrats, bureaucrats, military officers, businessmen: all could strive for both personal gain and, at the same time, advance the goals of the Führer, party, state, and nation.[52] The metaphor of "working towards the Führer" can explain to some extent, although not entirely, the frequently baffling and at times shocking behavior of those who formulated and executed Nazi policy in the Warthegau, whether the local member of the gendarmerie, the sadistic guard in Fort VII, the minor official compiling lists of allegedly subversive priests, the bureaucrat in the Reichsstatthalter's office, the city commissioner in Włocławek, or the Gauleiter himself.

By the middle of 1940, Helmut Bischoff, chief of the Poznań Gestapo, could report on significant progress toward the goals for the Polish clergy set out in Himmler's November 12, 1939, decree. In a letter dated June 4, Bischoff declared the "ordered internment of the Polish Catholic clergy implemented and concluded."[53] Himmler's edict had not specified how many, or what percentage of clergy were to be deported or interned, and it remains impossible to determine, as of June 1940, how many from the Warthegau were being held in prisons and camps, how many had been released and when, how many had been deported to the General Government, and how many had simply fled or gone into hiding.

Moreover, it is not entirely clear that the goal of removing 80 percent of the clergy set out in the Poznań Gestapo order of December 13 had been reached, although such was the conclusion of a December 1940 report of the Polish underground resistance.[54] Kazimierz Śmigiel has estimated, based on a variety of sources, that of the 1,366 secular clergy from the Częstochowa, Poznań, Gneizno, and Łódź dioceses who resided in the territory of the Wartheland, 277, or about 20 percent, had either voluntarily relocated to the General Government or had been forcibly deported there.[55] Hundreds more were either already dead, or had been incarcerated in camps and prisons. In an October 1940 report to a German bishop, Poznań's suffragan Walenty Dymek stated that in his diocese, of the 681 secular clergy active in September 1939, 275, or 40 percent, were still in office, while 170, or 25 percent, had been deported to concentration camps.[56] Two months later, a report from the Poznań SD stated that 380, or 80 percent, of the clergy from the Poznań Regierungsbezirk, had been interned in cloisters and "recently" sent to concentration camps in the Altreich,[57] although neither the geographic scope nor exact dates of the deportations to camps were specified. Describing the removal of priests on a more local level, a Vatican report from October 1940 states that in the Kutno deanery, where 40 priests had been active, only two remained, while in the city of Włocławek, seat of a diocese and an important center of theological training and research, only one aged and infirm priest was available.[58]

In short, the sources provide a confusing array of data, and these variations are related to four characteristics of the Warthegau church's situation under German control. First, under the conditions of the occupation, communication between local parishes and diocesan leadership was poor, so the numbers cited by, for example, Bishop Dymek, are not necessarily accurate. Second, regional variations in the treatment of the clergy were common. For example, a February 1940 report sent by Heydrich to Kerrl stated that in Łódź District, sixty-two clergy had been interned, and in Inowrocław District, 50 percent of the clergy had been interned, while *all* the clergy in Włocławek and the surrounding subdistrict had been interned. In some areas of the Warthegau, such as in the Inowrocław Subdistrict, a high number of priests were released from captivity and were even permitted to return to their former parishes.[59] Third, it is clear that local authorities were not necessarily rigorous or consistent in enforcing orders from above.[60] Finally, the distinction between secular clergy and monastic clergy was significant: given the German administration's long-term goal of shutting down and banning all religious orders in the Wartheland, a higher percentage of regular (i.e., monastic) clergy was incarcerated and deported.[61]

Even if German measures had not brought about (to echo Hitler's August 1939 demand) the entire "liquidation" of the Warthegau clergy, the Polish Catholic Church was an institution severely diminished after such a high percentage of priests had been deported or incarcerated. Summarizing the catastrophic situation of the Warthegau church only one year after the invasion and occupation, a 1940 report from the Vatican stated, "The churches, which are only permitted to open for two hours, once per week, remain closed because of the lack of officiants [priests]. No sacraments, no preaching, no religious instruction. Absolute destruction of the once-flourishing Catholic press with its world-renowned publishers. . . . No seminaries. No convents. Restrictions, humiliation, oppression are no more: it is absolute and complete devastation."[62]

The report's language may have been dramatic and even hyperbolic, but it points to the shock that Vatican officials likely felt when learning of the church's situation in the Wartheland. One year into the occupation, the "devastation" may not have been complete, but the Nazi authorities had successfully attacked the church on multiple fronts, not only neutralizing the clergy but also limiting the church's accessibility, economic viability, and legal status.

Notes

1. Jacewicz and Woś, *Martyrologium*, vol. 2, no. 1, 80–81.
2. Fijałkowski, *Kościół*, 237–39. On the early 1940 arrests, see also Wełniak, *Duchowieństwo*, 9.
3. Fijałkowski, 237–38.
4. Śmigiel, *Die katholische Kirche*, 171.
5. Lagebericht des Landrats von Hohensalza, November 6, 1939, in Łuczak, *Dyskryminacja Polaków*, 105; Śmigiel, *Die katholische Kirche*, 172.
6. Franciszek Korszyński, *Jasne promienie w Dachau* (Poznań: Pallotinum, 1957), 17.
7. Stadtkommissar des Stadtkreises Leslau, Tätigkeitsbericht, November 15, 1939, APP, 299/0/1.39/1832, microfilm no. O-60675, 7; Stadtkommissar Leslau (Cramer), Tätigkeitsbericht, December 13, 1939, APP, 299/0/1.39.1832, microfilm no. O-60675, 25; Śmigiel, *Die katholische Kirche*, 172.
8. Tätigkeitsbericht des Stadtkommissars (Cramer) in Leslau zum 13. Dezember 1939, December 13, 1939, APP, 299/0/1.39.1832, microfilm no. O-60675, 25.
9. Śmigiel, *Die katholische Kirche*, 172–73.
10. Kuria Biskupa Łódzka, Sprawozdanie o diecezji pod okupacją, IPN, GK 196/19, 158; Budziarek, "Zarząd," 308, 311–12. See also Ryszard Iwanicki, Grażyna Janaszek, and Andrzej Rukowiecki, *A Book of Łódź Martyrdom: A Guide to Radogoszcz and Sites of National Remembrance* (Łódź: Museum of the Independence Traditions in Łódź, 2005), 94–95. The November 9 and 10 arrests were coincident with the announcement of the incorporation of Łódź into the Reichsgau Wartheland, and therefore into the Reich.
11. Rutherford, *Prelude*, 47.
12. Rutherford, 6–7, 9.
13. On resettlement agreements between Germany and the Soviet Union, see Rutherford, 112, 174–75, and 263, note 9.
14. I am grateful to Dr. Agnieszka Łuczak for her insights on the expulsion and resettlement program, and for noting to me that among Polish historians, use of the terms *expulsion* (wypędzenia), *resettlement* (wysiedlenia), and *deportation* (deportacja) for the removal of Polish citizens remains open to debate. For some, use of the term *expulsion* likens the expulsion of Germans from Poland after 1945 to the treatment of Polish citizens in 1939–1940. The term *deportation* is most often used to describe the deportation of Polish citizens to the east by Soviet authorities. Łuczak, deferring to Maria Rutowska, a Polish expert on the program, prefers the term *resettlement*. To the reader of English, however,

the term *resettlement* might appear benign and even euphemistic in describing the forced relocation or incarceration experienced by Polish citizens from the Warthegau. With the above in mind, I generally use the term *deportation* to describe both the forced expulsions and the removal of Polish citizens, the clergy among them, to prisons, to the various types of Nazi camps, and to killing centers. On the deportation program, see, in addition to Rutherford, Maria Rutowska, *Wysiedlenia ludności polskiej z Kraju Warty do Generalnego Gubernatorstwa 1939–1941*, Prace Instytutu Zachodniego, vol. 71 (Poznań: Instytut Zachodni, 2003).

15. Kerrl to Greiser, October 26, 1939, BAB, R 5101/22185, 33.

16. Himmler, Anordnung 1/II, October 30, 1939, Abschrift, IPN, GK 196/28, 149.

17. Kerrl to Greiser, October 26, 1939, BAB, R 5101/22185, 33.

18. On Kerrl's diminishing status see Siegmund, *Rückblick*, 248; Conway, *Nazi Persecution*, 246–53.

19. Anordnung, Der Höhere SS- und Polizeiführer, Posen (Rapp), November 12, 1939, IPN, GK 196/28, 150–51.

20. "Katholische Geistliche im Kreise Kempen," n.d., IPN, GK 70/44, 5–8. The document is undated, yet its location in the file suggests that it originates from November 1939.

21. Geheime Staatspolizei, Staatspolizeistelle Posen, Aussendienststelle Schroda, an den herrn Landrat des Landkreises Schrimm in Schrimm, IZ, dok. I-445, 9; Śmigiel, *Die katholische Kirche*, 183.

22. Rundschreiben des Höheren SS- und Polizeiführers im Wartheland (Rapp), November 16, 1939, in Łuczak, *Dyskryminacja Polaków*, 154.

23. Rundschreiben, Staatspolizeileitstelle Posen (Bischoff) an den Herrn Landrat in Schrimm, December 13, 1939, in Czesław Łuczak, ed., *Położenie ludności polskiej w tzw. Kraju Warty w okresie hitlerowskiej okupacji*, Documenta Occupationis, vol. 13 (Poznań: Zachodni, 1990), 115–18; Gestapo Posen, Aussendienststelle Schroda an den Herrn Landrat des Landkreises Schrimm, December 20, 1939, IZ, document I-445, 9. The largest and most notorious of the transit camps for Poles in the early phase of deportation was the "Lager Glowna" on the outskirts of Poznań. On this and other transit camps in the Reichsgau Wartheland see Rutherford, *Prelude*, 77, 87; Rutowska, *Wysiedlenia*, 93–194; Maria Rutowska, *Lager Glowna: niemiecki obóz przesiedleńczy na Głównej w Poznaniu dla ludności polskiej (1939–1940)*, Documenta Occupationis, vol. 16 (Poznań: Instytut Zachodni, 2008).

24. Śmigiel, *Die katholische Kirche*, 173; Jolanta Adamska and Jan Sziling, *Polscy księża w niemieckich obozach koncentracyjnych: transport 527 duchownych 13 grudnia 1940 r. z Sachsenhausen do Dachau* (Warszawa: Rada Ochrony Pamięci Walk i Męczeństwa, 2007), 12–13; Fijałkowski, *Kościół*, 238; Jacewicz and Woś, *Martyrologium*, vol. 2, no. 1, 24. On the incarceration of clergy and especially members of religious orders in Bruczków, Chludowo, and numerous additional smaller camps see Izabela Pieniężna, "Zakonnice i zakonnicy w niemieckich więzieniach i obozach zbiorczych w Kraju Warty 1939–1945," in Chruścielski and Owsiński, *Konferencja*, 243–47.

25. Śmigiel, *Die katholische Kirche*, 181–82.

26. Ministerstwo Spraw Wewnętrzych, Wydział Społeczny, Nr. 18/44, część I-sza. Londyn, 1944. Archiwum Akt Nowych, Warsaw (hereafter AAN), zespół 493/Konsulat Gen.-Nowy York, syg. 472, 26.

27. Śmigiel, *Die katholische Kirche*, 172–73; Sprawozdanie sytuacyjne z kraju 1939–1941, vol. 1, 106, PUMST.

28. Befehlshaber der Sicherheitspolizei und des SD in Posen to Chef der Sicherheitspolizei Berlin, November 9, 1939, USHMM, RG15.007M, reel 38, 466, 4; Breitinger, *Als Deutschenseelsorger*, 64.
29. Jan Krajewski, ankieta, AAP, zespół 133, syg. 220, 516/74.
30. Hlond, *Persecution*, 5.
31. Breitinger, *Als Deutschenseelsorger*, 64.
32. Śmigiel, *Die katholische Kirche*, 173; Breitinger, *Als Deutschenseelsorger*, 65.
33. "Ląd . . . ," 235–36; Józef Świniarski, "Ląd–niedawny etap męczeństwa," *Kronika diecezji włocławskiej* 50, no. 6–10 (June–October 1967), 225–35.
34. Wąsowicz, *Łądczy*, 9–11, 54; Świniarski, "Ląd–niedawny," 226–30. See also Korszyński, *Jasne promienie*, 17–19, and Śmigiel, *Die katholische Kirche*, 179.
35. Wąsowicz, *Łądczy*, 13–14.
36. Breitinger, *Als Deutschenseelsorger*, 66; "Ląd . . . ," 236; Wąsowicz, *Łądczy*, 14.
37. Reichsstatthalter, Gauselbstverwaltung Posen to Hitlerjugend Gebiet Wartheland, Posen, October 2, 1941, Abschrift, IPN, GK 62/202, 112; Lagebericht des Regierungspräsidenten Hohensalza für die Zeit vom 1.10 bis 31.12.1941, IPN, GK 62/210/CD, 49.
38. Budziarek, "Zarząd i organizacja," 308, 311–12.
39. Kuria Biskupia Łódzka, sprawozdanie, May 13, 1946, IPN, GK 196/19, 158.
40. Hlond, *Persecution*, 53. Details from Hlond's reports appear also in United States National Catholic Welfare Conference, *The Nazi War against the Catholic Church* (Washington, DC: The National Catholic Welfare Conference, 1943), 77–78.
41. Budziarek, "Zarząd i organizacja," 311–12. See also Iwanicki, Janaszek, and Rukowiecki, *Book of Łódź*, 94–95. According to Stanisław Lewicki, in January 1940, priests in the camp were given a choice: to remain in the camp or be released under the condition that they not return to their parishes but instead leave Łódź and its adjacent districts. Only one priest, Józef Krukowski, chose to remain in the camp. See also Sipowicz, *Prześladowania*, 152–53, and Stanisław Lewicki, *Radogoszcz* (Warszawa: Książka i Wiedza, 1971), 21. The event and Krukowski's decision are also described by an eyewitness in Stanisław Rapalski, *Byłem w piekle: wspomnienia z Radogoszcza* (Łódź: Wydawnictwo Łódzkie, 1963), 108–10.
42. Akt Oskarzenia Greisera, n.d., IPN, GK 196/34, 39–40. On the Radogoszcz camp, see also Główna Komisja, *Obozy hitlerowskie*, 298–99.
43. Główna Komisja, *Obozy hitlerowskie*, 399–400.
44. Akt Oskarzenia Greisera, n.d., IPN, GK 196/34, 36.
45. Prezydent Miasta Poznania (Środa) to Obyw. Kierownika Sądu Grodzkiego, April 12, 1946, IPN, GK 196/31/CD2; Serwański, *Wielkopolska*, 96; Główna Komisja, *Obozy hitlerowskie*, 400.
46. Marian Olszewski, *Straty i martyrologia ludności polskiej w Poznaniu 1939–1945* (Poznań: Wydawnictwo Poznańskie, 1973), 101. On the history of the Fort VII camp in general, see Olszewski, *Straty*, 39–104.
47. See Główna Komisja, *Obozy hitlerowskie*, 400; Serwański, *Wielkopolska*, 96–97; Śmigiel, *Die katholische Kirche*, 180. Śmigiel's source is Marian Olszewski, *Fort VII w Poznaniu* (Poznań: 1974), 58–61, and especially 59, note 72.
48. Florian Deresiński to Kuria Poznańska, AAP, zespół 133, syg. OK 121.
49. Zeznanie, Sylwester Marciniak, o ks. Małeckim, June 23, 1946, Odpis, IPN, GK 196/34, 200.

50. Testimony of Sylwester Marciniak, in an undated description of the martyrdom of Fr. Ludwik Mzyk, SVD, AAP, zespół 133, OK 121; Sylwester Marciniak to Benedicta Maria Kempner, February 17, 1967, AAP, zespół 133, OK 121.

51. Chef der Gestapo in Posen, VII Fort, wykaz zmarłych, X.1939–V.1940, Polish translation, IPN, GK 196/31/CD2.

52. Ian Kershaw, "'Working Towards the Führer.' Reflections on the Nature of the Hitler Dictatorship," *Contemporary European History* 2, no. 2 (July 1993): 116–17, passim.

53. Bischoff, Geheime Staatspolizei Posen, June 4, 1940, Abschrift, YV, TR.17, 72.

54. Sprawozdanie sytuacyjne z kraju 1939–1941, vol. 1, 106, PUMST.

55. Śmigiel, *Die katholische Kirche*, 184–85.

56. Dymek to Heinrich Wienken, October 14, 1940, document 19, in Volk, *Akten deutscher Bischöfe*, vol. 5, 1010.

57. Sicherheitsdienst des Reichsführers-SS, SD-Leitabschnitt Posen, to Reichssicherheitshauptamt Berlin, Amt II B/32, December 10, 1940, USHMM, RG 15.007M, reel 38, 471, 1.

58. "L'eglise catholique en Pologne occupée par les Allemands," October 8, 1940, AAN, zespół 497, syg. 32, 3.

59. Bericht über die Entwicklung der kirchlichen Lage im Reichsgau Warthland (Abschnittsbereich Hohensalza), n.d., BAB R 58/7581, 26–32. Although this report is not dated, its content makes clear that it postdates June 1940.

60. Śmigiel, *Die katholische Kirche*, 184.

61. Śmigiel, 185.

62. "L'eglise catholique en Pologne occupée par les Allemands," October 8, 1940, AAN, zespół 497, syg. 32, 3–4.

7

KULT

Restrictions on Public Religious Life

EXECUTION, INCARCERATION, AND DEPORTATION OF THE CLERGY WERE the most obvious and perhaps most effective means of curbing the power and influence of the church. This the German authorities in the Reichsgau Wartheland undertook with vigor and brutality. Also playing a crucial role in separating Warthegau Catholics from the traditions of the church and limiting their access to it were the countless ordinances, prohibitions, and regulations issued during the occupation, especially during its first two years. These measures were often implemented and enforced in an inconsistent manner, illustrating the lack of coherence and experimental nature of church policy in this "model Gau." Yet they also revealed the authorities' resolve in confronting the threat the church allegedly posed, for a lack of coherence or consistent application of policy need not suggest that it was anything short of oppressive or effective. In the end, all policies are, to some extent, developed via experimentation and precedent, and in this respect Kirchenpolitik in the Wartheland was no exception.

A case in point is the November 1939 memorandum of the Office of Racial Policy of the NSDAP on "The Question of the Treatment of the Population of the Former Polish Regions according to Racial-Political Considerations" referred to in chapter 2. The document is an example of emerging Nazi racial policy vis-à-vis the Poles, but it also gives a view into the regime's early attempts to formulate church policy in the context of both the developing civil administration and the Germanization plans for the Warthegau. Broad in scope, detailed in its prescriptions, and reflecting the "widespread euphoria of the late autumn of 1939 that followed the conquest of new lebensraum in the East,"[1] the thirty-six-page memorandum includes a discussion of the ethnic and racial structure of the Polish lands under occupation, as well as policy recommendations on treatment of ethnic and racial groups, legal affairs, economic measures, and cultural affairs. Noteworthy also is that it differentiates between the treatment of non-German populations in "Restpolen"—that is, in the region that would become the General Government—and in the Incorporated Eastern Territories annexed to the Reich, where, according to the memorandum, any Polish social, political, and religious associations were to be banned.

With respect to the churches in the Reichsgau Wartheland, the authors of the memorandum, Erhard Wetzel and Gerhard Hecht, recommended that worship services in the Polish language be forbidden and that both Protestant and Catholic services be led only by "specially selected, German-conscious German clergy." Significantly, the authors also suggested *limiting* the attack on the church. "Given the political significance and the related danger of the Polish Catholic Church in these areas," they stated, "one could conclude that the Catholic Church should not be allowed to exist here at all. One must consider, however, that the population is decidedly church oriented, and that such a measure would perhaps not advance Germanization, but have the opposite effect." They therefore suggested that select, patriotic German clergy could exert an effectively delicate influence on the Polish Catholic population, perhaps aiding in the process of Germanization by bringing those considered racially appropriate into the German fold.[2]

It is paradoxical that Wetzel and Hecht saw a possible role for the church in the Germanization process at the same time that they emphasized the dangers that Polish Catholicism allegedly posed. It is also interesting that the memorandum reveals a degree of tactical restraint,[3] suggesting that despite the occupation regime's brutalities thus far, simply shutting down or banning the church was not a desirable option. While Wetzel and Hecht's agenda, according to Epstein, "anticipated many of the anti-Polish measures soon put into place in the Warthegau,"[4] the Nazi authorities there pursued a Kirchenpolitik that was generally much more radical than the memorandum proposed, although church policy, as draconian as it may have been, was frequently implemented in an improvised and inconsistent manner.

Broad Germanization of the region and its racially appropriate populations remained the overarching goal, but a "Germanization" of the churches through, as Wetzel and Hecht proposed, the installation of German clergy to minister to Poles never came under serious consideration. Reich Minister for Church Affairs Hanns Kerrl had, in the fall of 1939, also advocated on several occasions supplanting Polish clergy with patriotic Germans,[5] but without success. The failure of such proposals points to the regime's basic animosity toward the Catholic Church: in the Warthegau it remained a foreign and hostile element, regardless of whether its clergy were patriotic Germans or allegedly subversive Poles.

It is also significant that Warthegau Kirchenpolitik, especially at this early stage, appears to have been guided by aggressively antichurch forces in the Nazi Party, and particularly Martin Bormann. Chief of staff in the Office of the Deputy Führer, Bormann would, as of May 1941, head the Party Chancellery after Deputy Führer Rudolf Hess's flight to Britain that same month. Bormann's fundamental hostility to the churches was well known, and there is general agreement in the scholarship that he exerted a significant influence over the antichurch policies in the Gau.[6] Moreover, Bormann and Greiser were clearly in agreement over the need to separate church affairs there from any jurisdiction or influence of Kerrl's Ministry for Church Affairs.[7] Interestingly, Bormann also appears to have been somewhat flexible—or tactical—with respect to the application of policy, noting in a letter to Albert Forster that church-political questions in the East should be governed by "local conditions."[8]

There is no doubt that the Office of the Deputy Führer, and subsequently the Party Chancellery, were intimately involved in Warthegau church policy, but crafting and implementing it remained the responsibility of Arthur Greiser and his associates. To put it another way, the goals and broader strategies of Nazi Kirchenpolitik may have originated in the power centers of the Nazi state, and Bormann's instructions may, in the words of one Warthegau official, have had a "nearly dictatorial character,"[9] but the application of its details on the ground in the Mustergau Wartheland were a local project. It is therefore important to bear in mind that policy was not always developed or implemented in a top-down manner. Rather, the myriad measures intended to limit Poles' access to the Catholic Church, although certainly ideologically driven, were applied on an ad hoc basis, and were not yet, in the first months of the occupation, part of a larger coherent plan.

By 1940, Kirchenpolitik in the Reichsgau Wartheland was coordinated and implemented by a central bureau (Department I/51 of the Reichsstatthalter's office) supervised initially by Wilhelm Dudzus. He was succeeded in early 1941 by Dr. Kurt Birk,[10] who was then replaced in late 1942 by

Dr. Heinrich Meyer (sometimes referred to as Meyer-Eckhardt).[11] These three bureaucrats were more or less loyal and effective over the course of the occupation, and at times showed significant initiative, but in the final analysis, matters of the churches, although perhaps broadly directed from the Party Chancellery in Munich, remained firmly under the control of Arthur Greiser and his deputy, August Jäger.[12]

Among the first measures imposed were restrictions on what Poles referred to as the church's *Kult*—that is, its public, corporate activities and rituals, including worship services, religious education, funeral processions, and burials, but also the seven sacraments of the Roman Catholic Church: baptism, confirmation, the Eucharist or Holy Communion, penance or reconciliation, anointing of the sick, and holy orders. Already on October 6, 1939, Arthur Greiser, in his capacity as chief of civilian administration for the Posen Military District,[13] ordered that worship services in Polish Catholic churches be restricted to Sundays between 9:00 a.m. and 11:00 a.m. and that public displays of religious devotion outside of churches be prohibited.[14] Three weeks later he reiterated this restriction in a secret order to all subdistrict commissioners (*Landräte*)[15] and, in addition, prohibited the celebration of Mass on weekdays, with an exception made for the Christmas holiday on December 25.[16] These restrictions severely limited Poles' participation in that allegedly un-German practice of attending public worship, and would limit their access to the church as a source of collective identity. Moreover, in an effort to curb conspiratorial activity, the German authorities were eager to prevent, as Heydrich noted in a February 1940 letter to Kerrl, "larger and daily mass gatherings" of Poles on the occasion of worship services.

Noteworthy is that Heydrich, in the same letter, appeared to downplay the perceived threat posed by the Polish Catholic clergy, observing that the only clergy who were actively attempting to change the current state of affairs were those among the Reichsdeutsche (that is, those clergy from the Altreich who had immigrated to the Warthegau), and that the population was not, as expected, demonstrating significant dissatisfaction over the removal of priests.[17] In the same vein, an untitled policy document issued in the weeks that followed described the behavior of "Catholicism" in the Warthegau as "relatively passive" due to the "liabilities of its Polish exponents."[18] Given the character of the occupation and persecution of the church already underway, it should come as no surprise that Polish Roman Catholics were not "demonstrating significant dissatisfaction" with the state of affairs, and that the German authorities may have found them "relatively passive." They were likely terrified.

In general, the reports and correspondence of military and civilian authorities in the early months of the occupation reveal, on the one hand, German concern about large numbers of Polish Catholics congregating in and around churches during services.[19] This the authorities had anticipated. On the other hand, these documents reveal, contrary to German expectations, a general lack of Polish Catholic dissent or resistance.[20] It appears, then, that the Polish church was living up to its reputation as a locus of identity and community, and that Catholic Poles remained, at least in terms of participation in public worship, committed to the practice of their faith, despite the restrictions placed on them and the persecution of their clergy. To some German authorities, however, the church was not living up to its reputation as a center of political and nationalist opposition.

Local occupation authorities remained nonetheless concerned about Polish Catholics migrating through the cities and countryside and crowding in and around churches. This was one reason behind the Reichsstatthalter's decision of July 1940 to relax earlier restrictions and allow for expanded "confessional activities" in Catholic parishes, which in effect increased the "supply" of worship opportunities. According to the new regulations, "Polish" parishes were now free to celebrate Mass from 7:00 a.m. to 11:30 a.m. (as opposed to 9:00 a.m.–11:00 a.m.) on Sundays and legal holidays, and sermons were to be allowed as well at these services. Priests could now celebrate Mass on weekdays from 7:00 a.m. to 8:00 a.m., although they were to be open to the public only on Wednesdays and Saturdays. In addition, parishes were permitted to provide religious instruction to youth on Wednesdays from 3:00 p.m. to 6:00 p.m. and hold confession on Saturdays from 3:00 p.m. to 8:00 p.m. There were no restrictions on marriages, burials, baptisms, or anointing of the sick.[21] Poznań's vicar general Walenty Dymek would relay the new regulations to parish provosts in his diocese a few days later but, ever alert to the dangers of violating the regime's dictates, reminded them that the terms of the ordinance had to be strictly enforced, lest infractions "result in severe penalties against the clergy and repressive measures against the church."[22]

It is perhaps significant that Greiser's orders for relaxing restrictions on worship were issued only days after an important policy planning meeting on July 20, 1940, between the Reichsstatthalter, members of his staff involved in church affairs, and representatives of Bormann's Office of the Deputy Führer. Less concerned with specific regulations and restrictions, this meeting, to be addressed in more detail in chapter 10, was intended to confront broader issues and general approaches to ecclesiastical affairs in the Wartheland. Agendas and opinions at this meeting varied and, significantly, members of Greiser's staff advocated for a more moderate approach to the Polish churches.[23] The extent to which the discussions at this meeting had a direct effect on the details of church policy on the ground in the Warthegau remains unclear, but they do reveal a lack of unity and a modicum of dissent among those responsible for formulating policy.

The new regulations of July 1940 may have been seen by some as a liberalization of policy, but they were also intended to undermine any real or potential expressions of Polish conspiracy and limit the Sunday "migrations" of the Catholic devout. According to a report on church affairs issued by the Poznań SD in December 1940, restriction of worship activities was one way to limit the "pilgrimages" to worship services that "had assumed the character of demonstrations."[24] Evidently, this had remained a concern throughout the year, for when the regulations were extended in October for the winter months of 1940–41, Greiser's office stipulated that Masses on Sundays and holidays could not begin until 8:00 a.m. (presumably, the authorities did not want Poles engaging in the potentially conspiratorial activity of attending church in the dark). In addition, Greiser ordered that services and other activities could be attended only by a given parish's members. To discourage Catholic Poles from traveling the Warthegau countryside in search of services, church authorities were to be held responsible for ensuring that priests were distributed effectively throughout the region.[25] This proved at times difficult, given the inconsistencies in applying and enforcing the regulations.

A case in point was the local parish in Mogilno, northwest of Gniezno. In August 1940, the parish priest was interned by the police, who also confiscated the keys to the church. Eduard van Blericq, the vicar general, had attempted to arrange for a priest from a nearby parish to serve there. The German mayor of Mogilno remained, however, unwilling to relinquish the keys to the church, even over the Christmas holidays.[26] In another instance, for reasons that are unclear, the Żnin (Dietfurt) *Landrat* (Kreis or subdistrict commissioner) issued shortly before Christmas 1940 a prohibition against holding church services in the entire subdistrict. Van Blericq then appealed to Greiser's office to have the Reichsstatthalter's regulations upheld, noting, however, that were services once again permitted, ministry to Polish Catholics would remain especially difficult: the Żnin subdistrict had twenty-one Catholic parishes, for which only three priests were allowed, leaving each priest responsible for seven parishes. Van Blericq also added that the prohibition against nonmembers attending services in a given parish was difficult to enforce because many Catholics had gone months without attending Mass.[27]

Other inconsistencies emerged in the months ahead, as the German authorities chose to apply the October 1940 regulations in a variety of ways, even as Polish clergy attempted to maintain some degree of stability and accessibility in what little church life remained. In the Inowrocław district, for example, the Gestapo ordered that priests were required to celebrate Mass in German only—a restriction that would facilitate more effective police surveillance.[28] In the Gniezno archdiocese, priests had permission to preach (in German) during Masses, but according to van Blericq, they were charged with serving multiple parishes on a given Sunday and thus felt compelled to forego homilies in favor of celebrating briefer Masses within the allotted time frame.[29] In Kępno Subdistrict, Hans Neumann, the Landrat and local NSDAP leader, was particularly ambitious and rigorous when it came to church matters. In a November 1940 memorandum, he related his grave concern about the "more generous treatment" offered the churches in connection with the new regulations on service times. Neumann then subsequently determined that in the Łódź District (of which Kępno was a part), regulations applied that were, in fact, different from those in the rest of the Warthegau, allowing him to maintain stricter standards for "confessional events" under his jurisdiction. Hence, as of October 1940, churches in his district were to remain closed without exceptions from Monday through Saturday, confession was permitted on Sundays only, and first Communion instruction for children was strictly limited to only five two-hour sessions.[30] He reiterated these regulations the following month, with clear instructions to local officials and the police to impress upon the Polish clergy the grave consequences of violating them.[31]

Neumann's restrictions on first Communion instruction were in keeping with a broader effort to curtail religious education at all levels. As noted above, the ordinances in July 1940 strictly limited instruction of youth to three, and later two hours on Wednesday afternoons.[32] It is also worth noting that the German authorities had already eliminated religious instruction in schools and prohibited any confessional activities in school buildings.[33] Again, local officials, such as the Kępno Landrat, adapted and enforced these regulations in the manner they saw fit[34]—that is, for the most part, rigorously, despite the petitions and pleas of church leaders.[35]

The following year, further restrictions on education were imposed, when Greiser's office stipulated that only Polish children preparing for confession and first Communion were permitted to receive instruction.[36] This, in effect, made any form of religious instruction for adults impossible and prevented priests from providing any instruction beyond that minimally required for Catholics to participate in the sacraments of reconciliation and the Eucharist. Limits on educational activities such as these remained in place for years to come.[37]

Polish Catholics were thus left few public opportunities to express their faith, and such was the intent and execution of Nazi policy. One opportunity for public worship that remained, however, was attendance at funeral services and burials, which became a matter of serious concern to the German authorities. According to Victor Böttcher, president of Poznań District, Poles were using funerals and burials as a "welcome opportunity for a closed gathering." Participation in these rituals was, he claimed, at times so extensive that they assumed a "demonstration-like character." Consequently, he ordered in October 1940 that funeral services be permitted only in cemetery mortuaries, that participants be limited to relatives of the deceased, and that funerals and burials be put under police surveillance.[38] In February of the following year, the police ordered that celebration of burial Masses be open only to the closest relatives of the deceased in order to prevent large, unauthorized gatherings of congregants.[39]

The following month, the town commissioner (*Amtskommissar*) of Ostrów (Ostrowo), in the western part of the Łódź district, voiced his concerns over burials to the Landrat. Because churches were generally closed on weekdays, Polish clergy were, he claimed, using burials to provide alternative worship opportunities. Giving voice to his anxieties in a March 1941 report, he stated, "The little group that was part of the burial was led, with the coffin, into the church, which was already full. Of the four Polish priests, one read the Mass, a second heard confessions in the confessional booth, a third busied himself with the coffin in order to lend the funeral the appropriate atmosphere, while the fourth applied ashes to the foreheads of those in the crowd." Moreover, the official related, "it is observed that the Polish clergy are being invited to visit Polish families. What is played out there is not clear, but it is to be assumed that small gatherings are held."[40]

In the months ahead, various authorities, ranging from the village commissioner in Ujście (Usch) in the far north of the Warthegau,[41] to the Order Police,[42] to the offices of the Inowrocław and Łódź district presidents,

Fig. 7.1. Burial procession in Tuliszków, 1941. Courtesy of Muzeum Miasta Turku im Józefa Mehoffera, MRZTT/HA/1073–Teczka nr. 02–029.

voiced similar concerns about the demonstration-like character of funeral processions and funeral services.[43] Finally, the Gestapo required in August 1941 that funeral processions be limited to immediate family members of the deceased, that they be silent, and that they take place without flags, crosses, or altar boys in vestments.[44] Two months later, after the mass deportation Aktion of October 1941, funerals would take place without priests.[45]

By removing priests, limiting the availability of worship services, and restricting religious education and funeral practices, the Nazi authorities in the Reichsgau Wartheland had severely impeded the accessibility and ministries of the church over the first two years of the occupation. Not content, however, to limit their antichurch measures to restrictions placed on people and practices, they also undermined the church's viability through the exploitation, confiscation, and wanton destruction of its property.

Notes

1. Rutherford, *Prelude*, 64.
2. E. Wetzel and G. Hecht, "Die Frage der Behandlung der Bevölkerung der ehemaligen polnischen Gebiete nach rassenpolitischen Gesichtspunkten," November 25, 1939, in Pospieszalski, *Hitlerowskie "Prawo,"* 12–13.

3. On the restraint exhibited in the memorandum, see Richard Breitman, *The Architect of Genocide: Himmler and the Final Solution* (New York: Knopf, 1991), 85–86, 118.

4. Epstein, *Model Nazi*, 198.

5. Reichsministerium für die Kirchlichen Angelegenheiten (Roth) to Oberkommando der Wehrmacht, Abteilung Inneres, September 23, 1939, BAB, R 5101/22185, 8; Kerrl to Reichsminister des Innernn, October 11, 1939, BAB R5101/22185, 14; Kerrl to Greiser, October 26, 1939, BAB, R5101/22185, 33.

6. See, for example, Broszat, *Nationalsozialistische*, 148; Conway, *Nazi Persecution*, 313; Sziling, *Polityka*, 54–55. Epstein attributes these authors' emphasis on Bormann's role to the then-dominant totalitarian interpretation of the Nazi regime. See Epstein, *Model Nazi*, 222–23, 398n185. See also Siegmund, *Rückblick*, 209, 247.

7. "Bericht über die Dienstreise nach Posen am 12.12.39," BAB, R 58/7578, 30–32. On the "decoupling" of Warthegau church policy from the control or influence of the Reich Ministry for Church Affairs, and the Party Chancellery's support in that process, see Pohl, "Die Reichsgaue," 401.

8. Bormann to Forster, December 29, 1939, Abschrift, USHMM, RG 15.007M, reel 38, 465, 4–5.

9. Siegmund, *Rückblick*, 209.

10. Dudzus was replaced because of poor and reckless job performance. Reportedly, in a speech at a party gathering in Munich, he represented measures planned for the churches in the Warthegau as if they had already been implemented. According to Kurt Krüger from the Party Chancellery, church officials became aware of his speech, making implementation of some policies more difficult. Aktennotiz (Frank) für den Reichsleiter betr. Abberufung von Dudzus, March 6, 1941, document 347, in Grünzinger, *Dokumente zur Kirchenpolitik*, 851–52.

11. Sziling, *Polityka*, 61–62; Hannelore Braun and Gertraud Grünzinger, *Personenlexikon zum deutschen Protestantismus* (Göttingen: Vandenhoeck & Ruprecht, 2006), 64; Volk, *Akten deutscher Bischöfe*, vol. 5, 565n6, vol. 6, 114n1.

12. "Bericht über die Besprechung am 8.11.40 mit dem Referenten des Reichsstatthalters in Posen, Wilhelm Dudzus (Stiller)," November 13, 1940, Abschrift, USHMM, RG 15:007, reel 15, file 216, 18–21.

13. Greiser was appointed to this post on September 8, 1939, and remained briefly under Hans Frank's authority as chief of civilian administration for all of occupied Poland until he was subsequently appointed Gauleiter and Reichsstatthalter. See Epstein, *Model Nazi*, 133, and Alexander Kranz, *Reichsstatthalter Arthur Greiser und die "Zivilverwaltung" im Wartheland 1939/1940: Die Bevölkerungspolitik in der ersten Phase der deutschen Besatzungsherrschaft in Polen* (Potsdam: Militärgeschichtliches Forschungsamt, 2010), 17.

14. Verordnung, Chef der Zivilverwaltung, Posen, October 6, 1939, Abschrift, AAG, zespół 0131, AKM I, syg. 2178, 39; Zarządzenie Wikariusza Generalnego Gniezno (Blericq), October 9, 1939, AAG, zespół 0131, AKM I, syg. 2178 40.

15. Der Befehlshaber der Sicherheitspolizei und des SD in Posen to Chef der Sicherheitspolizei Berlin, November 9, 1939, USHMM, RG15.007M, reel 38, 466, 5.

16. Zarządzenie Wikariusza Generalnego Gniezno (Blericq), November 4, 1939, AAG, zespół 0131, AKM I, syg. 2177, 2.

17. Heydrich to Reichsminister für die kirchlichen Angelegenheiten, February 13, 1940, BAB, R 5101/22185, 112.

18. Untitled document, n.d., APP, zespół 299, syg. 1191, 9. The content of the document reveals that it postdates March 14, 1940.

19. See, for example, Hauptamt Sicherheitspolizei, Berlin, Tagesbericht, September 6, 1939, document 2, in Lehnstaedt and Böhler, *Berichte der Einsatzgruppen*, 47; Lagebericht, Amtskommissar Ostrowo, March 1, 1941, IZ, Dok. I-903, 76–77; Lagebericht des Regierungspräsidenten in Posen für die Zeit vom 16. Mai bis 30. Juni 1941, June 30, 1941, IPN, GK 62/210/CD, 39.

20. Tagesbericht der Einsatzgruppe VI, September 25, 1939, document 50, in Lehnstaedt and Böhler, 234; Sicherheitsdients, Lagebericht Bromberg, November 14, 1939, BAB, R 70/83, 41–42; Landkreis Tureck, Lagebericht für Monat Mai 1940, June 8, 1940, IPN, GK 70/36, 114; SD-Außenstelle Tureck, Lagebericht für Monat Juli 1940, August 3, 1940, BAB, R 70-Polen, 634, 212; Gestapo Hohensalza to Reichsstatthalter, August 14, 1941, IPN, GK 62/196/CD, 4.

21. Mehlhorn to Herren Regierungspräsidenten in Posen, Hohensalza, Litzmannstadt, Herren Landräte und Oberbürgermeister, Amtskommissar Liebenau-Land to Katholisches Pfarramt Zeugnersruh, July 24, 1940, Abschrift, IPN, GK 831/169, 30.

22. Dymek to Proboszczów, AAP, zespół 133, syg. OK 3.

23. Vermerk über die Besprechung [of July 20, 1940] mit Gauleiter Greiser über die konfessionellen Maßnahmen im Reichsgau Wartheland, August 13–14, 1940, Abschrift, BAB, R58/7581, 61–74. The meeting described took place on July 20, 1940; the memorandum describing the meeting is signed and dated by the authors Fruhwirth and Hartl on August 13 and 14, respectively.

24. Sicherheitsdienst des Reichsführers-SS, SD-Leitabschnitt Posen to Reichssicherheitshauptamt—Amt II B/32, Berlin, December 10, 1940, BAB, R 58/7216, 23.

25. Dudzus to Inspekteur der Sicherheitspolizei und des SD, October 3, 1940, AAG, zespół 0131, AKM I, syg. 2177, 37; Bischoff to Dymek, October 24, 1940, AAP, zespół 133, syg. OK 3.

26. Van Blericq to Herrn Kirchenreferenten des Reichsstatthalters, January 9, 1941, IPN, GK 62/186/CD, 5.

27. Van Blericq to Herrn Kirchenreferenten des Reichsstatthalters, January 9, 1941, IPN, GK 62/186/CD, 4.

28. Van Blericq to Admodum Reverende Domine, October 28, 1940, AAP, zespół 133, syg. OK 122; van Blericq to alle katholische Pfarrämter der Erzdioezese Gnesen, December 3, 1940, IZ, syg. I-129, dok. 1.

29. Van Blericq to Dudzus, November 10, 1940, AAG, zespół 0131, AKM I, syg. 2178. A June 1941 report on church affairs in the Reichsgau Wartheland and Danzig-Westpreußen stated that sermons in Polish were forbidden in the Warthegau in general. The author was likely Heinrich Wienken, and the report was apparently submitted in preparation for the conference of German bishops late that month. "Bericht über die Lage der Kirche im Warthegau und in Danzig-Westpreußen," document 665b, in Volk, *Akten deutscher Bischöfe*, vol. 5, 407–10, here 408. For the attribution to Wienken see 407n1.

30. Neumann to Amtskommissare, Gendarmerieposten, October 18, 1940, APP, zespół 452, syg. 8, 8. Neumann's signature appears on this document but is limited to his surname. He is identified as Hans Neumann by Rolf Jehke at the website http://www.territorial.de/wart/kempen/landkrs.htm.

31. Neumann to Amtskommissare, Gendarmerieposten, November 25, 1949, APP, zespół 452, syg. 8, 10.

32. Mehlhorn to Herren Regierungspräsidenten in Posen, Hohensalza, Litzmannstadt, Herren Landräte und Oberbürgermeister, Amtskommissar Liebenau-Land to Katholisches Pfarramt Zeugnersruh, Abschrift, July 24, 1940, IPN, GK 831/169, 30; Dudzus to Inspekteur der Sicherheitspolizei und des SB, October 3, 1940, AAG, zespół 0131, AKM I, syg. 2177, 37.

33. Greiser, Vermerk, n.d., Abschrift, USHMM, RG 15.007M, reel 47, 581, 95. The memorandum is not dated, but the text accompanies a letter of the Reichssicherheitshauptamt of October 9, 1940.

34. Neumann to Amtskommissare, Gendarmerieposten, October 18, 1940, APP, zespół 452, syg. 8, 8.

35. Van Blericq to Dudzus, November 10, 1940, AAG, zespół 0131, AKM I, syg. 2178.

36. Mehlhorn to Regierungspräsidenten Posen, Hohensalza, Litzmannstadt, to Höheren SS- und Polizeiführer, Posen, June 26, 1941, APP, zespół 299, syg. 1176, film 60028, 42.

37. A report of the government-in-exile's Ministry of the Interior therefore claimed in 1944 that "the pedagogical activities of the clergy have been fully paralyzed." Ministerstwo Spraw Wewnętrznych, Wydział Społeczny, "Raport 'Straty Kulturalne,'" nr. 18/44, część I-sza, London, 1944, AAN, zespół 493, syg. 472, 16.

38. Böttcher to Landräte des Bezirks Posen, Polizeipräsident Posen, October 8, 1940, APP, zespół 299, syg. 1174, film 60026, 10; Marian Biesiada, "Moja parafia w latach okupacji (1939–1945)," AAP, zespół 133, syg. OK 128.

39. Dymek to Rządców kościoła, February 19, 1941, AAP, zespół 133, syg. OK 3.

40. Lagebericht, Amtskommissar von Ostrowo to den Herrn Landrat des Landkreises Ostrowo, March 1, 1941, IZ, dok. I-903, 76–77.

41. W. Hagt to Landrat Kolmar, April 25, 1941, Abschrift, IPN, GK 62/182/CD, II, 1.

42. Befehlshaber der Ordnungspolizei (Knofe) to Reichsstatthalter, March 19, 1941, Abschrift, IPN, GK 62/186/CD, 14.

43. Lagebericht des Regierungspräsidentens Hohensalza (Burckhardt), June 8, 1941, IfZ, Fb 125, 311; Ausschnitt aus dem Lagebericht des Regierungspräsident in Litzmannstadt, March 20, 1941, IPN, GK 62/186/CD, 4.

44. Dymek to Rządców kościoła, August 9, 1941, AAP, zespół 133, syg. OK 3.

45. Relacja, Władysław Zarachowicz, February 2, 1991, YV, M.49-ZIH, file 7116; Stefan Komorowski, "Moja parafia w latach okupacji 1939–1945," AAP, zespół 133, syg. OK 128; Tadeusz Fołczyński, "'Moja parafia' w latach okupacynych (1939–1945)," AAP, zespół 133, syg. OK 128.

8

PROFANACJA

Desecration and Plunder

THE DESECRATION, CONFISCATION, MISUSE, AND DESTRUCTION—WHAT POLES referred to as the *profanacja* of church property—was one aspect of the violence unleashed by the Germans during and immediately following the invasion in the fall of 1939, and it continued in a variety of forms in the years to follow.[1] Most common in the early months of the occupation was the destruction of sites of public piety and reverence—wayside shrines, crosses, statues, and memorials[2]—because the Gestapo feared that after restrictions were placed on the times and locations of traditional religious services, Catholic clergy would encourage their faithful to gather at these monuments for silent open-air devotion.[3] According to reports of the Polish underground, over the first two years of the occupation, the Germans had undertaken a "systematic destruction of all roadside crosses, shrines, and other markers of religious devotion located in public places."[4] In Poznań, for example, all public crucifixes and statues of saints, save two, were destroyed. The gilded crucifix at the Chwaliszewski Bridge was thrown into the Warta River. The "Christ the King" monument, a central site of devotion and congregation in central Poznań, was demolished, and the German authorities forced Poles to do the work.[5]

A report in the files of the Reich Ministry for Church Affairs, most likely originating from church rather than state sources, reveals that in the Łódź diocese nearly all crosses, images of saints, and statues on public streets were destroyed. In the Łęczyca (Lentschütz) Subdistrict, all such markers were, without exception, demolished on orders of the Nazi administration.[6] By December 1940, the eradication of Catholicism's physical markers had become a matter of official policy, when the Gestapo ordered that all objects

Figs. 8.1 and 8.2. Destruction of the Shrine of Saint Lawrence, Nowe Miasto nad Wartą. Courtesy of Muzeum Regionalne w Jarocinie, D-887-c, D-887-b.

Fig. 8.2

with Polish inscriptions and emblems—flags, paintings, monuments, and memorial plaques—be removed from churches. In addition, all Polish inscriptions were to be removed from gravestones, mausoleums, and cemetery monuments.[7] For the local population, and for the German authorities, these "public icons" were visible, physical reminders of the "Polish" character of the landscape and religious culture, illustrating the link between "Polishness" and Catholicism. Their eradication, it is important to note, coincided with the removal and replacement of countless other markers of "Polishness" in the Wartheland, such as street signs and signs of businesses, as well as the renaming, transformation, or destruction of cultural institutions such as concert halls, museums, and cinemas.

The German authorities were not, however, concerned only with altering the physical places and spaces of Polish Catholic devotion; they were also committed to the wholesale confiscation of church property. It is interesting to note that a 1944 report of the Polish government-in-exile in London cited *not* the hostilities of warfare in the fall of 1939 but the intentional confiscation and destruction of church property during the subsequent occupation as the main cause of damage to Polish Catholic churches.[8] Church institutions that provided valuable social services—charitable, educational, medical—were closed, as were religious orders and their houses, cloisters, and convents.[9] Their buildings were then turned over to the German military, police, and civil authorities. In September 1940, an ordinance required that all church property and property of church organizations in the Incorporated Eastern Territories be confiscated and put under the control of local National Socialist authorities, with the exceptions of churches in which services were regularly held, cemeteries, and homes in which active clergy were living.[10] Issuing his own such orders for the Warthegau,[11] Greiser would then report that although German "confessional organizations" in the Reichsgau Wartheland had not been subject to such plunder, the "assets and property of Polish confessional organizations had been completely confiscated."[12]

The variety of ways in which the Nazi authorities made use of Polish church properties is evident in a July 1942 Łódź District report. According to the report, which listed one hundred different properties, the National Socialist People's Welfare (NSV) was the most frequent recipient of church real estate and buildings, but the German police, schools, and other organizations also benefitted from the requisitions. In the Kalisz Subdistrict, for example, the rectory in Koźminek (Bornhag) was used as an NSV kindergarten. The rectory in Iwanowice (Feldenrode) became a temporary shelter for Volksdeutsche settlers. The local gendarmerie in Zbiersk (Vorwalde) used the parish rectory as a barracks. In Kępno Subdistrict, the seminary was turned over to the Hitler Youth, and in Łask Subdistrict, the Catholic parish hall in Buczek (Buscheck) became a meeting hall for the local NSDAP. It is also noteworthy that in some cases, "Polish" Catholic property was taken over by German Catholic communities, which did not assume ownership of the churches and facilities but had permission from local authorities to use them.[13]

The practical implications of these measures were enormous for the church, its religious orders, and the diverse social services that they provided. Already by late 1940, male orders in the Wartheland had been disbanded and their monasteries and friaries put to more "positive, official, and practical use," while the confiscation and transformation of women's convents—a larger project with perhaps less urgency—was still underway.[14] In November of that year, members of the Polish underground reported on the confiscations, informing the London government-in-exile that Poznań's Dominicans had been removed from their cloister, as were the Franciscans in Jarocin (Jarotschin); the Missionaries of the Holy Family in Wieluń (Welun), Kruszewo (Kruschendorf), and Bąblin (Bablin); and the Pallotines in Suchary (Suchenheim). According to the same report, the Poznań Sisters of Charity of St. Vincent de Paul were removed from their hospital and orphanage, while most of the Ursuline sisters in Pniewy (Pinne) were expelled to the General Government, as were the Carmelite sisters in Poznań. The Germans likewise closed and confiscated the Ursulines' boarding school for girls in Poznań.[15]

German documents also tell the story of these expulsions and confiscations. The Gestapo closed the Ursuline cloister in Łódź in late 1940 so that it could be transformed into a home for German children evacuated from cities threatened by aerial bombing. The cloister never, however, fulfilled this role but was instead used as an apartment building for unmarried German officials and, later, as a prison.[16] By December 1940, the Poznań SD would report to the RSHA that 248 institutions and cloisters of the Polish Catholic Church in the Reichsgau Wartheland had been seized. Of those, 198 had been placed under the "Gau Self-Administration" (*Gauselbstverwaltung*, or GSV, a branch of the Reichsstatthalter's office responsible for the management of properties and institutions taken over by the German authorities), while 30 others had been turned over to the Nazi Party. As for the more than 1,400 members of religious orders, some had been confined in two large cloisters, others had been sent to the General Government, and some were forced to work in hospitals.[17]

Cloisters were put to a variety of other uses in the year that followed. The Pauline cloister in Wągrowiec (Eichenbrück) was evacuated and then used as housing for Polish families turned out of their homes by the relocation of German settlers in the northern Warthegau. In late 1941, the Gau Self-Administration turned the cloister over to the Wehrmacht, which then used it for storage.[18] The cloister housing the Carmelite sisters in Poznań was transformed into the city's new *Gaumusikschule*.[19] The historic Salesian cloister in Ląd, like several other houses for the male religious, became a site for the internment of Polish Catholic clergy in the early years of the occupation, and in October 1941 was turned over to the Hitler Youth.[20]

Incarceration of prisoners in cloisters was not uncommon, likely because of their architecture and design, which facilitated confinement, regulation, and supervision. In March 1941 Greiser's office assigned two Franciscan friaries in Osieczna (Storchnest) and Miejska Górka to the Reich Judiciary Administration (Reichsjustizverwaltung) to be used as prisons.[21] In April 1941, the authorities deported the Carmelite sisters in Łódź to the General Government, plundered the convent, and then transformed it into a prison for women, which it remained for the duration of the occupation.[22] In July 1941, Hitler put a Reich-wide moratorium on the confiscation of cloisters,[23] but by then, the damage to these institutions in the Wartheland had been done.

Seizure of church property was not, however, limited to buildings and real estate. Already in the first weeks of the occupation, the German civil administration began to confiscate the church's assets, with the result that Polish priests received no salary and became dependent on donations and stole fees.[24] The Nazi authorities also confiscated livestock, vestments and liturgical linens, libraries, works of art, gold and silver Communion ware, parish records, and bells. In connection with the mass arrest of Polish clergy in October 1941, the police plundered priests' homes for cash, foreign currency, church records, and books, and also raided their churches for chalices, monstrances, candlesticks, candles, and linens. In the aftermath of the mass arrest, the latter were put to practical, wartime use, as twenty tons of candles and six tons of linens were sent to the front.[25]

Military needs were also the impetus behind orders from the Reich Ministry of Economics to requisition bells. Church bells had for centuries

Fig. 8.3. Requisitioned church bells in Turek, April 1942. Courtesy of Muzeum Miasta Turku im Józefa Mehoffera, MRZTT/HA/1073–Teczka nr. 07–100.

served as a military resource, but the systematic thoroughness of the process in the Warthegau was unique.[26] The initiative had its origins in Nazi Germany's Four Year Plan, which was intended to achieve, in preparation for war, a higher degree of economic independence. On March 15, 1940, Hermann Göring, as Plenipotentiary for the Four Year Plan, issued a decree for the collection of bells across the Reich,[27] and in November 1941, after the nearly wholesale closure of "Polish" Catholic churches, Arthur Greiser ordered the intensification of what was referred to as the "*Glockenabnahmeaktion*" ("bell removal action") in the Warthegau.[28] Bells designated as historically or artistically significant were exempt from the requisitions—unless they were the property of churches designated as "Polish."[29] The Aktion proceeded apace but, at times, with discretion, for the SD had noted that much of the Gau's German population was critical of the requisitions.[30] In conjunction with Arthur Greiser's postwar trial, the Poznań historic preservationist stated that the Germans had either melted down or removed to the Reich 986 historically significant bells in the Poznań voivodship.[31] A total of 1,370 bells were removed from churches in the Poznań and Włocławek dioceses alone.[32]

Requisition of church property was justified in a variety of ways. When the papal nuncio in Berlin, Cesare Orsenigo, issued in March 1941 a *note verbale* of protest against these measures,[33] the Reich minister for church affairs stated that because the Catholic Church in Poland and its clergy—from the secular and religious clergy to the bishops—was dependent on the Polish state and was active on its behalf, the German occupiers had a "natural right to reduce the property of the Polish church on the territory of the German Reich to that which is absolutely necessary (churches and rectories)." This was intended as a blow not only against the Catholic Church but also "against the Polishness [*Polentum*] with which the church has identified in these areas."[34]

The political rationale and link to the broader Germanization effort in the Gau are clear. Beyond that, however, Göring's office for the Four Year Plan provided a legal rationale as well, stating in May 1941 that the Polish church was so closely linked—ideologically, politically, and financially—to the prewar Polish state that confiscation of its property was easily justified.[35] This was supported by the German Foreign Ministry in a *note verbale* to the papal nunciature on May 19, 1941, which stated, "The Catholic parishes, foundations, orders, and associations in the incorporated eastern areas are considered a corporate body to which Section 10 of the decree [regarding the treatment of property of subjects of the former Polish state, of September 17, 1940] applies, because their administration has been predominantly influenced by subjects of the former Polish state—this with the close connection of the Catholic Church with the Polish element."[36]

The seizure of church property was not, however, only intended as a defensive measure against the perceived anti-German, Polish-national activism of the Catholic establishment; there was also an obvious economic motivation. As Greiser stated in a June 1942 speech, "If we have taken away the property of the Polish Church, this is not to punish faithful Catholics, but rather because economic resources for the political struggle against the German people were derived from this property. That is why there are no more monasteries and no more church properties left in the Reichsgau Wartheland. They have all been confiscated, and because of that, my Gau Self-Administration has become the biggest landowner in the Gau."[37] The Gauleiter's boast was perhaps not inaccurate. According to one scholar, the Nazi authorities expropriated six hundred square kilometers of land from the Catholic Church in the Reichsgau Wartheland.[38]

So broad and comprehensive was the Nazi effort to deprive the church of its property and wealth that it is difficult to get a sense of the effects of these measures on individual parishes, their clergy, and their parishioners. After the war, church leaders, parishes, and individual priests from across the former Warthegau submitted reports to church and state authorities on material and demographic losses during the occupation, and these reports provide a sense of the devastation experienced at the local level, even only during the first two years of the occupation. One such report from the Włocławek diocese stated that several dozen churches were demolished, and that the majority of churches were plundered of linens, vestments, silver, furniture, and bells.[39] Similarly, a priest from St. Lawrence parish in Gniezno testified to the Polish Main Commission for the Investigation of German Crimes in Poland that the church was robbed of bells, carpets, linens, paraments, Communion ware, parish books, office supplies, and banners. It was then used as a warehouse for confiscated items. According to the priest, a chapel in the nearby Dziekanka (Tiegenhof) neighborhood was turned into a cinema.[40] Likewise, the Germans requisitioned bells, paraments, Communion ware, banners, and furniture from Gniezno's downtown Church of the Holy Trinity, from the chapel of the nearby convent of the Sisters of Mercy of St. Vincent DePaul, and from the filial church in Zdziechowa, which was then used for the storage of grain.[41] In Rozdrażew (Albertshof), a small town in the southern part of the Warthegau, the authorities closed the parish church in October 1941 and transformed it into a warehouse for paper. They removed all the pews, liturgical linens, and bells, destroyed the parish's grotto of Our Lady of Lourdes, transformed the church offices into a school for German children, turned the rectory into a private home for the German mayor, and used the parish's home for the elderly as the new headquarters for the local Nazi Party.[42]

A report from the parish in Odolanów (Adelnau) offers a remarkably detailed account of its losses during the occupation. On October 6, 1941, the Nazi police closed both Odolanów churches and deported the provost, two vicars, and five nuns. The authorities then seized, confiscated, or destroyed the parish's property, valued at 261,700 złoty. Stolen or destroyed were five carpets, eight meters of firewood, one ton of coal, five sets of bedsheets, three bells, two metal spires from the churches' roofs, one gold chalice, sixty brass candlesticks, twelve silver-plated candlesticks, eleven altar crosses, eleven lace altar cloths, twenty-two linen altar cloths, five albs, seventeen surplices, twenty-five chasubles, two hundred bottles of Communion wine,

Fig. 8.4. Interior of the Church of Christ the King, Jarocin, used as a storage facility for furniture. Courtesy of Muzeum Regionalne w Jarocinie, D-421-a.

three banners, two organs, one desk, one table, one sofa, one cow, and fifteen chickens.[43]

Notes

1. Zeznanie, Ks. Dr. Józef Nowacki, June 11, 1946, IPN, GK 196/30, 22.

2. Dymek to Heinrich Wienken, October 14, 1941, document 19 (Anhang), in Volk, *Akten deutscher Bischöfe*, vol. 5, 1010; Ministerstwo Spraw Wewnętrznych, Wydział Społeczny, "Raport 'Straty Kulturalne,'" nr. 18/44, część I-sza, London, 1944, AAN, zespół 493, syg. 472, 14–15, 20.

3. Gestapo Litzmannstadt (Schefe) to Landräte in Kalisch, Ostrowo, usw., April 25, 1940, Abschrift, IPN, GK 755/129, 20.

4. Sprawozdanie sytuacyjne z kraju 1939–1941, vol. 1, 105, PUMST.

5. Zeznanie, Ks. Dr. Józef Nowacki, June 11, 1946, IPN, GK 196/30, 22; Ministerstwo Spraw Wewnętrznych, Wydział Społeczny, "Raport 'Straty Kulturalne,'" nr. 18/44, część I-sza, London, 1944, AAN, zespół 493, syg. 472, 20.

6. Kirchenaufstellung Litzmannstadt," n.d., BA Berlin, R 5101/22437, 14–16. The content of the document indicates that it postdates October 6, 1941. It also claims that in the *Kreise* of Łódź and Łask (Lask), the destruction of roadside statues was allegedly undertaken by Russian paratroopers dropped into the region at night.

7. Van Bléricq to alle katholische Pfarrämter der Erzdiezese Gnesen, December 3, 1940, AAP, zespół 133, syg. OK 122.

8. "Raport 'Straty Kulturalne,'" Ministerstwo Spraw Wewnętrzych, Wydział Społeczny, Nr. 18/44, część I-sza, Londyn, 1944, AAN, zespół 493/Konsulat Gen.-Nowy York, syg. 472, 20.

9. "Raport 'Straty Kulturalne,'" Ministerstwo Spraw Wewnętrzych, Wydział Społeczny, Nr. 18/44, część I-sza, Londyn, 1944, AAN, zespół 493/Konsulat Gen.-Nowy York, syg. 472, 15.

10. Schnellbrief, Beauftragter für den Vierjahresplan to Haupttreuhandstelle Ost, Treuhandstellen Danzig-Westpr., Kattowitz, Posen, Zichenau, Litz., September 10, 1940, Abschrift. Archiwum Państwowe w Łodzi (hereafter APŁ), zespół: Akta Miasta Łodzi, syg. 32463.

11. Erlass Greisers, September 9, 1940, Abschrift, APŁ, zespół: Akta Miasta Łodżi, syg. 32463.

12. Vermerk über Kirchenverhältnisse im Warthegau, n.d., Abschrift, USHMM, RG 15.007, reel 47, 93.

13. "Aufstellung über das von der TNL beschlagnahmte und verwaltete Kirchenvermögen," July 8, 1942, IZ, dok. III-147, 197–204.

14. Vermerk über Kirchenverhältnisse im Warthegau, n.d., Abschrift, USHMM, RG 15.007, reel 47, 93.

15. Sprawozdanie sytuacyjne z kraju 1939–1941, vol. 1, 107–8, PUMST.

16. Reichsstatthalter–Generalstaatsanwalt (Knobloch) to Reichsstatthalter, January 16, 1941, IPN, GK 62/208, 1; Oberbürgermeister Litzmannstadt, Liegenschaftsamt to Reichsstatthalter, March 29, 1941, IPN, GK 62/208, 24; Reichsstatthalter (Birk) to Oberbürgermeister Litzmannstadt, April 11, 1941, Abschrift, IPN, GK 62/208, 24; Reichsstatthalter I/51 to Oberbürgermeister Litzmannstadt, April 23, 1941, IPN, GK 62/208, 25.

17. Sicherheitsdienst des Reichsführers-SS, SD-Leitabschnitt Posen to Reichssicherheitshauptamt–Amt II B/32, December 10, 1940, USHMM, RG 15.007m, reel 38, 471, 3–4. Among the numerous institutions supervised by the Gauselbstverwaltung were, for example, the Gau Children's Hospital, the Gau Women's Hospital, the "Gauheilanstalt Tiegenhof" (a "euthanasia" installation), various orphanages, the Poznań School for the Deaf, the Kaiser-Friedrich-Museum, and the "Gauarbeitsanstalt Schmückert" (discussed in chap. 13 and otherwise known as the "Nonnenlager Schmückert"). See "Vermerk betr. 'Rückführung der Gauselbstverwaltung,'" March 27, 1945, in Joachim Rogall, ed., *Die Räumung des "Reichsgaus Wartheland" vom 16. bis 26. January 1945 im Spiegel amtlicher Berichte* (Sigmaringen: Jan Thorbecke Verlag, 1993), 39.

18. Amtskommissar Eichenbrück-Stadt to Reichsstatthalter Abt. I/51, September 10, 1941, IPN, GK 62/202, 105; Reichsstatthalter–Gauselbstverwaltung to Wehrkreisverwaltung XXI Posen, December 3, 1941, Abschrift, IPN GK 202, 110.

19. Relacja, Ks. Marian Frankiewicz, October 25, 1947, IZ, dok. II-123, 3; Report of a Poznań Carmelite, October 15, 1974, in Benedicta Maria Kempner, *Nonnen unter dem Hakenkreuz: die erste Dokumentation über das Schicksal der Nonnen im Dritten Reich* (Würzburg: Naumann-Verlag, 1979), 107–8.

20. Reichsstatthalter to NSDAP–Hitlerjugend, Gebiet Wartheland, October 2, 1941, Abschrift, IPN, GK 62/202, 112; "Ląd . . . ," 235.

21. Reichsstatthalter Abt. I/8 D-147 (Mehlhorn) to Reichsstatthalter–Generalstaatsanwalt, March 18, 1941, Abschrift, IPN, GK 62/208, 14; Landrat des Kreises Lissa (Köhler) to Gestapo Posen, September 3, 1941, APP, 53/1023/0/-/13, film O-83184, 124.

22. H. Andrysiak, OKBZH, opis zbrodnia popełnionego w dniu 4 kwietnia 1941, January 27, 1971, Instytut Pamięci Narodowej–Komisja Ścigania Zbrodni przeciwko Narodowi Polskiemu, Łódź (herafter IPN-Ł), 11/255, 2.

23. Bormann to Gauleiter der NSDAP über die Beschlagnahme von Klöstern, July 30, 1941, document 224, in *Katholische Kirche und Nationalsozialismus 1930–1945: ein Bericht in Quellen*, ed. Hubert Gruber (Paderborn: Ferdinand Schöningh, 2006), 443.

24. Vermerk, Dudzus, February 7, 1940, USHMM, RG 15.007, reel 21, 276, 50; Brief des Generalvikars Weihbischof Dymek an bischof Wienken, Posen, October 14, 1940, document 19 (Anhang), in Volk, *Akten deutscher Bischöfe*, vol. 5, 1011; Ministerstwo Spraw Wewnętrznych, Wydział Społeczny, "Raport 'Straty Kulturalne,'" nr. 18/44, część I-sza, London, 1944, AAN, Warsaw, zespół 493, syg. 472, 20; "Raport 'Straty Kulturalne'," Ministerstwo Spraw Wewnętrzych, Wydział Społeczny, Nr. 18/44, część I-sza, Londyn, 1944, AAN, zespół 493/Konsulat Gen.-Nowy York, syg. 472, 14. "Stole fee" refers to a fee or voluntary donation offered by a member of the laity to a priest for the administration of a sacrament or church rite.

25. Gestapo Posen, Vermerk Stossberg, March 21, 1942, IPN, GK 196/19, 96.

26. For a detailed and comprehensive account of the program to requisition bells in occupied Poland, see Jerzy Gołos, Agnieszka Kasprzak Miler, Tomasz Łuczak, and Przemysław Nadolski, *Straty wojenne: Zabytkowe dzwony utracone w latach 1939–1945 w granicach Polski po 1945 roku (z wyłączeniem ziem należących przed 1939 rokiem do Rzeszy Niemieckiej)*, vol. 2 (woj. poznańskie), *Wartime Losses: Historic Bells Lost between 1939–1945 within Post 1945 Borders of Poland (Except Those from Regions beyond the Pre-1939 Polish-German Border)*, vol. 2 (The Poznań Voivodship), Polskie Dziedzictwo Kulturalne, Seria A. Straty kultury polskiej, Polish Cultural Heritage, Series A, Losses of Polish Culture (Poznań: Ministerstwo Kultury i Dziedziectwa Narodowego, Departament do spraw Polskiego Dziedzictwa Kulturowego za Granicą, 2006).

27. "Anordnung zur Durchführung des Vierjahresplans über die Erfassung von Nichteisenmetallen vom 15. März 1940," in Reichsministerium des Innern, *Reichsgesetzblatt* 1940, I, (Berlin: Reichsverlagsamt, 1940), 510; Gołos et al., *Straty wojenne*, 58–60.

28. Greiser to Regierungspräsidenten, Gestapo Posen, SD Posen, November 21, 1941, Abschrift, IPN, GK 196/19, 90.

29. Greiser to Daenicke, Johannes, November 21, 1941, IPN, GK 196/19, 91; Rundschreiben Nr. 2/42, Gauleitung Wartheland, Gaubeauftragter für Altmaterialfassung, February 28, 1942, IPN, GK 62/153, 103.

30. "Lagebericht des Höheren SS- und Polizeiführers beim Reichsstatthalter in Posen im Wehrkreis XXI–Inspekteur der Sicherheitspolizei und des SD-Posen, vom 22.3. bis 4.4.42," April 4, 1942, IPN, GK, 62/153, 191–93; "Rundschreiben des Beauftragten für Altmaterialerfassung im Wartheland" (Daenicke), Landratsamt Kempen, October 1, 1942, in Łuczak, *Dyskryminacja Polaków*, 214–15.

31. Z. Kępiński, Konserwator Urządu Wojewódzkiego w Poznaniu to GKBZNwP, O. Sęsziego and J. Skorzyńskiego, June 22, 1946, IPN, GK 196/20, 6.

32. Kuria Metropolitalna Poznania, "Zestawienie Strat Archidiecezji Poznańskiej w latach wojny i okupacji 1939–1945," October 18, 1967, AAP, zespół 133, OK 121; Frątczak, *Diecezja Włocławska*, 284–91.

33. Nuntiatur Berlin, Verbalnote, March 15, 1941, BAB, R 5101/22185, 220–21.

34. Vermerk, Reichsministerium für die Kirchlichen Angelegenheiten, April 2, 1941, BAB, R 5101/22185.

35. Vermerk, Reichsmarschall des Grossdeutschen Reiches, Beauftragter für den Vierjahresplan (Gramsch), May 11, 1941, Abschrift, APP, zespół 301, syg. 285, 49–50.

36. Note Verbale to the Apostolic Nunciature, May 19, 1941, document 567, in United States Department of State, *Documents on German Foreign Policy 1918–1945*, series D, vol. 12 (Washington, DC: United States Government Printing Office, 1962), 916.

37. Greiser, *Aufbau im Osten*, 10. Most of the translated quotation here is found in Conway, *Nazi Persecution*, 319.

38. Porzycki, *Posłudzni*, 46; see also Sziling, *Polityka*, 218.

39. Kuria diecezjalna we Włocławku, Raport o prześladowaniu kościoła katolickiego, n.d., IPN, GK 162/558, 266.

40. Ks. Mieczysław Bogacz, świadectwo, Gniezno, Parafia Św. Wawrzyńca, n.d., IPN, GK 196/19, 181.

41. Ks. Antoni Wronka, "Wiadomość o prześladowaniu kościoła katolickiego przez okupanta niemieckiego na terenie parafii Farnej w Gnieznie," July 10, 1945, IPN, GK 196/19, 182–85.

42. Stefan Komorowski, "Moja parafia w latach okupacji 1939–1945," AAP, zespół 133, syg. OK 128.

43. Kwestionariusz strat–Parafia Odolanów, AAP, zespół 133, syg. OK 214.

9

NATIONALITÄTENPRINZIP

National Segregation in Church Life

THE DESTRUCTION AND CONFISCATION OF CHURCH PROPERTY—AS BUT one aspect of National Socialist Kirchenpolitik—would further separate Polish Catholics in the Wartheland from the worship sites and rituals of their faith. Nazi *Rassenpolitik*, or racial policy, would, however, also have an impact on the expression of their faith and access to the sacraments. This was manifested primarily in the Gau administration's strict isolation of Poles from their German coreligionists but also in the marriage restrictions placed on Warthegau Catholics.

Given the regime's broader goal of drawing distinct boundaries between Germans and Poles in public life, it is not surprising that it demanded strict division of Germans and Poles in religious life as well. The segregation of German from Pole and Jew was, of course, axiomatic in the racialized context that was the Reichsgau Wartheland. Germans, Poles, and Jews were not permitted to frequent the same restaurants, bars, cafes, swimming pools, or park benches--or churches. In accordance with Nazi racial goals, Germanization policy, and what they referred to as the *Nationalitätenprinzip* (literally, "nationality principle")—that is, the separation of Poles and Germans—Poles not only were denied access to churches designated as "German" but also were prohibited access to German Catholics, whether German priests, Reichsdeutsche, Volksdeutsche, or members of the German armed forces.[1]

In the fall of 1939, reports had emerged of German soldiers participating in the sacrament of confession and in worship services led by Polish priests, a practice condemned by Hitler and prohibited by an order of the supreme commander of the Wehrmacht, Wilhelm Keitel. This order was subsequently expanded to include the Order Police in all occupied eastern territories, as well as Reich officials and employees.[2] Additional orders for the separation of Germans and Poles were issued orally in the fall of 1939,[3] but apparently German Catholics long continued to participate in services among Poles, a practice later described by the Kępno Landrat Hans Neumann as "politically unacceptable" and "undignified of a German."[4]

Arthur Greiser agreed, and in April 1941 issued an order to combat the "outrageous and shameless occurance" of Germans participating in Polish worship services. To Greiser it was a matter of national honor. Any German who attended a Polish Catholic church, he argued, "committed a violation against the laws of the German *Volk* characteristic of the race" ["verstößt gegen die arteigenen Gesetze des deutschen Volkes"] and therefore excluded oneself from the German *Volksgemeinschaft*. The consequences of violating the prohibition were severe: a one-month sentence to a concentration camp in the Warthegau for the first offense, and for the second offense, imprisonment in a concentration camp in the Altreich.[5] The following month, Greiser issued a legal decree mandating the separation of Poles and Germans in corporate worship. It stated that German and Polish priests were permitted to minister only to Catholics of their own nationality, that Poles were permitted only in churches officially designated and marked by a sign reading "Polish Church," and that Germans were limited to attending services in churches marked "for Germans only."[6] These new regulations resulted in the transfer of dozens of churches, hitherto served by Polish priests and frequented by Polish parishioners, to German Catholics—typically one church in each city and town of significant size.[7] This meant, in effect, that neither Polish Catholics nor German Catholic Volksdeutsche had access to the churches to which they were accustomed, and that both would face severe consequences for violating the segregation policy.

Hilarius Breitinger, a German Franciscan who served in Poznań as the apostolic administrator[8] for German Catholics from 1942–1945, described in his memoir how the police frequently observed church services, with the result that ethnic Germans were arrested in Polish churches and imprisoned for a few days. According to Breitinger, these were usually visitors from the Altreich who were not aware of the regulations. Yet Poles, Breitinger reported, consistently violated the segregation order, and continued to attend Mass in his central Poznań "for-Germans-only" church. In some instances, Breitinger's acquaintances in the Gestapo would tip him off about an upcoming *Kontrolle* (i.e., verification of personal documents), enabling him to warn some Poles of the danger.[9] In other cases, German civilians were responsible for discouraging Poles from attending services. An August 1943 report of the Polish underground resistance stated:

> Already for some time now the Franciscan church in Poznań designated for Germans has been surrounded by German Catholics functioning as civilian patrols making sure that no Pole enters the church. The German authorities warned the church administration that they would close the church unconditionally if it were determined that Poles are participating in services. Since they also announced that they would be conducting searches during services, the German parishioners are forming a cordon so that under no circumstances a Pole can enter the church.[10]

The motives of the German "guards" are not clear. Were they patrolling the church at the behest of Father Breitinger, trying to protect the Poles, or simply keeping the Poles out so that their church would remain open? In any case, the situation eventually led to an official warning from the Gestapo and, in November 1944, a threat from Greiser to close "German" churches if Breitinger did not sufficiently enforce the prohibition against Poles in his own parish. The German priest's experience suggests that enforcement of Greiser's early regulations against "cohabitation" in the churches was at times inconsistent or dilatory, and while this may have been the case, the warning issued to Breitinger in 1944 is nonetheless telling of the long-term importance of this issue for the Nazi authorities.

Over the course of the occupation there were numerous instances of priests censured, churches closed, and worshippers imprisoned for violating the segregation policy. In May 1942, a local party official in Oborniki (Obornik), north of Poznań, reported the presence of Polish altar boys at "German" Catholic services. Eventually, the Gestapo became involved in the case and recommended that the church be closed and the German priest, who was on record as having intervened on behalf of Polish Catholics, be expelled from the Warthegau.[11] Johannes Snurawa, a Reichsdeutsche priest in the village of Wielki Buczek (Hohenbusch), was reported as having held services in which Poles participated, so the Gestapo closed his church.[12]

In the summer of 1942, Greiser's office reported to party headquarters in Munich on the procedures used for enforcing the separation of worshippers. It was already common for the German police to place themselves at the exits of churches on Sunday mornings and demand to see worshippers' identification and documentation of their work placement. A means of apprehending the "work shy" and corraling Poles for forced labor in the

Altreich,[13] this practice also proved effective at apprehending unauthorized worshippers of the wrong nationality. On one Sunday, twenty-eight Germans were found attending Polish services, and fourteen of them were sentenced to a month in a concentration camp. According to the report on "Separation of Germans and Poles in Church Affairs" sent to Munich, this proved to be an effective means of ensuring compliance with the prohibition against ethnic mixing of this kind.[14] A December 1942 report of the Polish underground likewise described the dual goals of the "notoriously recurring" roundups: to corral Poles for forced labor and to arrest Germans guilty of violating the segregation policy.[15]

Some Poles went to the extent of requesting special permission to enter a "German" church. In the fall of 1942, Kasimira Kosicka, who worked as a translator in Kalisz, sent a letter to the Reichsstatthalter's office requesting that she be allowed to enter daily the Church of Saint Joseph in Kalisz, which had been assigned to German Catholics. She justified her request by noting that she had gone to church every day since childhood, and that it aided in her work by providing strength and comfort. Her request was denied by Heinrich Meyer, who had recently been named head of the Reichstatthalter's Department I/51 and Greiser's advisor for church affairs.[16] In his letter to the Łódź Gestapo, which was supervising the case, he wrote, "I ask you to make clear, or have it made clear to the woman who has issued this petition that her request must, of course, be rejected, since the use by Poles of a church designated for German church services can, under no circumstances, be permitted. Moreover, I think it would be useful to get in touch with Kasimira Kosicka's employer, so as to arrange that the divine blessings she no longer receives be compensated for by additional work."[17]

Meyer's negative and mocking response aside, it is worth considering the extent to which Poles and Germans in the Warthegau were willing to violate the Reichsstatthalter's segregative policy and join their coreligionists in church. German documents suggest that the practice was common, and clearly a source of concern and frustration to the authorities. Such violations were also indicative of the ideological limitations of the *Nationalitätenprinzip*. For some German and Polish Catholics—we will, of course, never know how many—segregation was either so unnatural or inconvenient or contrary to their sensibilities that they were willing to violate the prohibition, and at great risk. Viewed from the angle of the Nazi authorities, nationality did not necessarily come naturally when it came to matters of the church. It had to be enforced.

Violation of the segregation policy may not be such a significant chapter in the story of the Warthegau church, but it does invite broader consideration of how effective the barriers of nationality actually were. Nazi occupation policy toward Poles was crushing, and toward Jews, genocidal. The alleged racial and national distinctions between these groups were, on the one hand, ideologically grounded and, allegedly, self-evident. On the other hand, it is clear that for some of the population (and some clergy among them), the church could erase, or at least blur, the linguistic, cultural, ethnic, and racial frontiers that the regime so rigorously imposed and defended. In his study of Upper Silesia, historian James Bjork has emphasized how "when one looks deeper into the role of the church . . . one starts to appreciate the capacity of confession to complicate the process of national polarization."[18] Indeed, for Bjork, the "frontier between German and Polish Catholicism" was "a fluid zone begging for scrutiny rather than an impermeable outer limit."[19] Other scholars have effectively explored the role of language in avoiding and eliding the demands of modern nationalism in central and east-central European borderlands,[20] while Chad Bryant, in his exploration of the Czech lands under Nazi and postwar Czech rule, has emphasized the importance of "amphibians," referring to those individuals "who could switch public nationalities or to people whose nationality was unclear."[21]

All these approaches should inform further consideration of identity, ethnicity, nation, and race in the Reichsgau Wartheland, which was, to be sure, a context quite different from that of prewar Upper Silesia or German-occupied Moravia. "Under Nazi rule," Bryant writes, "nationality, once something acted out in civil and political society, became something that state officials assigned to individuals."[22] Such was the case in the Warthegau, but what remains open to analysis is the extent to which Poles, Reichsdeutsche, and Volksdeutsche complied with their assigned nationality, and how this varied geographically, in terms of social context, or chronologically. Enforcement undoubtedly varied, for example, across districts and subdistricts. Were Catholics more likely to "cohabitate" in large urban churches like Breitinger's, or in remote rural parishes? We know that Germans and Poles sometimes mixed in Catholic churches, but was this any more common than illegal social interaction in taverns, restaurants, or cinemas? And if so, what does this mean? Did violations of the *Nationalitätenprinzip* in churches become more or less common over the course of the occupation, and why?

There remains much to explore, and perhaps the most remarkable aspect of the segregation policy was its longevity. Throughout the occupation, the policy, as Hilarius Breitinger protested to Greiser, discriminated against both Polish and German Catholics, "contradicted the essence of the Catholic Church," was enforced through "stringent measures and severe punishments," and was, in general, "implemented in a form unseen in the Altreich or in other incorporated areas."[23] Breitinger's laxity in restricting access of Poles to his church resulted in, as noted above, a threat to close "German" churches, even in the waning months of the occupation.[24] In November and December 1944, only weeks before Soviet forces would liberate eastern sections of the Warthegau and when German and Polish Catholics were likely anticipating relaxation of the policy, the Reichsstatthalter's office continued to demand that churches remain well marked as either "Polish" or "German," and reminded local officials of the punishments for priests who did not adhere to and enforce the *Nationalitätenprinzip*.[25] As late as December 16, 1944, when Greiser's office granted permission for a group of so-called *Schwarzmeerdeutsche* ("Black Sea Germans" who were recent Volksdeutsche immigrants to the Warthegau) to use a closed "Polish" church in Michorzewo (Michenau), the local authorities were reminded that they were responsible for monitoring services there to ensure that Poles did not participate.[26]

Once mandated by official decree, the segregation of Polish and German Catholics was rigorously enforced and was then even extended beyond their earthly lives to the grave.[27] The Reichsstatthalter ordered in October 1941 that Germans and Poles were to be buried in separate cemeteries.[28] These restrictions, too, were upheld until nearly the end of the occupation and were accompanied in some communities by mass exhumations and reburial of corpses.[29] The length of time that a corpse was permitted to decay undisturbed depended, of course, on that corpse's nationality: forty years for Germans but only fifteen for Poles.[30]

A further regulation instituted in 1941 not only illustrated Nazi Germanization policy but also reflected the regime's aggressive racial policy by restricting Polish Catholics from partipating in the sacrament of marriage. Marriages between Poles and Germans were initially discouraged in the early weeks of the occupation, and by the end of 1939, forbidden.[31] In the long run, however, Germanization of the "model Gau" was dependent on both the rapid and sustained growth of the German population and a concurrent decline in the Polish population. Addressing this issue, an August 1941 report of the Łódź SD stated that "despite the changed political conditions and the often difficult economic situation, the biological strength of the Polish people has in no way weakened." As the report related, neither Polish deaths during the September 1939 hostilities, nor mass deportation to the General Government, nor the removal of tens of thousands of Warthegau Poles for work in the Altreich, nor any of these in combination had brought about a significant reduction of the Polish population in the Warthegau. The report thus recommended, in addition to sterilization of the Polish "primitive classes," setting minimum ages at which Warthegau Poles were permitted to marry.[32]

Gau officials were not only concerned about the demographic situation outlined in the report; some were also convinced that Polish Catholic priests were engaging in anti-German agitation by encouraging their parishioners to bear children as a means of bringing about Poland's national renewal.[33] The Reichstatthalter's office therefore required in September 1941 that in order to marry, Polish men had to be at least twenty-eight years of age, and Polish women at least twenty-five.[34] Apparently the problem did not, however, disappear. Defending this measure a few months later, Greiser himself argued, "We can under no circumstances back down from our Polish policy where it is concerned with . . . biological struggle, where we intend to reach the point that the Poles have fewer children than we. The raising of the marriage age is part of this [struggle]."[35] A May 1943 decree of the Reich Ministry of the Interior set the minimum age for Poles to marry somewhat lower, at twenty-five for men and twenty-two for women, but in the Reichsgau Wartheland, the higher minimum ages set a year and a half earlier were maintained.[36] To some extent, the marriage restrictions were effective. According to a 1942 report issued by the Łódź District, the number of marriages among Poles dropped dramatically—between 60 and 80 percent—from the previous year. At the same time, however, the number of children born to unmarried couples increased. There were also cases of Polish couples from the Warthegau crossing into the General Government and, after finding an accommodating priest, marrying there and returning to the Warthegau.[37] Their marriage may not have been recognized in the eyes of the Nazi state but was legitimate in the eyes of the church.

The measures, restrictions, and ordinances outlined in this and the preceding three chapters represent only a fraction of the ways in which the

Nazi authorities worked to separate Warthegau Catholics from the traditions of their church and limit their access to it. Yet they testify clearly to both the perceived importance of Polish Catholicism and to the diversity of Nazi measures confronting it. Removal of priests, closure of churches, and restrictions on worship times and the availability of the sacraments limited Poles' access to the church's rites and the "means of grace" that they offered. Restrictions on the availability of religious instruction and closure of Catholic schools prevented indoctrination in the spirit of Polish nationalism even as it ensured a Nazi monopoly on education. Destruction of shrines and removal of inscriptions from churches emphasized political control over public devotion and worship life, and aimed to extinguish yet another expression of Polish national consciousness. Confiscation of church property impoverished the church even as it advanced the economic transformation of the Warthegau. Separation of Poles and Germans in public worship and the legal designation of "Polish" and "German" churches was in accordance with the broader *Nationalitätenprinzip* so rigorously applied by the Nazis in the Warthegau. Marriage restrictions further limited access to and participation the church's ministry, even as they were intended to advance the regime's racial agenda. Poles who marry later, according to its logic, bear fewer children.

Diverse discriminatory measures were characteristic of Nazi church policy, but in order to develop a comprehensive plan for the churches' future—or future demise—in the Mustergau Wartheland, officials in Poznań and Berlin needed to enact dramatic changes to the churches' financial and legal status. A secret position paper from early 1940 reveals much about the opportunities and challenges Nazi policymakers were facing and also shows that more formal proposals for future policy were—already early in the occupation—beginning to coalesce. According to this document, the collapse of the Polish state had rendered the laws and ordinances relating to the churches in Poland inconsequential, resulting in a situation "free of legal constraints." The freedom inherent in the Wartheland's Mustergau status was clear, for the Nazi authorities were not required to recognize the former Polish legal structures protecting the churches, nor were they compelled to implement the legal structures still regulating church-state relations in the Altreich. Rather, the goal was to "stem the existing confessional positions of power in order to keep open the path to an uncompromising development and restructuring of National Socialist life in the Gau."[38] That path would be marked, according to the position paper, by a series of programmatic principles in the future—principles that would come to be known as the "Thirteen Points" of Nazi Kirchenpolitik in the Reichsgau Wartheland.

Notes

1. In the Reichsgau Wartheland, the term Nationalitätenprinzip was generally applied to distinguish and separate Pole from German, but it could be used as a basis for prohibiting interaction between Germans and Jews or Poles and Jews.

2. Keitel to Regierungspräsidenten in den Reichsgauen Danzig-Westpreußen und Posen, November 14, 1939, IPN 831/177, 5; Reichsführer-SS (von Bomhard), December 27, 1939, Abschrift, IPN, 831/177, 5; Böttcher to Polizeipräsidenten in Posen, Landrat in Rawitsch, n.d., IPN, 831/177, 5.

3. Breitinger, *Als Deutschenseelsorger*, 58.

4. Landrat des Kreises Kempen (Neumann) to Sämtliche Gefolgschaftsmitglieder der Kreisverwaltung, February 9, 1941, IPN, GK 831/59, 8.

5. Greiser to alle Dienststellen der Partei und des Staates, April 24, 1941, APP, zespół 452, syg. 8, 50.

6. Erlass Greisers, May 26, 1941, in Volk, *Akten deutscher Bischöfe*, vol. 5, 743n2; Jäger to Regierungspräsidenten Posen, Hohensalza, Litzmannstadt, May 27, 1941, IPN, GK 196/19, 83.

7. APP, zespół 299, syg. 1181, microfilm 0-60033, documents the transfer of dozens of such churches from across the Gau.

8. An apostolic administrator is a member of the clergy appointed by the pope and given authority over an "apostolic administration," in this case, the territory of the Reichsgau Wartheland. Given the enforced segregation of Poles and Germans in church life, Breitinger was appointed to this office to minister to German Catholics but not Poles.

9. Breitinger, *Als Deutschenseelsorger*, 59.

10. "Raport o sytuacji na Ziemiach Zachodnich Nr. 6 (do 15.VIII.1943)," in *Raporty z ziem wcielonych do III Rzeszy (1942–1944)*, Biblioteka Przeglądu Zachodniego, vol. 20, ed. Zbigniew Mazur, Aleksandra Pietrowicz, and Maria Rutowska (Poznań: Instytut Zachodni, 2004), 149.

11. Gauschulungsleiter der NSDAP, Gauleitung Wartheland, to Amtsgerichtsrat Dr. Birk, May 22, 1942, IPN, GK 196/12/CD, 40; Birk to Abteilungsleiter I, Posen, May 27, 1942, IPN, GK 196/12/CD, 41; Gestapo Posen to Reichsstatthalter, Abtl. I/51, August 5, 1942, IPN, GK 196/12/CD, 45.

12. Reichsstatthalter (Birk) to Gestapo Hohensalza, June 9, 1942, IPN, GK 62/180, 30.

13. "Prześladowanie przez okupanta niemieckiego na terenie parafii św. Wawrzyńca w Gnieźnie," Relacja Ks. Mieczysława Bogacza, kościół św. Wawrzyńca w Gnieźnie, September 13, 1945, AAG, zespół 0131 (AKM 1), syg. 2177; "Wiadomości o prześladowaniu kościoła katolickiego przez okupanta niemieckiego na terenie parafii farnej w Gnieźnie," IPN, GK 196/19, 182–85.

14. Birk to Frühwirth, June 26, 1942, Abschrift, IPN, GK 196/37, 65.

15. "Raport o sytuacji na Ziemiach Zachodnich Nr. 1/30.IX.42," in Mazur, Pietrowicz, and Rutowska, *Raporty*, 27.

16. Vermerk Meyers, November 18, 1942, IPN, GK 62/153, 225.

17. Meyer to Gestapo Litzmannstadt, Abschrift, November 18, 1942, IPN, GK 62/153, 225.

18. James E. Bjork, *Neither German nor Pole: Catholicism and National Indifference in a Central European Borderland* (Ann Arbor: University of Michigan Press, 2008), 7.

19. Bjork, 13.

20. See, for example, Pieter Judson, *Guardians of the Nation: Activists on the Language Frontiers of Imperial Austria* (Cambridge, MA: Harvard University Press, 2006) and Tara Zahra, *Kidnapped Souls: National Indifference and the Battle for Children in the Bohemian Lands, 1900–1948* (Ithaca, NY: Cornell University Press, 2008).

21. Chad Bryant, *Prague in Black: Nazi Rule and Czech Nationalism* (Cambridge: Harvard University Press, 2007), 3.

22. Bryant, 5.

23. Auszug aus dem Schreiben des Vorstandes der röm.kath.Kirche deutscher Nationalität im Reichsgau Wartheland an den Herrn Reichsstatthalter, October 1, 1943, Abschrift, IZ, syg. I-358, 8.

24. Breitinger, *Als Deutschenseelsorger*, 59.

25. Reichsstatthalter (Reischauer) to Landräte, Oberbürgermeister, Gestapo Posen and Litzmannstadt, November 17, 1944, APP, zespół 465, syg. 110, 340.

26. Reichsstatthalter to Landrat des Kreises Grätz, December 16, 1944, Abschrift, IPN GK 62/170/CD, 36.

27. On policies regulating use of cemeteries see Jastrząb, *Archidiecezja Poznańska*, 77–79.

28. "Verordnung über Friedhöfe im Reichsgau Wartheland vom 3. Oktober 1941," October 3, 1941, APP, zespół: 299, syg. 1176, microfilm 60028, 82.

29. Zapisek z przesłuchania p. Leona Wilińskiego, zawiadowcy cmentarza parafii Bożego Ciała na Dębcu w sprawie losów cmentarzy poznańskich podczas okupacji, August 27, 1948, IZ, Dok. III-1. According to a report of the Polish underground, when the German authorities "liquidated" the cemetery of Poznań's St. Martin parish, they forced Jews to get drunk, exhume the corpses, and rob the corpses of valuables, including gold teeth and fillings. "Raport o sytuacji na Ziemiach Zachodnich Nr. 3 (do 31. grudnia 1942 r.)," in Mazur, Pietrowicz, and Rutowska, *Raporty*, 65.

30. SD-Leitabschnitt Posen to Reichsstatthalter Abt. I/51, August 16, 1944, IPN, GK 62/153, 293.

31. Tagesbefehl Nr. 28 des Reichsstatthalters im Wartheland, November 7, 1939, in Łuczak, *Dyskryminacja Polaków*, 359–60; Schnellbrief, Reichsminister des Innern to Herrn Reichsstatthalter des Reichsgaues Posen, December 24, 1939, IPN, GK 196/16/CD, 1. The prohibition was reiterated in March of the following year with greater specificity, designating as German ("deutsche Volkszugehörige") those with German citizenship, Volksdeutsche settlers, and those individuals who had been admitted to the Deutsche Volksliste. Considered "Poles" were those who prior to the occupation had Polish citizenship and were not in any of the "German" categories above. Under the occupation, they were not citizens but subjects of the German Reich. See Greiser, Verordnung an die Herren Regierungspräsidenten in Posen, in Hohensalza, in Litzmannstadt, mit Überdrucken für die Landräte und Oberbürgermeister, March 21, 1941, Abschrift, YV, TR.17, file 12309, item 4068282, frame 594.

32. Meldungen aus dem Abschnittsgebiet, Sicherheitsdienst des Reichsführers-SS, SD-Abschnitt Litzmannstadt, August 25, 1941, IPN, GK 196/16/CD, 146–62.

33. Bericht über die Entwicklung der kirchlichen Lage im Reichsgau Wartheland (Abschnittsbereich Hohensalza), n.d., BAB, 58/7581, 26–32. Although the document is undated, its content indicates that it postdates mid-1940. Greiser was apparrently convinced that priests were undertaking this sort of anti-German propaganda. See "Bericht über die

Tagung der Reichstreuhänder der Arbeit der Ostgebiete in Posen am 9. Oktober 1941," October 9, 1941, IPN, GK 196/37, tom IV, 41–50. In July of the following year, a local party leader near Poznań expressed concern about the rising birth rate among Poles, citing a rumor that every Polish girl was supposed to have a child by age eighteen. "I assume," the official wrote, "that these instructions come from the Polish church." Ortsgruppenleiter Mundt, NSDAP, Gau Wartheland, Kreis Posen-Land, Ortsgruppe Schönherrnhausen to NSDAP Kreisleitung Posen-Land, July 8, 1942, Abschrift, IPN, GK 62/187/CD, 5.

34. Reichsstatthalter (Jäger) to Regierungspräsidenten Hohensalza, Litzmannstadt, Posen, September 10, 1941, IPN, GK 196/16/CD, 11; Breitinger, *Als Deutschenseelsorger*, 46–47; "A Note of His Eminence the Cardinal Secretary of State to the Foreign Minister of the Reich about the religious situation in the 'Warthegau' and in the other Polish provinces subject to Germany," March 2, 1943, document 3264-PS, in IMT, vol. 32, 93–105.

35. Reichsstatthalter, Vermerk, I/50, December 10, 1942, IPN, GK 196/16/CD, 22.

36. Reichsstatthalter (Mehlhorn) to Regierungspräsidenten, Landräte, Oberbürgermeister und Standesbeamten im Warthegau, Abschrift, May 27, 1943, IPN, GK 196/16/CD, 27.

37. Regierungspräsident Litzmannstadt (Moser), Volkspolitische Lagebericht für die Zeit vom 1. Mai bis 31 October 1942, November 23, 1942, IfZ, Fb 53, 56, 60.

38. Aufzeichnung über Kirchenpolitik in Polen, n.d., APP, zespół 299/1191, 9–15, here, 9. The undated document's content makes clear that it postdates March 14, 1940.

10

DREIZEHN PUNKTE

From the "Thirteen Points" to the "September Decree"

The measures outlined in the previous chapters illustrate the diverse motives behind Nazi church policy in the Reichsgau Wartheland, but they also attest to the improvised and experimental character of that policy—especially in the early months of the occupation. To address the lack of coherence in Warthegau Kirchenpolitik, and to provide a template for the future, Greiser and his supervisors in Berlin and Munich worked throughout 1940 and 1941 to develop and enact regulations that would dramatically change the financial and legal status of all "confessional organizations," both Catholic and Protestant, both "Polish" and "German." With respect to the Polish Catholic Church, these regulations were intended to restrict Poles' day-to-day engagement in the life of the church, to defend against the oppositional and nationalist traditions of Polish Catholic culture and devotion, to discourage contact between Germans and Poles, and to weaken any sense of community or conspiracy associated with the church. With respect to Christian denominations in general, whether Catholic or Protestant, the regulations were intended as templates for undermining the churches' financial and legal status after the war in the Reich as a whole.

It is worth emphasizing, if only briefly, that although antichurch measures were applied most aggressively to the Polish Catholic Church, all confessions and church bodies felt the severity of Nazi Kirchenpolitik in the "model Gau." The two main Protestant bodies in the Wartheland were the Evangelical United Church in Poland, which was overwhelmingly German in tradition and membership, and the Evangelical Augsburg Church, more confessionally bound to the Lutheran tradition with a large percentage of ethnic Poles among its members and clergy. There were several smaller groups as well, such as the Evangelical Lutheran Church of Western Poland (so-called *Altlutheraner*) and the Evangelical Reformed Church. Śmigiel has estimated that some 9 percent of the Warthegau's population was Protestant,[1] but it is important to bear in mind that because of settlement and expulsion, immigration and emigration, and the regime's discriminatory policies, membership in these bodies fluctuated dramatically over the course of the occupation. Persecution of the Evangelical Augsburg Church—regarded by the Nazis as an aggressively Polish-nationalist body—was thorough and, at times, brutal. More than half of its pastors claimed to be Polish, more than a quarter were arrested, and nearly one-fifth were incarcerated in concentration camps.[2] "German" Catholic parishes and the "German" Protestant bodies in the Warthegau, although not subject to the wholesale closure of churches and mass incarceration of priests, suffered as well.[3] Even if German Catholics and Protestants were spared the brutality of the Volkstumskampf as it was being applied to Polish Catholics and Polish Lutherans, they nonetheless experienced the rigors of Nazi Kirchenpolitik via discriminatory measures and legislation that were to pave the way for secularization in the future Reich.

The first step toward a coherent church policy in the Warthegau was the enactment of a policy to curb the rights of churches to collect contributions from their members. The established churches in Germany had traditionally relied for their financing on a complicated "church tax" adminstered by the state, but the annexation of Austria (subsequently renamed the "Ostmark") in 1938 offered the Nazi leadership the opportunity to change radically the system of financing the churches in this new region of the Reich. The Austrian decree of April 28, 1939, gave the Catholic and Protestant churches the right to collect contributions from adult members but did away with previous structures for financing the churches. It also required the churches to submit for approval by state authorities an annual budget and document their expenditures.[4] This law, approved by Hitler,[5] would serve as the basis for the new church "contribution law" (*Beitragsgesetz*) in the Wartheland.[6]

With the Austrian law as precedent, Greiser and his deputy Gauleiter August Jäger met on December 13, 1939, with Bormann's representative, Gerhard Klopfer, to discuss ecclesiastical matters in the Reichsgau Wartheland. It is significant that, according to a report on the meeting, Klopfer informed Greiser and Jäger "in detail about the current church-political situation and the exigencies that arise from it in the Warthegau." Thus, Greiser was not reporting to Bormann's office on church affairs in the Warthegau. Rather,

Bormann's office was issuing instructions. Greiser was receptive and stated that his preference would be for a "total separation of church and state in his Gau area,"[7] a theme he would echo in the years ahead.

To that end, the conferees discussed the possibility of instituting a "contribution law" modeled on the Austrian approach,[8] which would, in effect, reduce the churches' status from public corporations to private associations, disassociate them from the state, diminish their financial viability, and deny Hanns Kerrl's Ministry of Church Affairs any authority over them.[9] The "contribution law" in the Reichsgau Wartheland would, however, go a step further than its counterpart in the Ostmark, for in the case of Greiser's Gau, religious organizations would not automatically have the right to collect contributions; rather, the Reichsstatthalter would have the power to decide which religious communities and organizations would be permitted to do so. Should Kerrl attempt to interfere in this process, Greiser was to issue the law on his own authority ("*auf eigene Faust*"). The consent of the Ministry of the Interior and the Finance Ministry had already basically been secured, and Klopfer would work to gain the support of the Reich Chancellery as well.[10]

Three months passed before a "contribution law" was issued, and the process surrounding its development is significant in a number of ways. First, the archival documentation reveals that the Nazi leadership at the highest level was involved in the issue of church financing and church policy in general in the Warthegau. Bormann was especially active in the negotiations over the law's formulation,[11] while Himmler[12] and Heydrich[13] were involved as well.

Second, the development of a church contribution law occured over the objections of Kerrl, and its approval and promulgation were a means of further reducing his influence. Already at the December 12, 1939, meeting, Gerhard Klopfer stated that he had essentially already obtained approval for the law from the Ministries of the Interior and Finance, thereby making it difficult for Kerrl to withhold his consent.[14] In the months ahead, Kerrl complained repeatedly to Greiser, to Minister of the Interior Wilhelm Frick, and to others about the course that church policy in the Wartheland was taking, and especially about plans to sever ties between "religious organizations" there and the larger German church entities in the Altreich.[15] Remarkably, Greiser did not hesitate to scold the Reich minister harshly in his correspondence, citing the "powers invested in him [Greiser] by the Führer" and noting that he, Greiser, certainly had, "in developing the Gau, concerns other than determining the number of available clergy, the number of clergy who had fled, and the number of unoccupied parishes."[16] In a March 1940 letter, Himmler also dismissed Kerrl's objections, stating that the contribution law for the Warthegau would move forward because of "political necessity."[17]

Third, the "political necessity" to which Himmler referred related to the role of Kirchenpolitik in constructing a "model Gau." As Bormann had made clear on numerous occasions, the "church struggle" in the Warthegau was intimately connected to the ethno-racial struggle there. Writing to the Danzig-Westpreußen Gauleiter Albert Forster, he stated, "It is for me beyond all doubt that in the new eastern Gaus the Volkstumskampf cannot at all be separated from church-political questions."[18] This distinguished the Warthegau's situation from that in the Ostmark (where the Volkstumskampf took much different form), and made it especially necessary to grant Greiser the power to act with dispatch and of his own accord in church affairs.[19] Moreover, it is clear that the contribution law was to serve as a model. According to Bormann, it was all the more necessary to give Greiser the power to bypass Kerrl's objections to the law "because the decree desired by the Gauleiter is, after all, intended to accomplish a regulation of church contributions in the future."[20] The new contribution law, with its concurrent demotion of church bodies to "religious organizations" and "religious societies," provided in the Warthegau "the most appropriate opportunity, since the German Reich has no legal obligations there vis-à-vis the church, and must therefore create a new legal foundation."[21]

The "Decree on the Collection of Contributions by Religious Organizations and Religious Societies of 14 March 1940" limited the ability of churches (although the word was not used) to collect dues from adult members. It stated that only the Reichsstatthalter had the authority to empower such organizations to collect contributions, and that the budgets of religious organizations were subject to the evaluation and control of the Reichsstatthalter's office. Moreover, religious organizations were no longer entitled to subvention from the state, local communities, or other public entities. Like the decree for the Ostmark that preceded it, the contribution law for the Warthegau required churches to submit for approval by state authorities an annual budget and to document their expenditures. Beyond that, however, the president of each Warthegau Regierungsbezirk, or District, was entitled to reject budget items, to undertake audits of the churches' financial affairs, and to approve or reject any gifts or bequests.[22]

What may appear on the surface as little more than a bureaucratic dictate would have enormous consequences for the life of all churches in the Wartheland. Deliberations over the law demonstrated its importance for the Nazi leadership and illustrated the waning significance of Kerrl and his ministry, while its content and urgency revealed the significance of church policy for the development of the "model Gau." On a more basic level, restrictions on collection of contributions, combined with the confiscation of the Catholic Church's property already underway, dramatically undermined the church's financial viability. The contribution law, in combination with a later prohibition against collections during services,[23] would make the Polish Catholic clergy, from the bishop down to the village priest, dependent on gifts in kind or, in the case of some priests, work as wage laborers.

But the church contribution law also left questions open. Which "religious organizations" and "religious societies" would the Reichsstatthalter recognize? On what criteria would their membership be based? To what extent would they be organized on doctrinal, geographic, or ethnic lines? How would they be governed? Would their governance and organization be based on precedents established in the former Polish Republic? Would they have any relationship at all to church bodies in the Altreich or abroad or, in the case of the Catholic Church, to the papacy?

On June 17, 1940, three months after Greiser's order on "Collection of Contributions," Kurt Krüger, a representative of the Office of the Deputy Führer and senior advisor (*Oberregierungsrat*) for church affairs at NSDAP headquarters,[24] traveled to Poznań to discuss with Greiser's staff and a representative of the SD a variety of issues related to subsequent church policy in the experimental field that was the Warthegau and, in the longer term, the Reich as a whole. At this meeting, Krüger emphasized the need to revise the legal status of the churches in the Warthegau so that "after the war a Reich-wide transformation can be carried out." "It is precisely during the war," Krüger reported in the aftermath of the meeting, "that much can be accomplished in the Warthegau that would be much more difficult after war's end." The participants in the discussion agreed on a number of principles and proposals, among them, that churches in the Warthegau should have no relations with organizations outside its boundaries, that it should no longer be possible for people to be "born into" membership in a religious community, that those desiring membership be required to provide a formal and legal declaration thereof, that all religious instruction in schools be prohibited, that collections of money during services be prohibited, that

Germans and Poles no longer be allowed membership in the same religious organization, and that all religious orders in the Reichsgau Wartheland be dissolved.[25]

These principles were developed in the weeks ahead, and when Greiser's advisor for church affairs, Wilhelm Dudzus, who was also employed by the SD,[26] met on July 10 with representatives of the consistory of the Posen Evangelical Church, he presented a programmatic list that became known as the "Thirteen Points" to guide church policy in the Warthegau. Dudzus's list stipulated the following:

1. Churches are to be accorded the legal status of juridical persons under private law but not under public law—that is, they will no longer exist as public corporations but as private associations.
2. Leadership of the churches will no longer reside in public authorities or offices.
3. Churches will be financed not by taxes but by members' contributions or dues.
4. The Evangelical churches in the Warthegau will maintain a spiritual relationship "in theory" ("*ideell*") to German Evangelical churches, but they will be organized as independent entities.
5. Adult church members responsible for providing contributions will be required to register in writing as members.
6. In the interest of education and upbringing in the spirit of "community" (*Gemeinschaft*), confessional associations for women, men, and youth will be forbidden.
7. A subsequent law regulating religious associations will uphold the "nationality principle," achieving a total ecclesiastical separation between Germans and Poles, in both the Protestant and Catholic Churches.
8. Religious instruction in schools is not to be tolerated.
9. A new regulation regarding collection of offerings in churches will be issued, with the intent of making such collections more difficult.
10. Religious organizations will not be permitted to own property such as buildings, houses, fields, or cemeteries.
11. Religious organizations will not be permitted to engage in social welfare activities, which are controlled by the NSV.
12. Religious orders will be abolished.
13. There will be no theological studies at Posen University, clergy for the religious associations must come from the Warthegau, and they should have other professions.

Dudzus related the above principles not in written form but orally. Documentation of them is therefore sparse, and the above list relies on and integrates several sources.[27] The basic source for all versions of the Thirteen Points are notes from the meeting by Erich Nehring, president of the Posen Evangelical Consistory, and his commentary on these notes reveals much about the place of the Polish Catholic Church in the regime's plans. Nehring stated, for example, that according to Dudzus, the Catholic Church was acting in opposition to the Nazi regime, and that Cardinal Hlond, the Polish primate, was working in Rome and receiving support from the papacy. Therefore, Dudzus had argued, the Catholic Church in the Wartheland would have to be independent from the Vatican in the future. According to Nehring, this was also the regime's goal for the Catholic Church in Germany as a whole. In addition, Nehring noted that a major confiscation of land from the Catholic Church in the Warthegau was in the offing. Finally, he cited Dudzus's recurring claims that these plans were not the result of a hostile position toward the church but were measures to benefit the *Volksgemeinschaft*, and that they did not originate in the Reichsstatthalter's office but elsewhere. Exactly where, however, was not clear.[28]

Never published as formal and official policy, the Thirteen Points nonetheless served as a guide for subsequent discussions on church affairs, as at a meeting between Krüger and Greiser that took place in Poznań only ten days later, on July 20, 1940. Called for the purpose of addressing "further measures regarding confessional affairs in the Wartheland," the meeting was also attended by members of Greiser's staff and, significantly, Albert Hartl, a former Catholic priest in the service of the Reich Security Main Office (RSHA),[29] as well as a certain Dr. Fruhwirth from the Deputy Führer's office. A fourteen-page memorandum describing the proceedings, written by Hartl and Fruhwirth, is especially informative, as it reveals a basic synergy with respect to church policy between the party leadership, SD, and Warthegau administration. Although the Thirteen Points are not referred to as such, Hartl's and Fruhwirth's notes suggest that they provided a basis for discussion of how to implement the measures and transform church-state relations in both the short and long term. The meeting considered measures against both Catholic and Protestant bodies in the Warthegau, but it is clear that the Polish Catholic Church took center stage. This was evident in, for example, the emphasis placed on the anti-Polish Volkstumskampf as a guide for church policy in the years ahead, whether with respect to the language used to describe church institutions, to the prohibition against membership in religious associations based on birth, to the "nationality principle" as a basis for separation of Polish and German Catholics, or to even funding for the maintenence of Polish churches.[30]

Several scholars have contended that the Thirteen Points were developed in the Nazi Party headquarters,[31] and although it is likely that Munich was the source, evidence of this is not entirely clear. What is clear, however, is that Martin Bormann was frequently in consultation with Greiser over church matters in the Warthegau,[32] that Hitler had approved of the notion of special church regulations in the Warthegau,[33] and that Kurt Krüger, at the June 17 meeting cited above, had in his sights a "Reich-wide transformation" after the war—a transformation for which regulations in the Warthegau could serve as a model. Furthermore, Hitler himself is reported to have envisioned the Warthegau playing a leading role in the secularization of German society, stating, "Therefore, as regards future relations between State and Church, it is highly satisfactory from our point of view that in nearly half the Reich, negotiations can now be conducted by the appropriate Reichsstatthalter, unfettered by the clauses of the central Concordat.[34] This means that in each district the Gauleiter can, according to the degree of emancipation acquired by the population of his Gau, lead the people forward step by step in the sense that we desire."[35]

Efforts in the spring and summer of 1940 to regulate the financial and legal status of the Warthegau churches and restrict their associational life point to three main conclusions. First, when viewed in conjunction with the individual measures taken against Polish Catholics and their clergy, these efforts should be understood as arising from a combination of Nazi national, political, economic, and racial imperatives. In other words, a narrow interpretation of the Nazi measures as merely an aspect of German nationality policy or an example of administrative restructuring misses the diverse motives for the regime's Kirchenpolitik as a weapon in the broader Volkstumskampf waged in occupied Polish territory.

Second, it is clear that the Nazi leadership was eager for the Wartheland, in keeping with its role as a "model Gau," to function as a testing and proving ground for policies hostile toward the churches that could be implemented after the war in the Reich as a whole. Ambitious leadership along with the Warthegau's unique status as an annexed territory predominantly populated by allegedly racially inferior Polish Catholics offered motive, opportunity, and means for a radical revision of traditional church-state relations and the status of Christian denominations in society. Warthegau

Kirchenpolitik was to provide both praxis and precedent for the application of such measures in the postwar Reich.[36]

Moreover, it is worth emphasizing that the measures taken in 1940, like the Thirteen Points, were directed against the churches both Catholic and Protestant, both "Polish" and "German." On the one hand, the "nationality principle" and demands of the broader Volkstumskampf were essential to antichurch policy in the Warthegau, especially as they were applied to Catholic Poles and members of the Evangelical Augsburg Church; on the other hand, minority German Catholics and Protestants also were subject—albeit to a lesser degree—to the Reichsstatthalter's restrictive and coercive policies. This was consistent with the regime's long-term goal of an ethnically German and racially homogeneous postwar Reich in which the Christian churches had no relevance whatsoever, and suggests as well that the measures against the Warthegau churches were, in effect, battlefield tactics in the service of a grand strategy of radical secularization and eventual de-Christianization.

Third, the pace and character of the legal restrictions illustrate that Kirchenpolitik in the Warthegau was *not* as linear and resolute as it may at first glance appear. It is commonly assumed that the Nazi regime was aiming, at least in the long run, for the total destruction of the Polish church, and that church policy was consistently and efficiently implemented under the clear direction of NSDAP headquarters in Munich and the Reich Chancellery in Berlin. The evidence, however, presents a more complex picture, for it appears that the Gau administration remained unconvinced of destruction of the Polish Catholic Church as its ultimate goal, that some policies were, and remained, open to debate, and that Arthur Greiser and local Warthegau officials, although hardly independent of party control, had considerable decision-making power over church affairs.

Hartl and Fruhwirth's report of July 20, 1940, reveals, as noted above, much about the direction and implementation of policy, and about the basic synergy between Gau and party in policy formation. The report suggests that Nazi Party and Warthegau officials had developed a rough blueprint for the future, but at the same time, it also reveals how the deliberations at that meeting showed a lack of unanimity over church policy and a degree of indecision over how to proceed in the years ahead. Participants in the July meeting differed, for example, over the issue of ecclesiastical leadership. The necessity of separating the Catholic Church into German and Polish entities was clear to all, but some advocated a single German bishop to supervise the two churches, while others supported the idea of appointing both a Polish and a German bishop to lead their separate bodies. Greiser's advisors, Wilhelm Dudzus and Herbert Mehlhorn, were of the opinion that a single German bishop would violate the segregative practices of the Nationalitätenprinzip. Hartl and Krüger saw—perhaps with a view to the future—the likely conflicts and struggles faced by a single German bishop attempting to shepherd both Poles and Germans as a desirable outcome that would, in effect, destabilize the church. Greiser stated his preference for a single German bishop supported by Polish and German vicars general, but the Gauleiter elected to delay a final decision on the matter, which was, significantly, left to him to resolve.[37]

Whether or not to allow Polish churches to collect contributions from parishioners was a further matter of contention. According to the March 1940 dictate from Greiser, religious organizations in the Warthegau could, with the Reichstatthalter's approval and the accompanying restrictions, solicit regular contributions from their members.[38] Greiser, Dudzus, and Mehlhorn were in favor of continuing to allow the churches to do so, while the ideologically more rigorous Krüger was opposed to such a privilege, lest "the Polish clergy turn into nationalist leaders, which could lead to a strengthening of the Polish Volkstumskampf."[39] According to Dudzus, it would be appropriate for Polish parishes to use such contributions for the maintenance of their church buildings—a responsibility that would otherwise fall on the Gau administration. Krüger, by contrast, saw no need to renovate Polish churches. If they were in a state of dangerous disrepair, they should, he argued, be closed or destroyed, for it was only while these churches were still in Polish hands that the authorities could tear them down for the purpose of erecting "National Socialist Community Houses." Once German settlers arrived, Krüger maintained, they would begin to use the churches and, in effect, defend the buildings against the authorities.[40] Like the question of episcopal leadership, the matter remained unresolved, and was, with the blessing of the Office of the Deputy Führer (most likely Bormann), handed over to Greiser.

Both the issue of church leadership and the disagreement over financing Polish churches illustrate Greiser's central role. Although often reliant on the consent of his superiors in formulating church policy, the Gauleiter emerges here as a motor rather than a mere instrument of policy. He was given authority to resolve differences between his Gau and the party, and he had the power to act on his own.

The July 20, 1940, meeting also revealed disagreement over the most fundamental of issues: whether or not it was in the interests of the Reich to allow the Polish Roman Catholic Church in the Warthegau to survive at all, and if so, in what form. This is particularly interesting in light of the common view that the regime was bent on the church's destruction, and it points to the centrality of the alleged Polish-Catholic nexus in Nazi ideology and policy, for here the survival of Protestant and Catholic churches for Warthegau Germans was not at issue. Dudzus and Mehlhorn argued that it was, in fact, in the interest of the Nazi state to maintain in some form the influence of the Catholic Church among the Polish population, for the church provided a "foothold" for the Pole, who would otherwise be susceptible to criminal influences.[41] In addition, the Polish-Catholic nexus, understood in Nazi ideology as a constituent element of Polish ethnicity, was one way to distinguish the Poles from the Germans who, ideally, should have understood themselves as atheist or simply "believers in God" (*Gottgläubige*).[42]

Again, the meeting's minutes point to contrasting views. The traditional and negative equation of Polishness with Catholicism had never, it was argued, in any way encouraged German Catholics (who were, at least in theory, anti-Polish), to give up their faith. Rather, the exposure to Polish Catholicism had undermined German Catholics' identity as Germans. More significantly, Catholicism had allegedly for centuries been the ideological "backbone" of Polish identity vis-à-vis the Germans, and any weakening of Polish *Catholic* identity would therefore mean a corresponding and desired weakening of Polish *national* identity. In the end, the minutes of the meeting stated that the goal was not to "take the Catholic Church from the Poles" or to turn them into *Gottgläubige* but to "undermine the power and influence of the Catholic Church" while, at the same time, "recognizing freedom of conscience" for Poles. In an interesting comparison, the situation in the Warthegau was likened to that in a colonial context, where allegedly the same logic allowed for the continued existence of religious organizations but rejected any form of "*Negermission*" as potentially strengthening the presence of Christianity among colonial native peoples.[43] The significance of this entire conversation is striking, for it appears that even among the Polish Catholic Church's most ardent opponents, there was a willingness to let the church survive, if only temporarily and in dramatically diminished form.

Less than a year after the establishment of the Reichsgau Wartheland, the conferees appeared to be approaching a turning point in policy toward the Polish Catholic Church. From the beginning of the occupation through the summer of 1940, Nazi measures had been restrictive and, at times, brutal, and they reflected the perceived role of the Polish church in the broader Volkstumskampf waged in the "proving ground" of the "new German East." They were also a testimony to the ambition and resolve of both the party leadership and its Gauleiter in Poznań. At the same time, however, there is in this narrative a lack of clear direction, reflected in institutional and administrative incoherence that, in effect, postponed the most aggressive initiatives in Nazi church policy until the fall of 1941.

The reasons for the delay appear various and diverse. One scholar has referred to the period as a "phase of stagnation" in policy resulting in part from the SD's preoccupation with affairs in the recently conquered areas in Western Europe.[44] An alternative explanation is evident in correspondence from the middle of 1941 between the Plenipotentiary for the Four-Year Plan (Göring), Reich Chancellery, Ministry of the Interior, and Bormann's office—correspondence that indicates concern about plans to change the status of the churches in the Warthegau only, rather than in all the Incorporated Territories at once.[45] Catherine Epstein, citing a lack of bureaucratic and institutional unanimity, contends that it proved impossible for Greiser to issue a comprehensive decree to regulate confessional matters because of objections from the Ministry of Justice and Reich Chancellery.[46] These ministries indeed voiced their opposition, as did Kerrl's Ministry of Church Affairs.[47] Without dismissing these broader political, bureaucratic, and administrative concerns, it is important to note the factors "on the ground" in the Warthegau that influenced the timing of measures against the churches, among them its role as a "model Gau," the complex demographic and political shifts there, and concern over public responses to any aggressive antichurch policy.

A lengthy memorandum authored by Greiser in the fall of 1940 gives a sense of what may have been standing in the way of yet more radical measures against the church, and also offers insight into what one might call Greiser's "philosophy of religion."[48] Confessional differences, according to Greiser, had for generations undermined German unity, and confession and church matters had exercised an inordinate influence over the *Volk*, overshadowing questions of ethnicity, nation, politics, or state.[49] National

Socialism, he argued, was the only valid German *Weltanschauung*, for "National Socialism exclusively is, from now on, the single life-determining and life-shaping power in the Warthegau." The new regulations for the churches would, then, demonstrate that confession and church could no longer provide the primary point of orientation for Germans; rather, they should instead be a private, incidental (*nebensächliche*) matter to the individual.[50]

In the memorandum Greiser also referred extensively to the measures outlined in the Thirteen Points and his office's past (much had already been accomplished, he claimed) and future efforts to implement them. Moreover, he cited the need for flexibility in the face of the dramatic population shifts in the Gau. Any response to the current church situation would, he argued, have to take into consideration developments associated with the program of mass expulsion, relocation, and new colonization. Between the fall of 1939 and the spring of 1941, the German authorities expelled to the General Government some three hundred thousand people from the Reichsgau Wartheland, the overwhelming majority of them ethnic Poles; by mid-1942, some three hundred thousand ethnic Germans from various regions in Eastern Europe had been relocated to the Gau.[51] These dramatic population changes of course affected the confessional composition of the Wartheland as much as the ethnic composition, for the overwhelming majority of expelled Poles were Roman Catholics, and the majority of the German settlers were Protestants. Many of these Volksdeutsche had been promised the freedom to practice their religion of choice in the Wartheland, and most expected to be able to do so. The Warthegau administration did not, however, wish to encourage this, which raised the issue of strategy and timing for implementing sweeping regulatory measures.

"In my opinion," Greiser wrote in his memorandum, "the target date for the basic finalization and practical execution of the planned new regulations will be immediately between the initiation of the final composition and distribution of the population on the one hand, and the consolidation of confessional tendencies in the individual German groups on the other. This moment may well by now have arrived."[52] In other words, these wide-ranging regulations should, Greiser believed, be implemented after final population movements had begun but before German settlers in the Wartheland had had the opportunity to reestablish in their new home their religious culture and practices, in effect presenting them with a fait accompli. Greiser also wrote, however, that it was necessary to remain flexible and subordinate any new regulations to the general political “necessities and expediencies” in the Gau.[53]

The “necessities and expediencies” to which Greiser referred undoubtedly took into account a variety of factors: population movements, the Wartheland’s role as a model Gau, the unique challenges of Germanization there, and the possible reactions of the majority Polish and minority German populations. With respect to public response, Greiser outlined two possible approaches to implementing the changes he desired: “force and decree” or “persuasion and agreement.” The former, he maintained, was to be used on the Poles, and the latter on the Germans, but in reverse order. Were the authorities to begin by imposing measures against the “Polish” churches by “force and decree,” or in Greiser’s words, “playing all the trump cards against the Poles,” they would run the risk of alarming and alienating the German population. A safer path would therefore be to undertake negotiations with the leadership of the established German churches and, after stabilizing affairs with the Germans in the Gau, implement aggressive measures against the Poles.[54]

The memorandum also reveals that Greiser’s course was, in fact, somewhat more “moderate” than that advocated by the higher authorities to whom it was addressed—likely Bormann or his assistant for educational and church affairs in the Office of the Deputy Führer, Kurt Krüger.[55] The need for flexibility, appropriate timing for the implementation of anti-church measures, and concern over ethnic Germans’ responses to them are all indicators of Greiser’s restraint. In addition, Greiser made clear his plans to sanction five new “confessional organizations” in the Gau according to the “nationality principle”: Protestant and Catholic bodies for the Germans, Protestant and Catholic bodies for the Poles, and an orthodox body for the Ukrainians.[56] Greiser also left open the possibility of offering state subsidies to German religious organizations,[57] and he made a case for allowing Polish religious organizations to collect contributions from parishioners, despite arguments to the contrary voiced by Krüger in July.[58] A structured system of funding the Polish churches would, according to Greiser, allow for greater control and would discourage informal financial support or gifts in kind to the clergy.[59]

Greiser’s relative moderation in these areas points to an approach that was perhaps less “hard line” and ideological than that of his superiors, but it should not in any way be understood as support for the churches. The Gauleiter’s goal of bringing about the churches’ demise remained consistent, the measures he continued to implement were often brutal, and if he showed at this stage what appears to be some degree of restraint, it was simply to bring church policy in line with the "necessities and expediencies" characteristic of his Gau.

Several of the goals and restrictions outlined in the Thirteen Points had been implemented over the course of 1940, but it was not until September 1941, more than a year after the summer 1940 meetings, that Greiser issued a clear directive regulating the legal status of church bodies in the Warthegau: "Decree No. 246 on Religious Associations and Religious Societies in the Reichsgau Wartheland of 13 September 1941." This directive did not refer to the Thirteen Points specifically (they had never been made public), but by redefining and diminishing the churches' legal status, it ratified indirectly the measures taken thus far, and facilitated the implementation of others. In the words of one Nazi official, the Thirteen Points "found their reflection" in the September 13 decree,[60] which called for the establishment of four new "religious associations" in the Warthegau. The decree, issued simply and rather vaguely "on the basis of authorization granted,"[61] stated that henceforth, to be recognized as juridical entities under private law (as opposed to public law), were (1) the Posen Evangelical Church of German Nationality in the Wartheland, (2) the Litzmannstadt Evangelical Church of German Nationality in the Wartheland, (3) the Evangelical Lutheran Church of German Nationality in the Western Wartheland, and (4) the Roman Catholic Church of German Nationality in the Reichsgau Wartheland. The order also legally codified a number of the goals outlined in the Thirteen Points by limiting new membership in religious organizations to German adult residents of the Warthegau who officially registered with the local authorities, by maintaining strict separation of Poles and Germans in worship life, by requiring the Reichsstatthalter's approval of members of church boards, and by severing any legal, financial, or administrative relationships between these bodies and church organizations outside the Warthegau, whether the German Protestant bodies in the Altreich, or the Vatican.[62]

Accurately described by Epstein as "a milestone in the Nazis' anti-church campaign," the decree "suggested how the Nazis would eventually 'de-church' German society."[63] It created, in the place of established churches, private religious associations that no longer had any legal or financial relationship to the state, and it gave Greiser sweeping powers over these bodies. Significantly, the order also stated that other religious associations (such as those bodies, both Catholic and Protestant, that would be designated for Poles) could be recognized under private law as the Reichsstatthalter saw fit.[64] Greiser never took this step, however, and according to historian John S. Conway, the omission of a Catholic Church for Poles from the September 13 ordinance "clearly foreshadowed the eventual abolition of Polish Church life in its entirety."[65]

To some observers, it may well have appeared that this was in the offing, for the day after the Gauleiter's decree was issued, he gave an aggressively antireligious speech to a gathering at the Gau Office for Educational Affairs. Gone was Greiser's restraint of the previous year, for in emphasizing the central role of church policy in the broader Volkstumskampf being waged in the Warthegau, Greiser appeared to be preparing educators and officials for a severe intensification of the campaign against the churches, and especially the Catholic Church. In his speech he stressed the need to proceed with the struggle against the churches in a manner much different from that in the Altreich. Party comrades had not, according to Greiser, received their authority from Hitler in order to permit the continued existence in their Gau of the same sources of trouble (i.e., the churches) that continued to exist in the Altreich. On the contrary, it was necessary to do away with them in the virgin territory that was the Warthegau. Although it might be appropriate to exhibit a certain tolerance toward Germans in the Altreich who remained in the churches, "there is no need whatsoever," he argued, "to take this into consideration here in the midst of the Volkstumskampf, for it matters not to us whether or not the Poles have a church, priest, or anything else." "Where wood is planed," he succinctly concluded, "shavings will fall."[66]

Notes

1. Śmigiel, *Die katholische Kirche*, 13–14.

2. Kloczowski, *History*, 301.

3. The most thorough treatment of German Protestant bodies in the Warthegau is Gürtler's *Nationalsozialismus*.

4. "Gesetz über die Erhebung von Kirchenbeiträgen im Lande Österreich," *Gesestzblatt für das Land Österreich*, no. 111, April 28, 1939 (Wien: Staatsdruckerei Wien, 1939), 1875.

5. Bormann to Forster, February 2, 1940, Abschrift, USHMM, RG 15.007M, reel 38, 465, 28–29.

6. According to Gürtler, the contribution law in the Reichsgau Sudetenland also served as a basis for the Warthegau decree. See Gürtler, *Nationalsozialismus*, 44.

7. "Bericht über die Dienstreise nach Posen am 12.12.39," BAB, R 58/7578, 30. A memorandum issued following the meeting also indicates that present at the meeting was SS-Sturmbannführer Albert Hartl, who may have been the author of this report. N.a., Vermerk, December 15, 1939, BAB, R 58/7578, 6. Attempting to absolve himself from charges that he had participated in the persecution of the churches in occupied Poland, Hartl later claimed in a postwar deposition that he was present at only one meeting with Greiser regarding church policy, and that this meeting concerned the issue of member contributions to the churches. It is clear, however, that Hartl was present not only at the December 1939 meeting but also at a meeting on July 20, 1940, discussed below. Polish Military Mission for the Investigation of War Crimes in Europe Attached to War Crimes Branch USFET APO 633 US Army (Pęchalski) to Głównej Komisji Badania Zbrodni Niemieckich w Polsce, May 29, 1946, IPN, GK 174/30, 132.

8. Reichsstatthalter to Reichsinnenminister, December 28, 1939, document 323.I., in Grünzinger, *Dokumente zur Kirchenpolitik*, 775.

9. Epstein, *Model Nazi*, 222.

10. "Bericht über die Dienstreise nach Posen am 12.12.39," BAB, R 58/7578, 30–31. On Kerrl's objections to the law and the circumvention of his authority, see Kerrl to Reichsminister des Innern, April 3, 1940, BAB, R 58/7468, 6.

11. See, for example, Bormann to Greiser, December 29, 1939, USHMM, RG 15.007M, reel 47, 578, 35–36; Bormann to Forster, December 29, 1939, Abschrift, USHMM RG 15.007M, reel 38, 465, 4–5; Bormann to Reichsminister des Innern, January 17, 1940, Durchschrift, USHMM, RG 15.007M, reel 47, 578, 66–67; Bormann to Forster, February 2, 1940, Abschrift, USHMM RG 15.007M, reel 38, 465, 28–29.

12. Bormann to Himmler, February 2, 1940, USHMM RG 15.007M, reel 38, 465, 26–27; Himmler to Greiser, February 14, 1940, USHMM RG 15.007M, reel 47, 581, 38.

13. "Bericht über die Dienstreise nach Posen am 12.12.39," BAB, R 58/7578, 30; Heydrich to Stabsleiter des Generalbevollmächtigten für die Reichsverwaltung, Staatsskretär Stuckart, February 28, 1940, BAB R 58/7468, 13; Heydrich to Himmler, April 16, 1940, BAB, R 58/7468, 11.

14. "Bericht über die Dienstreise nach Posen am 12.12.39," BAB, R 58/7578, 31.

15. Vermerk, June 21, 1940, BAB R 43-II/170, 25; Kerrl to Frick, April 3, 1940, BAB, R 58/7468, 6.

16. Greiser to Kerrl, February 5, 1940, BAB, R 58/7581, 40. Greiser's irritation likely refers to a request from Kerrl for detailed information about clergy in the Warthegau. See Reichsminister für die kirchlichen Angelegenheiten to Reichsführer-SS, Entwurf, February 3, 1940, BAB, R 5101/22185, 102.

17. Himmler to Kerrl, March 11, 1940, USHMM, RG 15.007M, reel 47, 578, 101.

18. Bormann to Forster, December 29, 1939, Abschrift, USHMM, RG 15.007M, reel 38, 465, 4–5.

19. Bormann to Greiser, December 29, 1939, USHMM, RG 15.007M, reel 47, 578, 35–36; Bormann to Himmler, February 2, 1940, USHMM, RG 15.007M, reel 38, 465, 26–27.

20. Bormann to Herrn Reichsminister des Innern, February 23, 1940, IfZ, MA 544, 872–73.

21. Stellungnahme zu dem Entwurf des GBV betr. Regelung der Kirchenverhältnisse im Warthegau, June 13, 1940, USHMM, RG 15.007M, reel 38, 468, 27.

22. "Verordnung über die Erhebung von Beiträgen durch religiöse Vereinigungen und Religionsgesellschaften vom 14. März 1940," in Reichsgau Wartheland, *Verordnungsblatt des Reichsstatthalters im Reichsgau Wartheland*, no. 13 (March 16, 1940): 229–30.

23. Mehlhorn to Bishop van Blericq, February 6, 1941, AAP, zespół 133, syg. OK 122.

24. On Krüger, see Ernst Klee, *Das Personenlexikon zum Dritten Reich: Wer war was vor und nach 1945* (Frankfurt am Main: Fischer Taschenbuch Verlag, 2003), 344.

25. Stab der Stellvertreter des Führers (Krüger) to SS-Stürmbannführer Hartl, June 17, 1940, BAB, R58/7581, 55–59.

26. Wolfgang Dierker, *Himmlers Glaubenskrieger: der Sicherheitsdienst der SS und seine Religionspolitik, 1933–1941*, Veröffentlichungen der Kommission für Zeitgeschichte, series B, vol. 92 (Paderborn: Ferdinand Schöningh, 2003), 510.

27. A version of the Thirteen Points, which is based on documents from the Evangelische Oberkirchenrat, Berlin, and was reproduced in Joachim Beckmann, ed., *Kirchliches Jahrbuch für die Evangelische Kirche in Deutschland, 1933–1944* (Gütersloh: C. Bertelsmann, 1948), 453, appears in Gürtler's appendix, *Nationalsozialismus*, 200–201. Conflating the Thirteen Points with the church contribution law discussed above, this publication erroneously states that they were issued by Greiser as law on March 14, 1940. Śmigiel reproduces the same version in *Die katholische* Kirche, 71–72. The list provided above is based predominantly on the notes of Erich Nehring, president of the Posen Evangelical Consistory, and what appears to be his confidential set of "talking points" prepared for the consistory. See Nehring, Protokoll, Abschrift, July 10, 1940, USHMM, RG 15.007M, reel 15, 216, 1–2; "Material für die Beratungen im Konsistorium," n.d., USHMM, RG 15.007M, reel 15, 216, 3. Interestingly, these two documents, apparently meant for internal use by the consistory, were located by the author in files of the RSHA. For two different versions of the Thirteen Points, as well as additional documentation relevant to their formulation and use, see documents 333.I, 333.II, 333.III, and 333.IV, in Grünzinger, *Dokumente zur Kirchenpolitik*, 807–19.

28. Nehring, Protokoll, Abschrift, July 10, 1940, USHMM, RG 15.007M, reel 15, 216, 1–2.

29. On Hartl see Spicer, *Hitler's Priests*, 254; Klee, *Das Personenlexikon*, 228–29; Hansjakob Stehle, "Ein Eiferer in der Gesellschaft von Mördern," *Die Zeit*, October 7, 1983.

30. Vermerk über die Besprechung [of July 20, 1940] mit Gauleiter Greiser über die konfessionellen Maßnahmen im Reichsgau Wartheland, August 13–14, 1940, Abschrift, BAB, R58/7581, 61–74. The meeting described took place on July 20, 1940; the memorandum describing the meeting is dated by the authors Frühwirth and Hartl, August 13 and 14, respectively.

31. Gürtler claims, "Die Herkunft der '13 Punkte' läßt sich z.Zt. nicht belegen, doch kann mit großer Wahrscheinlichkeit angenommen werden, daß sie der Parteikanzlei entstammen." Gürtler, *Nationalsozialismus*, 47n11. See also Stasiewski, 53; Śmigiel, *Die katholische Kirche*, 70; Breitinger, *Als Deutschenseelsorger*, 51; Conway, *Nazi Persecution*, 316–17; Epstein, *Model Nazi*, 224; and Grünzinger, *Dokumente zur Kirchenpolitik*, 807n1. Although not contesting this view, Dierker describes the Thirteen Points as "nothing other than the well-known church-political program of the Security Service and Staff of the Deputy Führer." Dierker, *Himmlers Glaubenskrieger*, 519.

32. The memorandum on the July 20, 1940 meeting between Greiser, Krüger, and others points several times to the engagement of Bormann's office in these issues. Vermerk über die Besprechung mit Gauleiter Greiser über die konfessionellen Maßnahmen im Reichsgau Wartheland, August 13–14, 1940, Abschrift, BAB, R58/7581, 61–74.

33. Alfred Rosenberg, *Das politische Tagebuch Alfred Rosenbergs, 1934/35 und 1939/40* (München: Deutscher Taschenbuch Verlag, 1964), 148.

34. Hitler refers here to the 1933 Reichsconcordat between the Holy See and Nazi Germany.

35. Adolf Hitler, entry 248, July 4, 1942, in *Hitler's Table Talk 1941–1944: His Private Conversations* (New York: Enigma, 2000), 416. Following this comment, Hitler noted his admiration for the regulation of church-state relations in the United States.

36. This became evident to church and party leaders in the Altreich, despite the fact that neither the Thirteen Points nor the details of church policy in the Warthegau were intended to be advertised to the German public at large. For example, in November 1940 a party leader in Limburg publically stated that there would be no Evangelical or Catholic churches in the "Germany of the New Order." For evidence that the disappearance of the churches was the Führer's will, he argued, one needed only to consider the churches' situation in the Warthegau. The Bavarian Lutheran pastor Wolfgang Niederstrasser argued in a June 1942 sermon that the "Thirteen Death Sentences" developed for the Reichsgau Wartheland would be put into practice in the Reich at large. See Grünzinger, *Dokumente zur Kirchenpolitik*, 818n14. In December 1940, Albert Stohr, bishop of Mainz, wrote to Pope Pius XII expressing his concern that party leaders and representatives had been speaking out about the Warthegau as a model for the future of church affairs in the Reich as a whole. Stohr to Pius XII, December 1, 1940, document 3*, in Volk, *Akten deutscher Bischöfe*, vol. 6, 876. See also Zipfel, *Kirchenkampf*, 257.

37. Vermerk über die Besprechung mit Gauleiter Greiser über die konfessionellen Maßnahmen im Reichsgau Wartheland, August 13–14, 1940, Abschrift, BAB, R58/7581, 65–67. See also Dierker, *Himmlers Glaubenskrieger*, 519.

38. "Verordnung über die Erhebung von Beiträgen durch religiöse Vereinigungen und Religionsgesellschaften vom 14. März 1940," in Reichsgau Wartheland, *Verordnungsblatt des Reichsstatthalters im Reichsgau Wartheland*, no. 13 (March 16, 1940), 229–30.

39. Vermerk über die Besprechung mit Gauleiter Greiser über die konfessionellen Maßnahmen im Reichsgau Wartheland, August 13–14, 1940, Abschrift, BAB, R58/7581, 67–69.

40. Vermerk über die Besprechung mit Gauleiter Greiser über die konfessionellen Maßnahmen im Reichsgau Wartheland, August 13–14, 1940, Abschrift, BAB, R58/7581, 68.

41. The notion of the church as social anchor for the Poles was subsequently echoed by August Jäger in a position paper submitted to the Reich Security Main Office, which was largely a revision and elaboration of the Thirteen Points. "When viewed as a whole," he argued, "confessional organization of the Poles appears desirable. Given the Polish mentality, the prohibition of confessional organizations would lead unconditionally to conspiracy." Reichsstatthalter (Jäger) to Reichssicherheitshauptamt, Berlin, December 18, 1940, document 343, in Grünzinger, *Dokumente zur Kirchenpolitik*, 837.

42. Some scholars translate the term *Gottgläubig* as, simply, "deist." See, for example, Evans, *Third Reich in Power*, 252.

43. Vermerk über die Besprechung mit Gauleiter Greiser über die konfessionellen Maßnahmen im Reichsgau Wartheland, August 13–14, 1940, Abschrift, BAB, R58/7581, 69.

44. Dierker, *Himmlers Glaubenskrieger*, 520.

45. Vermerk betr. Kirchenverhältnisse im Warthegau, June 11, 1941, Abschrift, IfZ, Fa 199/51, 14–17.

46. Epstein, *Model Nazi*, 224; see also Vermerk, July 5, 1940, BAB, R 43 II/170, 41–42, which concerns general opposition to implementing of the Thirteen Points; as well as Generalbevollmächtigter für die Reichsverwaltung, July 26, 1940, BAB, R 43II/170, 50.

47. Vermerk, June 21, 1940, BAB, R 43II/170, 25.

48. Greiser, Vermerk über Kirchenverhältnisse im Warthegau, n.d., USHMM, RG 15.007, reel 47, 581, 79–95. Although the memorandum is not dated, its content reveals that it postdates October 4, 1940.

49. Greiser, Vermerk über Kirchenverhältnisse im Warthegau, n.d., USHMM, RG 15.007, reel 47, 581, 80–81.

50. Greiser, Vermerk über Kirchenverhältnisse im Warthegau, n.d., USHMM, RG 15.007, reel 47, 581, 82.

51. Rutherford, *Prelude*, 9, 71.

52. Greiser, Vermerk über Kirchenverhältnisse im Warthegau, n.d., USHMM, RG 15.007, reel 47, 581, 79.

53. Greiser, Vermerk über Kirchenverhältnisse im Warthegau, n.d., USHMM, RG 15.007, reel 47, 581, 80.

54. Greiser, Vermerk über Kirchenverhältnisse im Warthegau, n.d., USHMM, RG 15.007, reel 47, 581, 85.

55. The document does not indicate a specific recipient or audience, but Greiser does address the recipient in the second person *you*; he refers to the July 20, 1940, meeting with Krüger, discussed above, at which plans for confessional matters in the Warthegau were discussed, and he notes the "common goals" he shared with the recipient of the memorandum. Moreover, Greiser refers to the recipient's assistant for confessional affairs, Dr. Fruhwirth. This suggests that the memorandum was directed to either Bormann or Krüger.

56. Greiser, Vermerk über Kirchenverhältnisse im Warthegau, n.d., USHMM, RG 15.007, reel 47, 581, 87. It is not clear what Greiser meant by an "Orthodox" organization for Ukrainians, but it is likely that he was referring to a local form of the Ukrainian Greek Catholic, or "Uniate" Church.

57. Greiser, Vermerk über Kirchenverhältnisse im Warthegau, n.d., USHMM, RG 15.007, reel 47, 581, 92.

58. Vermerk über die Besprechung mit Gauleiter Greiser über die konfessionellen Maßnahmen im Reichsgau Wartheland, August 13–14, 1940, Abschrift, BAB, R58/7581, 68.

59. Greiser, Vermerk über Kirchenverhältnisse im Warthegau, n.d., USHMM, RG 15.007, reel 47, 581, 88.

60. NSDAP-Gauleitung Wartheland, Gauhauptstelle für Sonderfragen (Meyer) to NSDAP-Gauleitung Bayreuth, Gauschulungsamt, June 18, 1943, APP, 53/299/0/1.30/1186, 13.

61. Epstein notes, however, that the decree was issued without the blessing of relevant government ministries. Epstein, *Model Nazi*, 224. See also Broszat, *Nationalsozialistische*, 153.

62. "Verordnung Nr. 246 über die religiöse Vereinigungen und Religionsgesellschaften im Reichsgau Wartheland vom 13. September 1941," *Verordnungsblatt des Reichsstatthalters im Warthegau*, BAB, R 5101/22437, 3. Both Martin Broszat and Catherine Epstein refer to Reich Chancellery chief Hans Lammers's concern over the bases of Greiser's authority to issue such a far-reaching decree, and the vagaries of Greiser's claim to have promulgated it with Hitler's approval. Bormann, however, had assured Lammers in October 1941 that already the previous winter (Bormann could not recall the date), Greiser had outlined to Hitler his plans for the churches in Wartheland "as expressed in the decree of 13 September 1941." Lammers to Bormann, November 11, 1941, document 374/II, in Grünzinger, *Dokumente zur Kirchenpolitik*, 900. Lammers then spoke about the matter with Hitler directly, who

confirmed his approval of the September Decree. Lammers to Bormann, November 11, 1941, document 374/IV, in Grünzinger, *Dokumente zur Kirchenpolitik*, 901–2. See also Broszat, *Nationalsozialistische*, 153–54; Epstein, *Model Nazi*, 225.

63. Epstein, *Model Nazi*, 225. As Epstein points out, in his monograph *The Holy Reich*, Richard Steigmann-Gall arrives at the opposite conclusion, namely, that establishment of the four "German" "religious associations" in the Wartheland was an indicator of the compatibility of National Socialism and Christianity. In other words, that the Nazis would establish such associations in the "paradise" of the Reichsgau Wartheland, where they could have eradicated all organized church organizations, reveals a fundamental tolerance rather than a long-term destructive agenda. See Steigmann-Gall, *Holy Reich*, 229, and Epstein, *Model Nazi*, 398n199.

64. "Verordnung Nr. 246 über die religiöse Vereinigungen und Religionsgesellschaften im Reichsgau Wartheland vom 13. September 1941," *Verordnungsblatt des Reichsstatthalters im Warthegau*, BAB, R 5101/22437, 3.

65. Conway, *Nazi Persecution*, 320. See also Broszat, *Nationalsozialistische*, 154. Steigmann-Gall offers a contrary point of view, as noted above. "The blank slate of the Warthegau," he writes, "suggests what the fate of the churches would have been in a 'pure' Nazi State, or at least Bormann's vision of one, unsullied by the forces of political 'reaction' or public opinion. . . . Just as noteworthy as the stringent prohibitions taken by Nazis, however, is the simple fact that the churches were allowed in: They were given a place in the Nazi paradise." "Carefully precluding any proclerical forces from adding their brushstrokes to the Wartheland palette," he continues, "Bormann and his associates still painted the Christian churches, even if in minimal form, into their picture." Finally, in concluding his study, he states, "The 'blank slate' of the Warthegau, the testing ground for the unhindered implementation of Nazi ideology, revealed that church institutions, although totally severed from the state and strongly curtailed in their activities, would nonetheless find a place in the future Nazi utopia." Steigmann-Gall, *Holy Reich*, 229, 260.

66. Greiser, speech at the Arbeitstagung des Gauschulungsamtes, September 14, 1941, IPN, GK 196/37, 87–98.

11

ZERSCHLAGUNG

The "Action for the Destruction of the Polish Clergy"

Less than three weeks later, on October 2, 1941, the Łódź Gestapo issued orders for the arrest and detention of Polish Catholic clergy throughout the entire Łódź District. Two days later, the Landrat in Kępno Subdistrict passed on the orders orally to the commander of the local gendarmerie charged with executing the arrests. At 4:00 a.m. on October 6, his men gathered at their headquarters and were ordered to arrest twenty priests in the subdistrict. Over the next several hours, they carried out their orders. Seventeen priests were arrested and detained in the Horst-Wessel Hall in Kępno. Another, from the village of Grabów (Grabow), fled in his nightshirt to the tower of his church, where he was discovered and arrested. Two priests, however, successfully escaped. Three were permitted to remain in the district—two because of poor health, and one to serve the entire subdistrict on his own.[1] So began the mass arrest of the vast majority of Polish Catholic clergy remaining in the Reichsgau Wartheland, what the German authorities referred to as the *Aktion zur Zerschlagung der polnischen Kirche*, or "Action for the Destruction of the Polish Church."

Early the following day, three Gestapo officers arrested Kazimierz Niesiołowski, a seventy-year-old priest in Pleszew (Pleschen), a small town between Jarocin and Kalisz. Together with Stanisław Herwart, a fellow priest, he was brought to Jarocin, which served as a collection point for clergy from the entire region. From there, the two were transported to Gestapo headquarters in Poznań, where they were registered, photographed, and forced to turn over their money and personal effects. They were then taken to Fort VII, the notorious prison on the outskirts of the city. When the priests arrived, they learned that among the approximately one thousand inmates were already more than one hundred clergy of the Poznań and Gniezno dioceses. Subject to the brutal conditions in the camp, they were housed in the underground bunkers of the old fort and forced to sleep on the floor. The priests were poorly fed, suffered from dysentery, and endured frequent humiliations and beatings. Objecting to such treatment, one cleric, Ludwik Rochalski, told a Gestapo officer that it was dishonorable to torment a defenseless old man. The policeman kicked Rochalski to death.

So dreadful were the conditions in Fort VII that, according to Niesiołowski, some of the clergy expressed the hope that they would soon be deported to Dachau, a likewise notorious destination, but a camp where they would not be "dependent on the whims of a horde of degenerates and sadists." The following month the majority—that is, the younger and healthier among the priests—were, in fact, sent to Dachau. Niesiołowski, however, was sent with some of the older priests to Bojanowo (Schmückert), a town in the southwestern Wartheland where there was a work camp for vagrants, the "work shy," and, significantly, nuns, which earned it the nickname *Nonnenlager Schmückert*, or "Schmückert Camp for Nuns."[2]

Franz Heinrich Bock, the German mayor and *Amtskommissar* in Poddębice, a town forty kilometers northwest of Łódź, described the October arrests dramatically in his diary:

> This morning the Gendarmerie informed me that overnight the Gestapo placed all Polish clergy in "protective custody" and deported them to the Altreich. The young priest of the town church also fell victim to this sudden Aktion. Restless nights, in which acts of violence are undertaken, which go unnoticed even by the mayor, who is responsible for the welfare of the city. While we peacefully sleep, henchmen are wreaking havoc among the Polish population like wolves in a herd of sheep.[3]

Poddębice was only one of many communities in the southeastern Warthegau targeted by the German authorities. A flyer distributed by the Polish underground described the breadth of the Aktion in the Łódź District:

> On 6.9 [*sic*: the arrests took place on October 6] all clergy in our region were arrested and brought to Konstantynów near Litzmannstadt, where they were housed in a camp. In all, 800 people. The first night they had to sleep without straw on the bare floor. They were treated poorly. Three of the priests already died. The Gestapo reported that four priests had fled, but this certainly referred to those who died. . . . During the arrests in Kutno a priest fled. In the entire Kreis only two priests remained.[4]

Stefan Bączyk was a military chaplain and one of three priests serving the parish in Rozdrażew (Brigidau), a village in the southern part of Poznań District. After the two other priests were arrested in March 1940, Bączyk served the parish alone until his own arrest on the morning of October 7, 1941. On that day, he was returning from a funeral with the parish organist when he was arrested by the Gestapo. The policemen were, however, willing to let him first eat breakfast at the organist's home. Hoping to escape, the priest claimed that he needed to relieve himself, but the Gestapo officer went with him. When they returned, Father Bączyk began to eat his breakfast. When the Gestapo officer stepped into the adjacent room, the priest fled the house and sought refuge in a shed across the road. The Gestapo searched throughout the day for the fugitive, who remained in the shed, hidden under a pile of beetroot leaves, for two days. Bączyk then lived in hiding in a nearby village until his arrest in March 1942. Imprisoned in Poznań, he was sent to Dachau in July of that year.[5]

Stefan Bączyk's flight and six-month reprieve was, of course, exceptional, for in general, Catholic priests were an easy target for the police. The German army and occupation authorities had been apprehending priests since the fall of 1939, but these individual and mass arrests were generally localized. By contrast, the scope of the "Action for the Destruction of the Polish Church" extended across the entire Wartheland. Centrally coordinated among police organs throughout the Gau,[6] it was, according to Polish historian Jan Sziling, the "coronation" of Nazi Kirchenpolitik in the region,[7] for over the course of only forty-eight hours, the German police had arrested more than five hundred clergy[8] and interned them in three existing camps specially activated for the Aktion.[9] In the aftermath of the arrests, they closed nearly all "Polish" churches in the Warthegau that had thus far remained open.

Little evidence remains of the specific orders for the Aktion, although local Warthegau officials may have known in advance about the impending arrests. Some members of the clergy were also aware that brutal measures were in the offing. According to one Poznań priest, some clergy knew already two weeks prior to the event that a mass arrest was to take place. The priest also reported that the source of this information was Franz Wolf, the Gestapo officer responsible for church affairs in Poznań.[10]

An October 7, 1941, report from the Kępno gendarmerie indicates that orders were issued by the Łódź Gestapo on October 2, that these were discussed among party officials in Kępno the following day, and that instructions to execute the arrests were conveyed orally to police commanders on October 4.[11] In his account of the arrests, Hilarius Breitinger claimed to have seen the Gestapo's order in a document provided to him by an employee of the Poznań District offices. It is worth noting that the description "Action for the Destruction of the Polish Church" did not originate among persecuted Polish Catholics or in the writings of historians; rather, it was referred to as such in the order Breitinger described[12] and appears frequently in German reports submitted in the days and weeks after the arrests.

The Aktion—the most dramatic and violent intensification of antichurch measures thus far—took place at a time when the Nazi regime was, in fact, moderating its policies toward the churches in the Altreich. The growing importance of Himmler and Bormann, as well as an intensification of antichurch policy since the beginning of the war that was nowhere more evident than in the Reichsgau Wartheland, suggested to some that a "final settlement" with the churches was in the offing. In June 1941, Bormann issued to the Reich's Gauleiters a secret order that appeared to point in that direction. A policy directive of sorts, the decree on "the relationship between National Socialism and Christianity" emphasized the irreconcilability of the Christian faith and Nazi ideology and demanded that the churches' influence in society be "completely eliminated." Only in this way, Bormann argued, could National Socialist rule be secured.[13]

Hitler was, on the one hand, eager to give Bormann, Himmler, and Greiser significant freedom in the formulation and execution of Kirchenpolitik, but he remained skeptical about the wisdom and efficacy of broad and violent measures against the churches, believing instead that they would inevitably "die off." Moreover, relations between the Nazi government and German Catholics were particularly strained in the summer of 1941—strained by the confiscation of cloisters in western Germany and the Ostmark, as well as by revelations about the "euthanasia" program responsible for the murder of tens of thousands of disabled and allegedly disabled Germans. Not eager to escalate the conflict with the German churches, Hitler therefore instructed Bormann to order all Gauleiters to suspend the expropriation of church property and demanded that persecutory measures against the churches cease.[14] On September 22, Albert Hartl, head of antichurch counterintelligence in Section IV-B-1 of the Reich Security Main Office, convened in Berlin some twenty church specialists from among the police. The former priest then ordered that major measures against the churches be avoided, that actions against monasteries and convents cease, and that the focus of police forces be intelligence gathering about the churches rather than aggression against them.[15] The following month, Reinhard Heydrich made a call before SD and SS leaders for not only ideological consistency but also practical expediency in matters related to the churches. "Our fundamental attitude to denominational opponents," he stated, "has been clearly and unambiguously laid down. The practical regulations for guarding against actions of denominational groups hostile to the state must, however, be guided by tactics of expediency."[16] Thus, it appears that even for antichurch zealots like Heydrich, the hour of reckoning for the German churches would come after the war, or at least not while the 1941 invasion of the Soviet Union was underway.

For the Polish clergy remaining in the Reichsgau Wartheland, the hour of reckoning arrived in early October 1941, yet the concrete motives for the Aktion against them remain elusive. Martin Broszat placed the mass arrests in the context of the military campaign against the Soviet Union, a consequence of which was the expansion of persecutory measures in the east: in addition to the mass killing of Jews and Soviet officials as the front moved into Soviet territory, there was also an increase in aggressive actions against the Catholic clergy in the occupied territories. It was in this context that on August 7, Gestapo chief Heinrich Müller issued an order of Heinrich Himmler's on "the arrest of subversive elements following the invasion of the Soviet Union." The order stated, "In light of the proliferation of subversive activities and utterances since the beginning of the campaign against the Soviet Union, the Reichsführer-SS and Chief of the German Police has now reached the basic decision that all incendiary clergy,[17] anti-German Czechs and Poles, as well as communists and similar rabble will, as a matter of principle, be sent to a concentration camp for an extended period."[18]

A consequence of this order was, according to Broszat, the use of "police preventative measures," to use a Nazi-favored term, in the mass deportation of Poles in the annexed territories to concentration camps. Broszat also concluded that Himmler's order encouraged Greiser and the Warthegau police organs to move forward with the Aktion,[19] although clear evidence for this is lacking.

Jan Sziling has argued that the Aktion was the initiative of both Greiser and Himmler and suggests that it was the logical consequence of Greiser's September 13, 1941, decree that created four new "religious associations" in the Warthegau and firmly established state control over them.[20] The decree, as noted in the previous chapter, did not establish a Roman Catholic association for Poles, and the arrest of more than five hundred Catholic priests less than a month later suggests that this was not in the offing. It is also worth recalling in this context Greiser's ominous words from his September 14 speech: "Where wood is planed, shavings will fall." [21] If this was a call for draconian measures, events of the following weeks appeared to confirm it.

German documents from the weeks before and after the arrests indicate more basic ideological and political motives. In mid-September, the office of the Kępno Landrat requested from all police precincts detailed information on Polish Catholic clergy, targeting especially those who "were actively anti-German or currently exert a negative influence on the Polish population." Local officials were to provide written reports on such clergy that included personal data, addresses, the parishes they served, and precise information on which charges could be brought against them.[22] As has been noted, the Kępno commissioner was unusually rigorous in applying measures against the Polish church and clergy, and it is possible that this order was simply maintaining his hitherto aggressive stance. It is also possible, however, that the order was issued in preparation for the mass arrests that would follow three weeks later.

In the aftermath of the Aktion, the Hohensalza district president, Hans Burkhardt, offered his interpretation of the motives and desired effects of the arrests. In Burkhardt's words, "The Catholic clergy remains as ever the backbone of Polish national identity. As always, the churches are very well attended by the Poles, and for anyone who feels Polish, it is a matter of honor to appear in church on Sundays. Thus, for Poles, attendance at church extends beyond the realm of religion." According to Burkhardt, the closing of churches in years past had led to a certain "pacification" of the population on the one hand, but on the other, it had also resulted in many Poles traveling great distances "in a demonstrative manner" to neighboring communities to attend services. "In order to attain consistency of enforcement," Burkhardt continued, "all Polish clergy, but two for each Kreis, were arrested by the Gestapo and sent to an internment camp. It is expected that an essential pacification of the Poles will occur, and that the very powerful influence of the clergy will to a great extent be broken, above all as a result of the size of the region that they now have to serve."[23]

The head of the Poznań Police, Helmut Bischoff, put it more succinctly, stating in a memorandum to his subordinates two weeks after the Aktion, "The internment of the Polish clergy was a blow against the last remaining basis of Polish common identity and the spirit of resistance."[24] German officials on the ground may have seen the October Aktion as a practical, and indeed aggressive, extension and amplification of antichurch measures undertaken in the first two years of the occupation. It is worth considering, however, the scope, coordination, and broader effects of the Aktion, which suggest that the high-level Nazi leadership responsible for the basic outlines of Kirchenpolitik in the Warthegau was undertaking a much more comprehensive project.

The timing of that project is significant. Over the course of 1940, it had become clear that it would not be possible to deport as many Poles as originally planned, and that the Reichsgau Wartheland would remain, at least for the time being, overwhelmingly Polish in terms of its population. The Polish population had not stopped attending church or conceiving children—two phenomena that were, in the minds of some Nazi policymakers, closely linked and markers of Polish nationalism and hostility toward the occupation regime. Tens of thousands of Reichsdeutsche and Volksdeutsche were arriving from the Altreich and eastern Europe, and most of the Volksdeutsche were eager to become part of church communities in their new homeland. In September, the German army had encircled Leningrad and taken Kiev; in early October, the march on Moscow resumed, and it appeared to some that victory by the end of the year was possible. In short, the war was going well.[25] It was in this context that the regime issued the September Decree, a template for future church-state relations that only applied to "religious organizations" defined as "German," and from which any provision for "Polish" churches was conspicuously absent. And it was in this context that the regime undertook its most violent and comprehensive attack on the clergy.

The results were dramatic in all three Warthegau *Regierungsbezirke*. In Łódź District, where the Aktion began on October 5, more than three hundred diocesan priests and religious were arrested, including 175 from the Łódź diocese, fifty-eight from the Częstochowa diocese, and several dozen from the Włocławek and Warsaw dioceses. All were initially taken to the Konstantinow (as of May 1943, Tuchingen) camp near Lódź, where they were prohibited from any contact with other prisoners.[26] Konstantinow, along with the Fort VII prison on the outskirts of Poznań and the cloister in Ląd, was one of three "holding pens" for Warthegau clergy arrested in the Aktion.[27] Located in a converted textile factory, it had functioned since January 1940 primarily as a transit camp, holding on average some eight hundred prisoners under consistently deplorable conditions.[28] Documents of the Polish underground report that several hundred priests from across the Wartheland were interned there in the fall of 1941,[29] and although these numbers may be inflated, records do indicate that well over 300 priests were interned in Konstantinow as a result of the October arrests,[30] including nearly all remaining priests of the Łódź diocese.[31] After two weeks, 296 were deported to Dachau. Thirteen were released, 6 had escaped, and 4 had died while in Konstantinow.[32]

Arrests in Inowrocław District commenced on October 6, when German police arrested some seventy clerics from the Poznań, Gniezno, Warsaw, Włocławek, and Płock dioceses and interned them in the former Salesian cloister in Ląd. As discussed in chapters 1 and 6, the cloister had already served as an internment camp for clergy beginning in January 1940, and October 1941 marked the beginning of its "second phase," when priests arrested in the Aktion were incarcerated there. Records of the Inowrocław arrests also offer evidence that Nazi policymakers at the highest level were involved in the Aktion, for Reinhard Heydrich, head of the RSHA, issued on November 10 a directive ordering that the seventy-eight detained priests remain in "protective custody."[33] In fact, at the end of the previous month, 117 clergy in the camp had been deported to Dachau, while 35 were released, and most of them subsequently expelled to the General Government.[34]

In Poznań District, police arrested 141 diocesan priests and religious from the Poznań and Gniezno dioceses and held them temporarily in the Poznań Gestapo headquarters, where they were registered, photographed, and given medical examinations. They were then sent to Fort VII, from which the vast majority were likewise deported in a three-day journey to Dachau.[35] Ewaryst Nawrowski, a priest from Zaniemyśl (Santomichel), a village twenty miles southeast of Poznań, described in his 1942 memoir of Fort VII the experiences of the newly arrived clergymen in the camp. According to Nawrowski, the priests were rather docile prisoners, but this did not stop the German guards from terrorizing them over the course of their three weeks in the prison. For his amusement and as a demonstration of his authority, one particularly depraved guard would shoot his revolver over the heads of marching priests, which caused the death of at least one priest who suffered already from a weak heart. "The criminal Nazis," Nawrowski wrote, "undertook the taunting, degradation, and evocation of an atmosphere of dread and terror with unheard-of skill. Nearly every day there was news of new methods."[36]

In the days following the October mass arrests, the German Franciscan Hilarius Breitinger decided to investigate the circumstances of priests in the Poznań archdiocese. Researching diocesan records, and with the assistance of a tight-lipped Volksdeutsche woman who traveled the region collecting information, Breitinger arrived at some startling statistics that attest to the scale of the Aktion. While at the outbreak of war there were 681 secular clergy and 147 male members of religious orders in the archdiocese, as of October 10, 1941, there remained only 34 priests to minister to Polish Catholics. Seventy-four priests had been shot or had died in concentration camps, 120 had been deported into the General Government, and 451 were currently interned in prisons and concentration camps.[37]

The mass deportation of Warthegau priests in October 1941 was, of course, devastating to the church. The German authorities had planned for only two officially active priests (as opposed to those working clandestinely) to remain in each subdistrict to minister to Polish Catholics. In some cases, however, there were no active priests in a given district, and in other cases, priests had to serve more than one district. Only seventy-three active priests remained in the entire Gau to minister to Poles—eleven in the Gniezno archdiocese, thirty-four in the Poznań archdiocese, twelve each in the Łódź and Włocławek dioceses, and four distributed among the small sections of the Warsaw, Płock, and Częstochowa dioceses within the Gau's territory.[38]

The demand for priests and their ministry was enormous, and this is evident when one considers population figures in relation to the number of priests. For example, according to German statistics, as of October 1, 1941, there were 360,437 ethnic Poles in the city of Łódź. After the Aktion, only eight priests remained to minster to them, or one priest for roughly every 45,000 Poles.[39] By way of comparison, in the Altreich there was, on average, one priest for every one thousand Catholics.[40] For priests in urban areas, the numbers were overwhelming, but the distances to cover were relatively short. Priests in rural areas often faced numbers as large, but they also had to cover much longer distances in order to celebrate Masses, distribute the sacraments, and attend to other aspects of their work. A case in point was that of the village of Mikstat (Mixstadt), located in Ostrów Subdistrict. On October 13, 1941, two clerics were installed there. These "official" priests, and the Mikstat village church, were to serve the entire Ostrów Subdistrict, with its population of more than one hundred thousand.[41] Significantly, their church was not located in the central and larger town Ostrów but in a hard-to-reach village on the outskirts of the subdistrict. The goal here for the German authorities was to minimize contact between the clergy and the Catholic population and, quite simply, to make church attendance more difficult.[42] In light of challenges such as these, it is not surprising that many of the few remaining clerics in the Gau undertook their ministry, in the words of one priest, "with a backpack and on a bicycle."[43]

Corollary to the removal of priests in the Aktion was the closure of hundreds more churches, as well as additional plunder and confiscation of church property. The closure of Warthegau churches during the first two years of the occupation had often occurred on an ad hoc basis and independently of the arrest of priests, but in October 1941, the German authorities began to close systematically all churches that had been served by priests removed in the Aktion.[44] It is not clear precisely how many were closed, but in the aftermath of the Aktion, only twenty-nine churches remained available in the Gniezno diocese, and eleven of these were restricted to Germans only.[45] In the Poznań archdiocese, of the 441 churches available to the public prior to the war, only 30 churches remained open as of October 10, 1941. Within the Poznań city limits, of the thirty churches and forty-seven chapels open in September 1939, only two churches and one chapel remained available for Polish Catholics as of October 10, 1941[46]—this for a population of approximately 180,000 Poles remaining in the city.[47]

With respect to other forms of church property, a Gestapo order issued a week after the arrests stipulated that the property and resources of Catholic parishes either be confiscated, turned over to police authorities, or put, for the time being, under lock and key. Thus, harvested grain and livestock were to be turned over to the county farm commission, while mail, parish records, hymnals, books, candles, and linens were to be turned over to the police.[48] This process continued in the weeks that followed across the Gau,[49] as priests' apartments and rectories were registered with local police for confiscation, while churches and chapels were put under the authority of the Gau Self-Administration.[50] As a leaflet distributed by the Polish underground following the Aktion claimed, "After the arrests, the plunder of the churches began. All carpets, vestments, and liturgical instruments were removed. In addition, parchment books from the middle ages were destroyed in the church in Last [*sic*: presumably Łask/Lask], and other churches were totally looted. The Bernardin cloister in Kolo [Koło/Warthbrücken] was transformed into a warehouse for furniture."[51] According to a report of the Poznań Gestapo, the German police had, in conjunction with the mass arrests, confiscated from the homes of priests and parish offices money, foreign currency, certificates of credit and stocks, titles and deeds, parish records, and libraries. From the churches the police removed chalices, candlesticks and candelabra, monstrances, and linens, six tons of which were sent to the front.[52] In some cases, liturgical linens from churches and books from parish libraries were simply sent to paper factories for recycling.[53]

Word of the brutal measures of October 1941 spread, and the information compiled by Hilarius Breitinger in the aftermath of the Aktion did not remain secret. Intent on communicating the dramatic losses among the Polish clergy, Breitinger engaged the help of German soldiers heading to the Altreich on leave and succeeded in sending his information to the papal nuncio in Berlin and to German bishops. The statistics he had compiled, distributed covertly, appear to have circulated widely among church leaders in Germany.[54] They also fell into the hands of Nazi authorities in Berlin[55] and were eventually made public in a BBC radio report.[56] Breitinger's report also appears to have been the impetus for a letter from Adolf Cardinal Bertram, chair of the Fulda Conference of German Bishops and the highest authority of the Catholic Church in Germany, to Hanns Kerrl, Reich minister for church affairs. Bertram noted in his letter, written only two weeks after the Aktion, that it had been impossible for the German church leadership to investigate fully the church's situation in the formerly Polish dioceses but that much information about the Warthegau had spread to the Altreich, causing among the German bishops considerable unease about further developments, especially in the Poznań and Gniezno archdioceses. Hardly a consistent voice of opposition to the regime,[57] Bertram nonetheless addressed in his letter a wide variety of broad concerns, from the closure of churches to the deportation and internment of priests, from confiscation of church property to limitations on religious instruction. But it is also clear from the cardinal's letter that he had been informed about specific events of the October Aktion which, in combination with other measures over the past two years, had resulted in what he described as "a violent suppression of all Catholic religious life in the Warthegau."[58]

By the end of 1941, reports were also emerging in the foreign press about the new wave of arrests. This prompted the German Foreign Office to inquire in December at the Reich Security Main Office about the veracity and extent of the measures taken in the Warthegau. An official from the RSHA offered the following laconic and understated reply: "In response to the query . . . I inform [you] that in the Reichsgau Wartheland a large number of Polish Catholic clergy were, for political-security reasons, arrested and transferred to a concentration camp."[59] The "large number" was at least five hundred, and the concentration camp was Dachau.

Notes

1. Gendarmerie Kreis Kempen to Kommandeur der Gendarmerie in Litzmannstadt, October 7, 1941, BAB, R 70/Polen, 252, 1115-01.

2. Świadectwo K. Niesiołowskiego, Pleszew, July 20, 1945, IPN, GK 196/19, 180; Budziarek, "Geneza," 41–42. On the development, organization, prisoners, and conditions of the Fort VII prison, see Olszewski, *Fort VII*, 34–58.

3. Alexander Hohenstein (Franz Heinrich Bock), *Wartheländisches Tagebuch aus den Jahren 1941/42*, Veröffentlichungen des Instituts für Zeitgeschichte, Quellen und Darstellungen zur Zeitgeschichte, vol. 8 (Stuttgart: Deutsche Verlags-Anstalt, 1961), 188–89. Bock erroneously dated the mass arrest of Polish clergy as occurring in the night of September 8–9, 1941. Moreover, the arrested clergy were not deported immediately to the Altreich. When Bock referred in this excerpt of his diary to the "mayor," he was referring to himself. On the dates, see Broszat, "Verfolgung," 78n4.

4. Lagebericht des Höheren SS- und Polizeiführers beim Reichsstatthalter in Posen im Wehrkreis XXI.-Inspekteur der Sicherheitspoizei und den SD, June 24, 1942, IPN, GK 62/210/CD, 112.

5. The story of Bączyk's apprehension and escape is reported, on the basis of the testimonies of two of his colleagues in the parish, Fr. Jan Kujawa and Józef Mettler, in Stefan Komorowski, "Moja parafie w latach okupacji 1939–1945," 1973, AAP, zespół 133, OK 128. On Bączyk's arrest see Domagała, *Ci, Którzy Przeszli Przez Dachau*, 71; Jastrząb, *Archidiecezja Poznańska*, 550, 1155.

6. Budziarek, "Geneza," 39.

7. Jan Sziling, "Hitlerowska polityka eksterminacji duchowieństwa katolickiego w Kraju Warty," in *Akcje okupanta hitlerowskiego wobec Kościoła katolickiego w Kraju Warty*, ed. Antoni Galiński and Marek Budziarek (Łódź: Okręgowa Komisja Badania Zbrodni Przeciwko Narodowi Polskiemu w Łodzi–Instytutu Pamięci Narodowej/Muzeum Historii Łodzi, 1997), 22.

8. Breitinger estimated that some five hundred clergy were arrested over the course of the Aktion, a number substantiated by the postwar testimony of Franciszek Jedwabski, a canon of the Poznań Cathedral Chapter. See Breitinger, *Als Deutschenseelsorger*, 68, and on Jedwabski, Broszat, "Verfolgung," 78. Jan Sziling sets the number of clergy arrested in the Aktion at 540, while Marek Budziarek counts 560. See Sziling, "Hitlerowska," 22; Budziarek, "Geneza," 41.

9. Sziling, "Hitlerowska," 22.

10. Stanisław Poczta, Ankieta, June 1, 1974, AAP, zespół 133, syg. OK 224, 497/74. Poczta's report of the alleged tip remains unconfirmed by other sources, and the Gestapo officer's motives for allegedly providing the alleged information remain unclear.

11. Gendarmerie Kreis Kempen to Kommandeur der Gendarmerie in Litzmannstadt, October 7, 1941, BAB, R 70/Polen, 252, 1115-01.
12. Breitinger, *Als Deutschenseelsorger*, 68.
13. Bormann to Gauleiter, "Verhältnis vom Nationalsozialismus und Christentum," June 6–7, 1941, document 075-D, in IMT, vol. 35, 7–13, here 12.
14. Conway, *Nazi Persecution*, 279, 284. See also Broszat, "Verfolgung," 26–30.
15. Vermerk über die Arbeitstagung der Kirchenarbeiter bei den Staatspolizei (leit) stellen am 22. und 23. September 1941, document 1815-PS, in IMT, vol. 28, 447; Stehle, "Ein Eiferer," 12.
16. Quoted in Conway, *Nazi Persecution*, 287.
17. In German, *Pfaffen*, a derogatory term for preachers, priests, or pastors.
18. Chef der Sicherheitspolizei und des SD (Müller) to Staatspolizei(leit)stellen et al., August 27, 1941, IfZ, Nürnberg document no. NO-1653.
19. Broszat, "Verfolgung," 76–77.
20. Sziling, *Polityka*, 259; Budziarek, "Geneza," 39.
21. Greiser, speech at the Arbeitstagung des Gauschulungsamtes, September 14, 1941, IPN, GK 196/37, 87–98.
22. Landrat des Kreises Kempen (Wolf) to Ortspolizeibehörden des Kreises, September 15, 1941, IPN, GK 831/59, 48.
23. Lagebericht des Regierungspräsidenten Hohensalza, October 20, 1941, IfZ, Fb 125, 383. Similar sentiments are evident in an October 1941 report of the Litzmannstadt *Regierungspräsident* Friedrich Uebelhoer in Łuczak, *Położenie*, 346.
24. Quoted in Fijałkowski, *Kościół*, 239.
25. Christopher R. Browning and Jürgen Matthäus, *The Origins of the Final Solution: The Evolution of Nazi Jewish Policy, September 1939–March 1942* (Lincoln: University of Nebraska Press, 2004), 427, 546n1.
26. Budziarek, "Geneza," 40; "Raport Nr. 20 za czas od 16.XI.-30.XI.1941 r." in Sprawozdanie sytuacyjne z kraju, vol. 2, no. 1–6, 1941–1942, 67–70, PUMST.
27. Sziling, "Hitlerowska," 22.
28. Główna Komisja, *Obozy hitlerowskie*, 240–41. On the Konstantynów camp see also Serwański, *Wielkopolska*, 136, 140–41.
29. "Raport Nr. 20 za czas od 16.XI.-30.XI.1941 r." in Sprawozdanie sytuacyjne z kraju, vol 2, no. 1–6, 1941–1942, 70, PUMST; "Pro Memoria o sytuacji w kraju w okresie 1 listopada - 15 grudnia 1941" in "Materiały o sytuacji kraju w okresie od 1 listopada 1941 roku do 15. I. 1942 roku," in Sprawozdanie sytuacyjne z kraju, vol. 2, no. 1–6, 1941–1942, 3, PUMST; Lagebericht des Höheren SS- und Polizeiführers beim Reichsstatthalter in Posen im Wehrkreis XXI.-Inspekteur der Sicherheitspolizei und den SD, June 24, 1942, IPN, GK 62/210/CD, 112.
30. Śmigiel, *Die katholische Kirche*, 179–81. Śmigiel here sets the number of clergy arrested in the Litzmannstadt Regierungsbezirk at 317. Budziarek sets the number at 350. See Budziarek, "Geneza," 40.
31. Jan Zdżarski, zeznanie, Radca Kurii Biskupiej, Kanclerz Kurii Biskupiej, Łódź, n.d., IPN, GK 162/558, 213.
32. Budziarek "Geneza," 40; Śmigiel, *Die katholische Kirche*, 175.
33. Heydrich to Staatspolizeistelle Hohensalza, November 10, 1941, in Łuczak, *Położenie*, 31.
34. "Ląd . . . ," 235–36; Budziarek, "Geneza," 40.
35. Ankieta, Ks. Marian Józef Bogacki, April 10, 1975, AAP, zespół 133, syg. OK 215, 191/75; Budziarek, "Geneza," 40; Śmigiel, *Die katholische Kirche*, 175. Budziarek sets the number

of clergy arrested in the Poznań District at 141, and Śmigiel at 123. A report from the Polish underground indicates that 144 priests from the Poznań diocese were deported to Dachau: "Pro Memoria o sytuacji w kraju w okresie 1 listopada - 15 grudnia 1941," in "Materiały o sytuacji kraju w okresie od 1 listopada 1941 roku do 15. I. 1942 roku," in Sprawozdanie sytuacyjne z kraju, vol. 2, no. 1–6, 1941–1942, 1–4, PUMST.

36. Ewaryst Nawrowski, *W szponach gestapo. Urywki z moich przeżyć w obozie Fort VII (Übergangslager S. S. Posen)* (Poznań: Muzeum Martyrologiczne w Żabikowie, 2008), 78.

37. "Aufstellung Priester und Kirchen in der Erzdiözese Posen," October 10, 1941, BAB, R 5101/22437, 13; Aufstellung Breitingers über die Lage der Erzdiözese Posen," document 706, in Volk, *Akten deutscher Bischöfe*, vol. 5, 568–69; Breitinger, *Als Deutschenseelsorger*, 69; Broszat, "Verfolgung," 79.

38. Kuria Biskupia Łódzka, May 13, 1946, IPN, GK 196/19, 160; Jolanta Adamska, *Reżimy totalitarne wobec duchownych kościołów chrześcijańskich okupowanej Polski 1939–1945* (Warszawa: Rada Ochrony Pamięci Walk i Męczeństwa, 2008), 8; Sziling, *Polityka*, 261.

39. Budziarek, "Zarząd i organizacja," 314.

40. Breitinger to Himmler, document 938a, in Volk, *Akten deutscher Bischöfe*, vol. 6, 396.

41. Statistische Angaben zur Bevölkerung im Gau, January 17, 1941, IPN, GK 62/19, 10. According to this document, the population of Ostrów county in 1931 was 104,000.

42. "Raport o sytuacji na Ziemiach Zachodnich Nr. 5 (do 31.X.1943 r.)," in Mazur, Pietrowicz, and Rutowska, *Raporty*, 289; Tadeusz Fółczyński, "Moja parafia w latch okupacynych (1939–1945)," 1973, AAP, zespół 133, syg. 128.

43. Budziarek, "Zarząd i organizacja," 314.

44. Śmigiel, *Die katholische Kirche*, 242.

45. Kazimierz Śmigiel, "Walka władz hitlerowskich z katolickim kultem religijnym na terenie archidiecezji gnieźnieńskiej w latach 1939–1945," Towarzystwo Naukowe Katolickiego Uniwersytetu Lubelskiego–Rozprawy Wydziału Historyczno-Filologicznego, vol. 34, *Studia Historyczne* 2 (Lublin: Towarzystwo Naukowe Katolickiego Uniwersytetu Lubelskiego, 1968), 280.

46. "Aufstellung Priester und Kirchen in der Erzdiözese Posen," October 10, 1941, BAB, R 5101/22437, 13; "Aufstellung Breitingers über die Lage der Erzdiözese Posen," document 706, in Volk, *Akten deutscher Bischöfe*, vol. 5, 568–69. Breitinger, *Als Deutschenseelsorger*, 69.

47. "Pro Memoria o sytuacji w kraju w okresie 1 listopada - 15 grudnia 1941," in "Materiały o sytuacji kraju w okresie od 1 listopada 1941 roku do 15. I. 1942 roku," in Sprawozdanie sytuacyjne z kraju, vol. 2, no. 1–6, 1941–1942, 1–4, PUMST.

48. Geheime Staatspolizei, Staatspolizeistelle Posen (Bischoff) to Landräte des Bezirks, October 16, 1941, Abschrift, IfZ, Fb 95/39.

49. Landrat des Kreises Schrimm to Gendarmerieposten des Kreises, Schutzpolizeidienstabteilung Schrimm, October 29, 1941, APP, 53/465/0/2/105, 136; Gendarmerie-Posten Schmückert, Lagebericht für den Monat Oktober 1941, October 31, 1941, IPN, GK 736/2, 138–39; Einschreiben, Gestapo Hohensalza, November 14, 1941, IPN, GK 713/9, 31–32; "Raport Nr. 20 za czas od 16.XI.-30.XI.1941 r." in Sprawozdanie sytuacyjne z kraju, vol., 2, no. 1–6, 1941–1942, 69–70, PUMST.

50. Gestapo Litzmannstadt (Schefe) to Landrat Kempen, November 24, 1941, Abschrift, IPN, GK 831/59, 58; Greiser (Birk) to Hauptvermessungsabteilung VXI, Gruppe B (Kat.Verm.), November 27, 1941, IPN, GK 62/166/CD, 31.

51. Lagebericht des Höheren SS- und Polizeiführers beim Reichsstatthalter in Posen im Wehrkreis XXI.-Inspekteur der Sicherheitspolizei und den SD, June 24, 1942, IPN, GK 62/210/CD, 112.

52. Vermerk, Stossberg, March 21, 1942, IPN, GK 196/19, 96; Akt oskarzenia Artura Greisera, June 10, 1946, IPN, GK 196/34, 14.

53. "Raport Nr. 20 za czas od 16.XI.-30.XI.1941 r." in Sprawozdanie sytuacyjne z kraju, vol. 2, no. 1–6, 1941–1942, 70, PUMST.

54. Volk, *Akten deutscher Bischöfe*, vol. 5, 568n1; Broszat, "Verfolgung," 78–79.

55. Breitinger's statistics can be found in the files of the Reich Ministry for Church Affairs in the Bundesarchiv Berlin: "Aufstellung Priester und Kirchen in der Erzdiözese Posen," October 10, 1941, BAB, R 5101/22437, 13.

56. Breitinger, *Als Deutschenseelsorger*, 70. Once it learned of the information leaked by Breitinger, the Posen Gestapo did its own research into missing, deported, and murdered priests and arrived at essentially the same statistics as Breitinger. They strongly suspected that he was behind the document and searched his apartment in vain for evidence to that effect. They also searched the quarters of the Poznań suffragan Walenty Dymek but to no avail. See Breitinger, *Als Deutschenseelsorger*, 69–70.

57. On Bertram's role in the church during the Nazi era, and the ambivalence in the scholarship surrounding his relationship to the regime, see, for example, Joachim Köhler, "Adolf Kardinal Bertram (1859–1945). Sein Umgang mit dem totalitären System des Nationalsozialismus," in *Katholische Kirche unter nationalsozialistischer und kommunistischer Diktatur. Deutschland und Polen 1939–1945*, ed. Hans-Jürgen Karp and Joachim Köhler (Köln: Böhlau, 2001), 175–93, and more recently, Sascha Hinkel, "'Vielleicht werden Kirchenhistoriker in hundert Jahren über mich auch so urteilen; dabei habe ich nur das Beste gewollt'. Adolf Kardinal Bertram im Spiegel neuer Forchsungsergebnisse," in *Die Kirchen und die Verbrechen im nationalsozialistischen Staat*, ed. Thomas Brechenmacher and Harry Oelke, Dachauer Symposien zur Zeitgeschichte, vol. 11 (Göttingen: Wallstein Verlag, 2011), 201–18.

58. Adolf Cardinal Bertram to Hanns Kerrl, October 22, 1941, BAB, R 5101/22437, 5–6.

59. Broszat, "Verfolgung," 78.

12

DACHAU

Polish Clergy in the Concentration Camp Dachau

IT REMAINS UNCLEAR PRECISELY HOW MANY CLERGY WERE arrested in the "Action for the Destruction of the Polish Church," but estimates run from 500[1] to 560,[2] of whom 474 were subsequently sent to Dachau.[3] This means that between 85 and 95 percent of the Aktion's victims were, after their temporary incarceration in one of three Warthegau camps, deported to this single destination. Of the more than 2,700 clergy from across Europe imprisoned in Dachau, two-thirds were from Poland, nearly half of whom died there.[4] The experience of Polish clergy in the camp, an important story unto itself, is also central to the history of the Catholic Church in the Warthegau. As Martin Broszat noted already sixty years ago, "The persecution of the Polish clerics, who alone composed 68 percent of all incarcerated Catholic clergy in Dachau and who amounted to 83 percent of the priests who died there, was of an entirely different magnitude than that of German clergy or the clergy from other countries. This holds especially true for the Polish Catholic clergy of the 'annexed eastern territories,' nearly half of whom were prisoners in Dachau."[5] It is only natural, then, that since the Second World War, Poles have identified Dachau as the most important site of Nazism's persecution of the Polish and Warthegau clergy, and the most important *locus memoriae* of what many have commemorated as their martyrdom.

When the victims of the Warthegau Aktion began their three-day journey[6] to Dachau in late October 1941, they had little sense of what awaited them. Some had experienced the appalling conditions of Fort VII or the camp in Konstantynow, others the milder conditions in the Ląd cloister, but few had any sense of the enormous size of the Dachau camp, the number of inmates, or the omnipresence of suffering and death there. Opened already in March

1933, Dachau was initially intended as a camp for some 5,000 prisoners. By early 1940, it housed at least 12,000 prisoners, and some 32,000 were there when the camp was liberated in April 1945.[7] Between 1933 and 1945, there were approximately 190,000 imprisoned in the camp, among them, 40,404 Poles, or roughly one in five inmates.[8] The first clergyman arrived in Dachau in December 1935,[9] and the first Poles in September 1939, only weeks after the German invasion. The vast majority of Polish clergy arrived, however, in one of two mass deportation actions.[10] The first of these was in December 1940 and was part of an effort to concentrate in Dachau hundreds of priests already incarcerated in various other Nazi camps, an initiative that earned Dachau the ironic designation "the largest cloister in the world."[11]

For most priests deported there, Dachau was the last among multiple destinations in Nazi Germany's network of prisons and camps. One Warthegau priest, Wiktor Sobecki, passed through several already in the first months of the occupation. Arrested and imprisoned in Inowrocław in November 1939, held for three months in the former monastery in Górna Grupa, deported to the Stutthof concentration camp near Gdańsk, and incarcerated in the Sachsenhausen camp near Berlin in April 1940, Sobecki finally arrived in Dachau on December 14, 1940, where he remained until its liberation.[12] Florian Deresiński, a Poznań priest, was arrested by the Gestapo on April 11, 1940, and temporarily held in Fort VII. Sent later that month on a transport with 1,600 other Poznań prisoners to Dachau, Deresiński was quarantined there before his transfer to Gusen I, part of the Mauthausen camp complex in upper Austria, where he remained until he was transferred back to Dachau in December 1940.[13] His transfer from Dachau to Gusen was part of larger effort to destroy members of the Polish intelligentsia, and in all, 5,782 Poles were sent there.[14]

In Gusen, Deresiński had been subjected to bone-crushing labor in the quarries,[15] and conditions there were exceptionally brutal, even in comparison to other concentration camps. Włodzimierz Laskowski, a village priest from west of Poznań, arrived in Gusen on a transport from Dachau on August 2. He died six days later. Ludwik Bielerzewski, another priest, recalled Laskowski's demise:

> "Who are you?"—The question fell—"A priest. . . ." This answer was sufficient. They ordered him to lift a huge, hundred kilo stone. When he was not able to lift it . . . then "Tygrys" . . . one of those kapos[16] who should be avoided at all costs, since a mere encounter with him heralded an inevitable death, together with his colleagues placed this stone on the back of the unfortunate prisoner.

> The stone fell, Father Laskowski was knocked down. The torturers beat and kicked the prostrated victim. When he got up with difficulty, they weighed him down again. Another fall. After the third time they put him out of his misery.[17]

When Deresiński was sent back to Dachau in December 1940, he likely found conditions there an improvement over Gusen.[18] Such was the intent, for his transfer to Dachau was actually the result of negotiations between Vatican representatives and the Reich Security Main Office. The concentration of priests from across Nazi-occupied Europe in Dachau was, in fact, intended to improve the circumstances of their incarceration, and to some extent this was successful: the clergy were housed together in barracks 26, 28, and 30—the so-called *Priesterblocks* or *Pfarrerblocks*[19] ("priest blocks" or "pastor blocks"), they had a small chapel at their disposal, were not required to work as much as "normal" prisoners, were given time to rest at midday, and had better, if still insufficient, provisions.[20] These concessions were, however, only temporary, and were never really fully enjoyed by the Polish clergy, whose status was considerably lower than that of the German clergy.[21]

By the end of 1941, the vast majority of Polish clergy imprisoned under the Nazi regime had been concentrated in Dachau.[22] Whether they arrived over the course of 1940, at the end of that year, or in the aftermath of the October 1941 Aktion in the Reichsgau Wartheland, Dachau would, for nearly all, be their final destination. Nearly half died there, slightly more survived, and all were subject to poor living conditions, inadequate diet, and mistreatment at the hands of the guards and fellow inmates.

In keeping with the SS principle of *divide et impera*, the camp administration worked to sow division and encourage competition among the prisoners.[23] Clergy in the camp had, for a time, certain privileges, which led to hostility and resentment on the part of other inmates and some guards. The camp authorities also treated the Polish clergy more severely than those of other nationalities, strictly separating them from the German clergy,[24] and often withdrawing their privileges or singling them out for more demanding labor.[25] German priests were permitted to celebrate Mass, attend services, and receive the sacraments, while Polish and Czech priests were not.[26] In April 1942, Himmler ordered that German, Dutch, and Norwegian clergy be assigned to lighter work in the herb "plantation" at the camp, but at the same time he demanded that Polish priests be subject to the same strenuous work assignments as other prisoners.[27] In fact, the Polish clergy were often assigned some of the worst tasks: cleaning the streets of the camp, cleaning latrines, and hauling buckets of human waste.[28]

The Polish clergy were frequently subjected to other abuses. In March 1942, a priest was discovered with American dollars.[29] As a consequence, on the day before Palm Sunday, the Polish clergy were mustered for "gymnastics" or "*Sport machen*." For the next nine days, from morning to evening, the priests were forced to perform in this way before the Dachau guards—this during Holy Week (from Palm Sunday to Easter), the most important week in the liturgical calendar. At this spectacle, the Polish clergy were also subject to the derision of other prisoners. One priest recalled, "The camp is in an uproar! Aspersions, calumnies, slanders, verbal abuse, malicious remarks, and jeers pour down in a torrent on the ill-treated priests! 'It serves them right! All their lives they chased money, robbed the poor, provided no ministry without a payment, and their greed showed up even here in camp! It serves them right!'"[30] Some forty priests died as a result,[31] among them Stanisław Wierzbowski, the priest in possession of the money.[32] Their confrères were singled out for the same treatment during Holy Week of the following year.[33]

Despite such abuses, the camp authorities considered the Polish clergy to be relatively healthy and well nourished. Dachau physicians therefore frequently subjected them to medical experiments,[34] infecting them with bacteria, subjecting them to x-rays, using them to test human responses to low air pressure, or exposing them to malaria.[35] One Polish priest, Leon Michałowski, testified in 1946 at the Nürnberg "Doctor's Trial" about how he was used as a subject for experiments measuring human tolerance of cold water: "I was freezing badly in this water, my feet became stiff as iron, my hands too, I was breathing very shallowly. I started again to tremble badly, and cold sweat ran down my head. I felt like I was about to die. And then I pleaded once more to be pulled out, because I could not bear the water any longer."[36] Subjects of such experiments were often referred to as "*Versuchskaninchen*" ("guinea pigs" or, literally, "experimental rabbits")—a bitterly sardonic designation, for the Dachau camp actually had, among its economic and experimental enterprises, a rabbit-breeding operation. As the Polish priest Henryk Malak recalled, "Real rabbits had a different price. They were raised in rabbit pens built with our hands. The select 'angora' species received tender care. And although there were five thousand of them [at Dachau], if even one died, the prisoner in charge could pay with his life. A rabbit is considered by the SS men more valuable than a human being."[37]

The value of human life at Dachau was well illustrated by the so-called *Invaliden-Transporte*, which subjected the Polish clergy to direct extermination. The *Einsatzgruppen* had executed priests in the fall of 1939 because they were regarded as insurgents and the bearers of Polish national identity; at Dachau, the SS sent hundreds of Polish clergymen to be gassed to death because they were no longer economically viable and were therefore a drain on resources. Among its thousands of prisoners, Dachau had long had a high number of "invalids" who were unable to work,[38] and beginning in 1942, the camp authorities initiated "invalid transports" to rid the hospitals and convalescent barracks of inmates regarded as too old, ill, or incapacitated—what Franz Hofmann, commandant of the "Protective Custody Camp" at Dachau, referred to as "ballast burdening the German state."[39] These transports took place in the context of the "Aktion 14f13," a centrally directed program of mass killing according to which "useless" prisoners in concentration camps were examined by medical personnel, selected for death, and sent away for *Sonderbehandlung*, or "special treatment"—the term prescribed for mass killing in the gas chambers.[40]

The overwhelming majority of Dachau prisoners killed as a result of these transports, which were essentially an extension of the "euthanasia" program in the Altreich in 1940 and 1941, died in the Hartheim killing center, near Linz.[41] "Selection" of these deportees began in September 1941, and resulted in a list of some two thousand inmates for the transports, which began in January 1942. Over the course of 1942, there were thirty-two transports to Hartheim, and although researchers have not agreed on the total number of deportees, it is clear that at least 2,593 Dachau prisoners fell victim to the Aktion 14f13.[42] The Polish clergy were especially targeted by the program, and in particular, those deported to the camp in the aftermath of the October 1941 "Aktion for the Destruction of the Polish Church," many of whom were elderly and incapable of work. According to the former prisoner and historian Stanislav Zámečník, of the more than seven hundred Dachau prisoners sent to Hartheim from May to August 1942, nearly half were clergy. Among them were seven Germans, six Czechs, four Luxembourgers, three Dutch, two Belgians, and 310 Poles.[43] More Polish clergy died in those four months of 1942 than had died in Dachau over the previous two years,[44] and most awaiting their transport to Hartheim knew their fate. In August 1942, a Dachau prisoner recorded the following prayer, recited by a group of Polish priests awaiting their deaths:

Pójdę za Tobą, Chryste, drogą krzyż,	I follow you, Christ, on the way of the Cross
bo krzyź najlepiej mnie do Ciebie zbliża.	For the cross brings me closer to you.
Daj mi, o Chryste, przez Twą świetą mękę,	Grant me, O Christ, through your holy passion
gazowej męki zwyciężyć udrękę.	Victory over the torment of the gas.[45]

Postwar testimonies, questionnaires, and published memoirs all have much to tell us about how Polish clergymen responded to their incarceration and persecution in Dachau, and reveal that despite the many abuses they endured, there existed among most a sense of community. This sense of community—unusual among inmates in Dachau, and among inmates of the camps in general—was manifested in a variety of ways. The Czech priest, historian, and former Dachau inmate Reimund Schnabel has referred to the "*una vox*" among the clergy in general—that is, the communication and community that arose from common proficiency in Latin and spanned the barriers of national origin, culture, and native language.[46]

It stands to reason, however, that a sense of community was more evident among the clergy of a specific national group. To this the Poles were no exception, and the sense of solidarity they experienced was arguably strengthened by the camp's regime and conditions. Segregated from other prisoners (and often, other clergy) with respect to their housing, work, and privileges, and at the same time subjected to collective reprisals and group punishments for infractions,[47] many among the Polish clergy lived, suffered, and died as a collective.

That "collective" was expressed in a variety of charitable ways. Polish priests provided medical assistance to other prisoners, clergy and laity alike, and were known for sharing with other inmates the food that they received in packages.[48] Many also engaged in small acts of defiance or resistance in the camp, and these included efforts to maintain intellectual life, clandestine seminary instruction,[49] and especially covert worship and celebration of the Mass.[50]

Solidarity in defiance of the camp authorities was especially evident in an incident only weeks before the arrival of hundreds of priests in connection with the October 1941 Aktion. On September 18, the Polish clergy were asked if they wished to apply for admission to the Volksliste. For many

Poles, signing on to the Volksliste was considered treasonous, but for many in the annexed territories such as the Warthegau, it was perhaps a means of avoiding persecution or deportation, or for others, was perhaps a path to social and economic advancement. When offered the opportunity to sign on and thereby gain their release from the camp, only two or three of the roughly 1,200 priests agreed to do so. The motivations for the offer are not clear, but it is possible that the camp authorities were notified that a mass transport of Warthegau priests was in the offing. In any case, the nearly total rejection of the offer is also remarkable and testifies to a high level of patriotism, solidarity, mistrust, or a combination of the three among the clergy. The consequences for rejecting the offer were severe: the Poles lost any special privileges they had as clergymen, had to surrender their prayer books and rosaries, and were given more difficult labor assignments.[51]

Expressions of altruism, community, and solidarity among the Polish clergy—as important as these are to the Dachau story—have led to a tendency in the literature, and in some of the clergy's own reporting of their experiences in the camp, to uphold them as selfless, model prisoners, thereby idealizing their behavior in a somewhat hagiographic representation of their roles in the camp, or what Reimund Schnabel has referred to as "romantically enthusiastic accounts of fraternal coexistence."[52] Acts of altruism and solidarity were indeed many, and worthy of admiration, but it is also important to bear in mind that the general operation of the camp, its prisoner hierarchy, and the cruel and inhuman treatment of inmates were intended to encourage not solidarity but competition, not altruism but self-interest, not cooperation among the inmates but antagonism. "In the writings of the clergy," Schnabel has argued,

> is found at times a certain tendency to elevate the priest over the mass of the [camp] population, representing him as "blessed" and, in terms of character, superior to his fellow men. In the concentration camp it was revealed, for all to see, that clerics are normal people with all their weaknesses. And if a cleric has claimed that "no group loomed so exalted as the priesterly class," then this is false. It simply contradicts the reality of Dachau. . . . In the final analysis, it is clear that the clergy in the camps revealed themselves to be human, and that their coexistence under such extreme circumstances was likewise human—as human as the coexistence among prisoners in the other blocks of the Dachau concentration camp.[53]

In short, the behavior of the clergy in Dachau was at times less exemplary than has often been portrayed. There was, for example, friction between "regular" prisoners and the clergy, some of whom revealed a lack of sympathy with and even selfishness toward their fellow inmates.[54] Meindert Hinlopen, a Dutch clergyman, recalled that there were arguments and animosities among Polish and German clergy and theological disagreements between Catholic and Protestant clergy, as well as egotism, self-interest, and a general lack of solidarity.[55] In particular, national distinctions and prisoner hierarchies in the camp also contributed to discord among the priests. One particularly telling example of this concerned use of the *Lagerkapelle*, or "camp chapel." Beginning in September 1941, the camp administration prohibited Poles from entering or using the chapel. This was discussed among the clergy of other nationalities, who, according to a German priest, concluded that "one should not endanger possession of the chapel by allowing Polish priests and laity to participate in worship. If, during an inspection, the SS were to find prisoners of other blocks [i.e., prisoners other than the non-Polish clergy], they could order the destruction of the chapel. For this reason, priests were posted as sentries at the entrance to prevent prisoners from the wrong blocks from entering."[56]

Schnabel's designation of the clergy in Dachau as "human" also suggests that summary characterizations of their behavior as either altruistic or egotistic are misleading. Under the circumstances in the camp, clergy, like other prisoners, exhibited both extremes and, of course, the wide range of behaviors in between. "The special status of the clergy in the Dachau concentration camp," Schnabel concludes, "was only external. They lived in isolated blocks, yet were also prisoners like all the others. It would be as wrong to elevate them to heaven (as has often been the case) as it would be (as has likewise been the case) to condemn them."[57] Or, as the Dutch author and journalist Nico Rost described one of the *Priesterblocks* in his Dachau diary: "No, Block 26 is not a uniform whole. Here are also, in the end, only people! People with all their good and bad human characteristics! Here are simple, even willfully narrow-minded village priests and chaplains, and yet also Jesuits with astoundingly great knowledge in the most diverse areas. Here are unusually well-educated clergy, and yet also monks whose horizons are shockingly limited. Her are reactionary elements who dream of a 'feudal-state,' but also pastors who were with the partisans."[58]

To address the complexities of behavior in the camp is not to judge the clergy, Polish or otherwise, but to remain mindful, as Rost suggests, of the diversity of their biographies, political orientations, and responses to incarceration. One is also reminded in this context of Primo Levi's claim, in discussing his "gray zone" of moral culpability in the camps, that "it is naive, absurd, and historically false to believe that an infernal system such as National Socialism sanctifies its victims: on the contrary, it degrades them, it makes them resemble itself, and this all the more when they are available, blank, and lacking a political or moral armature."[59] Clergymen in Dachau may, in fact, have had a moral armature at their disposal, and this is perhaps what sustained many of them over the course of their incarceration, but they remained, as other prisoners, subject to both the brutalities of the camp and the frailties of their human condition.

For moral leadership and support in these challenging circumstances, many of the Polish clergy in Dachau looked to Michał Kozal, the auxiliary bishop of Włocławek. Deported to Dachau in April 1941, Kozal was, until his death in January 1943, central to spiritual and intellectual life among the priests there. His experience under the occupation was remarkable in a number of ways: it was an example of the treatment of the Polish Catholic hierarchy, for he was one of numerous bishops imprisoned under the Nazis, and one of three killed in concentration camps[60]; it was an odyssey through a complex network of prisons and camps much like that experienced by hundreds of Polish clergymen; and it revealed the inability of the larger Roman Catholic hierarchy—in this case, the Vatican and its representatives—to act effectively on behalf of a member of the Polish episcopate.

"I was consecrated a bishop only to be arrested immediately thereafter,"[61] Michał Kozal was reported to have remarked in 1940. Consecrated as suffragan bishop on August 13, 1939, Kozal was forced, only weeks later, to assume the leadership of the Włocławek diocese after the German invasion and departure of his superior, Bishop Karol Radoński.[62] Like his colleague in Poznań, suffragan bishop Walenty Dymek, Kozal was labeled by the Nazi authorities a dangerous nationalist and "fanatical Pole,"[63] "an enemy of Germany" who was "clever and to be treated with caution."[64] Following the invasion and in the weeks prior to his incarceration, Kozal had emerged as an active opponent of the Nazi occupiers, intervening with the authorities in numerous ways[65] until he was arrested, along with forty to fifty other Włocławek priests, on November 7 1939.[66] First detained in a local prison, the bishop was then transferred to the Ląd cloister along with some eighty other priests.[67] He remained there until May 1940, when he was transferred to a prison in Poznań. Beginning in April 1941, he was imprisoned in a camp in Inowrocław, and then held in prisons in Poznań,

Berlin, Halle, Weimar, and Nürnberg,[68] before his deportation to Dachau in April 1941.

The Vatican was aware of the bishop's initial arrest and imprisonment[69] and made several attempts to secure his release. In early 1940, Kozal was visited in Ląd by a German priest named Eberhard Wigge, who had been charged by the papal nuncio in Berlin, Cesare Orsenigo, with convincing the bishop to take on the role of apostolic administrator in the Lublin diocese. Kozal, not understanding that this was, in fact, a "rescue mission" of sorts, was highly mistrustful of the pope's German emissary. When asked about conditions in his diocese, he stated that he had "nothing to communicate to the nuncio," and when presented with the prospect of a transfer to a diocese "farther east," the bishop dismissed the offer, and stated that he would accept such an assignment "only if the pope commands it."[70] In retrospect, this maneuver by the Berlin nunciature might appear clumsy and naive, and suggests as well that Orsenigo and his representative were not fully cognizant of the bishop's circumstances or, more broadly, the character of German Kirchenpolitik in the Warthegau.[71] It also foreshadowed subsequent and futile attempts by the Vatican to act on Kozal's behalf.

The bishop arrived in Dachau on April 25, 1941, was given prisoner number 24,544, and was assigned to *Priesterblock* 28 where, because of his status, he was frequently mistreated by the SS and functionary prisoners.[72] According to a fellow priest in Dachau, when a *kapo* was asked if he could accommodate Kozal in his labor commando, he responded, "You know, however, what a sensation that would cause . . . . The bishop would be thrown out, and I would catch hell . . . . You see, a Bishop in Dachau is like a raisin that has found its way into a loaf of whole-wheat bread. It attracts the attention of everyone."[73] Whether despite or because of his office, Bishop Kozal suffered the same labor demands, discipline, and beatings as his fellow prisoners, receiving from the *kapos* and camp guards no preferential treatment.

Aware of the bishop's incarceration in the camp, the Vatican attempted to intervene on his behalf. On at least three occasions, Pius XII's representatives issued diplomatic notes to the German Ministry of Foreign Affairs protesting against Kozal's treatment, but to no avail.[74] Once in Dachau, the bishop's only contact with the outside world would remain his correspondence with a friend in Włocławek. In that city's diocesan archive are twenty-two of Kozal's letters from Dachau, written from May 1941 until

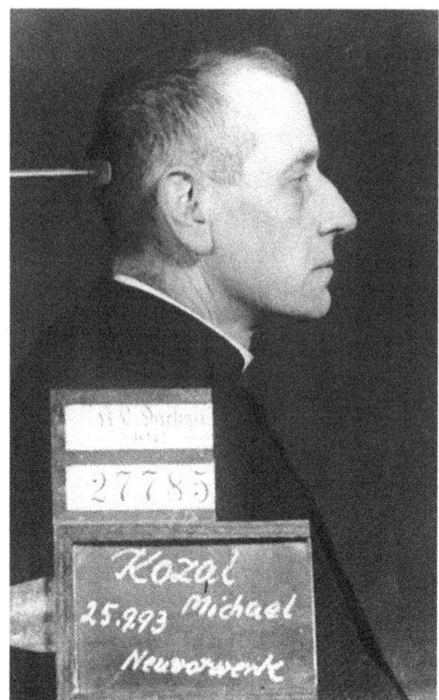

Figs. 12.1 and 12.2. Bishop Michał Kozal in Dachau, April 1941. Courtesy of Włocławskie Muzeum Diecezjalne.

January 1943, all addressed to Father Ignacy Zięciak. The bishop's correspondence reveals on the surface perhaps little—inquiries about relatives and friends, blessings on the occasion of holidays, thanks for packages sent and additional requests—but on closer look, the letters, written in German and subject to camp censors, show his grave concern about matters in his diocese and his stoicism in the face of maltreatment and illness. Also evident are the coded ways in which the bishop reported on conditions in the camp and the fate of fellow clergy there.[75]

Kozal's last letter was posted on January 10, 1943, but revealed nothing about his health, which was declining rapidly. He died in Dachau sixteen days later. His cause of death was officially listed as typhus, although there remains controversy over whether he died as a result of an ear infection, or whether he was killed by a lethal injection, as some of his companions and early biographers claimed.[76] The Vatican proved unable to secure the bishop's release, yet Pope Pius XII publicly recognized his suffering and death in a 1945 speech to the College of Cardinals,[77] marking the beginning of

Kozal's postmortem prominence in the commemorative culture of postwar Polish Catholicism. A church leader who defied the Nazis, suffered their persecution, and died in the camp best known for the incarceration of Polish priests, the bishop would, in the years that followed, be venerated, along with the Franciscan Maksymilian Kolbe, who was killed in Auschwitz in 1941, as one of the great Catholic martyrs of the faith, church, and Polish nation.

Michał Kozal may have been the most prominent among Polish Catholic clerics in Dachau, but he was, of course, one among many. His story, like all such stories, is unique, but it also remains strikingly ordinary, for the bishop's demise was much like that of hundreds of other Polish priests whose health and spirit succumbed to the rigors and brutality of life and death in Dachau. While statistics certainly do not capture the character of human experience, they illustrate how the Nazi regime targeted at Dachau Polish priests, and especially those from the Reichsgau Wartheland. They also point to the significance of Dachau as their "final destination." Over the course of the occupation, 234 secular priests had been killed in camps on Polish territory,[78] but by 1944, nearly all Polish clergy from the entire network of Nazi camps had been concentrated in Dachau. Of the more than 1,700 Polish Catholic priests registered as prisoners in Dachau, some 850, or roughly half, did not survive the camp.[79] They accounted for 83 percent of all Catholic clergy killed there.[80] Statistics also testify to the rigor and severity of Nazi policy toward the church in the "model Gau." The Dachau camp had assembled secular clergy from twenty-one Polish dioceses: 60 percent of them came from the four main Warthegau dioceses (Poznań, Gniezno, Łódź, and Włocławek) alone, and the Warthegau clergy accounted for more than 65 percent of the deaths there.[81]

Among them was Jan Pewniak, provost in Zduny (Treustadt), who wrote from Dachau on July 12, 1941, to the Sisters of Charity of Saint Vincent de Paul at his home parish, "The single experience of martyrdom may be more resplendent, but it is often more difficult and meritorious to bear, in silent fulfillment of one's duty and according to Christ's instructions, our daily cross."[82] Father Pewniak died in Dachau in December of the following year.[83] We do not know how his words were received by the nuns in his parish, but it is likely that they would take on a special relevance for the many sisters of their order, dozens of whom would be deported in the months that followed to the "Nonnenlager Schmückert."

Notes

1. Breitinger, *Als Deutschenseelsorger*, 68.
2. Sziling, *Polityka*, 260.
3. Sziling, 260.
4. Beate Kosmala, "Polnische Häftlinge im Konzentrationslager Dachau 1939–1945," *Dachauer Hefte* 21 (November 2005): 106.
5. Broszat, "Verfolgung," 84.
6. Józef Bogacki, Ankieta, April 10, 1975, AAP, zespół 133, syg. OK 215.
7. Schnabel, *Macht*, 39.
8. Kosmala, "Polnische Häftlinge," 96.
9. Paul Berben, *Dachau 1933–1945: The Official History* (London: Comité International de Dachau, 1980), 144.
10. Schnabel, *Macht*, 96.
11. Kosmala, "Polnische Häftlinge," 106.
12. Wiktor Sobecki to Kuria Poznań, AAP, zespół 133, syg. OK 121.
13. Florian Deresiński to Kuria Poznań, January 9, 1947, AAP, zespół 133, syg. OK 121. The Dachau-Gusen-Dachau pattern was not uncommon among priests from the Poznań archdiocese, as reports from priests issued in 1947 demonstrate. See, i.a., Paweł Zydor to Kuria Poznań, AAP, zespół 133, syg. OK121; Marian Magnuszewski to Kuria Poznań, AAP, zespół 133, OK 121; Jolanta Adamska and Jan Sziling, *Man to Man . . . : Destruction of the Polish Intelligentsia in the Years 1939–1945. Mauthausen/Gusen* (Warszawa: Rada Ochrony Pamięci Walk i Męczeństwa: 2009), 34.
14. Stanislav Zámecník, *That Was Dachau 1933–1945* (Paris: Fondation internationale de Dachau/le cherche midi, 2004), 167n7.
15. Florian Deresiński to Kuria Poznań, January 9, 1947, AAP, zespół 133, syg. OK 121.
16. A functionary prisoner, usually assigned to supervise the labor of other prisoners.
17. Quoted and translated in Adamska and Sziling, *Man to Man*, 63.
18. One Polish priest has recalled in his memoir the better conditions, food, and relaxed discipline in Dachau in comparison to Gusen. See Ludwik Bielerzewski, *Ksiądz nie zostaje sam. Wspomnienia* (Poznań: Księgarnia Św. Wojciecha, 1976), 160–61. See also the testimony of the Polish priest Henryk Malak, who described the frail condition of inmates recently transferred from Gusen to Dachau, in Adamska and Sziling, *Man to Man*, 34.
19. The vast majority of clergy were housed first in Block 26, although a small number were also housed in other camp barracks among "regular" prisoners. See Domagała, *Ci, którzy przeszli przez Dachau*, 52.
20. Berben, *Dachau*, 146; Schnabel, *Macht*, 96, 125, 154–55; Zámečnik, *That Was Dachau*, 169; Kosmala, "Polnische Häftlinge," 106.
21. The Polish clergy were housed together in Block 28, separate from the German priests in Block 26. Berben, *Dachau*, 146; Johannes Neuhäusler, *What Was It Like in the Concentration Camp at Dachau? An Attempt to Come Closer to the Truth* (München: Trustees for the Monument of Atonement in the Concentration Camp at Dachau, 1973), 51. On the privileged status of German clergy, see Broszat, "Verfolgung," 81.
22. Raport 'Straty Kulturalne,' Ministerstwo Spraw Wewnętrzych, Wydiał Społeczny, Nr. 18/44, Część I-sza, Londyn, December 30, 1944, AAN, zespół 493/Konsulat Gen.-Nowy York, syg. 472, 26; Schnabel, *Macht*, 88.

23. Kosmala, "Polnische Häftlinge," 95; Schnabel, *Macht*, 60.

24. Broszat, "Verfolgung," 82.

25. Schnabel, *Macht*, 142.

26. Wienken to Bertram, September 15, 1943, document 883, in Volk, *Akten deutscher Bischöfe*, vol. 6, 227; Schnabel, *Macht*, 152.

27. Robert Sigel, "The Cultivation of Medicinal Herbs in the Concentration Camp: The Plantation at Dachau," *Dachau Review* 2 (1990): 84; Broszat, "Verfolgung," 81.

28. Kosmala, "Polnische Häftlinge," 106.

29. Henryk Malak recalled that one dollar was discovered. Zámečnik set the number at seven hundred. Historian Florian Schwanninger claims that the camp authorities confiscated eight hundred dollars. See Henryk Maria Malak, *Shavelings in Death Camps: A Polish Priest's Memoir of Imprisonment by the Nazis, 1939–1945* (Jefferson, North Carolina: McFarland and Company, Inc., 2012), 253–54; Zámečnik, *That Was Dachau*, 171; Florian Schwanninger, "The Murders of Priests at Hartheim Castle under 'Sonderbehandlung 14f13," *Studia nad Totalitaryzmami i Wiekiem XX—Totalitarian and 20th Century Studies* 2 (2018), 167.

30. Malak, *Shavelings*, 254.

31. On the priests' ten days of *Sport* in 1942, see Malak, *Shavelings*, 252–55; Franciszek Korszyński, *Jasne promienie w Dachau* (Poznań: Pallotinum, 1957), 46–48; Zámečnik, *That Was Dachau*, 171–72; Schnabel, *Macht*, 121.

32. Stefan Biskupski, *Księża polscy w niemieckich obozach koncentracynych* (London: F. Mildner and Sons, 1946), 23, 62.

33. Florian Deresiński to Kuria Poznań, January 9, 1947, AAP, zespół 133, syg. OK 121.

34. Bedrich Hoffmann, *And Who Will Kill You: The Chronicle of the Life and Sufferings of Priests in the Concentration Camps* (Poznań: Pallottinum, 1994), 159.

35. Florian Deresiński to Kuria Poznań, January 9, 1947, AAP, zespół 133, syg. OK 121; Stanisław Szymański to Kuria Poznań, January 11, 1947, AAP, zespół 133, syg. OK 121; Edmund Bartosiak to Kuria Poznań, January 13, 1947, AAP, zespół 133, syg. OK 121; Marian Magnuszewski to Kuria Poznań, January 14, 1947, AAP, zespół 133, syg. OK 121. On the various experiments using Polish clergy as subjects, see also Malak, *Shavelings*, 269–75.

36. Michałowski's testimony took place on December 21, 1946. See United States, *Trials of War Criminals before the Nuernberg Military Tribunals under Control Council Law No. 10*, vol. 10 (Washington, DC: US Government Printing Office), quoted in Nikolaus Wachsmann, *KL: A History of the Nazi Concentration Camps* (New York: Farrar, Straus and Giroux, 2015), 431.

37. Malak, *Shavelings*, 274–75.

38. Eugen Kogon, *Der SS-Staat: das System der deutschen Konzentrationslager* (München: Kindler Verlag, 1997), 281.

39. Konstanty Pankiewicz, in Katolicki Ośrodek Wydawniczy Veritas, ed., *Cudem ocaleni: wspomnienia z kacetów. Praca zbiorowa* (London: Katolicki Ośrodek Wydawniczy Veritas, 1981), 254. On Hofmann, see Klee, *Personenlexikon*, 266.

40. On the "selections" and "euthanasia" in the camps, including Dachau, see Wachsmann, *KL*, 243–55. On "*Aktion* 14f13" see Henry Friedlander, *The Origins of Nazi Genocide: From Euthanasia to the Final Solution* (Chapel Hill: University of North Carolina Press, 1995), 142–50.

41. Two Polish scholars have claimed that the Polish clergy who were taken for the "invalid transports" were killed mainly in mobile gas vans, such as had been used in the "euthanasia" program in the Altreich in 1940 and 1941. See Jacewicz and Woś,

Martyrologium, vol. 2, no. 1, "Straty," 26, 29, 40. As noted below, however, the consensus among scholars and former Dachau prisoners is that the transports were destined for Hartheim. On the history of the Hartheim facility see Brigitte Kepplinger, Gerhart Marckhgott, and Hartmut Reese, eds., *Tötungsanstalt Hartheim*, Oberösterreich in der Zeit des Nationalsozialismus, vol. 3 (Linz: Oberösterreichischen Landesarchiv/Lern- und Gedenkort Schloss Hartheim, 2008).

42. Florian Schwanninger, "'Wenn Du nicht arbeiten kannst, schicken wir Dich zum Vergasen.': Die 'Sonderbehandlung 14f13' im Schloss Hartheim 1941–1944," in Kepplinger, Marckhgott, and Reese, *Tötungsanstalt Hartheim*, 191–93. See also Schwanninger, "Murders," 163–68.

43. Zámečník, *That Was Dachau*, 209–11; Schwanninger, "Murders," 164. For a list of Polish clergymen taken in these transports see Hoffmann, *And Who Will Kill You*, 556–78. A commemorative tablet installed in 2005 at the Hartheim memorial site states that 297 Polish priests were killed there. See Adamska and Sziling, *Polscy księża*, 182. On the experience of Polish clergy designated for the *Invaliden-Transporte* and awaiting deportation to Hartheim, see the recollections of Tadeusz Gaik in Katolicki Ośrodek Wydawniczy Veritas, *Cudem ocaleni*, 73–76.

44. Jacewicz and Woś, *Martyrologium*," Straty," 26, 29. On the number of Polish clergymen killed in the transports, see "Eidestattliche Erklärung eines polnischen Priesters (Gerald Mizgalski) über die Ausrottung polnischer Geistlicher, July 1, 1946, document B 15, in Schnabel, *Macht*, 398; Berben, *Dachau*, 157, 277; Neuhäusler, *What Was It Like*, 29–30. See also Domagała, who sets the total number of Dachau prisoners killed in the transports at roughly 3,166, among them approximately 700 Poles: Domagała, *Ci, którzy przeszli przez Dachau*, 45.

45. Quoted by Tadeusz Gaik, in Katolicki Ośrodek Wydawniczy Veritas, *Cudem ocaleni*, 75–76.

46. Schnabel, *Macht*, 126.

47. Hoffmann, *And Who Will Kill You*, 141–42, 144.

48. Kosmala, "Polnische Häftlinge," 108. On the charitable activities of the clergy in the camp, see also Korszyński, *Jasne promienie*, 86–93.

49. On the intellectual pursuits of clergy, see Korszyński, *Jasne promienie*, 99–104.

50. Schnabel, *Macht*, 152. In October 1941 the non-German priests were removed from Block 26 to Block 28, and were denied access to the small chapel in Block 26. See Neuhäusler, *What Was It Like*, 51–53. On the Polish clergy's worship activities and spiritual ministry to other inmates, see Sławomir Kęszka, "Posługa polskich księży w KL Dachau i jej upamiętnienie," *Biuletyn Instytutu Pamięci Narodowej*, no. 146–147 (January–February 2018): 49–59.

51. Korszyński, *Jasne promienie*, 44–46, 70; Schnabel, *Macht*, 142; Hoffmann, *And Who Will Kill You*, 180. Leo Michałowski, in his testimony at the Nürnberg "Doctors Trial," also briefly described the incident: Testimony of Leo Michalowski, December 21, 1946, 885, trial transcript, accessed on February 11, 2018 via Harvard Law School, Nuremberg Trials Project, http://nuremberg.law.harvard.edu/transcripts/1-transcript-for-nmt-1-medical-case?seq=889&q=miochalowski.

52. Schnabel, *Macht*, 126.

53. Schnabel, 126–29.

54. Berben, *Dachau*, 147.

55. Schnabel, *Macht*, 127.

56. Johannes Sonnenschein, interview with Christian Frieling, October 5 and 7, 1989, quoted in Christian Frieling, *Priester aus dem Bistum Münster im KZ: 38 Biographien* (Münster: Aschendorff, 1992), 64, quoted in Thomas Rahe, "Die Bedeutung von Religion und Religiosität in den KZs," in *Die nationalsozialistischen Konzentrationslager-Entwicklung und Struktur*, vol. 2, ed. Ulrich Herbert, Karin Orth, and Christoph Dieckmann (Göttingen: Wallstein Verlag, 1998), 1018.

57. Schnabel, *Macht*, 136.

58. Nico Rost, *Goethe in Dachau* (Berlin: Volk und Welt, 1999), 190. The source of the quoted English translation is the German translation cited here. That translation refers not to a "feudal state," but a "city state" ("*Städte-staat*"). In the original Dutch edition, Rost uses the term *Stände-staat* in German—i.e., "feudal state." See Nico Rost, *Goethe in Dachau: Literatuur en Werkelijkheid* (Amsterdam: L.J. Veen's Uitgeversmaatschappij N.V., 1948), 152.

59. Primo Levi, *The Drowned and the Saved* (New York: Summit, 1980), 40.

60. The other two bishops were Antoni Julian Nowowiejski, ordinary of the Płock (during the German occupation, Schröttersburg) diocese, and the Płock suffragan Leon Wetmański.

61. Breitinger, *Als Deutschenseelsorger*, 66.

62. Stanisław Librowski, *Ofiary zbrodni niemieckiej spośród duchowieństwa diecezji włocławskiej 1939–1945* (Włocławek: Księgarnia Powszechna i Drukarnia Diecezjalna, 1947), 72–73; Wojciech Frątczak, *Diecezja Włocławska*, 73.

63. Kerrl to Reichsministerium des Innern, October 11, 1939, BAB, R 5101/22185, 14.

64. Hawranke, Bericht über die Kirchenlage im Gebiet der Militärbefehlshabers Danzig-Westpreußen, October 9, 1939, BAB, R 5101/22185, 17.

65. Testimony of Fr. Dr. Stefan Biskupski, June 27, 1946, IPN, GK 196/38/CD 1, 93–95; Librowski, *Ofiary zbrodni*, 73.

66. Stadtkommissar des Stadtkreises Leslau, Tätigkeitsbericht zum 15. November 1939, December 13, 1939, APP, 53/299/0/1.39/1832, microfilm O-60675, 7. While this document notes the arrest of approximately fifty Włocławek clerics, the postwar testimony of a Włocławek resident reported that forty-four Włocławek priests were arrested on November 7: Jadwiga Toporowska, relacja, February 1, 1948, IZ, Dok. II-94.

67. "Ląd-niemieckie obóz przejściowy," 235–36; Świniarski, "Ląd–niedawny," 225–35.

68. Testimony of Fr. Dr. Stefan Biskupski, June 27, 1946, IPN, GK 196/38/CD 1, 93–95; Korszyński, *Jasne promienie*, 147–50. On Kozal's imprisonment in these locations, see Wojciech Frątczak, *Biskup Michał Kozal: życie-męczeństwo-kult* (Włocławek: Wydawnictwo Duszpasterstwa Rolników, 2009), 145–47; Stefan Biskupski, "Męczeńskie biskupstwo księdza Michała Kozala," *Atheneum Kapłańskie*, vol. 45, nos. 1–2 (August–September 1946): 52–66.

69. Orsenigo to Maglione, December 7, 1939, document 62, in *ADSS*, vol. 3, no. 1, 143.

70. Orsenigo to Maglione, May 24, 1940, document 140, in *ADSS* vol. 3, no. 1, 244.

71. See Breitinger, *Als Deutschenseelsorger*, 67. The visit and the bishop's mistrust are described as well by a fellow priest in the camp. See Władysław Bartoń, "Życie lądzkich więźniów (wspomnienia ks. W. Bartonia SDB)," in Wąsowicz, *Łądczy*, 53.

72. Malak, *Shavelings*, 218–19, 250. On Kozal's arrival in Dachau, see Frątczak, *Biskup*, 147–48, 150–51; Malak, *Shavelings*, 206–9.

73. Malak, *Shavelings*, 250.

74. The Vatican's protests are described in "A Note of His Eminence the Cardinal Secretary of State to the Foreign Minister of the Reich about the religious situation in the

'Warthegau' and in the other Polish provinces subject to Germany," document 3264-PS, in IMT, vol. 32, 95.

75. The letters in the Archiwum Diecezjalne we Włocławku are reproduced (in Polish translation) and annoted in "Listy biskupa Michała Kozala z obozu koncentracyjnego w Dachau," *Studia Włocławskie* 17 (2015): 539–61. For further interpretation of them see Wojciech Frątczak, "Listy obozowe biskupa Michała Kozala," *Atheneum Kapłańskie* 472 (1987): 532–38. I am grateful to Father Krzysztof Kamiński and Sister Bernadeta Żabierek of the library of the Wyższe Seminarium Duchowne, Włocławek, for alerting me to these sources.

76. Librowski, *Ofiary zbrodni*, 76. On the controversy over Kozal's death, see Frątczak, *Biskup*, 169–74.

77. "Excerpts from the allocution of His Holiness Pope Pius XII to the Sacred College, June 2, 1945, on the persecution of the Catholic Church during the period of the National Socialist Government in Germany," document 3268-PS, in IMT, vol. 32, 112–15.

78. Stanisław Batawia and Janusz Gumkowski, Oświadczenie Głównej Komisji Badania Zbrodni Niemieckich w Polsce, January 7, 1946, IPN, GK 162/468, 2.

79. Statistics on the number of clergy, Catholic priests, and members of religious orders in Dachau differ, but not dramatically. Jan Domagała set the number of Polish clergy (of all faiths) in Dachau at 1,780 (among them 1,748 Catholic clergy), claiming that 868 died. See Domagała, *Ci, którzy przeszli przez Dachau*, 54, 57. Emil Thoma has claimed that among the Catholic secular and religious clergy in Dachau, 1,773 were Poles. See Emil Thoma, *Die Geistlichen in Dachau sowie in anderen Konzentrationslager und Gefängnissen* (Mödling: Missionsdruckerei St. Gabriel, 1971), 45. The Polish priest Gerard Mizgalski concluded, based on his research in 1946 at the behest of the American occupation authorities in Germany, that 846 religious and secular Polish Catholic clergy died in Dachau. See "Eidestattliche Erklärung eines polnischen Priesters (Gerald Mizgalski) über die Ausrottung polnischer Geistlicher, July 1, 1946, document B 15, in Schnabel, *Macht*, 398. Wiktor Jacewicz and Jan Woś state that 860 Polish clergymen incarcerated in Dachau died, although this number includes sixty who were in Dachau and subsequently died after being transferred in 1940 to the Buchenwald and Gusen camps. See Jacewicz and Woś, *Martyrologium*, "Straty," 41. An affidavit submitted by the Polish Main Commission for the Investigation of German Crimes in Poland sets the number at 851: Stanisław Batawia and Janusz Gumkowski, Oświadczenie Głównej Komisji Badania Zbrodni Niemieckich w Polsce, January 7, 1946, IPN, GK 162/468, 2.

80. Broszat, "Verfolgung," 83.

81. Domagała, *Ci, którzy przeszli przez Dachau*, 54–60; Jacewicz and Woś, *Martyrologium*, "Straty," 34.

82. German, from Pewniak's letter: "Das einmalige Martyrium mag zwar glänzender sein, aber oft ist es schwerer u. verdienstvoller im stiller Pflichterfüllung das tägliche Kreuz zu tragen, der Weisungen Christi entsprechend." Jan Pewniak to Sióstr Miłosierdzia św. Wincentego i Paulo, July 12, 1941, AAP, zespół 133, syg. OK 235.

83. Domagała, *Ci, którzy przeszli przez Dachau*, 190.

13

NONNENLAGER

Women Religious in the Bojanowo Labor Camp

On June 11, 1941, the papal nunciature in Berlin issued a protest to the Reich Ministry for Foreign Affairs regarding the existence of a camp in Bojanowo, a small town known in German as Schmückert, located near the southern border of the Reichsgau Wartheland. The nuncio's representation claimed that approximately four hundred women religious were incarcerated there.[1] In response, the Foreign Ministry replied on September 28 that the facility was "a temporary measure for the Reichsgau Wartheland, undertaken with the consent of the Reich lieutenant [Reichsstatthalter], in order to address the problem of homelessness among Polish Catholic sisters."[2] More than a year and a half later, the Vatican secretary of state, Cardinal Luigi Maglione, issued a note verbale to the Reich minister for foreign affairs, Joachim von Ribbentrop. This expansive document was a clear and detailed protest against German measures against the Roman Catholic Church in occupied Poland, and the Wartheland in particular. One illustration of the brutality of German policy was, according to Maglione, the ongoing existence of the Bojanowo camp, where, he claimed, hundreds of women religious were still incarcerated as of the end of 1942.[3]

There were, in fact, hundreds of nuns in the camp at that time,[4] and the facility was more than a temporary homeless shelter. The cardinal secretary of state was referring to a labor camp that had, since February 1941,[5] been used for the incarceration of the Warthegau's women religious who had been deported there after being expelled from their convents, cloisters, and religious houses. In all, more than six hundred sisters and nuns[6] were incarcerated in the Nonnenlager Schmückert, where they worked under difficult conditions for the German authorities in agricultural work, munitions manufacturing, garment production, and other capacities. The camp remained in operation until early 1945.[7]

One might approach the story of the Nonnenlager as an odd curiosity, as if to say, "So bad were the Nazis that they even had a camp for nuns." Or one might choose to compare it to other prisons and camps in the Warthegau, concluding that life there was hard for the nuns, but not nearly as difficult as in most other sites for the incarceration of the Polish secular clergy and male religious. The camp was indeed an oddity, but its little-known history is well worth investigating, on the one hand, in the context of National Socialist Kirchenpolitik and, on the other, in relation to the labor needs of the German war economy. While the broader persecution of the Warthegau church and its attendant goal of Germanization was the impetus for establishing the camp, labor utilization appears to be the reason for expanding and maintaining it.

Point twelve of the Thirteen Points of church policy introduced in 1940 called for the dissolution of all religious orders in the Wartheland, and the Nazi authorities nearly accomplished this goal. Women religious were not subject to the same level of persecution as their male counterparts, but they were far more numerous, for religious orders for women were many and expansive in interwar Poland. Prior to World War II, there were eighty-four different orders, of which ten were cloistered, and their 21,914 sisters (including professed nuns, novices, and postulants) lived in 2,289 religious houses and convents across the country.[8] The overwhelming majority were "active"—that is, not cloistered, and engaged in a variety of social services, such as education, medical care, support and care for the elderly and orphans, or service to the poor and homeless. They operated more than 1,800 preschools, 232 orphanages, and hundreds of schools, hospitals, and soup kitchens.[9]

With the Nazi invasion of Poland, their circumstances changed dramatically, especially in the Reichsgau Wartheland, where the German military and, later, occupation authorities often terrorized the women religious and subjected them to various indignities. Describing an episode in the fall of 1939, a Carmelite nun from Poznań recalled, "Later the Gestapo came. They wanted us to undress. Among them was a physician who was supposed to examine us. We said: 'You cannot demand that of us. We are nuns—unless you intend to commit violence against us.' They limited [the examinations] to shoulders or heads or in some cases feet. At every turn we felt that they wanted to humiliate us, to degrade our human dignity."[10] Most of the nuns among the Poznań Carmelites were eventually sent to the General Government, where they found refuge in other cloisters of their order. Others were not so fortunate, for beginning in 1939, the German authorities closed 294 houses belonging to the women religious across occupied Poland.[11] Housing the expelled sisters in alternative religious communities was seldom an option, and many did not have family nearby. Often, the German authorities simply decided where the nuns would go, and often, their destination was the camp in Bojanowo. When, for example, members of the Franciscan Sisters of the Family of Mary were evicted from their convents in 1939, they were initially permitted to resettle in the Warthegau. In 1940, the Germans began to deport the nuns to the General Government, and in 1941, they sent the remaining nuns to Bojanowo.[12] The Congregation of the Sisters Servant of the Immaculate Conception of the Blessed Virgin Mary included 466 sisters spread across eight dioceses, where they operated sixty-six preschools serving four thousand children, four primary schools, and five orphanages serving 222 children. Forty-five of their houses and more than half their sisters were located in the Warthegau. Five of the houses had been closed already in September and October 1939; another twenty-six were closed between December 1939 and September 1942. The authorities subjected sisters from another twelve houses to various forms of repression—placing them under house arrest, prohibiting them from providing social services, and forcing them to sign on to the Volksliste—before they were finally deported to Bojanowo.[13]

The Congregation of the Sisters of the Common Labor of Mary Immaculate, a relatively small order based in the Włocławek diocese, operated eleven houses, four orphanages, three facilities for the elderly, and two schools for girls. Under the German occupation, all 246 sisters of the order were expelled from their houses, and all but one house, located on the territory of the General Government, were "Germanized" and put to secular use. The house in Poznań was turned into a hotel and cafeteria for Germans; a house in Kalisz was likewise used as a hotel; five of the order's institutions were transformed into homes for Volksdeutsche children; one was converted to a hospital for German children.[14] The fate of the "mother house" and sisters in Włocławek is instructive. The house was closed already in 1939 and remained so for the duration of the occupation. The sisters of the order also operated in Włocławek a child-care facility for sixty children, which was closed in 1940. Fifteen children lived in the order's orphanage, which the Germans closed in 1941. The order's home for the elderly was also closed, and the twenty-five residents were reportedly taken away to be gassed. Of the eighty-five sisters residing in the "mother house" in 1939, only fifty-three had returned by 1947. During the occupation, twenty-six had been sent to the Nonnenlager.[15]

The Nazi authorities expelled women religious from their institutions and restricted or prohibited their social ministries, but their spiritual work continued, and often illegally, as they were required to take on many of the duties traditionally undertaken by priests who had been killed, incarcerated in prisons and camps, or prohibited from serving their parishes. These responsibilities included children's catechetical instruction and preparation for first Communion, care for and administration of the Eucharist to the dying, officiating at burials, maintaining parish life in the absence of priests, and keeping churches and chapels accessible to the public—and all of these in, at times, clandestine ways.[16] In effect, nuns were carrying on much of the work of priests, and as public ministers of the church, were visible and active members of the community. For the occupation authorities, this was a cause for concern. In Rogoźno (Rogasen), a small town in Oborniki Subdistrict, the parish priest had been deported to a concentration camp. According to the report of an alarmed local Nazi Party leader, the nuns in the community were, in effect, working in his place. "Through them," the official claimed, "solidarity among the Poles is becoming stronger." Moreover, he claimed, the nuns were responsible for spreading rumors and anti-German propaganda and should therefore be removed from the town as soon as possible.[17]

Ardent Roman Catholic educators, evangelizers, social servants, and, in the eyes of the German authorities, bearers of Polish national identity, women religious in the Warthegau were subject to persecution, deportation, and incarceration, although to a lesser degree than their counterparts among the male religious and secular clergy. Of the 2,666 nuns in the Warthegau,[18] more than 1,500 were deported to the General Government.[19] While more than two-thirds of the Warthegau's monastic and secular clergy were subject to the brutalities of Nazi prisons and camps[20] across the Altreich and Incorporated Territories, only roughly one-fourth of the nuns in the Warthegau were incarcerated. They were confined not in conventional Nazi prisons and camps but in the comparatively mild conditions of the Nonnenlager Schmückert.

Scholarly analysis of the Nonnenlager is sparse. A few synthetic histories of the German occupation in Poland and a number of church histories refer to the camp, but only in passing.[21] The well-known Polish reference work *Obozy hitlerowskie na ziemiach polskich 1939–1945* (Nazi Camps in the Polish lands 1939–1945), published in 1979, includes an entry on the camp that describes it as a facility where Poles, Jews, Roma, and Germans were subjected to forced labor, but it does not note the presence of nuns there.[22] There is a Polish-language literature on women's religious orders under the occupation, and it includes a small number of articles and book chapters that refer to the camp as a destination for nuns.[23] In addition, a local historian in the town of Bojanowo has published a study of the Nonnenlager.[24] Although quite concise, it remains the most extensive analysis to date.

The origins of the Bojanowo camp go back to the late nineteenth century, when the town, like most of the territory of the subsequent Reichsgau Wartheland, was part of what historians of Poland would refer to as the Prussian or German Partition. In 1889, the German army built barracks there. A few years later, these were transformed into a "forced labor house" for vagrants and beggars. During World War I, a German infantry battalion was stationed there, and after the reestablishment of the Polish state (and the renaming of the town "Bojanowo"), the compound was used again as a correctional institution for the indigent. After the German invasion of September 1939, the town once again assumed its former German name (Schmückert), and the inmates there were freed.[25] There is record of the complex being used for the mentally ill in 1940,[26] but it was not transformed into a labor camp until February 1941, when the first transports of women religious arrived there from Poznań and Lisków (Schönort), a village east of Kalisz.[27]

The nuns were sent to Bojanowo following an order of Reichsstatthalter Greiser on September 24, 1940, calling for the dissolution of all confessional institutions in the Warthegau, including hospitals, orphanages, cloisters, and religious houses.[28] Greiser's instructions were consistent with the Thirteen Points outlined in the summer of that year, which stated that religious organizations would not be permitted to own property such as buildings, that they would cease any social welfare activities, and that all religious orders were to be abolished. The Nazi authorities acted swiftly: according to a December 1940 SD report, over the course of only three months, 248 Roman Catholic religious houses and institutions in the Warthegau had been closed and seized by the police. Thirty were turned over to the party, and the overwhelming majority (198) were put under the control of the *Gauselbstverwaltung* (the Gau Self-Administration, or GSV, which was responsible for managing properties and institutions taken over by the German authorities).[29] It is significant that the camp, at that time officially referred to as the "Gauarbeitsanstalt Schmückert" ("Gau Labor Facility Schmückert"), was also placed under the authority of the Gau Self-Administration. This put the Reichsstatthalter's office in control of both the vacated cloisters and the camp where the expelled sisters were to be interned.

Although under the control of the GSV, which was a state entity, the Nonnenlager Schmückert was one of hundreds of camps developed to provide prisoner labor for the benefit of private firms or individuals. To that extent, it can perhaps be considered part of what Christopher Browning, in his examination of the Starachowice factory camps, has referred to as the "privatization" of the camp system. Such camps were typically built, managed, and guarded by those individuals and firms that exploited laborers who were essentially owned and "rented out" by the SS.[30] In the case of the Bojanowo camp, however, the Reichsstatthalter's office, via the Gauselbstverwaltung, owned the camp, and it was the local Gestapo that made the nuns available to a number of different enterprises as forced laborers.

For the nuns sent to Bojanowo, their arrest and deportation was dramatic, and even terrifying. Accounts of the Sisters of the Common Labor of Mary Immaculate in Włocławek describe how on August 5, 1942, the German authorities arrived, surrounded the entire convent, and ordered the nuns to assemble in the courtyard. They then went in search of the old and infirm and, according to one witness, "tore them from their beds and threw them in the truck like animals." "We wept," she continued, "because someone said that they were being taken to their deaths. All were taken away and gassed."[31]

That night, a local parish priest secretly entered the convent to celebrate Mass with the sisters, and at four the following morning, the police appeared again.[32] Wakened by a whistle, the nuns were given thirty minutes to pack their bags, and were then ordered to assemble again in the courtyard, where they were checked off a deportation list.[33] Two were missing. A German policeman pulled aside the mother superior, bloodied her nose, knocked her down, and sent her to search for the missing nuns. They had apparently escaped, so the sisters were marched away, unaware of their destination, and guarded by Germans with rifles. Assuming they were to be shot, the nuns were preparing to die and began to sing. Instead of facing a firing squad, however, they were brought to the Włocławek train station,

Fig. 13.1. An exterior wall of the former Nonnenlager Schmückert, Bojanowo. Photo by the author.

where they were locked into a railroad car without food or water and transported to Poznań, and from there to Bojanowo.[34]

When the first women religious arrived at the Nonnenlager in February 1941, they found a rectangular compound encircled by fences, walls, and barbed wire. Some of the brick and stone structures in the compound were used for labor, and others for housing the prisoners. Older, weaker nuns were assigned to the "white pavilion" or, in camp slang, "Kraków," while the younger and healthier were assigned to cells in the three-story "red house," or "Warszawa." Wooden barracks were used to house a small number of inmates of both sexes assigned to the camp for "correctional purposes."[35] The nuns were not permitted contact with these "politicals," who were beaten, mauled by dogs and, according to one of the sisters, "treated like beasts."[36]

Conditions for the nuns in Bojanowo were difficult, although not brutal in comparison to other prisons and camps in the Warthegau, such as Fort VII, Radogoszcz, or the Żabikowo (Lenzingen) labor camp near Poznań.

Nonetheless, as one sister recalled, "all the rigors and attributes of a [forced labor] camp were there . . . prisoners in a sealed camp secured by sentries, work under the supervision of guards with dogs, lack of any remuneration for work, prohibition of visitors, pitiful provisions, crowding of hundreds of sisters in tight rooms, vulgar and insulting treatment of the female prisoners by the German supervisors."[37] Food, although sometimes prepared by the sisters, was poor,[38] and was similar to what prisoners in other camps were offered: for breakfast, twelve grams of black bread and black coffee; for the noon meal, a soup with potatoes, turnips, or bran; for supper, black coffee and black bread, sometimes served with jam or margarine.[39] At times inmates were permitted to receive packages, but these were often confiscated, or the contents were distributed to other inmates.[40] The harsh conditions in the camp were reflected in a report of October 1941, in which an inspector from the Gau administration indicated that the facility was designed for 100 *Zwangspfleglinge*, or "compulsory wards," but currently held 286 inmates, among them 232 Polish nuns.[41]

The daily routine in the Nonnenlager also reflected the rigor and discipline of other camps: from Monday to Saturday the nuns had to appear at 7:00 a.m. for roll call, which was always supervised by two Germans with dogs. They were then sent to work. There was a noon break of one hour for lunch, and the workday ended at 6:00 p.m. After supper, the nuns had free time, which they used primarily to attend to their "spiritual duties": prayer, devotions, and study.[42] Work assignments varied, depending on the labor needs of the camp and the capabilities and health of the nuns, who were assigned to work in the camp kitchen, in a garment workshop and laundry on the premises, and in a small factory in the facility's former chapel that manufactured munitions and airplane propellers. Other nuns were sent outside the camp grounds for agricultural work in the gardens and fields,[43] for work in nearby hospitals,[44] or for domestic service in the homes of party officials, Gestapo officers, and members of the SS.[45]

The Gau Self-Administration imposed numerous restrictions on the sisters incarcerated in Bojanowo. Although discipline and abuse were not at the level of other Warthegau camps and prisons, regulations in the Nonnenlager testify to the authorities' anxiety over possible conspiratorial activities among the inmates. In early 1941, the local NSDAP *Ortsgruppenleiter* Großman complained that conditions in the camp were entirely too lax, as some sisters were permitted out of the camp for visits to a doctor or dentist—excursions that, he claimed, allowed them to post uncensored

Figs. 13.2 and 13.3. Nuns from the Bojanowo camp at work. Courtesy of Zgromadzenie Sióstr Wspólnej Pracy od Niepokolanej Maryi, Włocławek.

Fig. 13.3

mail. Moreover, nuns were periodically given furloughs and allowed into the village of Bojanowo for a few hours at a time, giving them the opportunity to communicate with the local Polish population. Finally, the official noted, a Polish priest had on occasion been allowed into the camp to hear confessions and celebrate Mass among the sisters, giving him the opportunity to report on conditions in the camp to the outside. According to Großman, his own "National Socialist bearing" made it impossible to tolerate a situation in which "nuns would be given the opportunity to undertake espionage."[46]

Later in the year, new restrictions were imposed to undermine group identity and solidarity among the "former Polish Catholic sisters of religious orders": they were no longer permitted to share cells with members of their own orders; religious images were to be removed; correspondence was limited to one censored letter per month to immediate family members, and one letter or package per month from family members. Moreover, sisters were prohibited from leaving the camp, and clergymen were prohibited from entering it.[47] In January 1942, the nuns were prohibited from wearing habits, their traditional religious clothing.[48] Six months later, a new *Lagerordnung*, or set of camp regulations, was issued, and it is significant that by the summer of 1942, German documents regularly referred to the complex as a *Lager*, as opposed to the more neutral *Anstalt*, or "facility." The regulations, developed by the Poznań Gestapo,[49] built on the restrictions imposed the previous year and included additional demands for immediate compliance with all German orders and rules, cleanliness, order, diligent fulfillment of work assignments, and appropriate deportment vis-à-vis the German personnel.[50] The impetus for these new regulations emerged out of concerns over possible espionage and sabotage in connection with munitions manufacturing in the camp.[51]

Munitions production in the Nonnenlager appears to have resulted from a relationship of convenience between a Karlsruhe-based company, the Deutsche Waffen- und Munitionsfabriken, A. G. (German Weapon and Munitions Manufacturing, or "DWM"), and the Reichsstatthalter's office. In July 1941, only weeks after the German invasion of the Soviet Union, representatives of the Reichsstatthalter's office, the Poznań Gestapo, and the DWM met in Poznań to discuss how the nuns' labor was to be deployed. One proposal called for the sisters to be employed in military hospitals, but this was rejected, as it was deemed inappropriate for Poles to care for wounded German soldiers. The Gestapo representative requested that nuns not be employed outside of the camp, as it would be nearly impossible to oversee their activities. The director of the DWM then put forth his proposal: the nuns would labor for the DWM, and the DWM would undertake the renovations necessary for munitions production in the camp.

But could the nuns be trusted? Representatives from the Gau Self-Administration then reminded those present that these sisters "were among the most fanatical Poles," and that it was not necessarily desirable to have them work with dangerous explosives. The DWM representative then assured those present that it would be possible to determine which nuns were reliable enough to take on such work. This seems to have satisfied all concerned, and it was agreed that five hundred nuns were to be made available to the DWM.[52] With this agreement reached, renovations were to proceed, as was the deportation of more nuns to the facility. The sudden demand for them as laborers appears to have been the reason for an *Erfassungsaktion* only a few weeks later—a mass arrest that set out to apprehend all women religious remaining in the Gau.[53]

Historian Ingo Loose has referred to a "spirit of optimism" that animated commercial enterprises from the Altreich as they expanded their business activities to the incorporated territories in the East.[54] Such optimism appears to have been at work in Bojanowo, as the DWM and other enterprises seized the opportunity to exploit the inexpensive labor of the nuns. Addressing a broader, yet related phenomenon, Phillip Rutherford has explored what he has described as the "enduring tension between the regime's ideological goals and the hard realities of the German war economy,"[55] as well as the ways in which economic demands undermined the broader Germanization process in the Warthegau.[56] By the late winter of 1941, Rutherford has argued, "Polish workers were remaining in Wartheland not because they could no longer be deported; they were remaining because the Gau economy desperately needed their labor."[57] The same might be said of Warthegau nuns, for the perspectives of both Loose and Rutherford provide an economic-military context for the small-scale efforts toward labor exploitation in Bojanowo.

Ambitious measures, heady optimism, and the exigencies of the military economy notwithstanding, the deployment of prisoner labor at the Nonnenlager was neither effective nor profitable. Renovations did not proceed apace,[58] it proved difficult to remove "unproductive" nuns from the camp,[59] and because of the lack of police resources and manpower, plans for the mass apprehension and deportation of Warthegau nuns stalled.[60] Production of munition parts—in this case, springs—began on December 15, 1941, but as of the following month, only some ten nuns were working for the DWM.[61] Yet the demand for more persisted, to the extent that the authorities in Inowrocław District were unwilling to approve the deportation of local nuns to the General Government. Instead, they required that the nuns be sent to Bojanowo, citing as justification the "shortage of labor" in the Gau,[62] and invalidating the Foreign Ministry's claim of the previous year that the camp was but a response to a lack of housing for women religious.

A call for the police to "apprehend without exception" the remaining nuns in the Gau was repeated in 1942[63] but failed to improve the level of production in the camp. Low production capacity was in large part the result of the nuns' alarmingly poor state of health and the inability of many of them to work. Moreover, those who could not work were expensive to maintain, for the cost of feeding and housing them was not covered by the DWM. To address the problem, the Gauselbstverwaltung, in early May 1942, subjected some two hundred nuns to humiliating medical examinations, according to which they were classified in five categories as "fully capable of work," "requiring a chest x-ray," able to work "in a warm and dry room," "capable of light work," or "unable to work." Detailed records of each of the exams are available in the Poznań State Archive, and these records state that only seventy-two nuns were "fully capable of work," seventy were capable of "light work," and twenty-six were unable to work at all.[64]

The frenzy to assemble and deploy industrial labor at the Bojanowo camp in 1941 and 1942 proved futile, as munitions manufacturing appears to have proceeded only in fits and starts. Production of springs was ineffective and was halted in May 1942. That decision may have been due in part to a case of sabotage uncovered early in the year. It was never determined who among the nuns was responsible, but the German production supervisor, Georg Berg, was sent to the eastern front as punishment for the incident that had occurred on his watch.[65] There were subsequent attempts in the fall of 1942 to have the nuns work on cleaning shell casings and diffusing unspent ammunition,[66] but these plans were scrapped when representatives from the GSV and DWM concluded that it had become "politically impossible for the nuns to be working with munitions." Better, they decided, that the sisters be occupied with garment production instead,[67] and this appears to have been the main work assigned to the nuns in the months that followed.[68]

Plans then emerged in the summer of 1943 to close the camp, assign some of the nuns to alternative forced labor duties, turn others over to family members in the Warthegau or other Incorporated Eastern Territories, and send the rest to cloisters in the General Government.[69] Nuns were indeed released from the camp. Some were sent to relatives and others to the General Government. Some were given alternative work assignments, but the Nonnenlager was not closed. Instead, over the course of 1943 and even well into 1944, the authorities continued to send the Warthegau's women religious to the camp.[70] Not only was there an ongoing demand for their labor; the nuns were still regarded by some as a security risk.

An exchange of correspondence in the second half of 1944 is illustrative. In July of that year, an official of the Poznań SD expressed concern about the continued presence of nuns from an Ursuline convent in the Szamotuły (Samter) Subdistrict. The local ethnic German population, he claimed, did not understand that allowing these women religious to continue to work in the area would only work to the advantage of the Polish underground and hostile foreign press. Seeing potential resistance fighters and agents among the nuns, he therefore recommended an immediate investigation and, if necessary, a ban on their activities.[71] Heinrich Meyer, the official then responsible for church affairs in Greiser's office, shared these concerns and was perplexed that the nuns had not already been sent to Bojanowo. He determined that it would be unacceptable for them to remain in the Wartheland.[72] After investigating the matter further—albeit at a deliberate pace—the Poznań Security Police informed Meyer in December that there remained fifty-two Ursuline sisters in the Szamotuły area. When their convent was closed in 1942, those sisters unable to work had been sent to Bojanowo, while the others were put to work in agriculture. According to the SiPo official issuing the report, the nuns' labor was very much in need. "Even if," he concluded, "this kind of aggregation of former members of Polish religious orders is undesirable from a state-security point of view," the removal of the nuns would cause significant disruptions in the local agricultural economy. They would, he assured the Reichsstatthalter's office, be continually supervised and guarded.[73]

This seemingly routine correspondence is remarkable in several respects. First, it reveals the German authorities' enduring identification of the Polish Catholic clergy and members of religious orders as security risks. Second, it suggests a desperate need for labor—even that of nuns—in a collapsing wartime economy, prompting the question: What sort of agricultural labor was so crucial to the Warthegau economy in December of 1944? Finally, the above exchange illustrates a persistent tension in the Warthegau—even at this late juncture, when the Third Reich was collapsing on all fronts—between perceived security needs and the demands of the late wartime economy. As late as December 1944, Polish nuns were in demand as laborers, even as they were regarded as security risks to the occupation regime and required constant supervision. When it came to the incarceration and exploitation of women religious in the Warthegau, whether in the Nonnenlager or elsewhere, the Nazi authorities appeared motivated not only by an ideologically principled paranoia or racialist rigor but by economic practicality as well.

The number of women religious interned in Bojanowo fluctuated dramatically over time, and the available documentation provides a confusing array of figures. The first transport in February 1941 brought 56 sisters to the camp,[74] and that number was increased to 200 in the course of the following month.[75] In June of that year there were still 200 sisters in the camp, among them only 80 who were *einsatzfähig*—that is, "deployable" for work.[76] One source from October 1941 lists 260 sisters in the camp, among them only 72 able to work[77]; another source from the same month states that among the inmates were 232 sisters and 54 nonreligious prisoners.[78] By December 1941, the number of sisters was down to 169[79] and then remained at around 100 through much of the spring of 1942.[80] As of May 12, 1942, however, there were at least 192 nuns in the camp, and according to a former prisoner, there were more than 300 in the camp when she arrived in September 1942.[81] Another inmate estimated that in August 1942 the Nonnenlager held more than 400 women religious from some twenty congregations. When the camp was liquidated in early 1945, there were 50 sisters there.[82]

In comparison to other camps and prisons in the Reichsgau Wartheland, deaths were rare in the Nonnenlager, and sources indicate that between eight and eleven sisters died there. In his brief work on the camp, local historian Henryk Duda lists eight nuns who died during their incarceration,[83] while Wiktor Jacewicz and Jan Woś set the number at nine.[84] The total number of sisters incarcerated in Bojanowo remains unclear as well, but the most reliable estimate is that provided by Duda, who has listed by name, order or congregation, and date of release or death 615 sisters incarcerated there.[85] This number represents approximately 23 percent of women religious in the Reichsgau Wartheland.[86]

Viewed in context, the Nonnenlager emerges as a peculiar marker at the intersection of Kirchenpolitik, Volkstumspolitik, and Nazi labor and industrial policy in annexed Polish territory. Its existence illustrates the occupation regime's commitment to incarcerating and exploiting its alleged enemies, and that regime's obsession with Polish Catholicism as an inherently dangerous and conspiratorial locus of anti-German, Polish-national sentiment. At the same time, the Bojanowo camp invites us to consider the relationships—and conflicts—between ideology and economic rationality, even in this microhistorical context. If the fight against Polish Catholicism and the broader Germanization program in the Gau provided the impetus for the Nonnenlager's creation, economic opportunity and, later, necessity brought about its expansion and justified its continued existence.

Notes

1. The June 11, 1941, protest is cited in Maglione to von Ribbentrop, March 2, 1943, document 480, in *ADSS*, vol. 3, no. 2, 745.

2. Maglione to von Ribbentrop, March 2, 1943, document 480, in *ADSS*, vol. 3, no. 2, 745. Maglione's note verbale of March 2, 1943 refers as well to the September 28, 1941, reply.

3. Maglione to von Ribbentrop, March 2, 1943, document 480, in *ADSS*, vol. 3, no. 2, 745.

4. S. M. Fidelis, "Wspomnienie z obozu w Bojanowie," *Homo Dei* 18, no. 3–4 (1949), 460. In this memoir, the author, who was deported to the camp on September 19, 1942, claimed that there were more than three hundred sisters there as of that date. The introduction to a collection of brief memoirs compiled and printed by the mother house of the Congregation of the Sisters Servant of the Immaculate Conception of the Blessed Virgin Mary in Luboń also describes the presence of more than three hundred sisters in the camp by the end of 1941. "Wstęp," unpublished memoir collection, Archiwum Zgromadzenia Sióstr Służebniczek Niepokalanego Poczęcia Najświętszej Maryi Panny, Luboń (hereafter AZSS), 1.

5. Vermerk, Gauselbstverwaltung (Wilborn) to Bartels, May 23, 1942, APP, zespół 301, syg. 285, 80; Józef Kubów, "Parafia Gołaszyn-Bojanowo w latach okupacji," AAP, zespół 133, OK 128; Henryk Duda, *Nonnenlager Schmückert. Obóz sióstr zakonnych w Bojanowie*, Skice Bojanowskie 1 (Bojanowo: Urząd Miasta i Gminy w Bojanowie, 1999), 8; "Wstęp," unpublished memoir collection, AZSS, 1.

6. On the terms *sister* and *nun*: Canon Law states that technically only women religious who take what are known as "solemn vows" and live in enclosed convents of a religious order are nuns, but the convention in the English-language scholarship (and among many women religious) is to refer to all female members of Catholic religious orders and congregations, including those officially designated as sisters (who take "simple vows" and who are not cloistered in the same way) as nuns. In this work, therefore, the terms *nun* and *sister*, and *order* and *congregation*, will be used interchangeably. Similarly, as is conventional in the scholarship, the terms *convent*, *abbey*, *religious house*, and *cloister* are used here interchangeably. I am grateful to Dr. Martina Cucchiara for her instruction and insights on these issues.

7. It is not clear when the camp was liberated or liquidated. Henryk Duda states that the Soviet army liberated the Schmückert/Bojanowo camp on January 23, 1945, and that a hospital functioned in one of the camp pavilions until March of that year. See Duda,

Nonnenlager Schmückert, 9, 21. German correspondence from late March 1945 indicates that the camp had been dissolved by that time and had most recently served as a military hospital. See Vermerk, Gauselbstverwaltung, March 27, 1945, document 2, in Rogall, *Die Räumung*, 39. Izabela Pieniężna states that as the Soviet army approached, the "director" of the facility, Erich Fischer, ordered relevant documents to be burned, and that he then fled to Wrocław on January 20, 1945: Pieniężna, 254. In a postwar testimony, a former inmate of the camp stated that she was released on February 24, 1945 as a result of the Soviet army's invasion: M. Petronela Dyderska, handwritten manuscript, photocopy, AZSS. Another scholar maintains that the liquidation of the camp occurred in February 1945. See Krystyna Winnicka, "Camp pour les religieuses organisé par les Allemands à Bojanowo," *Miscellanea Historiae Ecclesiasticae* 9, Bibliothèque de la revue d'histoire ecclésiastique, fascicule 70 (Bruxelles: Éditions Nauwelaerts, 1984), 434. A legal attestation issued by the Bojanowo city administration on behalf of a former inmate of the camp, Sister Anna Agata Zalewska, states that the camp was dissolved on February 28, 1945, although this may refer to the date on which the facility was closed and the former inmates were dispersed. See Zaświadczenie, Urząd Miasta i Gminy Bojanowo, August 26, 1999, Archiwum Zgromadzenia Sióstr Wspólnej Pracy od Niepokolanej Maryi, Włocławek (hereafter AZW). Zalewska's own personal recollections of the camp indicate that Soviet soldiers entered the camp complex in early February: Życiorys Siostry Anny Agaty Zalewskiej, 2006, AZW. Józef Kubów, a local priest, recorded that the first postliberation Mass was celebrated in the camp on February 10, 1945. Józef Kubów, "Parafia Gołaszyn-Bojanowo w latach okupacji," 1973, AAP, zespół 133, OK 128.

8. Krystyna Dębowska, "Les congrégations féminines religieuses en Pologne au cours des années 1939–1945 (données statistiques fondamentales)," *Miscellanea Historiae Ecclesiasticae*, vol. 9, Bibliothèque de la revue d'histoire ecclésiastique, fascicule 70 (Bruxelles: Éditions Nauwelaerts, 1984), 370.

9. Maria Lucyna Mistecka, "Zakony żeńskie w życiu religijnym okupowanej Polski," in *Życie religijne w Polsce pod okupacją hitlerowską 1939–1945*, ed. Zygmunt Zieliński (Warszawa: Ośrodek Dokumentacji i Studiów Społecznych, 1982), 795.

10. Report of a Poznań Carmelite, October 15, 1974, in Kempner, *Nonnen*, 106–8, here 107.

11. Kłoczowski, Müllerowa, and Skarbek, *Zarys dziejów*, 352; Śmigiel, *Die katholische Kirche*, 34.

12. Teresa Frącek, "Franciszkanki Rodziny Maryi," in Zieliński, *Życie religijne*, 828.

13. Waleria Syksta Niklewska, *Służebnicki Niepokalanego Poczęcia Najświętszej Maryi Panny (Pleszew)*, Żeńskie zgromadzenia zakonne w Polsce 1939–1947, vol. 3 (Lublin: Redakcja Wydawnictw Katolickiego Uniwersytetu Lubelskiego, 1985), 34–35; Małgorzata Wirgilia Wrońska, "Służebniczki Maryi (pleszewskie)" in Zieliński, *Życie religijne*, 913.

14. Maria Jędrzejczak, "Siostry Wspólnej Pracy," in Zieliński, *Życie religijne*, 893–95.

15. Ankieta Strat Wojennych Diecezji Włocławskiej w l. 1939/45, przeprowadzona przez Archiwariusza Diecezjalnego w r. 1947, tom 1, ADW, 1.

16. Mistecka, "Zakony żeńskie," 802–8.

17. NSDAP Kreis Obornik, Kreisschulungsleiter to Gauleiter der NSDAP/Gauschulungsamt, October 9, 1941, IPN, GK 62/197, 29.

18. Śmigiel, *Die katholische Kirche*, 34, 161.

19. Łuczak, *Pod niemieckim jarzmem*, 302.

20. Śmigiel, *Die katholische Kirche*, 186.

21. See, for example, Conway, *Nazi Persecution*, 325; Kłoczowski, *History*, 299; Kłoczowski, Müllerowa, and Skarbek, *Zarys dziejów*, 352; Richard Lukas, *The Forgotten*

Holocaust: The Poles under German Occupation 1939–1945 (New York: Hippocrene, 1997), 14; Śmigiel, *Die katholische Kirche*, 163–64; Edward Serwański, *Wielkopolska*, 176.

22. Główna Komisja, *Obozy hitlerowskie*, 113.

23. See, for example, Olga Abramczuk, "Magdalenki," in Zieliński, *Życie religijne*, 858–80; Frącek, "Franciszkanki," 828; Jędrzejczak, "Siostry," 893–95; Mistecka, "Zakony żeńskie," 800; Alicja Prawdzić, "Hitlerowska obóz dla sióstr zakonnych w Bojanowie 1941–1943," *Chrześcijanin w świecie* 10 (1978), 21–40; Wrońska, "Służebniczki Maryi," 906, 920.

24. Duda, *Nonnenlager Schmückert*.

25. Duda, 6–8.

26. Bericht, Gendarmerie-Posten Schmückert, Kreis Rawitsch, Reg. Bez. Posen, April 19, 1940, IPN, GK 736/2, 23.

27. Józef Kubów, "Parafia Gołaszyn-Bojanowo w latach okupacji," 1973, AAP, zespół 133, OK 128; Stanisław Jędraś, *Miasto i Gmina Bojanowo* (Leszno: Nakładem Gminy Bojanowo, 2005), 127.

28. Gauselbstverwaltung, Abt. II (Ventzki) to die Herrn Oberbürgermeister und Landräte im Reichsgau Wartheland, January 2, 1941, APP, zespół 465, syg. 110, 44; Gestapo Posen (Bischoff) to Gauleitung der Nationalsozialistischen Arbeiterpartei in Posen, die Herren Landräte in Jarotschin, Kosten, Lissa, Samter, January 11, 1941, IPN 831/177, 136; Verfügung, Gauselbstverwaltung, Abt. III-S-, November 4, 1941, APP, zespół 301, syg. 284, 29; Vermerk, Gauselbstverwaltung, June 23, 1942, APP, zespół 301, syg. 284, 65–66.

29. Sicherheitsdienst des Reichsführers-SS, SD-Leitabschnitt Posen, to Reichssicherheitshauptamt, Amt II B/32, December 10, 1940, USHMM, RG 15.007, reel 15, 216, 24.

30. Christopher R. Browning, *Remembering Survival: Inside a Nazi Slave-Labor Camp* (New York: W. W. Norton, 2011), 3–4.

31. Życiorys Siostry Agaty Anny Zalewskiej, 2006, AZW. Another eyewitness, sister Hilaria Bojakowska, reported that those nuns who had not appeared in the courtyard as ordered were tossed "into the truck like wood" and "taken in the direction of the woods (Chełmno)." Życiorys Siostry Hilarii Bojakowskiej, December 12, 1999, AZW.

32. Życiorys Siostry Hilarii Bojakowskiej, December 12, 1999, AZW.

33. Życiorys Siostry Hilarii Bojakowskiej, December 12, 1999, AZW; Oświadczenie Bernardy Sobańskiej, September 24, 1980, AZW.

34. Oświadczenie Bernardy Sobańskiej, September 24, 1980, AZW; Życiorys Siostry Agaty Anny Zalewskiej, 2006, AZW.

35. S. M. Loyola Sommerfeld sł. M., "Wspomnienia z Bojanowa," Manuscript, September 1, 1946, AZSS; idem., Wspomnienia z obozu–Schmückert, n.d., AZSS. See also Pieniężna, 249–50. On the nicknames given to the various buildings in the camp see Jędraś, *Miasto*, 129.

36. Oświadczenie Bernardy Sobańskiej, September 24, 1980, AZW; Oświadczenie Teresy Jakubka, handwritten manuscript, October 5, 1980, AZW.

37. Anna Zalewska to Naczelny Sąd Administracyjny, Ośrodek Zamiejscowy Wydz. II w Łodzi, May 22, 2001, AZW.

38. S. M. Fidelis, "Wspomnienie," 460–61; Oświadczenie Heleny Bojakowskiej, August 19, 1999, AZW.

39. Oświadczenie Bernardy Sobańskiej, September 24, 1980, AZW.

40. Gauanstalt Schmückert to Gauselbstverwaltung, September 12, 1942, APP, zespół 301, syg. 285, 96; Oświadczenie Jozefiny Styśkiej, September 25, 1980, AZW; Fidelis, "Wspomnienie," 460.

41. Meinke, report to Reichsstatthalter/Gauselbstverwaltung, October 29, 1941, APP, zespół 301, syg. 284, 31–32.
42. Życiorys Siostry Agaty Anny Zalewskiej, 2006, AZW; Oświadczenie Jozefiny Styśkiej, September 25, 1980, AZW; Oświadczenie Bernardy Sobańskiej, September 24, 1980, AZW.
43. Oświadczenie Jozefiny Styśkiej, September 25, 1980, AZW; Oświadczenie Bernardy Sobańskiej, September 24, 1980; Oświadczenie Teresy Jakubkiej, October 5, 1980, AZW; Życiorys Siostry Agaty Anny Zalewskiej, 2006, AZW.
44. S. M. Loyola Sommerfeld sł. M., "Wspomnienia z Bojanowa," Manuscript, September 1, 1946, AZSS; S. M. Loyola Sommerfeld sł. M., Wspomnienia z obozu-Schmückert, n.d., AZSS.
45. Zeznanie, Ks. Dr. Józef Nowacki, June 11, 1946, IPN, GK 196/30, tom IV, 23–24.
46. NSDAP Ortsgruppe Schmückert (Großmann) to Reichsstatthalter, Gauselbstverwaltung (Schulz), March 27, 1941, APP, zespół 301, syg. 285, 1–2.
47. Gauselbstverwaltung to Leiter der Gauanstalt Schmückert, July 14, 1941, APP, zespół 301, syg. 285, 31–32.
48. Reichsstatthalter to Gauanstalt Schmückert, January 30, 1942, APP, zespół 301, syg. 284, 8.
49. Gestapo Posen to Gauselbstverwaltung, July 13, 1942, APP, zespół 301, syg. 285, 86–88.
50. Gauselbstverwaltung (Bartels), Lagerordnung für Schmuckert, Abschrift, July 30, 1942, APP, zespół 301, syg. 285, 90–91.
51. Vermerk, Gauselbstverwaltung, über die Besprechung am 23.06.1942, APP, zespół 301, syg. 284, 65.
52. Vermerk, Reichsstatthalter, Gauselbstverwaltung, Abt. III -S-, July 21, 1941, APP, zespół 301, syg. 284, 9–10.
53. Gauselbstverwaltung to Leiter der Gauanstalt Schmückert, August 16, 1941, APP, zespół 301, syg. 285, 33–34.
54. Ingo Loose, "Wartheland," in *The Greater German Reich and the Jews: Nazi Persecution Policies in the Annexed Territories 1935–1945*, ed. Wolf Gruner and Jörg Osterloh, translated by Bernard Heise (New York: Berghahn, 2015), 200.
55. Rutherford, *Prelude*, 7.
56. Rutherford, 198. For a succinct discussion of the tension between ideology and economics, between racial goals and production imperatives, see Jens-Christian Wagner, "Work and Extermination in the Concentration Camps," in *Concentration Camps in Nazi Germany: The New Histories*, ed. Jane Caplan and Nikolaus Wachsmann (London: Routledge, 2010).
57. Rutherford, *Prelude*, 205.
58. Vermerk, November 24, 1941, APP, zespół 301, syg. 284, 35–36.
59. Protokoll über einer Besprechung über den Einsatz von Ordensangehörigen, November 26, 1941, APP, zespół 301, syg. 285, 68–69; Vermerk, Bartels, December 1, 1941, APP, zespół 301, syg. 285, 75–76.
60. Gauselbstverwaltung to Inspekteur des Sicherheitsdienstes Posen, July 9, 1942, APP, zespół 301, syg. 285, 92.
61. Vermerk (Bartels), APP, zespół 301, syg. 284, 47.
62. Gauselbstverwaltung to Regierungspräsidenten Hohensalza, July 9, 1942, APP, zespół 301, syg. 285, 92.
63. Gauselbstverwaltung to Inspekteur des Sicherheitsdienstes Posen, July 9, 1942, APP, zespół 301, syg. 285, 92.

64. Gauselbstverwaltung Posen to Gauarbeitsanstalt Schmückert, May 12, 1942, APP, zespół 301, syg. 273, film 0-69955, 3–81.

65. Duda, *Nonnenlager Schmückert*, 14.

66. DWM to GSV (Bartels), September 28, 1942, APP, zespół 301, syg. 284, 86; Vermerk, GSV, APP, zespół 301, syg. 284, 88; Gauarbeitsanstalt Schmückert to GSV, November 26, 1942, APP, zespół 301, syg. 284, 104–5.

67. Vermerk, Gauselbstverwaltung, December 7, 1942, APP, zespół 301, syg. 284, 96.

68. GSV(?) to Landesarbeitsamt, z. Hd. von Herrn Oberregierungsrat Dr. Schadow, May 15, 1943, APP, zespół 301, syg. 284, 114.

69. Verfügung, July 27, 1943, APP, zespół 301, syg. 284, 118.

70. Gestapo Litzmannstadt to Gauselbstverwaltung Posen, September 16, 1943, Durchschlag, APP, zespół 301, syg. 284, 120; Gauselbstverwaltung Posen to Gestapo Litzmannstadt, October 15, 1943, APP, zespół 301, syg. 284, 121. See also Duda, *Nonnenlager Schmückert*, 25–64, which provides dates of arrival for deportees to Bojanowo.

71. SD Posen to Reichsstatthalter Abteilung I/51, July 21, 1944, IPN, GK 62/200, 5.

72. Reichstatthalter (Meyer) to Kommandantur der Sicherheitspolizei Posen, October 18, 1944. IPN, GK 62/200, 6.

73. Kommandeur der Sicherheitspolizei Posen to Reichsstatthalter (Meyer), December 10, 1944. IPN, GK 62/200, 8.

74. Józef Kubów, "Parafia Gołaszyn-Bojanowo w latach okupacji," 1973, AAP, zespół 133, OK 128; Duda, *Nonnenlager Schmückert*, 8.

75. Vermerk, Gauselbstverwaltung (Wilborn) to Bartels, May 23, 1942, APP, zespół 301, syg. 285, 80.

76. Gauselbstverwaltung to Herrn Gaumedizinalrat Dr. Freimert, June 26, 1941, APP, zespół 301, syg. 285, 42.

77. Vermerk (Wilborn), October 23, 1941, APP, zespół 301, syg. 285, 56.

78. Bericht (Meinke) to Reichsstatthalter, Gauselbstverwaltung, October 29, 1941, APP, zespół 301, syg. 285, 31.

79. Gauarbeitsanstalt Schmückert to Gauselbstverwaltung, November 26, 1942, APP, zespół 301, syg. 284, 103.

80. Gauarbeitsanstalt Schmückert to Gauselbstverwaltung, November 26, 1942, APP, zespół 301, syg. 284, 103.

81. Fidelis, "Wspomnienie," 460.

82. Duda, *Nonnenlager Schmückert*, 21.

83. Duda, 25, 26, 29, 30, 35, 39. Jacewicz and Woś, *Martyrologium*, "Straty," 87. Kłoczowski, Müllerowa, and Skarbek claim eleven deaths in Bojanowo. See Kłoczowski, Müllerowa, and Skarbek, *Zarys dziejów*, 352.

84. Jacewicz and Woś, *Martyrologium*, "Straty," 87.

85. Duda, *Nonnenlager Schmückert*, 25–64. A number of scholars, likely relying on Maglione's March 1943 note verbale to von Ribbentrop, have stated that some four hundred sisters were in Bojanowo. See Lukas, *Forgotten Holocaust*, 14; Breitinger, *Als Deutschenseelsorger*, 72; Fijałkowski, *Kościół*, 240. Jerzy Kłoczowski offers the more accurate, if imprecise, estimate "more than 600." See Kłoczowski, *History*, 299.

86. According to Kazimierz Śmigiel, in 1939 there were 2,666 female members of religious orders in the territory of the Reichsgau Wartheland. See Śmigiel, *Die katholische Kirche*, 34.

14

SPÄNE

Kirchenpolitik *in the Warthegau, 1942–1944*

"Wo gehobelt wird, da fallen Späne." "Where wood is planed, shavings will fall," Arthur Greiser had proclaimed in a speech a few weeks before the "Action for the Destruction of the Polish Church" in October 1941.[1] For Greiser, the Volkstumskampf—a battle over race, culture, and power—required that the Reichsgau Wartheland be smoothed, refined, and purified. Purification often required violent means, while the scraps and residue of that process were to be discarded. The Gauleiter was referring here specifically to the Polish Catholic Church, and suggesting that in the future, only remnants of it, or "shavings," would remain.

Greiser's prediction was confirmed in the aftermath of the Aktion by regional officials in the Gau administration. In the weeks after the mass arrests, Łódź District President Friedrich Uebelhoer echoed the Gauleiter's aggressive optimism, stating, "Since all rights of organization and assembly were taken from Poles, they see in the church the final and only possibility of association. Participation in worship was therefore . . . a demonstration of Polishness. It was clear that this had to be impeded. Therefore, on 6 October of this year the Polish churches were, save for a few minor exceptions, suddenly closed and the Polish clergy taken into custody. The Pole is therefore robbed of his last and only means of Polish support."[2] Similarly, Hans Burkhardt, president of the Inowrocław District, voiced the expectation that the Aktion would usher in "an essential pacification of the Poles" and break "the very powerful influence of the clergy," who "remain as ever the backbone of Polish national identity."[3]

These are telling descriptions of the motives and intended results of the October 1941 events, and they also express a certain finality, as if the

Nazi leadership in the Gau were operating under the assumption that the short-term goals of Nazi Kirchenpolitik in the Warthegau had largely been achieved. With the September decree regulating the legal status of the churches, and the mass arrests and deportations of priests in early October, the fall of 1941 marked the apex of the Nazi regime's persecution of the Polish church. It is, however, also worth noting that neither Uebelhoer nor Burkhardt referred to the church's destruction as a goal or result of the Aktion. Destruction appears to have been the long-term objective, but the aims expressed here simply appear consistent with the main currents of Nazi church policy since German forces took control of the region in 1939: neutralization of the anti-German, nationalist threat posed by Polish Catholicism; restriction of Poles' access to their main locus of association and potential resistance; and restriction of their access to the traditions, rituals, ministries, and institutions of the church.

By the fall of 1941, this was largely accomplished, for church-state ties had been severed, the Polish church had no legal recognition, the overwhelming majority of churches were closed, and their priests were incarcerated. In the words of a December 1941 report compiled by the Polish government-in-exile, German measures had resulted in the "near total restriction of public religious life in Polish society" ("do całkowitego niemal zahamowania publicznego życia religijnego polskiego społeczeństwa").[4] The phrase "near total restriction of public religious life" reflects the scope and consequentiality of Nazi policy, but at the same time, it points to its limitations. If the dissolution of Polish Catholicism and its institutions was the long-term goal, the goal in the short term was the near-total removal of the clergy and near-total inaccessibility of the churches. The church had been reduced to virtual inactivity, yet a vestige of it was permitted to survive. Kirchenpolitik in the Reichsgau Wartheland therefore remained business unfinished, a work in progress. From the German perspective, a decimated Polish Catholic Church was tolerated, if scarcely so; from the Polish perspective, the church was, simply put, in "survival mode." This explains, in part, why the years 1942–1945 figure much less prominently in both German archival documentation and in the secondary literature on the Catholic Church in the Warthegau.

Focused on the "shavings"—that is, the remnants of the Warthegau church during the later years of the occupation—this chapter is guided by two basic themes. First, if Nazi measures toward the Warthegau church during the first two years of the occupation were distinguished by their increasing intensity and brutality, the regime's Kirchenpolitik after the fall of 1941, although not entirely stagnant, was characterized by its consistency. Revisiting some of the themes emerging in the foregoing analysis—the deportation of priests, *profanacja* of church property, measures to restrict the worship life of Warthegau Catholics—this chapter will illustrate that the Nazi administration was committed to continuing its persecution of what little remained of the church without destroying it immediately or entirely. Second, there were limitations to what the Gau authorities wished to or could accomplish with respect to the church. For the most part, these limitations were internal and self-imposed, although to some extent they were the result of external circumstances.

Consistency in Nazi policy was perhaps most evident in the Gau administration's unrelenting emphasis on the Wartheland's role as Mustergau. As discussed in chapter 4, the notion of the Reichsgau Wartheland as "model Gau" was founded on the conviction that this "virgin territory," marked for political, cultural, economic, and racial Germanization, was to function as a "parade ground" of ambitious Nazi policy, including policy toward the churches. Arthur Greiser and his administration would cling to this ideal for as long as they were able—that is, until the tide of the war had put Nazi Germany on the defensive and, eventually, in a fight for its survival.

In the heady optimism of 1941 and 1942, however, the Wartheland's salient role was not in question. In a highly publicized speech of June 1942, the ever-ambitious Greiser outlined his enduring commitment to the above principles, emphasized the Warthegau's singular responsibility, and stressed the sacrifice necessary for Germany to prevail in its ethno-racial struggle. "It is therefore necessary," he stated in characteristically portentous rhetoric, "that those who initiate such a struggle proceed from the start with full severity, in order that the foundation on which the house is to stand, and the house in which later generations are to reside, be built for eternity." For the Gauleiter, this was not a time for compromise or shortcuts but a time for resolve and continuity in the conflict against the Polish people and nation. The Polish Catholic clergy, Greiser claimed, were the "bearer of the greatest struggle against the German *Volk*." Reflecting on the measures his office had thus far implemented in the ongoing struggle against the church, he continued, "It was therefore necessary to exclude, in a sensible manner, the clergy from political life, and this we have accomplished. We have not forced politics into religion; rather, the Polish Catholic clergy has attempted to force its religion into our politics, and in a time of war, one cannot tolerate institutions that exist to work against the German *Volk* and its policies."[5]

Such was the approach in the Warthegau, but the broader agenda was, of course, to evaluate Greiser's experimental measures against the church and consider them for subsequent implementation in other occupied territories and the Altreich—another mark of continuity in Nazi policy.[6] High-level Reich authorities, whether in the Reich Security Main Office or Nazi Party, continued to monitor church affairs in the Warthegau, and as ever, Bormann's influence remained strong. As Greiser was delivering the June 1942 speech quoted above, the Party Chancellery in Munich was corresponding with the Reichsstatthalter's office about the relative success of the Warthegau's policy of segregating Germans and Poles in public worship. The Chancellery had requested from Dr. Kurt Birk, Dudzus's successor as head of the Reichsstatthalter's Department I-51,[7] copies of documents and decrees relating to the segregation policy and the designation of churches as "Polish" and "German." The request was for the explicit purpose of evaluating these practices for possible implementation "in other regions."[8] Birk's successor in Department I-51, Dr. Heinrich Meyer, likewise corresponded with party authorities elsewhere in the Reich about the relative effectiveness of the Gau's church policy, the Thirteen Points developed in 1941, and the role of the September 1941 decree on "Religious Associations and Religious Societies in the Reichsgau Wartheland" in facilitating their implementation.[9]

Moreover, the influence of Bormann's Party Chancellery does not appear to have waned. In May 1943, for example, a high-level meeting between representatives of the Party Chancellery and the officers for church affairs from the various "eastern Gaus" took place in Poznań. The agenda for the meeting clearly illustrated, in the words of one official, "how intensively and to the smallest detail church policy in the annexed territories is directed by party offices,"[10] and the discussions covered issues both minute and broad: from the use of automobiles by clergymen to the legal status of the Warthegau "religious associations," from the ringing of bells at burials to "confessional influence" on Poles, from candle consumption to the ongoing seizure of church property.

With respect to church property, the reach of the September Decree of 1941 was broad and deep, and its regulation of the legal status of "religious associations" paved the way for more aggressive appropriation of church property in the years that followed. Plunder, confiscation, requisition, and "secularization," which had begun during the 1939 invasion and had reached their apex in the aftermath of the October 1941 Aktion, continued unabated. In August 1942, the Reich government issued an order that further authorized and expedited the appropriation of church property "on account of hostility to the people and Reich." Thus, in the wake of this decree, property designated both "Catholic" and "Polish" was by definition *reichsfeindlich*, or "hostile to the Reich," and became the property of the state. Because the "religious associations" were, according to the September 1941 decree, juridical entities under private law (as opposed to public law), Polish Catholic parishes and communities were therefore required to rent from the state authorities the few dozen churches available for their use on Sunday mornings.[11]

If church buildings became the property of the state, the authorities could do with them as they pleased. Consequently, beginning in 1942, and particularly in the later years of the occupation, hundreds of churches and chapels were transformed into warehouses, magazines for any variety of goods, and storage facilities for clothing and furniture confiscated from deported Jews and Poles.[12] A list compiled in November 1942 by the Poznań Gestapo recorded thirty-seven churches in the city that were being used as storage facilities for everything from grain, to furniture for Volksdeutsche settlers, to cement, to vegetables.[13] The large interior spaces of churches could also be used in a variety of ways. For example, Poznań's Bernardine Church—one of the city's most important baroque architectural monuments—was converted to a workshop for the *Reichsgautheater*, and in May 1944, its eighteenth-century altar was destroyed and used for firewood.[14] Poznań's Church of Saint Michael was turned into a repository for confiscated books; the Church of Saint John Kantius in Poznań was used for equestrian instruction; the Carmelite Basilica of Saint Joseph housed the new Gau music school.[15] In Turek, a small town northwest of Łódź, the parish church was used to process and house German settlers from the east.[16] Churches were even used as sites of incarceration, as in, for example, Blizanów (Schrammhausen), Nowogród, and Dobra (Doberbühl), where a church temporarily functioned as part of a ghetto for Jews.[17] In Łask, more than 3,000 Jews from the ghetto were confined in the town's Catholic church before their deportation, most likely to the Chełmno nad Nerem (Kulmhof) killing center.[18] At Chełmno, the Church of the Nativity of the

Fig. 14.1. Interior of the Church of Saint Michael, Poznań, 1942. Courtesy of Instytut Zachodni, IZ, Dział IV, 135.

Blessed Virgin Mary was used as a holding pen for Jews—up to 700 at a time—waiting to be killed in mobile gas vans. More than 150,000 Jews died at Chełmno in this way.[19]

In a curious development, by the second half of 1943, a "competition" of sorts had developed among various state, party, and private agencies for the use of vacant and shuttered Polish Catholic churches. As bombing raids in the Altreich brought increasing numbers of German families into the Warthegau, as the eastern front neared and refugees poured in, and as military needs assumed ever greater priority, such space was at a premium. All these factors resulted in an ever-shrinking supply of housing, storage, and production facilities, resulting in what the German documentation refers to as a *Raumnotstand*, or "space emergency." Accordingly, applications to the Reichsstatthalter's Department I/51 for the use or conversion of churches increased dramatically.[20] One such application is illustrative. In September 1943, Heinrich Meyer received from a grocery wholesaler a request to use the Church of St. Stanislaus Kostka in Poznań as a

Fig. 14.2. Volksdeutsche settlers temporarily housed in the Church of the Sacred Heart, Turek, 1942. Courtesy of Muzeum Miasta Turku im Józefa Mehoffera, MRZTT/HA/1073–Teczka nr. 07–170.

Figs. 14.3 and 14.4. Entrance to the Church of the Sacred Heart, Turek, with Volksdeutsche settlers guarded by members of the Reichsarbeitsdienst (Reich Labor Service), Turek, March 1942. Courtesy of Muzeum Miasta Turku im Józefa Mehoffera, MRZTT/HA/1073–Teczka nr. 05–192, 195. Note the sign reading "Polnische Kirche" (Polish church), indicating that before it was used to house Volksdeutsche settlers, the church was exclusively for the use of Polish Catholics.

Fig. 14.4

warehouse. For Meyer this was problematic, because the Reichsstiftung für deutsche Ostforschung (Reich Foundation for German Research on the East)[21] was using the massive sanctuary for a public exhibition on, coincidentally, "resettlement issues." In the end, the request was denied,[22] but the matter points to an emerging tension in Warthegau church policy between its "practical" and "ideological" aspects—a tension that only increased in the months ahead.

It is also worth noting that all requests for the secular use of Polish churches had to be submitted to Department I/51 of the Reichsstatthalter's office. Whether an application came from a private citizen (as in the above example); the National Socialist People's Welfare, which assisted bombed-out Germans arriving from the west; the Ethnic German Liaison Office (Volksdeutsche Mittelstelle, or VoMi), which was responsible for coordinating the settlement of ethnic Germans from the east; or the Wehrmacht, the application was dependent on the disposition of Greiser's main advisor on church affairs, Heinrich Meyer. Not until July 1944, when German forces had been pushed back to Poland's former prewar eastern border, was this regulation modified to allow the Wehrmacht to make use of any and all Polish churches still remaining vacant.[23]

Particularly offensive to Catholic Poles was the *profanacja* of cathedrals in the Warthegau. These churches functioned as the bishops' sees, were among the largest churches in a given diocese, were historically significant, and generally contained the most valuable treasures and works of art. Poznań's gothic cathedral, home to a parish of twelve thousand, had been closed already in 1939 under the pretext that it was unsafe.[24] It was, however, used for the storage of especially valuable plundered goods and museum pieces: works of art, furniture, antique weapons, and armor.[25] The fourteenth-century Gniezno cathedral, used temporarily by the Wehrmacht for worship services, was designated in 1942 a "German architectural monument and site of German art,"[26] to be "freed of all Polish defacement."[27] Its most important artistic treasures—altarpieces, paraments, sculptures—were either destroyed or sent to Germany, and it was transformed into a concert hall.[28] Temporarily used for the storage of plundered goods,[29] furniture,[30] and later grain,[31] the cathedral in Włocławek subsequently served as part of a military hospital.[32] After it was plundered in the fall of 1941,[33] the Łódź cathedral was transformed into a military magazine, while its underground chambers were used for the cultivation of mushrooms.[34] During the occupation as a whole, the German authorities closed at least twelve hundred churches and chapels. As of December 1944, some five hundred of these had been converted to storage facilities of one kind or another, seventy had been made available to German Catholics, and a few others had been made available to German Protestant communities.[35]

The small number of churches still open in the Gau after 1941, and the small number of active priests, remained under strict surveillance. Filing hundreds of reports on Sunday worship services, the Gestapo and SD continued to register concern and even alarm at the throngs of Poles packing the churches and gathering by the hundreds outside of them. As in the past, agents continued to voice concern over the mass Sunday "migration" of Poles from surrounding communities to churches open for services. The phenomenon caused traffic problems, allegedly undermined productivity in the agricultural economy, and, of course, brought hundreds of potentially conspiratorial Poles together in the same place at the same time. Local police therefore banned Poles from gathering outside of churches during services.[36]

As a means of reducing the number of worshippers in general, the Poznań Gestapo chief Karl-Heinz Stossberg ordered in the summer of 1942 a reduction in the times for Sunday services, set those times earlier in the morning, and restricted attendance to members of the parish where services were held[37]—a restriction that was, apparently, frequently violated. Police authorities also closely monitored the activities of the few dozen Polish priests still active in the Warthegau. Otto Bradfisch, commander of the Security Police and SD in Łódź, reported in the summer of 1942 that his men were engaged in "continual surveillance of church life and the religious activities of Polish Catholics." According to Bradfisch, Polish priests in his district were required to file monthly reports on how often they held services, the number of attendees, and how many baptisms, weddings, and burials had taken place.[38]

The deportation of the Polish clergy had largely concluded by October 1941, but not entirely, as arrests and incarcerations continued, not only among the few remaining active priests in the Warthegau but also among those who were staying with relatives and friends, or had been living in hiding. Some, like the Rozdrażew priest Stefan Bączyk described in chapter 11, had evaded arrest or escaped (Bączyk was arrested again in March 1942). Some priests ran afoul of the authorities for having too great an influence on the local Polish population,[39] while others were charged with violating restrictions on their ministerial activities. Father Alfons Jankowski, one of only two priests serving one of only two Poznań churches remaining for Poles, was arrested in October 1943 for undertaking unauthorized charitable work and performing a wedding ceremony without permission. Jankowski, who was also involved in resistance activities and was a chaplain in the Armia Krajowa (or AK, usually referred to in English as the "Home Army"—the principal Polish underground resistance organization, formed in 1942 and loyal to the Polish government-in-exile),[40] was held in a Poznań prison, sent to Fort VII, interrogated, and tortured. He died there the following month.[41]

Father Czesław Cofta served a church in Lubasz (Lubasch), a village in the Czarnków (Scharnikau) subdistrict in the northwest of the Gau. Also active in resistance activities and clandestine ministry,[42] Cofta was denounced by one of his parishioners,[43] and in early 1944, officers of the SD searched his home and found various contraband: a camera, butter, bacon, and 1,650 Reichsmark in cash. They also found evidence that he had, over the past four years, sent some thirteen thousand Reichsmark to individuals in occupied Poland and the Altreich.[44] Cofta was sent to the Żabikowo camp outside of Poznań, where he reportedly died while being tortured in the camp's infamous "barbed wire barrel."[45]

Although a relatively small camp, Żabikowo has an important place in the history of the Warthegau church, as it was the main destination for clergy in the Poznań district arrested in the later years of the occupation.[46] Opened in the summer of 1943 and officially known as the Polizeigefängnis der Sicherheitspolizei und Arbeitserziehungslager in Posen-Lenzingen (Police Prison of the Security Police and Corrective Labor Camp in Posen-Lenzingen), or PGuAL, the camp operated in conjunction with Poznań's Fort VII until the spring of 1944, when it effectively superseded Fort VII as the main prison and corrective labor camp for the Warthegau capital and its environs. The camp generally held between 1,700 and 2,000 prisoners, and was, like Fort VII, known for its poor conditions, poor provisions, and sadistic guards.[47]

Far fewer clergy were held in Lenzingen than in Fort VII or other prisons and camps for the simple reason that far fewer Warthegau clergy were arrested and deported in the later years of the occupation. The work of neutralizing the clergy had largely been done, and if the authorities were willing to allow for a tiny remnant of pastoral ministry to remain in the

Gau, then there were limits as to how many more among the few dozen remaining priests they could arrest and remove. As noted in chapter 11, after October 1941, the few remaining priests in the city of Łódź were each responsible for some forty-five thousand souls. These proportions appear to have remained relatively consistent throughout the duration of the occupation, so that as late as 1944, there were still only approximately seventy priests—about 3 percent of the prewar number—to minister to more than three million Catholic Poles in the Reichsgau Wartheland.[48]

The Nazi authorities in the Reichsgau Wartheland remained consistent in their policy toward the Polish Catholic Church after October 1941, and this was the case with respect to the treatment of priests, appropriation of property, restrictions on public religious activity, segregation of Poles and Germans, and ideological bases of their policies. There were, however, limits to what the Gau administration could and chose to accomplish, and if that was the case, then to what extent did the "destruction" of the church proclaimed in connection with the October 1941 arrests remain the goal? The answer is complicated, for "consistency" in the application of policy, and a willingness to allow a vestige of the Polish Catholic Church to remain, appear to challenge the axiom, dominant in the literature, that Nazi policy in the Warthegau was clearly aimed at destroying the church. Did the fall of 1941 signal, in the words of one historian, "the eventual abolition of Polish Church life in its entirety,"[49] or was it a clear step toward, as some scholars have claimed, the even more radical goal of eradicating Christianity altogether?[50]

Despite the hyperbolic declarations and aggressive resolve of Arthur Greiser and others, Nazi Kirchenpolitik in the Warthegau was always a work in progress, and this is illustrated to some extent by the deliberate pace and incongruities of Nazi policy in the two years following the invasion. As discussed in chapter 10, already in July 1940 there were those in the Gau administration who considered it advisable to maintain a church for Polish Catholics as a social "foothold" and as a barrier to otherwise subversive or criminal activities.[51] Paradoxically, even after the fall 1941 events, the Reichsstatthalter's office also remained open to the idea of granting legal status to a Catholic Church for Poles.

The 1941 September Decree on "Religious Associations and Religious Societies in the Reichsgau Wartheland" had provided the opportunity for Greiser to grant legal status to religious associations other than those listed in the document (which included three German Protestant "associations" and one for German Roman Catholics), and such a step remained under consideration for many months to follow. Only a week after the decree was issued, Greiser's deputy, August Jäger, reminded local district officials that despite their antichurch enthusiasm, the decree had not prohibited holding services in Polish Catholic churches, and those religious associations not named in the decree would, in the future, have the opportunity to apply for legal status.[52]

The minutes of a conference of district police chiefs meeting more than a year later, in November 1942, to discuss the current state of religious affairs in the Warthegau, attest to this. At this meeting, Heinrich Meyer introduced Greiser's intent to grant legal status to a church for Catholic Poles. To some, this undoubtedly appeared a radical and ideologically inconsistent proposal. According to Meyer, however, such a step, which, significantly, already had the approval of the Party Chancellery and Bormann, would not in any way result in the Polish church gaining the same status and recognition of the four German religious associations that had been permitted in September 1941. Moreover, the current restrictions on the religious life and religious activities of Poles were to remain in effect.

Meyer also noted during the meeting that resistance against the proposal was to be expected from certain quarters, despite the blessing of Bormann and the party. He therefore asked the three police chiefs to compile, for their respective districts, reports and documentation on the number of churches open, the number of Polish priests available, the level of Polish participation in Catholic religious life, the extent to which Poles had come to rely on the services of laypeople and spiritual "self-help" in the absence of priests, and the extent to which religious practice among Poles had led to the development of resistance activities and organizations. The goal of this effort, according to Meyer, was to assemble evidence that could demonstrate to skeptics that the Polish church was *not*, in fact, a forum for anti-German resistance, and did *not* pose a threat to the security of the Reich.[53] The significance of this meeting, largely overlooked in the literature, should not be underestimated. Not only did Meyer's initiative run counter to the conventional antichurch tropes consistently employed by Nazi functionaries in the Warthegau, it also casts doubt on the prevailing interpretation that Nazi policy consistently aimed to destroy the Polish church. Moreover, the minutes of the meeting confirm the intimate involvement of Martin Bormann and the Party Chancellery—involvement not only in the development of

Warthegau Kirchenpolitik but also in an effort to sustain the Warthegau church, if only in its most vestigial and rudimentary form.

Although plans for formal recognition of a Polish Catholic "religious association" appear to have remained on the table at least until March 1943,[54] the Gau administration never succeeded in establishing a functional and legal relationship with the Roman Catholic Church as a whole in the Wartheland. For Polish Catholics, their national "branch" of the church remained in legal limbo until the end of the occupation. One reason for this was the failure to reach agreement on a required statute (*Satzung*) for the Polish church.[55] Resistance to this from Polish church leaders and the Vatican was to be expected, for to accede to any German demands for such an arrangement would have meant offering a measure of loyalty to the Nazi state in the place of loyalty to God, Canon Law, and the traditions and structures of the church. More specifically, the Vatican required that any Polish church body remain subject to the Roman Catholic hierarchy and in communion with the Holy See, and that its internal organization be guided by Canon Law.[56]

Options were limited. To reject outright the opportunity to reach a highly unsatisfactory agreement with the Gau administration ran the risk of foregoing any possible concessions and losing the ability to maintain current pastoral functions, circumscribed as they were. It is therefore likely that Polish church leaders and the Vatican, seeing no benefit to such an agreement, regarded the status quo, tragic as it was, as their best or only option. Bishop Walenty Dymek, vicar-general in Poznań and, as of May 1942, apostolic administrator for Polish Catholics in the Warthegau,[57] was required that month to submit to the Reichsstatthalter's office a proposed statute for the Polish church.[58] His statute stated that such an organization would "form a part of the entire Roman Catholic church" and would order its affairs according to the "precepts of the Codex Iuris Canonici."[59]

In October 1942 Dymek met with Kurt Birk, who treated the bishop in a dismissive manner and rejected many elements of his proposed statute. Birk remained inflexible, as did the bishop, who bore no illusions that Nazi efforts toward any sort of arrangement had as their goal anything but even more rigid German control and further persecution. Better, then, for the church to attempt to carry on its work as long as possible under the circumstances. Dymek also regarded it as a foregone conclusion that the few remaining active priests in the Gau—himself included—would ultimately be arrested.[60] Already in September 1942, the papal nuncio in

Berlin, Orsenigo, had reported to the Vatican secretary of state, Maglione, that Dymek was "waiting for Dachau."[61] Following his meeting with Birk, the bishop, still under house arrest, wrote to the Berlin nuncio in a manner illustrating both his unwillingness to compromise with the Nazi authorities and his pessimism regarding his own fate:

> The situation of the Polish church is bleak. I myself will likely not enjoy freedom much longer. I have come to the conviction that the Holy See cannot, or on higher grounds will not help us. . . . In the event that I should be arrested and then shall leave this life, I would, in all subservience, ask His Excellency to assure His Holiness that in my life I have continually strived to spread the kingdom of God, that I will gladly suffer and die for Christ, but that I also will never be a traitor to my people and fatherland.[62]

The bishop would survive, and the church as well. Why, then, did the regime not attack the church more aggressively? Measures in the fall of 1941 marked the institutionalization of existing antichurch policy and the stabilization of state control, and they may have been understood as a portend of what some referred to as the "final solution"[63] of the church question in the Third Reich. Greiser, Bormann, and others directing Warthegau Kirchenpolitik remained consistently hostile toward the Polish church in the years that followed—after all, they had closed nearly all of the Warthegau's churches and had removed nearly all of the priests. Yet they also exercised a small degree of restraint, suggesting that the regime's aim was not to destroy what remained of the Polish church but to assist it in dying a slow death. This appears consistent with the views of Adolf Hitler, who is recorded as remarking, only a week after the October 1941 Aktion against the Polish clergy, that "the best thing is to let Christianity die a natural death. A slow death has something comforting about it."[64]

Kazimierz Śmigiel has concluded, based on the trajectory of antichurch measures beginning already in 1939, that the long-term goal of German policy was, in fact, the destruction of the Warthegau church, and that any tolerance of church activities in the latter years of the war was but a temporary concession to the Warthegau population and public opinion in the Reich.[65] Such a conclusion may be correct, but it remains speculative, and in the final analysis, the fundamental issue is not what the future of German policy would have been but what the goals of existing policy were, how it was implemented, and how the Catholic Church and its adherents responded to that policy. It may appear remarkable that the Polish church was allowed to exist at all in the experimental field that was the Warthegau, and its continued existence is a reminder that there were limits to what Greiser and the Party Chancellery could and did accomplish—limits that raise important questions about the subsequent course of Nazi policy toward the church and church responses to it.

Not until the waning months of the war did the Gau authorities relax restrictions on the church—a theme addressed in chapter 18—and it appears that in the meantime, the limits placed on Nazi policy were largely self-imposed. The motives for restraint after the fall of 1941—that is, in the aftermath of such hitherto aggressive antichurch persecution—are unclear, however, especially in light of the broader Nazi goal of the Reich's secularization. In this context, it is worth reemphasizing that there were indeed those in the Gau administration who saw the value of maintaining a minimally functional Polish church as an instrument of social stabilization among the Polish population.

Greiser himself was a proponent of such an approach and recognized that Volkstumspolitik in the "model Gau," although deadly in its application to Wartheland Jews, had to proceed pragmatically and at a more moderate pace with respect to Poles. In a March 1943 speech, for example, he emphasized the fundamental ethnic and racial irreconcilability of German and Pole and stated the firm goal of extirpating Polish *Volkstum* in his Gau. In the same speech, however, Greiser also noted the value of a "transition period" (*Übergangszeit*) for the economic exploitation of the Poles.[66] To what extent, then, was the restraint in post-1941 Kirchenpolitik driven by the goal of maintaining social peace among an economically valuable Polish population; to what extent was it simply the result of a lack of unanimity or coherent agenda on the part of the Nazi leadership, whether in Poznań or Berlin; and to what extent did new concerns and new priorities overshadow church policy in the Gau?

Several authors refer to changes in Germany's military situation as central to the regime's post-Aktion restraint and later shifts in Warthegau Volkstumspolitik and Kirchenpolitik,[67] but there is no consensus on the issue of precisely how struggles on both the battlefield and the home front had an impact. It is clear, however, that one consequence of the changing tide of the war was the influx of settlers and refugees. Gau officials had long had to contend with challenges to their church policy posed by German settlers from eastern Europe and the Soviet Union. Brought to the Warthegau in the context of a broader Germanization program, many of these Volksdeutsche were forced to live in squalid resettlement camps, saw their home communities broken up and distributed throughout the Gau, and faced hostility from both the Polish population and the Warthegau Reichsdeutsche.[68]

Having been promised access to churches and the freedom to worship as they pleased, ethnic German settlers were also often bitterly disappointed by the harsh antireligious reality in Greiser's domain. In April 1942 a group of seventy-seven German Catholic settlers from the Soviet Union issued a petition to the Gauleiter, stating, "Prior to our resettlement we were promised that here we would get back not only our possessions and livelihood but also our churches and our priests."[69] Later that year, a German clergyman from Bessarabia complained to the Poznań Gestapo: "Now we have come here—left our homeland, our beautiful, rich land, our villages, our church—and now we sit here, abandoned. We have no church, no services. Our children grow up like the heathen, without reverence, without religious instruction, without song and prayer. Yet all this was promised us."[70] Party officials apparently took these concerns seriously, instructing their operatives to proceed with "exceptional reserve" when it came to addressing church issues among Volksdeutsche settlers.[71] This did not mean that the authorities suddenly made churches available to settlers or other German communities in the Gau—they would not do so until the final months of the occupation—but it did mean that the authorities were loath to alienate even further these "new" Germans through intensified antichurch rhetoric and policies.

The situation became more difficult as Germany's forces retreated westward and tens of thousands of German refugees from the east flooded the Warthegau.[72] Moreover, in response to Allied bombing raids in the west, the Nazi government began evacuating thousands from the Altreich eastward, evacuees who then became acquainted with the grim reality of the Warthegau. Not only would settlers and refugees be confronted with barriers to the practice of their faith; they would also have the opportunity to report on the persecution of the church to friends and relatives at home, in effect breaching the cordon that had existed for years between the Warthegau and rest of the Third Reich.[73]

The documentation also makes clear that the Gau authorities were, paradoxically, frequently concerned about public opinion and the responses of Germans in the Gau toward secular use of Polish churches. In May 1941, Bormann had prohibited the conversion of churches for use by the Nazi Party,[74] and authorities in the Reichsgau Wartheland held rigorously to this dictate.[75] It was acknowledged that use of Polish churches for purposes some would regard as inappropriate ran the risk of stimulating enemy propaganda, and that the use of churches for secular purposes be limited to alleviation of the current "space emergency" in the Gau,[76] even if this restriction was not rigorously enforced. Similarly, in the summer of 1942 the Reichsstatthalter's office instructed the Inowrocław District Gestapo to prohibit the use of "Polish" churches by the Hitler Youth, or the conversion of churches into gymnasiums or kindergartens.[77]

Concerns over responses to the regime's Kirchenpolitik from abroad may also have played a role in the regime's restraint. Hilarius Breitinger noted in his memoir the regime's desire to maintain the appearance of a functional Polish church so as to avoid international condemnation.[78] This perspective is substantiated by a memorandum written already in April 1942 by an undersecretary of state of the German Foreign Office, Ernst Woermann. Expressing concern over the negative reactions to treatment of the Catholic Church abroad (especially in Spain and Italy, two countries normally not negatively disposed toward Nazi Germany), the memorandum noted that enemy propaganda had quite effectively seized on Germany's repressive measures. Moreover, the Reich's relations with the Vatican were imperiled, and Japan and Finland had recently embarked on diplomatic relations with the Holy See. Woermann therefore recommended that any antichurch measures in the Warthegau be suspended at least until the end of the war.[79] Evidence that Greiser, Bormann, or anyone else in the higher Nazi leadership was significantly influenced by the Foreign Office in their dealings with the Warthegau remains lacking. It is, however, clear that German officials in the Warthegau were well aware of the questionable "optics" associated with their policies and measures toward the Polish church and were eager to avoid backlash, either among the German populations in the Warthegau and Reich as a whole, or abroad.[80]

It is also worth considering the extent to which, as Michael Phayer has argued, a shift in German occupation priorities in 1941 and 1942 reflected the emerging commitment to the total annihilation of Europe's Jews, the resulting need to replace Jewish labor with that of non-Jewish Poles, and a post-Stalingrad German effort to gain Polish sympathy in the war against the Soviet Union.[81] For Phayer, the convergence of these three factors resulted in an improved situation for Polish Catholics beginning in 1942. The decision to eliminate Europe's Jews and the resulting need to supplant Jewish labor with Polish labor may be linked to policies toward the churches. But the link remains, at best, unclear and is not necessarily evident in the unique context of the Warthegau, where the Łódź ghetto remained an enduring reservoir of Jewish labor well into the summer of 1944,[82] where brutal suppression of Polish culture persisted, and where, simply put, church policy differed significantly from elsewhere in occupied Poland because it was more comprehensive and severe. More importantly, the evidence does not indicate any significant improvement in the status of the Warthegau church (in contrast to the church in the General Government[83] and other incorporated territories[84]). We know that some Nazi administrators were interested in the legal establishment and stabilization of the church after the October 1941 Aktion, but the absence of a destructive agenda is not synonymous with an attempt to improve the church's situation. As Heinrich Meyer made clear at the November 1942 meeting discussed above, the granting of legal status to the Polish church would in no way result in an increased number of available churches or active priests. "Nothing," Meyer emphasized, "shall change with respect to church life or the religious activities of the Poles."[85]

This meant that churches would not be opened, priests would not be returned to their parishes, and church property would not be restored. The church as an organization had, according to a German report of March 1943, been "nearly completely crippled" ("*fast vollständig lahmgelegt*"),[86] and so it would remain until the occupation neared its end, when Greiser would find it expedient, or perhaps in his view necessary, to loosen some restrictions on the church. Until then, however, the church's survival depended largely on efforts at the parish level to maintain its ministries under extraordinarily difficult conditions.

Notes

1. Greiser, speech at the Arbeitstagung des Gauschulungsamtes, September 14, 1941, IPN, GK 196/37, 96.

2. Friedrich Uebelhoer, report of October 1941, document XII-8, in Łuczak, *Położenie*, 346.

3. "Lagebericht des Regierungspräsidenten Hohensalza," October 20, 1941, IfZ, Fb 125, 383.

4. "Pro Memoria o sytuacji w kraju w okresie 1 listopada—15 grudnia 1941," in "Materiały o sytuacji kraju w okresie od 1 listopada 1941 roku do 15. I. 1942 roku," in Sprawozdanie sytuacyjne z kraju, vol. 2, Nr. 1–6, 1941–1942, 3, PUMST. The Polish verb *zahamować* can be translated variously as, for example, to brake, stop, retard, impede, rein, hinder, or restrict.

5. Greiser, *Aufbau im Osten*, 6.

6. See Sziling, *Polityka*, 273; Broszat, "Verfolgung," 30–32.

7. Birk succeeded Wilhelm Dudzus in this office, where he remained until October 1942, when he was replaced by Dr. Heinrich Meyer. See Volk, *Akten deutscher Bischöfe*, vol. 5, 565, note 6.

8. NSDAP Partei-Kanzlei (Frühwirth) to Amtsgerichtsrat Dr. Birk, June 25, 1942, IPN, GK 196/37, NTN 37; 585/zIV, tom IV, 63–64.

9. NSDAP-Gauleitung Wartheland, Gauhauptstelle für Sonderfragen (Meyer) to NSDAP-Gauleitung Bayreuth, Gauschulungsamt, June 18, 1943, APP, 53/299/0/1.30/1186, 13.

10. Vermerk, Kirchenpolitik in den neuen Gebieten, May 25, 1943, BAB, R43II/170, 274–76.

11. Reichsstatthatler Abt. I/51, "Rechenschaftsbericht für die Zeit vom 1. Oktober 1941 bis 1. Oktober 1942," IPN, GK 62/153, 215; NSDAP Partei-Kanzlei (Krüger) to Reichstatthalter, Herrn Ministerialdirektor Jäger, September 19, 1942, IPN, GK 196/19, 46–48.

12. Relacja Władysława Zarachowicza, YV, M.49-ZIH, file 7116, 9; Marian Biesiada, "Moja parafia w latach okupacji (1939–1945)," AAP, zespół 133, OK 128. Extensive documentation on the utilization of Polish church buildings as storage facilities is found in IPN, GK 62/218/CD, 62/219/CD, 62/222/CD, and 62/223/CD.

13. Gestapo Posen to Reichsstatthalter, November 18, 1942, APP, zespół 299, syg. 1187, film 0-60039, 1b-2.

14. Z. Kępiński, Konserwator Urządu Wojewódzkiego w Poznaniu, to Głowna Komisja Zbrodni Niemieckich w Poznaniu, June 22, 1946, IPN, GK 196/20, 3–4.

15. Breitinger, *Als Deutschenseelsorger*, 69; Aufstellung Priester und Kirchen in der Erzdiözese Posen, October 10, 1941, BAB, R 5101/22437, 13.

16. "Raport o sytuacji na Ziemiach Zachodnich Nr. 3 (do 31. grudnia 1942 r.)," in Mazur, Pietrowicz, and Rutowska, *Raporty*, 64.

17. Frątczak, *Diecezja Włocławska*, 273.

18. Amtskommissar der Stadt Lask to Herrn Landrat des Kreises Lask, September 19, 1942, IPN, GK 62/223/CD, 53. On the August 1942 deportation of Jews from Łask, see Michael Alberti, *Die Verfolgung und Vernichtung der Juden im Reichsgau Wartheland 1939–1945* (Wiesbaden: Harrassowitz Verlag, 2006), 446–47.

19. On the church's use in the killing process at Chełmno, see Patrick Montague, *Chelmno and the Holocaust: The History of Hitler's First Death Camp* (Chapel Hill: University of North Carolina Press, 2012), 158–59. On the number of Jews killed at Chełmno, see Raul Hilberg, *The Destruction of the European Jews*, vol. 3 (New Haven, CT: Yale University Press, 2003), 1320.

20. In the archive of the Instytut Pamięci Narodowej, Warsaw, are hundreds of such requests, which usually met with approval from the Reichsstatthalter's office with the words "In view of the space emergency prevailing in the Warthegau, I give permission for the use of the church in. . . ." See IPN, GK 62/218/CD, 62/219/CD, 62/222/CD, 62/223/CD, 62/225.

21. Meyer referred, in fact, to the Reich Institute for Research on the East ("Reichinstitut für Ostforschung") which, to the best of this author's knowledge, did not exist. On the Warthegau's Reichsstiftung für deutsche Ostforschung in Poznań, to which Meyer was likely referring, see Michael Burleigh, *Germany Turns Eastward: A Study of* Ostforschung *in the Third Reich* (Cambridge: Cambridge University Press, 1988), 290–97.

22. Meyer, Vermerk, September 15, 1943, IPN, GK 62/222/CD, 118.

23. Reichsstatthalter Abt. I/51 (Jäger) to Landräte and Oberbürgermeister im Reichsgau Wartheland, July 18, 1944, APŁ, zespół: Akta Miasta Łodzi, syg. 32473.

24. Dymek to Orsenigo, February 8, 1940, document 112, in *ADSS*, vol. 3, no. 1, 214; Hlond, *Persecution*, 12; Sprawozdanie sytuacyjne z kraju 1939–1941, vol. 1, 105–11. PUMST.

25. Ks. Dr. Józef Nowacki, Zeznanie, IPN, GK 196/30, tom IV, 22–27. Nowacki was professor at Poznań's Archdiocesan Seminary and director of the Archdiocesan Archive and Archdiocesan Museum.

26. Vermerk, Dr. Neumann-Silkow, January 6, 1942, IPN, GK 196/20, 17–18.

27. Lagebericht des Gaukonserwators Dr. Johannes über die Denkmalpflege im Warthegau, January 8, 1942, IPN, GK 196/20, 9–10.

28. Józef Nowacki to GKBZNwP, June 1, 1946, IPN, GK 196/19, 145. For the history of the Gniezno cathedral during the occupation, see Janusz Powidzki, "Losy katedry gnieźnieńskiej podczas okupacji 1939–1945," in *Święty Wojciech 997–1947: księga pamiątkowa*, ed. Zbigniew Bernacki (Gniezno: Wydawnictwo Kurii Metropolitalnej w Gnieźnie, 1947). On its symbolic value for both Poles and Germans, see Michał Sołomieniuk, "Katedra gnieźnieńska: polsko-niemieckie zmagania o symbole w czasie zaborów, dwudziestolecia międzywojennego i okupacji hitlerowskiej," *Seminare* 39, no. 3 (2018).

29. Frątczak, *Diecezja Włocławska*, 272.

30. Lagebericht des Regierungspräsidenten Hohensalza für die Zeit vom 1.10 bis 31.12.1941, IPN, GK 62/210/CD, 49.

31. Reichsstatthalter to Kreisbauernschaft in Leslau über Verwendung der Kathedrale in Leslau, April 29, 1942, IPN, GK 62/218/CD, 129.

32. Reichsstatthalter, Abteilung I/51 to Wehrmachtkommandantur Posen, October 22, 1943, IPN, GK 62/223/CD, 50.

33. "Raport Nr. 20 za czas od 16.XI.-30.XI.1941 r.," in Sprawozdanie sytuacyjne z kraju, vol. 2, Nr. 1–6, 1941–1942, 70, PUMST.

34. Budziarek, "Geneza," 45; Reichsstatthalter Abteilung I/51 to SS-Abschnitt XXXXIII, Litzmannstadt, January 29, 1943, IPN, GK 62/222/CD, 9.

35. Vermerk, Dr. Meyer-Eckhardt, December 22, 1944, IPN, GK 196/19, 58. Meyer-Eckhardt bases his estimate of 1,200–1,300 churches on statistics provided by the Gau Self-Administration. These were also the figures that appeared in the letter of indictment against Arthur Greiser in his postwar trial. See Akt oskarzenia Artura Greisera, June 10, 1946, IPN, GK 196/34, 14.

36. ADW, Ankieta Strat Wojennych Diecezji Włocławskiej w l. 1939/45, przeprowadzona przez Archiwariusza Diecezjalnego w r. 1947, tom 1, 6.

37. Gestapo Posen (Stossberg) to Herrn Landräte, Aussendienststellen des Bezirks, June 13, 1942, APP, zespół 465, syg. 110, 263.

38. Handwritten margin notes, "Niederschrift über die Besprechung der Leiter der Staatspolizei(leit)stellen Posen, Hohensalza und Litzmannstadt mit dem Sachbearbeiter für kirchliche Fragen beim Reichsstatthalter im Warthegau am 19.11.1942 in Hohensalza," November 19, 1942, IPN, GK 196/19, 118.

39. NSDAP Kreisleitung Obornik to Gauschulungsamt NSDAP Posen, January 16, 1942, IPN, GK 62/197, 50.

40. On Jankowski's resistance activities and service in the Home Army, see Nikodem Kowalski, "Jankowski Alfons," in *Encyklopedia konspiracji Wielkopolskiej 1939–1945*, ed. Marian Woźniak (Poznań: Instytut Zachodni, 1998), 227.

41. "Raport o sytuacji na Ziemiach Zachodnich (nr. 10), grudzień 1943–styczeń 1944," in Mazur, Pietrowicz, and Rutowska, *Raporty*, 463; Jastrząb, *Archidiecezja Poznańska*, 385, 1197; Relacja Mariana Frankiewicza, October 25, 1947, IZ, Dok. II-123, 1; Fijałkowski, *Kościół*, 240. According to Wełniak, one eyewitness account maintains that Jankowski was incarcerated and died in the nearby Żabikowo camp. See Wełniak, *Duchowieństwo*, 49.

42. Nikodem Kowalski, "Cofta Czesław," in Woźniak, *Encyklopedia konspiracji*, 124–25.

43. Jastrząb, *Archidiecezja Poznańska*, 345, 446.

44. Sicherheitsdeinst des Reichsführers-SS to Reichsstatthalter Abteilungsleiter I/51, March 17, 1944, IPN, GK 62/197, 57.

45. Alfons Miśko to Przewielebny Ksiądz Archybiskup Antoni Baraniak, Metropolita Poznański, February 28, 1972, Odpis, AAP, zespół 133, syg. OK 117; Jastrząb, *Archidiecezja Poznańska*, 1191. The letter of indictment against Arthur Greiser describes the device as a "barrel made of barbed wire, in which prisoners were held several days without food or drink in a hunched-over position." Akt oskarzenia Artura Greisera, June 10, 1946, IPN, GK 196/34, 14. The cause of Cofta's death remains open to dispute, for according to an alternative source, he died of tuberculosis in the camp. See Kowalski, "Cofta," 125.

46. For biographies of clergy in the Lenzingen camp, see Wełniak, *Duchowieństwo*, 42–66.

47. On the history of the camp, see Albin Wietrzykowski, *Zbrodnie niemieckie w Żabikowe: zeznania-dokumenty* (Poznań: Nakładem Księgarni Wydawniczej w Poznaniu, 1946); Armin Ziegler, *Wer kennt schon Zabikowo . . . : Ein Bericht über das "Polizeigefängnis der Sicherheitspolizei und SS-Arbeitserziehungslager Posen-Lenzingen"* (Schönaich: Armin Ziegler, 1994); Stanisław Nawrocki, *Policja Hitlerowska w tzw. Kraju Warty w latach 1939–1945*, Badania nad okupacją niemiecką w Polsce, vol. 10 (Poznań: Institut Zachodni, 1970), 211–14; Olszewski, *Straty*, 105–69; Główna Komisja, *Obozy hitlerowskie*, 595.

48. Łuczak, *Pod niemieckim jarzmem*, 302; Sziling, "Hitlerowska," 22; Adamska, *Reżimy*, 8.

49. Conway, *Nazi Persecution*, 320. See also Kłoczowski, *History*, 298.

50. Sziling, "Hitlerowska," 23; Stasiewski, "Kirchenpolitik," 74.

51. Vermerk über die Besprechung mit Gauleiter Greiser über die konfessionellen Maßnahmen im Reichsgau Wartheland, August 13–14, 1940, Abschrift, BAB, R58/7581, 69.

52. Reichsstatthalter (Jäger) to Herren Landräte and Oberbürgermeister, September 20, 1941, APP, zespół 465, syg. 110, 196.

53. "Niederschrift über die Besprechung der Leiter der Staatspolizei(leit)stellen Posen, Hohensalza und Litzmannstadt mit dem Sachbearbeiter für kirchliche Fragen beim Reichsstatthalter im Warthegau am 19.11.1942 in Hohensalza," November 19, 1942, IPN, GK 196/19, 116–18. Father Józef Nowacki, professor at the Poznań seminary and director of the Poznań archdiocesan archive, also referred, in his June 24, 1946, testimony at the trial of Arthur Greiser, to the November 19 meeting: IPN GK 196/38/CD1, 60. See also Śmigiel, *Die katholische Kirche*, 75–76.

54. "Darlegung betr. die Rechtslage der katholischen Kirche im Reichsgau Wartheland," March 5, 1943, BAB, R5101/22437, 28–33, here 30. This document in the files of the Bundesarchiv Berlin is not dated, but it is reproduced in Volk, *Akten deutscher Bischöfe*, 28–36, and dated March 5, 1943.

55. Śmigiel, *Die katholische Kirche*, 112.

56. Kazimierz Śmigiel, "Losy Kościoła katolickiego w okupowanym Poznaniu," *Kronika miasta Poznania* 77, no. 3 (2009): 67.

57. Dymek was appointed to this post on April 9, 1942. Orsenigo to Maglione, April 11, 1942, document 373, in *ADSS*, vol. 3, no. 2, 563. His ability to fulfill this office was limited, however, because he had, since October 1939, been under house arrest. For his protection and to preserve any authority at his disposal, his appointment as apostolic administrator was not made public until after the occupation. See Zofia Waszkiewicz, *Polityka Watykanu wobec Polski 1939–1945* (Warszawa: Państwowe Wydawnictwo Naukowe, 1980), 118–19.

58. Reichsstatthalter, Referat I/51 (Birk), Lagebericht zur kirchlichen Angelegenheiten, May 6, 1942, IPN, GK 62/153, 138.

59. Śmigiel has maintained that the proposed statute submitted by Dymek is unavailable, and that it was likely submitted to the Reichsstatthalter's office in September 1942. See Śmigiel, *Die katholische kirche*, 109–10. In fact, Dymek's proposed statute, dated May 22, 1942, can be found in the IPN archive: Dymek, Weihbischof, to Reichsstatthalter, May 22, 1942, IPN, GK 62/153, 207. It is accompanied by a memorandum from Birk noting that "The statute remains in need of extensive revision": Birk to Herrn Referenten I/50, May 31, 1942, IPN, GK 62/153, 206. An undated additional draft in the same archive: IPN, GK 62/186/CD, 35–38.

60. Dymek to Orsenigo, n.d., document 39, in Volk, *Akten deutscher Bischöfe*, vol. 5, 1054–56. Although the letter to the papal nuncio is undated, it is clear from its content that it postdates the October 18, 1942, meeting with Birk. See also Śmigiel, *Die katholische Kirche*, 111–12.

61. Orsenigo to Maglione, September 24, 1942, document 417, in *ADSS*, vol. 3, no. 2, 645.

62. Dymek to Orsenigo, n.d., document 39, in Volk, *Akten deutscher Bischöfe*, vol. 5, 1055–56.

63. The phrase "final solution of the religious question" appears to have originated with Albert Hartl. See Dierker, *Himmlers Glaubenskrieger*, 528.

64. Entry 39, October 14, 1941, in *Hitler's Table Talk 1941–1944: His Private Conversations*, ed. Hugh Trevor-Roper, trans. Norman Cameron and R. H. Stevens (New York: Enigma, 2008), 47–50, here 48.

65. Śmigiel, *Die katholische Kirche*, 316.

66. Greiser, speech, in "Bericht über die Arbeitstagung des Gauamtes für Volkstumspolitik am 20. u. 21.3.1943 in Posen," IPN, GK 196/37, 104.

67. See, for example, Fijałkowski, *Kościół*, 376; Gürtler, *Nationalsozialismus*, 114, 142; Stasiewski, "Kirchenpolitik," 60.

68. On the challenges faced by Volksdeutsche settlers see Epstein, *Model Nazi*, 170–76.

69. Ludwig Wurzer et al. to Reichsstatthalter, April 15, 1942, IPN, GK 62/176/CD, 8.

70. Otto Kersten to Gestapo Posen, June 23, 1942, Abschrift, IPN, GK 62/214/CD, 58–59.

71. SD-Abschnitt Litzmannstadt (Schwark) to SD-Aussenstellen January 30, 1943, IPN, GK 70/73, 1.

72. One scholar has included among those immigrants to the Warthegau 51,000 Volksdeutsche from Lithuania, Latvia, and Estonia; 125,000 Volhynian and Galician Germans (so-called *Wolhyniendeutsche* and *Galiziendeutsche*); 72,000 ethnic Germans from Dobrudja, Bessarabia, and Bukowina; and 50,000 so-called Black Sea Germans. See Rogall, *Die Räumung*, 26.

73. Birk, Vermerk, March 17, 1942, IPN, GK 62/218/CD, 90; Gürtler, *Nationalsozialismus*, 114.

74. Bormann, NSDAP Parteikanzlei, Rundschreiben Nr. 57/41, May 11, 1941, Abschrift, IPN, GK 62/218/CD, 6.

75. Reichsstatthalter to Landrat des Kreises Lask, March 24, 1942, IPN, GK 62/218/CD, 97.

76. Vermerk, Reichsstatthalter (Birk), June 12, 1942, APP, zespół 299, syg. 1176, film 60028, 154.

77. Reichsstatthalter to Gestapo Hohensalza, July 25, 1942, IPN, GK 62/218/CD, 258.

78. Breitinger, *Als Deutschenseelsorger*, 142.

79. "Aufzeichnung des Leiters der Politischen Abteilung im Auswärtigen Amt, Unterstaatssekretär Ernst Woermann," April 21, 1942, document 238, in Gruber, *Katholische Kirche*, 474.

80. Pressebericht, February 22, 1943, BAB, R 5101/22181, 48–49; Vermerk, Reichsstatthalter Abt. I/51, March 12, 1943, IPN, GK 62/222/CD, 15–16.

81. See Michael Phayer, *The Catholic Church and the Holocaust, 1930–1965* (Bloomington: Indiana University Press, 2000), 29, where, citing Sziling, "Die Kirchen im Generalgouvernement," 282, Phayer argues for a post-Stalingrad shift in German policy. His claim that the shift was related to the advent of the "final solution" and annihilation of Polish Jewry is advanced in chap. 2 of Michael Phayer, *Pius XII, the Holocaust, and the Cold War* (Bloomington: Indiana University Press, 2008), 16–41.

82. On the use of Jewish and Polish labor in German-occupied Poland, see chap. 3 of Christopher R. Browning, *Nazi Policy, Jewish Workers, German Killers* (Cambridge: Cambridge University Press, 2000), 58–88.

83. On Nazi church policy in the General Government see Sziling, "Die Kirchen im Generalgouvernement," 277–88; Madajczyk, *Okkupationspolitik*, 362–64; and the numerous essays in Zieliński, *Życie religijne*. According to reports of the Polish underground from July 1941, the situation of the Catholic Church in the General Government had, in contrast to the situation in the Warthegau, improved already in the first seven months of that year: "Raport Sytuacyjny okupacji niemieckiej za czas od 1.I. do 1.VII.1941 r." in Sprawozdanie sytuacyjne z kraju 1939–1941, vol. 1, 49–53, PUMST.

84. In the words of Martin Broszat, "While church affairs began to normalize in the other Gaus of the incorporated eastern territories, the essentially antichurch and unique church policy in the Warthegau emerged ever more prominently." Broszat, *Nationalsozialistische*, 148.

85. "Niederschrift über die Besprechung der Leiter der Staatspolizei(leit)stellen Posen, Hohensalza und Litzmannstadt mit dem Sachbearbeiter für kirchliche Fragen beim Reichsstatthalter im Warthegau am 19.11.1942 in Hohensalza," November 19, 1942, IPN, GK 196/19, 117. Quoted here is the meeting's protocol and not Meyer's words. See also Śmigiel, *Die katholische Kirche*, 75–76.

86. "Darlegung betr. die Rechtslage der katholischen Kirche im Reichsgau Wartheland," March 5, 1943, BAB, R5101/22437, 28–33, here 31.

15

PARAFIA

Parish Life

In 1946, the diocesan archivist in Włocławek set out to document the experience of each parish in his diocese during the German occupation. Asked to respond to detailed questionnaires, priests in individual parishes chronicled the losses, both human and material, in the years 1939–1945. The surveys are especially informative for the historian. For example, the report provided by the parish in Białotarsk (Weißenmarkt), a village southeast of Włocławek, is illustrative of the experiences of many Polish Catholic communities. According to the report, the German authorities deported the parish priest, Father Ignacy Bronszewski, to the General Government on March 7, 1941. Worship services then ceased in the parish until February 1945. Over the course of the occupation, a total of 900 families from the parish had been deported; as of January 1947, only 750 of them had returned. Among the parishioners, nineteen had died in concentration camps, twenty-five had lost their homes, and fifteen were crippled during the occupation. The church's sanctuary was plundered and the bells taken. Church records, which dated back to 1650, were confiscated, as were approximately three hundred books from the parish library. Parishioners who wished to attend services after the church was closed in March 1941 had to travel to Włocławek, thirty kilometers away. According to the report, the vast majority of parishioners simply did not attend church.[1]

Although the challenges faced by the Białotarsk parish were dramatic, losses such as these were not unusual. Many parishes saw their priests deported and murdered in camps. Others experienced more significant losses among parishioners, while still others saw their churches and facilities damaged or demolished. Viewed as an aggregate, the postwar questionnaires assembled for the Włocławek diocese, as well as parish reports from other dioceses filed in subsequent decades, demonstrate that parish life in the conventional sense did not exist in the Reichsgau Wartheland, for it was nearly destroyed by the closure of churches, countless restrictions issued during the first two years of the occupation, and the mass arrests of priests culminating in October 1941. In effect, one could not really speak of parishes after 1941 but only of a few dozen scattered, individual churches available for occasional services.[2]

There is perhaps the tendency to view the life, challenges, or even dissolution of Catholic communities in the Warthegau solely in terms of conventional categories and measures, such as the number of open churches, the presence or absence of priests, the availability of the sacraments, or attendance at public worship services. Church life during the occupation was, however, extraordinarily challenging and highly complex. Only remnants of the institutional church remained, but its ministries did persevere, if in strictly limited ways. The few dozen remaining active Polish priests in the Warthegau, despite their severely reduced numbers and the myriad of restrictions imposed on them, continued to celebrate Mass, baptize infants, educate the young, conclude marriages, and bury the dead. Perhaps more significantly, many Catholic devout strove to hold to their traditions and express their faith in diverse ways, both public and private, legal and illegal.

It remains difficult, however, to elaborate on parish life in the Warthegau because of the paucity of sources. Because activities associated with the church's ministry were considered hostile to the state and were in most cases illegal, they were usually undertaken privately or in secret. Such activities are therefore not well documented, but Polish and German sources do exist in a variety of forms. In the archdiocesan archives in Gniezno and Poznań are, for example, administrative ordinances issued by the vicars general, as well as correspondence between the vicars general and clergy. Documentation such as this is sparse, however, because bishops in the Warthegau—with the exception of Walenty Dymek, the Poznań auxiliary and vicar general during the occupation—had either fled, were dead, or were incarcerated. The priest Edward van Blericq served as vicar general in the Gniezno diocese, but he was removed to a parish in Inowrocław in early 1941 and thereafter had only limited contact with the rest of the clergy.[3] The paucity of documentation is also due to the fact that after October 1941, there were, quite simply, hardly any priests remaining in these dioceses to advise or with whom to correspond. For its part, the German documentation consists mostly of reports on parish life and the clergy submitted by the police, as well as ordinances intended to curb or eliminate clandestine church activity. These sources are extensive and informative but are also limited in value to the extent that they express the perspective of the hostile "outsider" to the parish community and reflect, of course, the ideological orientation of the Gestapo, SD, or Nazi administration.

A further source of information on parish life consists of testimonies, questionnaires, and reports submitted after the war to state investigative offices, legal authorities, and church authorities. Beginning already in 1945, prosecutors, archivists, historians, and seminarians went to great efforts to survey and document the parish experience during the occupation. The collection in the Włocławek diocesan archive mentioned above, for example, consists of some three hundred reports from parishes and religious orders; a similar effort was undertaken in the Poznań diocese in the 1970s. While these reports are, of course, subject to the mutations and partialities of individual and collective memory, they nonetheless remain important eyewitness accounts that provide a wealth of information.

At a basic level, a parish's vitality depends significantly on the presence of a priest, and after the fall 1941 Aktion, few priests remained available in the Reichsgau Wartheland. A comparison of priests active in 1939 and 1944 in dioceses either fully or partially in the Warthegau reveals dramatic disparities:[4]

Table 15.1

Diocese	Active Priests in 1939	Active Priests in 1944
Częstochowa	86	2
Gniezno	306	11
Łódź	300	11
Płock	30	1
Poznań	681	28
Warsaw	30	1
Włocławek	400	8
Total	1833	62

It is also worth noting that there were dozens of clerics remaining in the Warthegau who had been prohibited from carrying out their duties and were living with friends, relatives, or in hiding.[5] Some voluntarily took on or were forced into "secular" professions, and among them, many continued to offer their services, ministering to Polish Catholics in secret.[6]

Fewer active priests meant, of course, fewer worship services, and this is one of the reasons why German surveillance reports consistently refer to the "crowds," "throngs," or "multitudes" of Poles congregating on Sundays in and around Polish churches. At the center of parish life was the Sunday Mass, and regular attendance at services among Polish Catholics had always been strong. It appeared to remain so throughout the occupation, as confirmed by dozens of reports from local Warthegau officials and the Gestapo. Early in the occupation, for example, a Kępno SD officer reported that "the Polish Catholic services are invariably overcrowded. Despite the severe cold, the Poles still travel in throngs the many kilometers through deep snow in order to attend church."[7] For all the restrictions imposed by the Gau administration, Inowrocław District President Hans Burkhardt reported in January 1941 that attendance at services had actually recently increased, especially among the Polish youth. "The Poles," he wrote, "emerge out of distant villages in spite of unfavorable weather and bad traffic conditions." According to Burkhardt, so massive was the turnout on Sunday mornings that a local official in Żnin had, like other officials around the Gau, gone so far as to forbid Polish Catholic services in his subdistrict in order to prevent "mass migrations" to those towns and villages where services had been permitted. And Burkhardt noted an additional concern: attending church services had become, for Poles, a "silent demonstration of protest."[8]

That same month, Helmut Bischoff, head of the Poznań Gestapo, noted that "the previous year has shown that the Polish Catholic population is under no circumstances willing to forgo Sunday worship. It has been determined that the entire populations of villages where there are no priests travel to the next village where there is." To remedy traffic problems, increase Polish worker productivity, and maintain public order, Bischoff ordered that Polish Catholic clergy would henceforth be permitted to hold services in neighboring parishes, but only under the existing time restrictions—that is, on Sundays between 8:00 a.m. and 11:00 a.m.[9]

As a means of discouraging church attendance, countering alleged idleness among Poles, and assembling labor for the wartime economy, the Poznań District President Viktor Böttcher ordered, beginning on July 29, 1941, *Kontrolle* of Polish churchgoers. Those who could not prove on the spot (with an identification card or work certification) that they were employed, were to be apprehended and taken to the district labor offices.[10]

These roundups were particularly dangerous for Poles who did not have the necessary documentation on hand, for they were sometimes marked for deportation to the Altreich for forced labor.[11]

Attendance at services was, of course, dramatically diminished after the mass deportation of priests in October 1941, but the available evidence makes clear that the few churches remaining open were full or overflowing on Sunday mornings. The crowds did not, however, signal an increase in the number of those attending church; on the contrary, they reflected the dramatic reduction in the number of priests and open churches. With, for example, only two churches available to 230,000 Polish Catholics in the city of Poznań, those churches naturally filled on Sunday mornings.

In order to attend Sunday services, many Polish Catholics living in close proximity to the Altreich simply crossed the border to a neighboring parish. This was problematic for the authorities in a number of ways: it violated regulations against unauthorized crossing of the frontier, it gave Warthegau Poles the opportunity to experience the church's better circumstances elsewhere, and worst of all, it resulted in Poles and Germans sharing the same worship space. On, for example, the frontier between the Reichsgau Wartheland and Lower Silesia, large numbers of Poles were reported traveling every Sunday the fifteen kilometers from the Warthegau village of Głuszyna (Glausche) to the Lower Silesian village of Namysłów (Namslau).[12] These Sunday "migrations" led the Gestapo in 1943 to require clergy in Lower and Upper Silesia to announce to their congregations at the beginning of services that Poles were not permitted. This elicited a number of protests from the cardinal Adolf Bertram of the Wrocław archdiocese,[13] but these were ineffective, for the German authorities held fast to the "nationality principle" of separate worship well into 1944, when the occupation was nearing its end. As an RSHA official wrote in June of that year, any integration in the churches would "blur the boundaries between Germans and Poles that have, in ethno-racial respects, been drawn and so strictly enforced in the Warthegau." "It is clear," he continued, "that the Catholic Church again and again attempts to violate the ordinances issued regarding confessional support for Poles. It has no understanding of ethno-racial concerns."[14]

It is impossible to determine with precision what motivated Poles to take the risky, "oppositional," and at the very least inconvenient step of attending church, but the issue is worth consideration. Beyond the demands of the faith and traditional religious devotion, participation in corporate worship was a way for some Poles to confess publicly not only to the Catholic faith but also to the language, culture, and traditions of the nation. To put it another way, participation in worship was not only a customary and obligatory demonstration of a common religious identity; it was also the expression of a common national identity. The extent to which this was a motivation for attending services cannot, of course, be documented effectively, but it is evident that throughout the entire occupation, the German authorities continued to see Polish church attendance as an expression of nationalism. The Poznań District president referred to it in a June 1941 report as an "active profession of allegiance to Polishness,"[15] while in Inowrocław, Hans Burkhardt reported only weeks after the October 1941 arrests that "for anyone who feels Polish, it is a matter of honor to go to services on Sundays. Thus, the Poles' attendance at church goes far beyond the religious element."[16]

Nazi officials were not necessarily incorrect in viewing expressions of religious identity in this way, but attendance at worship offered other benefits, despite the risks. Some Poles likely found in the collective ritual of the Catholic Mass an elevation of cultural expression that was sorely lacking in everyday life under the occupation. Cultural institutions such as theaters, cabarets, cinemas, concerts, and sporting events were closed to Poles, so for many, the church was the single institution and "Polish" social forum that remained available amid the deprivation and isolation that was the occupation. It was, simply, the only location outside the workplace where Poles could gather legally in large numbers. To that extent, the Sunday service could function—just as the Gau administration and police feared and believed—as an incubator and forum for conspiracy and resistance. In some instances, it undoubtedly did. For many, participation in a public ritual that the Germans barely tolerated and treated with hostility was a mark of independence or even defiance. It may not have been an illegal, conspiratorial act, but it was at the least an oppositional gesture.

In the final analysis, however, one has to acknowledge multiple motives on the part of both individual Catholics and the collective of Polish Catholics in the Warthegau. Giving voice to the variety of factors that were to motivate and maintain Poles' allegiance to their faith and church, an anti-Nazi, patriotic "Christian Broadcaster" in October 1943 stated:

> In western Poland the Enemy attempts to eradicate the Christian faith by all means possible. . . . Although the invader has forbidden that homilies and services take place in the Polish language, the Polish population streams

> into the churches in droves in order to pray, for the Enemy will never succeed in tearing the Lord Jesus and his Mother from the hearts of Poles. He will never succeed in eradicating our beautiful language—the language of the Priest Skara[17] and the poet Adam [Mickiewicz].[18] Brothers and Sisters! Go to church, and raise your prayers to the dear Lord God. May he hasten this war of our liberation. May he grant us faith in victory and inspire us in the struggle against the Enemy.[19]

Transmitted in Polish and, of course, illegally, the broadcast exhorted Poles to be loyal and zealous in the Catholic faith, yet at the same time appealed to their linguistic heritage, awareness of cultural history, and, not least, their sense of national outrage at the "Enemy."

Practice of the faith could be a demonstrative political and oppositional gesture, yet for many—and likely the majority who attended services—participation in public worship simply marked their devotion to the faith and responsiveness to the spiritual and sacramental benefits it provided. To put it another way: while it is important to acknowledge the oppositional and potentially conspiratorial motives for church attendance, it is equally important to recognize the purely spiritual motives of Catholic Poles in the Warthegau.

Attendance at Sunday services may have been the most public expression of religious devotion, but attention to the spiritual needs of the faithful also took less visible, more private, and even illegal forms. Religious education for children was permitted, but there were severe constraints as to when and where it could take place. In October 1940, Greiser issued an order stipulating that religious education and first Communion instruction was permitted only on Wednesdays between 2:00 p.m. and 4:00 p.m., that it could take place only in church buildings, and that it was to be limited to members of a given parish.[20] Due to the lack of priests and small number of open churches, after 1941 it was impossible to provide even this minimal level of instruction, so the work went underground. An extensive survey of priests in the Poznań diocese revealed that a significant number provided religious education to children and adults secretly and in private homes, and that many clerics in prisons and camps provided instruction while incarcerated.[21]

Other elements of spiritual and parish life were likewise forced underground. Among them, perhaps the most common were the sacraments of penance or reconciliation and the Eucharist, or Holy Communion. Father Mieczysław Posmyk, a priest in the northwest of the Wartheland, recalled secretly hearing confessions during the Easter season in four different communities, as well as in the Chodzież sanitorium.[22] Sometimes ministries such as these were provided by priests who had evaded arrest or deportation, and who were living in hiding. According to the testimony of Father Stanisław Cichy, there were at least four young priests living underground in his parish, all of whom secretly heard confessions and celebrated the Eucharist in private homes.[23] Henryk Kaliszan, who served seven different parishes until his arrest in October 1941, recalled that often a healthy parishioner would feign sickness so as to give the priest the opportunity to visit her or him at home in the company of other visitors. On the occasion of such visits, Kaliszan would then illegally celebrate the Eucharist among several dozen parishioners at a time.[24]

Particularly active in this regard was Father Marian Samoliński. On the run from the beginning of the occupation, Samoliński, according to several of his colleagues, tirelessly provided pastoral care and the sacraments across several Warthegau subdistricts until he was arrested in 1944.[25] The consequences for his illegal activities were severe, as he was sent on an odyssey illustrative of the chaos and severity of the Nazi penal system in the waning months of the war. In his own 1947 account, Samoliński reported that after his April 1944 arrest he was incarcerated and tortured in the Kościań (Kosten) prison, then spent eight months in Żabikowo, three weeks each in Sachsenhausen and Bergen-Belsen, and two months in Dachau, where he was liberated in April 1945.[26]

The difficult circumstances of parish life under the occupation demanded at times unusual and unorthodox practices. In the village parish of Ołobok (Ollebach) in the southern Warthegau, mass confessions with a general absolution were common, first Communion instruction for children was simply left to parents, and priests conducted weddings in secret, without the knowledge of state authorities. A priest was seldom available for burials, so the village gravedigger usually officiated at the graveside ceremonies.[27] When, in fact, priests were available, they were often required to administer the sacraments to large groups of people at the same time. This applied not only to the sacraments of penance and Holy Communion but to baptism as well. On Easter Sunday in 1942, between 200 and 250 children were baptized in the Catholic church in Chlebów, a tiny village in the Turek subdistrict,[28] and in June of that year, a parish priest in Konorzewo (Konradsfeld) baptized some 80 children on one Sunday.[29]

After the 1941 closure of nearly all churches, when at most two remained open in any given subdistrict, numbers such as this were not

Fig. 15.1. A clandestine marriage ceremony, Ostrzeszow, 1942 or 1943. Courtesy of Instytut Zachodni, IZ, Dział IV, 133.

all that unusual. They also reveal the important role of open churches as regional gathering points and centers of "sacramental migration" for Polish Catholics. The Catholic parish in Grabowo, a village in the Września subdistrict, provides a dramatic illustration. Parish records indicate that in 1938 there were 17 baptisms, and all the baptized were from the parish. In 1939 there were 25 baptisms, and in 1940, 60. In 1941, there were 187 baptisms. Among the baptized, however, 161 were from outside the parish. The numbers increased dramatically over the years ahead. In 1942, for example, there were 605 baptisms, and only 32 of the baptized were members of the parish. The following year the priest in Grabowo baptized twenty-eight infants from his parish, and 1,932 others.[30] On average, then, 37 baptisms took place in the Grabowo church every week during 1943.

Extreme circumstances also brought women to the fore of parish life and service. Limited by Catholic doctrine and tradition to certain forms of service and ministry, they took on unconventional roles in sustaining the religious communities of which they were a part. Janina Bzyl, a member of the Wielichowo (Wiesenstadt) parish, made her home available for clandestine confession, celebration of Holy Communion, and baptisms.[31] In the same parish, Antonina Radziemska provided first Communion instruction to some two hundred children.[32] According to records of the Rozdrażew (Albertshof/Brigidau) parish in Krotoszyn subdistrict, baptisms were frequently performed by Katarzyna Król, a local midwife.[33] Often, women religious were particularly engaged in ministries that had previously been undertaken solely by priests. In Rakoniewice (Rakwitz), a village in the far west of the Warthegau, Sister Piątkówna of the Sisters Servants of the Immaculate Conception of the Blessed Virgin Mary played an essential role in the life of the parish, preparing children for their first Communion and distributing the Eucharist to the sick, which was permitted by a special decree issued by the auxiliary bishop and vicar general Walenty Dymek. She continued these services until she was deported for forced labor in the Altreich in 1944.[34]

A close look at the life of a single parish under the occupation can offer an even clearer sense of the challenges faced by Polish Catholics in the Warthegau, and their responses to those challenges. Our Lady of Sorrows parish in Poznań's Łazarz district (under Nazi occupation, *Posen-Hermannstadt*) was typical in many ways. The German authorities severely restricted parish activities, plundered the church, and rounded up Sunday worshippers for labor. The majority of priests were arrested and imprisoned, and two died. Attendance at Sunday services was consistently strong. On the other hand, the parish was also unusual because of its size, urban location, and role as a "flagship" of sorts among functional parishes in the Warthegau in the latter years of the war. Also unique are the available sources—postwar testimonies and reports of priests—that depict parish life during the occupation and provide an unusually detailed and vivid account of their experiences.[35]

Prior to the outbreak of the war, there were five priests serving Our Lady of Sorrows parish. Shortly after the invasion, the parish's provost

Józef Gorgolewski and vicar Edmund Lorkiewicz were arrested. Both were interned in the cloister in Kazimierz Biskupi. Gorgolewski was subsequently deported to Dachau, where he was gassed in October 1942 among hundreds of other priests in the "invalid transports."[36] Lorkiewicz was released and sent to the General Government. The Gestapo arrested Father Roman Hildebrandt in August 1940 and sent him to Dachau, where he remained until the liberation. This left administration of the parish to Fathers Alfons Jankowski and Marian Frankiewicz. The two worked together until October 1943, when the Gestapo arrested Jankowski. Frankiewicz then served largely on his own until October 1944, when he was joined by Father Józef Sarniewicz, who remained until the city was liberated in February 1945.

The parish church was one of two in Poznań that remained open to the city's roughly 230,000 Polish Catholics. According to Józef Sarniewicz, the church had to serve some 150,000 of them, representing the membership not only of Our Lady of Sorrows parish but of twelve other Poznań parishes as well. Not surprisingly, turnout on Sundays was enormous. Initially there were six services on Sundays at Our Lady of Sorrows church, but after Alfons Jankowski's arrest, only four. Services were permitted only in a limited time frame (beginning in 1942, from 6:00 a.m. to 10:00 a.m. in the summer, and from 7:00 a.m. to 10:30 a.m. in the winter). Huge lines formed, and young people were enlisted to usher visitors in and out so as to keep the breaks between the Masses as brief as possible. Priests even went to the extent of asking people to attend services only once on holidays, so that all who wished to do so could be accommodated in the building.[37] According to Marian Frankiewicz, an average of 2,500 people received the Eucharist on any given Sunday.

In preparation, priests heard hundreds of confessions on Saturday afternoons. According to an order issued by Greiser in October 1940, this was permitted only between 2:00 p.m. and 6:00 p.m.,[38] but priests would typically continue for hours more. Parishioners were asked to keep their confessions especially brief, noting only the length of time since the previous confession and the sins worthy of confessing. After Alfons Jankowski's arrest in 1943, Bishop Dymek tried to assist with confessions and pronouncing absolution. This practice ended quickly, however, because people began to boast that the bishop had heard their confessions, and if word of this spread, it could put the bishop, already under house arrest, in further danger. Other priests remaining in the area came to the parish to help, illegally, with Saturday confessions.

Preparation of Poznań children for their first Communion was also unconventional. Catechisms had to be shared among the pupils, and lessons took place for two hours on Wednesday afternoons. After October 1943, when Marian Frankiewicz was the sole priest serving the parish, instruction was moved inside the church itself, which could accommodate hundreds of children at once. By the end of the occupation, Frankiewicz was giving first Communion instruction to four hundred children at a time.

Infants and others entered the community through the sacrament of baptism on Sunday afternoons, when the priests would baptize up to twenty children per hour. Burials were not as rapid but sometimes were nearly as frequent. According to a 1943 report issued by the underground resistance, burials could take place only on weekdays between 6:00 a.m. and 8:00 a.m., and only close family members who had obtained special permission from the authorities were permitted to attend.[39] The priest Józef Sarniewicz recalled conducting as many as sixteen burials per day in October 1944.

The parish was also engaged in charitable work of various kinds. Although collection of offerings during services was prohibited, the parish had at its disposal significant secret funds—one scholar has claimed as much as twenty thousand German marks per month[40]—that it used for the particularly needy in the community, for the support of priests' families, to provide medical care and pharmaceuticals, and for other charitable causes, some of them quite unconventional. One parishioner, for example, received thousands of Reichsmarks out of parish coffers in order to buy her daughter out of the Żabikowo concentration camp—an undertaking that was, remarkably, successful. In another initiative, an Ursuline nun connected to the parish was effective in organizing the shipment of packages to priests in the Dachau camp.

One peculiarity of Our Lady of Sorrows Parish was that it housed the auxiliary bishop Walenty Dymek. Under house arrest on the "Cathedral Island" since October 1939, he was moved in January 1943 to a third-floor apartment in the parish house, directly above Franz Wolf, the Poznań Gestapo officer responsible for church affairs. Intending to keep the bishop, who was known to have contacts with the Polish resistance, under close Gestapo observation, the German authorities even went to the extent of installing a listening device in his quarters.[41] The bishop's presence in the parish, although not public, was significant, and invites further consideration of his role and activities during the occupation, as he functioned, on the one

Fig. 15.2. Church of Our Lady of Sorrows, Poznań. Photo by the author.

hand, as an administrator seemingly compliant with German demands, and on the other, as a member of the church hierarchy acting in opposition to the occupation regime.

Notes

1. ADW, Ankieta Strat Wojennych Diecezji Włocławskiej w l. 1939/45, przeprowadzona przez Archiwariusza Diecezjalnego w r. 1947, tom 1, 7–8.
2. Serwański, *Wielkopolska*, 421.
3. Report of Stanisław Adamski, January 1943, document 472, in *ADSS*, vol. 3, no. 2, 731; Madajczyk, *Okkupationspolitik*, 358.
4. Sziling, *Polityka*, 101–2. In "Hitlerowska," published much more recently (1997), Sziling states that in 1944 there were approximately seventy priests available in the Warthegau: Sziling, "Hitlerowska," 22.
5. Józef Nowacki, Raport to Główna Komisja Badania Zbrodnich Niemieckich w Polsce, June 1, 1946, IPN, GK 196/19, 141. Nowacki's report cites fifty-four such priests in the Poznań archdiocese alone.
6. Feliks Michalski, Ankieta, June 20, 1974, AAP, zespół 133, syg. OK 222.

7. Lagebericht, SD-Aussenstelle Kempen, March 4, 1949, IPN, GK 70/48, 15.

8. Lagebericht des Regierungspräsidentens Hohensalza, January 18, 1941, IfZ, Fb 125, 203.

9. Helmut Bischoff, Verordnung, IPN, 831/177, 139; Bischoff to Dymek, October 24, 1940, AAP, zespół 133, OK 3.

10. Regierungspräsident Posen (Böttcher) to Herren Landräte des Bezirks, Amtskommissare, Gendarmerie-Kreisführer, Schutzpolizei-Dienstabteilungen, APP, 53/1023/0/-/13, film O-83184, 91; Świadectwo Ks. Józefa Sarniewicza, n.d., IPN, GK 196/19, 169; Marian Frankiewicz, Relacja, October 25, 1947, IZ, Document II-123, 2.

11. Lagebericht des Regierungspräsidentens Hohensalza (Burkhardt), October 8, 1941, IfZ, Fb 125, 344.

12. Anonymous report, Kalisch, SD Abschnitt Litzmannstadt, SD Hauptaussenstelle Kalisch, YV, TR. 17, JM 12083, frame 453.

13. Bertram to Reichsminister für die Kirchlichen Angelegenheiten, April 6, 1944, BAB, R 5101/22437, 57.

14. RSHA to Reichsministerium für Kirchliche Angelegenheiten, June 5, 1944, BAB, R 5101/22437, 59.

15. Ausschnitt aus dem Lagebericht des Regierungspräsidenten in Posen für die Zeit vom 16. Mai bis 30. Juni 1941, June 30, 1941, IPN, GK 62/210/CD, 39.

16. Lagebericht des Regierungspräsidentens Hohensalza (Burkhardt), October 20, 1941, IfZ, Fb 125, 383.

17. The text here quoted is an awkward German transcription of a broadcast in Polish. It can be assumed that the broadcast was referring not to "Skara," but to Piotr Skarga, a late sixteenth- and early seventeenth-century Polish Jesuit associated with the Counter-Reformation in the Polish-Lithuanian Commonwealth.

18. The text is missing a surname following "Adam," but it is likely that the broadcast was referring to Adam Mickiewicz, the most revered Polish romantic poet and dramatist of the nineteenth century.

19. NSDAP Partei-Kanzlei (Birk) to Herrn Regierungsrat Meyer, October 18, 1943, IPN, GK 62/215/CD, 67–68. The correspondence includes the quoted text, which is a transcription of a broadcast on October 9, 1943. According to Kurt Birk (who was, as of October 1942, in the NSDAP Party Chancellery), the radio station issued regular broadcasts on confessional matters and was a "Bolshevik" propaganda tool. The broadcast did, in fact, exhort its listeners to pray for the Kościuszko Division, which was fighting under Red Army command on the Eastern Front. On Birk's biography, see Volk, *Akten deutscher Bischöfe*, vol. 5, 565n6.

20. Dudzus to Inspekteur der Sicherheitspolizei und des SD, October 3, 1940, AAG, zespół AKM I, syg., 2177, 37; Bischoff to Generalvikar der Erzdiözese Posen-Gnesen, October 24, 1940, AAP, zespół 133, syg. OK 3.

21. See, for example, Jan Kujawa, Ankieta, May 28, 1974, AAP, zespół 133, syg. OK 220, 471/74; Stanisław Poczta, Ankieta, June 1, 1974, AAP, zespół 133, syg. OK 224, 497/74; Bernard Langkau, Ankieta, June 28, 1974, AAP, zespół 133, syg. OK 221, 567/74; Marian Koszewski, Ankieta, June 30, 1974, AAP, zespół 133, syg. OK 220, 557/74.

22. Mieczysław Posmyk, Ankieta, May 17, 1974, AAP, zespół 133, syg. OK 224, 450/74.

23. Stanisław Cichy, Ankieta, March 28, 1974, AAP, zespół 133, syg. OK 216, 404/74.

24. Henryk Kaliszan, Ankieta, June 18, 1974, AAP, zespół 133, syg. OK 220, 519/74.

25. Stanisław Cichy, Ankieta, March 28, 1974, AAP, zespół 133, syg. OK 216, 404/74; Stanisław Kaczmarek, Ankieta, May 1974, AAP, zespół 133, syg. 220, 475/74; Władysław

Pawelczak, Ankieta, April 20, 1975, AAP, zespół 133, syg. OK 224, 531/75; Janusz Sobczak, "Moja parafie w latach okupacji (1939–1945)," AAP, zespół 133, syg. OK 128; Marian Biesiada, "Moja parafia w latach okupacji (1939–1945)," AAP, zespół 133, syg. OK 128.

26. Marian Samoliński to Kurii arcyb. w Poznaniu, January 11, 1947, AAP, zespół 133, syg. OK 121.

27. Tadeusz Fołczyński, "Moja parafia w latach okupacynych (1939–1945)," AAP, zespół 133, syg. 128.

28. NSDAP Kreisleiter Turek (Schlemper) to NSDAP Gauschulungsleiter Brixner, n.d., Abschrift, IPN, GK 62/197, 62. Evident from the content of the communication is that it postdates September 24, 1942. Records do not show that there was a German name assigned to Chlebów.

29. Stanisław Hartlieb, Ankieta, May 15, 1974, AAP, zespół 133, syg. 218.

30. Śmigiel, "Walka władz," 366.

31. Marian Biesiada, "Moja parafia w latach okupacji (1939–1945)," AAP, zespół 133, syg. OK 128.

32. Marian Biesiada, "Moja parafia w latach okupacji (1939–1945)," AAP, zespół 133, syg. OK 128.

33. Stefan Komorowski, "Moja parafia w latach okupacji 1939–1945," AAP, zespół 133, syg. OK 128.

34. Janusz Sobczak, "Moja parafie w latach okupacji (1939–1945)," AAP, zespół 133, syg. OK 128; see also Jastrząb, *Archidiecezja Poznańska*, 57.

35. Unless noted otherwise, the following description of this parish is based on Marian Frankiewicz, Relacja, October 25, 1947, IZ, Dok. II-123, 1; Józef Sarniewicz, Świadectwo, n.d., IPN, GK 196/19, 168; Marian Frankiewicz, Ankieta, January 19, 1974, AAP, zespół 133, syg. OK 217, 517/74.

36. See Domagała, *Ci, którzy przeszli przez Dachau*, 111.

37. Jastrząb, *Archidiecezja Poznańska*, 384.

38. Dudzus to Inspekteur der Sicherheitspolizei und des SD, October 3, 1940, AAG, zespół AKM I, syg. 2177, 37; Bischoff to Dymek, October 24, 1940, AAP, zespół 133, syg. OK 3.

39. "Raport o sytuacji na Ziemiach Zachodnich Nr. 5 (do 15.VIII.1943 r.)," in Mazur, Pietrowicz, and Rutowska, *Raporty*, 149.

40. Serwański, *Wielkopolska*, 421.

41. Bishop Stanisław Adamski to Pius XII, n.d., document 472, in *ADSS*, vol., 3, no. 2, 730; Jastrząb, *Archidiecezja Poznańska*, 58, 114, 386; Śmigiel, "Die apostolischen Administratoren," 260.

16

KONSPIRACJA

Resistance and Conspiracy

Walenty Dymek's role and activities during the occupation—a theme to be addressed in more detail below—invite a broader investigation of the role and nature of resistance among Polish Catholics in the Warthegau. Such an exercise presents, however, some challenging questions, most of which do not lend themselves to clear and precise answers. What constituted "resistance" in this context? What made resistance "Polish," what made it "Catholic," and to what extent did the two intersect? Can one speak of an "institutional resistance" on the part of the Catholic Church? Does an act of resistance on the part of a church authority or member of the episcopate "institutionalize" that act? If so, is that act of resistance of different or greater significance than were it initiated by a layperson?

Analyses of resistance in occupied Poland have tended to focus on more conventional categories such as organized conspiracy, sabotage, and armed, violent rebellion. Such an approach is, however, too restrictive when considering the actions of Polish Catholics in the Warthegau. In addressing the phenomenon of resistance as it relates to the Polish church, the work of West German scholars working in the 1970s and 1980s on resistance in Nazi Germany[1] is instructive, and can inform discussions of oppositional behavior that took place beyond the borders of the Altreich. To a great extent, it was these historians who broadened the notion of resistance to emphasize activities and behaviors not traditionally included in more conventional definitions. For example, scholars associated with a project on "Resistance and Persecution in Bavaria 1933–1945," initiated by Munich's Institute for Contemporary History in 1973, defined resistance as "every form of active or passive behavior which allows recognition of the rejection of the National Socialist regime or a partial area of National Socialist ideology and was bound up with certain risks."[2] The emerging emphasis in those years on *Alltagsgeschichte*, or the "history of everyday life," thus offered a whole range of noncompliant behaviors that could be described variously as violent, active, passive, or simply oppositional. In line with this approach, Holocaust historian Doris Bergen has defined resistance broadly as "any actions taken with the intent of thwarting Nazi German goals in the war, actions that carried with them risk of punishment."[3]

In the early 1980s, German historian Detlev Peukert described a range of dissident responses in the Third Reich that ranged from "nonconformist behavior" (e.g., choosing not to greet others with the "Heil Hitler" salute) to "refusal" (e.g., refusing to enlist one's son in the Hitler Youth) to "protest" (yet more political, and farther in the direction of broad rejection of the regime—e.g., the churches' protests against the "euthanasia" program) to "resistance" that grew out of rejection of the regime and that aimed at its overthrow. Peukert developed this spectrum of responses in describing Germans' oppositional behavior during the Third Reich, but his categories of analysis are also applicable to other contexts, such as that of Polish Catholics in the Warthegau. Moreover, Peukert emphasized that opposition-minded people at times took refuge in social-cultural institutions and structures that offered strength, solidarity, and encouragement, and among such institutions was the Catholic Church.[4]

Given these diverse responses, it should be clear that resistance could be the work of a group or organization, or the work of an individual. It could be armed or unarmed, violent or nonviolent. It could be motivated by patriotism and founded on a Christian moral armature, even as it could, at the same time and in the same individual, be the work of a radical xenophobic nationalist or antisemite. None of this is intended to diminish the sacrifice or heroism of those who defended their neighbors, country, or church in the face of Nazi persecution. Rather, the intent is to acknowledge the complexity of the issue. To acknowledge the possible coexistence of sacrifice and opportunism, of resistance and compliance in the same community or individual—to recognize such coexistence is to recognize both the brutality of Nazi rule and the humanity of its victims.

With the above in mind, it is useful to consider the extent to which the Catholic Church in the Warthegau can be considered a "resistance organization" or institution fundamentally and actively opposed to Nazi rule. Clearly, it did not, as an institution, pose any significant challenge or threat to the occupation regime. It did, however, provide a subculture and milieu that could, at some risk, counter the wishes or dictates of the occupation regime and its claims on Warthegau Poles. After 1941, however, the church—whether as institution, spiritual ministry, or building—was inaccessible for the majority of believers, further driving the Catholic community into the private sphere and underground.

The situation of the Catholic Church in the Warthegau also points to the importance of context, for whether or not an action can be classified as opposition or resistance depends on time, place, and circumstances.[5] Oppositional behavior is received, tolerated, or punished in a police state differently from in a democracy governed by rule of law. Acts of resistance were punished differently in occupied France, in the Altreich, and in the General Government. Public displays of Catholic devotion at roadside shrines remained common in East Upper Silesia but were forbidden in the Reichsgau Wartheland. Ultimately, then, it was the Nazi authorities who defined the risks and set the punishments. In the words of Hans Mommsen, "The power to define what in the narrow sense constituted actual resistance lay in the end of the day with the Gestapo."[6]

It was also the regime that erected barriers against resistance—barriers faced by Warthegau Poles in general, and by devout and oppositional Catholics in particular. Such barriers were particularly extensive in the Warthegau and ranged from specific consequences and punishments for oppositional behavior to the mundane yet discriminatory and burdensome aspects of everyday life under the Nazi occupation, such as poor housing and nutrition, prohibitions against the use of telephones, or restrictions on the use of bicycles and automobiles.[7] Opportunities for conspiracy and resistance were generally more limited in the Warthegau than in other regions of annexed and occupied Poland. According to Catherine Epstein, there were some fifty resistance groups organized in the Warthegau, and some six thousand Poles were arrested for their oppositional activities.[8] These numbers may at first glance appear high, but they pale in comparison to the number of organizations and number arrested in, for example, the General Government. Rigorous restriction of the Poles' movement and activities, comprehensive and severe Germanization measures, the relatively efficient authoritarianism of Greiser's regime, and the perpetual threat of incarceration and deportation—all were certainly effective barriers to resistance, as were the retributive "justice" and collective reprisals undertaken by the Gau administration and police. One priest from the Poznań diocese recalled that he had been involved in the distribution of underground newspapers early in the occupation but later gave this up in order to "stop exposing myself and others to an unnecessary death."[9]

In short, the barriers were great and the risks deadly for all Poles in the Warthegau, and this was no less the case for the clergy and others who opposed the occupation regime on behalf of the church and its ministries. Hostage taking and summary executions of priests were common during and in the weeks following the invasion. Roundups of churchgoing Poles for forced labor were frequent. Merely the untimely public expression of one's faith or devotion was dangerous. Throughout the occupation, violation of restrictions on the church's ministries resulted for many clergy in arrest, deportation, and death. Moreover, it is worth noting that, from the perspective of the institutional church and its hierarchy, removal of the clergy was perhaps the worst possible form of persecution of the church because it limited, or even denied, access to the sacraments.

It should therefore come as no surprise that active resistance was not the norm. In fact, accounts of German police officials after the 1941 Aktion consistently describe the Polish churchgoing population as generally apathetic and resigned to the new order. "The Polish population has finally realized," a report from the Bojanowo gendarmerie stated in late October of that year, "that they have nothing left to hope for. . . . The closure of the churches has embittered them even more, but they recognize that they can do nothing about it."[10] A month later, the same official ascribed the Poles' more passive bearing to the closure of churches in October: "The police are increasingly occupied with the task of keeping a close watch on the Poles and giving them no opportunity to increase their level of confidence. Because of the closure of churches, they have become somewhat tamer, for one used to notice how, when they emerged from a church, they appeared much more confident than otherwise."[11] The following June, a report of the Poznań Gestapo observed that "contrary to our expectations, with the closing of churches some time ago, the broader mass of the Polish population has, after some initial bewilderment, resigned itself to the current situation."[12]

Conditioned to believe that Poles congregating in Catholic churches fostered dissent and rebellion, it is not surprising that these officials associated the Aktion of October 1941 with what they perceived as passivity and resignation in its aftermath. In the small town of Aleksandrów

(Weichselstädt) on the northern border of the Gau, the local gendarmerie issued dozens of reports attesting to the timid and resigned behavior of the Polish population.[13] According to these accounts, organized resistance was absent, and acts of defiance against German authority were confined to individual infractions such as illegal butchering or distillation of alcohol. The general mood, the reports contended, was influenced by concern that there would be further deportation of Poles from the region. "The Poles," one such report claimed, "are unexacting and withdrawn."[14] Clearly, the Polish population was not as docile and compliant as here described. It may well have been in the interest of the German authorities to exaggerate to their superiors the level of Polish passivity, thereby suggesting a high level of success in their efforts to pacify the local population, even as it would have been in the interest of Poles engaged in resistance to mask their activities with a façade of compliance.

Resistance was therefore seldom obvious, open, or violent, but if one is willing to designate as resistance any action intended to undermine, thwart, or combat Nazi measures and policies designed to discriminate against or persecute the church, it is clear that Catholic Poles in the Reichsgau Wartheland, both clergy and laity, engaged in a wide spectrum of oppositional activities, from participating in secret worship services to fighting in partisan organizations, from sheltering a priest to serving as a chaplain in the Home Army, from illegally distributing the sacraments to sabotaging munitions production. Some of these activities were of course "secular" in nature, while others were specifically intended to maintain or advance the cause of the faith and church.

The complexities of resistance as it related to the Warthegau church are well illustrated in the person and role of the Poznań auxiliary bishop Walenty Dymek, the dilemmas he faced, and the degree to which his role under the occupation should be characterized as compliant or oppositional. In fact, his responses to the persecution of the church reflected both compliance and opposition, and to that extent, his role was in some respects not unlike that of many lower-level Polish clergy in the Reichsgau Wartheland.

In the early months of the occupation, Bishop Dymek may have given the impression of reflexive outward compliance with the authorities. For example, in September 1939, after Cardinal Hlond's departure and in the first days of German military rule, he arranged a meeting with the German military commander in Poznań, Lieutenant General Max von

Schenkendorff. According to Hilarius Breitinger, Dymek presented the general with a declaration to be read in churches of his diocese on the following Sunday, a declaration that reportedly urged Poles to remain loyal to the German military authorities. The general expressed his thanks and promised that the Poles would be treated justly.[15]

Moreover, the bishop's limited correspondence with clergy in the diocese during the early weeks of the occupation suggests a rather mechanical acquiescence to German demands and restrictions on church activities, as he dutifully instructed priests to avoid expressions of Polish nationalism,[16] to restrict sermons to purely theological themes,[17] and to avoid any activities that would conflict with the wishes of the occupation authorities or German police.[18] Reinhard Heydrich had even once gone so far as to refer to the bishop's "resigned behavior," claiming that some regarded him as a "weakling" who did not enjoy the support of the clergy under his authority.[19] For the bishop, however, and for any other church authorities from Pius XII on down, maintaining the ministries of the church was of paramount importance. In most cases, outward compliance with the dictates of the regime helped in achieving this goal. The bishop may have appeared compliant, but at the same time he was working to subvert Nazi authority and policy, although not always in obvious or discernable ways.

Walenty Dymek bore no illusions about the character of Nazi rule after the October 3, 1939, "Cathedral Island Action," when he was placed under house arrest. This made him largely invisible, which likely reinforced an impression of his outward compliance with the authorities. The sources make clear, however, that the bishop was engaging in illegal activities in the service of the diocese and, later, on behalf of Our Lady of Sorrows parish. He was, for example, illegally ordaining priests[20] and, in the latter years of the occupation, using his residence in the parish house to minister illegally to parishioners by hearing confessions and secretly celebrating Masses.[21] The bishop also provided spiritual and practical assistance to priests in hiding, and facilitated their escapes to other regions of occupied Poland. Such was the case of Father Władysław Pawełczak who, because of his impending arrest, was forced to flee the Wartheland for the General Government in May 1941.[22]

Dymek's activities also included the gathering of information from and for the Polish underground state[23]—information about church affairs and the church's persecution that he included in clandestine reports to the Vatican

Fig. 16.1. Rectory of Our Lady of Sorrows Parish, Poznań, where Bishop Walenty Dymek remained under house arrest in a third-floor apartment. The second floor was occupied by the Gestapo's officer for church affairs, Franz Wolf. Photo by the author.

issued on December 1, 1939; February 9, 1940; and September 26, 1941.[24] The last of these, signed by both the bishop and Edward van Blericq, vicar general for the Gniezno diocese, was sent to Pius XII shortly after Greiser's September 13 edict regulating the legal status of the churches. A highly detailed account of the disastrous situation in the Warthegau, it outlined both the Reichsgau Wartheland's status as a "model Gau," and the extensive powers available to the Gauleiter and Reichsstatthalter, who, as Dymek and Blericq clearly understood, was pursuing his Kirchenpolitik largely independently of Berlin ministries.[25]

The German authorities were well aware of the bishop's contacts with the Polish resistance, and were eager to exploit their knowledge of his activities. At the November 1942 meeting described in chapter 14, the district police chiefs devoted part of their discussion specifically to Dymek and his role in church affairs. According to the meeting's minutes, Gauleiter Greiser had decided that because the bishop was politically compromised, he

Fig. 16.2. A plaque on the rectory of Our Lady of Sorrows Parish, Poznań, commemorating Bishop Walenty Dymek. The tablet erroneously states that Bishop Dymek was placed under house arrest in the building in 1939. He was, in fact, moved there in January 1943. Photo by the author.

would be the most appropriate choice for head of a Polish Catholic religious association should one be established under the current structure. Not only had Dymek emerged as hostile to Germans during the "Polish times" (i.e., during the interwar years in independent Poland); he had also exhibited under the occupation "verifiable sympathies for the Polish resistance movement." As far as Greiser and the German authorities were concerned, Dymek was therefore relatively "safe" as a leader of Polish Catholics because they had a simple and convenient justification for taking measures against him should the need arise.[26] In other words, they saw in the bishop an easy target for extortion.

The Gau authorities continued in their efforts to control, influence, and at the same time, exploit the bishop. In 1943, after the German defeat at the Battle of Stalingrad, the Gestapo turned to him with the request that he sign an anticommunist public declaration. Dymek refused, responding, as one scholar has alleged, with the provocative suggestion that it would instead be better if the Nazi authorities opened all the Warthegau churches and released all priests from concentration camps.[27] The following year, after an Allied air raid on April 9, Nazi officials organized, for propaganda purposes, a public ceremony of burial for the Polish victims of the bombing. Although under house arrest, Bishop Dymek was briefly taken from his quarters in the parish house in order to conduct the ceremony. Whether the event succeeded in appealing to the religious sensibilities of Warthegau Poles, Catholics elsewhere in the Reich, or Catholics and governments abroad is not clear, but the authorities certainly went to great lengths to choreograph and publicize the event. They even permitted the bishop to offer a homily in Polish, marking the first time since the beginning of the occupation that a priest had done so in public. Gau officials, probably hoping for a condemnation of the attack, were likely disappointed, for Dymek reportedly kept his words decidedly spiritual and nonpolitical.[28] Just prior to the liberation, a final effort was made to gain the bishop's support for German purposes. On January 26, 1945, Major General Ernst Matern called on Dymek to issue with him an "Appeal to the Polish Population." Again, the bishop refused, stating that as a cleric, he prays for all people, but as a Pole, there was no way he could cosign a document with a Nazi general.[29]

Dymek's colleagues in the Łódź diocese, Bishop Włodzimierz Jasiński and his suffragan Kazimierz Tomczak, faced similar challenges but also enjoyed considerably more freedom to carry out their duties, if for only the first year

Fig. 16.3. Bishop Walenty Dymek officiating at a mass burial of Polish victims of an Allied bombing, Poznań, April 1944. Courtesy of Instytut Zachodni, IZ, Dział IV, 123–4.

and a half of the occupation. Ever negotiating the balance of resistance and compliance, both were engaged in oppositional activities from the start. When the German invasion began, Jasiński and Tomczak both called on the clergy in their diocese not to flee the Germans but to remain in their parishes to continue their ministry. They were also instrumental in establishing the Łódź District Committee for Social Service to Soldiers and their Families (Okręgowy Łódzki Komitet Społecznego Niesienia Pomocy Żolnierzom oraz ich Rodzinom), with Tomczak at its head.[30] On September 5, Bishop Jasiński issued a radio address calling for the population to resist what he called the "new Teutonic invasion," which earned him, in the eyes of the authorities, the reputation of an aggressive German hater, and resulted in his being placed under house arrest.[31] Jasiński was freed from house arrest at the end of January 1940 and, from then until mid-1941, was able to administrate affairs in his diocese more or less normally.[32] It is not clear what was behind this more tolerant approach, but in any case, it allowed the bishop to maintain contact with the clergy who remained, and gave him the opportunity to provide the sacrament of confirmation to 2,700 Catholics in the diocese through the end of 1940,[33] to facilitate hundreds of illegal marriages, to cultivate contact with the Home Army, and perhaps most significantly, to inform the Vatican of church affairs in his diocese and the Warthegau in general.[34]

There were two basic channels that allowed Bishop Jasiński to communicate with Rome. The first of these was via a Volksdeutscher priest, Roman Gradolewski, who on at least three occasions relayed information to Cesare Orsenigo, the papal nuncio in Berlin.[35] In addition, the bishop relied on a courier—likely an Italian industrialist in Łódź—who passed information on to the Vatican secretary of state Maglione.[36] While the content of most of Jasiński's communications is unknown, it is nonetheless clear that Orsenigo attempted on numerous occasions to intervene on his behalf with the German authorities.[37] The bishop's role as a conduit of information for the Vatican, and his administration of the Łódź diocese, came to an abrupt end when he was required on May 5, 1941 to appear before the German authorities. Jasiński, along with fifteen other clergymen, was sent to the General Government, where he remained for the duration of the occupation.

Like many local parish priests, Walenty Dymek and Włodzimierz Jasiński generally complied with German demands but also defied the Gau authorities in maintaining the church's ministries and even engaging in the illegal and more dangerous work of intelligence gathering, secret reporting, and other forms of resistance. The details of their relationships to the Polish underground or the extent of their activities on behalf of the Delegatura, Home Army, or other organizations are not well known,[38] but this is hardly surprising, as such activities were rarely documented at the time, and in the aftermath of the occupation, these men would likely refrain from making them public.

More is known about nuns and priests at the parish level engaging in clandestine ministry and conspiratorial work on behalf of the underground resistance, work that could take many forms. Among the women religious, many were active in conveying information to resistance organizations, others were instrumental in illegal distribution of food and other necessities among the Polish population, while still others sheltered fugitives. In some cases, nuns paid for such risks with their lives. Maria Wiśniewska, a member of the Sisters of Charity of Saint Vincent DePaul, or "Gray Sisters," was deeply involved in the work of Our Lady of Sorrows parish in Poznań and, at the same time, served as a messenger for the Home Army's Poznań-Łazarz district. In July of 1942 she was summoned to the Gestapo and informed that she would thereafter be working (presumably as a domestic) in the home of Franz Wolf, the chief officer for church affairs, who, of course, also lived in the parish house. This provided her with the opportunity to convey information about Wolf to Walenty Dymek, who could then relay it to others in the resistance or wider church hierarchy beyond the borders of the Warthegau. Wiśniewska was arrested in October 1943 and taken to the Fort VII prison, where she died the next month following a brutal interrogation.[39]

Helena Dąbrowska, also a member of the Gray Sisters, worked in a supervisory role in a Poznań workhouse, and used her position there to purchase far more food for the residents than was needed. She then channeled the extra supplies to the needy in the Poznań population. Arrested and imprisoned in July 1941, she stood trial for theft and embezzlement as well as for relaying to a colleague in Danzig-Westpreussen information about conditions in the Warthegau, including the execution of dozens of priests. The court sentenced Helena Dąbrowska to ten years imprisonment. In her case, that meant deportation to Auschwitz, where she died on January 31, 1943.[40]

The Sisters Servant of the Immaculate Conception of the Blessed Virgin Mary in Poznań used their convent as a refuge for at least five priests fleeing from the Gestapo, hiding the fugitives in concealed rooms in the nearby church tower or in the church itself. This lasted until the convent was requisitioned on April 1, 1942. In October of the previous year, Sister Maria Róża Woźniak was the victim of a denunciation and was arrested by the Gestapo. Subsequently tortured and deported to the Ravensbrück concentration camp, she remained there until the camp's liberation on April 25, 1945. Woźniak died the following day.[41]

Some women religious were involved in harboring Jewish fugitives and sheltering Jewish children, but such assistance was far less common in the Reichsgau Wartheland than in other regions of occupied Poland. This reality encourages consideration of an important and much broader issue: the responses of Catholic laypeople, clergy, and institutions to the Nazi treatment of Jews in the Warthegau. The matter is sensitive and remains insufficiently charted in the literature. Despite the emergence of important research over the last two decades on the role of antisemitism in the Polish church[42] and on the Shoah in the Reichsgau Wartheland,[43] and although there is a significant recent literature on the responses of non-Jewish Poles (the vast majority of whom were Roman Catholics) in other regions of occupied Poland to the persecution of Jews in their midst,[44] analysis of institutional Catholic responses to the persecution and annihilation of the Jews in the Polish lands, or of the relationship between Polish Catholic tradition or theology and these responses, remains lacking.

In general, for many years Western scholars of the Shoah tended to focus their research not on the Reichsgau Wartheland but on the persecution of Jews in other parts of occupied Poland, especially the General Government, where there were more Jews, more and larger ghettos (with the important exception of the Łódź ghetto in the eastern Wartheland), and four of the six centers for industrialized mass killing: Bełżec, Sobibór, Treblinka, and Majdanek. In addition, because Governor General Hans Frank was tried at the Nürnberg International Military Tribunal, extensive source material on this region was available to Western scholars.[45]

The Warthegau had, however, a crucial place in the planning and execution of the "Final Solution." When German forces entered the region in September 1939, there were approximately 435,000 Jews in the territory of the future Reichsgau Wartheland (the vast majority in the eastern Warthegau, with 233,000 in Łódź alone). Of these, only 10,000 to 15,000 survived.[46] The first ghettos were established in the Warthegau, the Łódź ghetto was the last to be "liquidated," and the National Socialists established in Chełmno nad Nerem the first center for the mass killing of Jews, where more than 150,000 died.[47] Moreover, Gauleiter Arthur Greiser had tremendous authority and liberty to implement the concentration, exploitation, and destruction of Jews under his authority, functioning as, in the words of Ian Kershaw, a "motor of the 'Final Solution.'"[48]

Despite the Warthegau's importance in the history of the Holocaust, contacts between the Jewish and Polish populations were limited, and instances of aid and rescue were less common than in the other regions of occupied Poland. The reasons for this were many. The Warthegau's Jewish population was not as great or as dense as in some other regions of Nazi-occupied Poland, and the overwhelming majority of Warthegau Jews lived in Łódź District.[49] Significant as well were the regime's policies toward Poles and Jews—policies that were, toward the former, restrictive and murderous, and toward the latter, in the end, annihilationist. Timing was also a factor, as Jews were ghettoized, sent to forced labor camps, and murdered earlier in the Warthegau than in other regions, so that by September 1942, nearly all Warthegau Jews were either in the Łódź ghetto, in forced labor camps, or dead.[50] With respect to Catholic Poles, persecution of their church, its institutions, and its religious orders was more severe in the Reichsgau Wartheland than elsewhere in occupied Poland, and there were, as elsewhere, strict and enforced prohibitions against Poles offering aid to Jews. Finally, as elsewhere in Poland and elsewhere in Europe, relations between the two groups were burdened by traditions of distance, aloofness, or hostility.

Several factors make it impossible to gauge with precision the responses of Warthegau Catholics and their church to the persecution of the Jews. Catholics and representatives of the church who aided Jews may not have been eager or willing to document their actions, which were undertaken in secret and at great risk. Poles who were indifferent to or even supportive of Nazi measures against Warthegau Jews would likewise not have left behind record of their attitudes or actions, or testified to them after the occupation. And in the end, the Catholic clergy were first and foremost responsible for ministering to their faithful and providing them with the sacraments, rather than aiding Jews. There also remains, of course, the possibility that a lack of documentation simply reflects a lack of action on behalf of Jews, especially when one considers how other forms of resistance undertaken at great risk were, in fact, recorded both during and after the occupation. All of these factors suggest why, after years of research for this book, no more than a few dozen references to Jews have emerged in the sources documenting the history of the Catholic Church in the Warthegau. Exploration and interpretation of that silence are necessary but remain desiderata beyond the scope of the archival sources and secondary literature on which this monograph is based.

Such barriers and uncertainties notwithstanding, there were indeed instances of Polish Catholic clergy, laypeople, and institutions providing aid and assistance to Jews, most of which have remained outside the historical record, and relatively few of which, in comparison to other regions of occupied Poland, are recorded as emerging from the Reichsgau Wartheland. Relying on an admittedly limited source base, church historian Zygmunt Zieliński has listed ninety-one religious houses across Poland that were engaged in aid and rescue efforts on behalf of Jews. Of these, only one—the "Gray Ursulines" in Sieradz (Schieratz)—was located in the Reichsgau Wartheland.[51] Another account notes only one religious house in the Warthegau—the orphanage of the Sisters Servant of Mary Immaculate in Łódź—involved in the rescue of Jewish children. In this case, the nuns were able to place the children, both Polish and Jewish, with Polish families before the German authorities closed the orphanage and sent the nuns to Bojanowo.[52] In the literature and documentation there are also references to assistance offered to Jews by Polish religious and secular clergymen:

Father Jan Jazdończyk was known to have supplied medicines to Jews at the forced labor camp in Boguszyń (Buchenhof);[53] another priest prepared Jews for baptism;[54] the Franciscans at the Niepokolanów monastery, although known for their prewar antisemitic publications, provided Jews expelled from Poznań with food and medicine.[55]

There is, not surprisingly, far more extensive documentation of priests' illegal efforts to maintain the church's ministries, and of their illegal work on behalf of resistance organizations. As described in the previous chapter, priests regularly violated restrictions on their ministries, frequently providing clandestine religious instruction, distributing the sacraments, officiating at illegal worship services, or ministering to German Catholics in violation of the "nationality principle." The risks associated with any such activities were significant. For example, in the Chlebów parish, the local priest was not only responsible for the baptism of hundreds of children on one day; he was also known to provide his services to devout Volksdeutsche settlers in the area—settlers who had a Polish priest baptize their German children, and who, according to a local Nazi Party official, "could not be kept away [from the church], even with brute force." Any ministry to German Catholics was, of course, forbidden, posing a danger to both the priest and the Volksdeutsche he was serving. "It is," the same party official continued, "therefore impossible to tolerate these matters any further, and I am requesting that immediate steps be taken to see to it that the church is closed and the priest be assigned more useful work."[56] The Gestapo's response to the official's demands was perhaps unexpected. Because only one or two "Polish" churches remained open in each subdistrict, the Gestapo was reluctant to close the Chlebów church, as doing so would result in Poles streaming to churches in the neighboring subdistricts. Moreover, the Gestapo expected that closing the church "would elicit disquiet, which, in light of the integration of Polish labor into the war economy, must be avoided." The issue of the priest was simpler to resolve: the Gestapo arrested him and dispatched him to a concentration camp.[57]

Clergymen were also involved in a wide variety of activities on behalf of the Polish resistance, and although the documentation of such activities is not extensive, it does offer a view into the large- and small-scale conspiratorial work they undertook. For example, the Koryta (Krippenfeld) priest Henryk Kaliszan recalled securing false documents for individuals at risk, and assisting in their escape to the General Government.[58] Some priests, like Tadeusz Malinowski in Poznań, sheltered not only fellow priests who

Fig. 16.4. Father Józef Adamek celebrating an Easter Mass in a private home, Ostrowo, April 1943. Courtesy of Muzeum Miasta Ostrowa Wielkopolskiego, Ostrowo, Foto-Nr. 1753.

were hiding from the authorities but also members of the underground resistance.[59] A significant number of priests also served as chaplains for underground military organizations. Henryk Szklarek, for example, served as both a leader and a chaplain in the Wojsko Ochotnicze (WO) or Volunteer Army in the western Polish territories. Sought by the Gestapo, he fled in 1941 to the General Government and later served as a Home Army chaplain during the 1944 Warsaw Uprising.[60] Other Catholic priests such Bolesław Jordan in Ostrowo, Czesław Cofta in Czarnków, and Alfons Jankowski in Poznań—the latter two discussed briefly in chapter 14—were active in assisting partisans and troops in various underground organizations. All three were eventually imprisoned in the Żabikowo camp.[61]

"I did not formally belong to any conspiratorial organization," wrote Father Marian Kowalewski in response to a question in a survey about his wartime experiences. This may have been true, but his activities during the occupation were nonetheless remarkable. A priest in Mosina (Moschin) just south of Poznań, Kowalewski was arrested twice in December 1939 and held each time as a hostage. In March 1940 he evaded a third arrest, escaping minutes before the arrival of the police, and then lived until early 1941 in Poznań under a false identity. Working as a carpenter under the assumed name Zbigniew Babst, he secretly celebrated Masses in a nearby village, and in January 1941, made his way illegally into the General Government. He eventually settled in Kraków, where he served a parish in the southern part of the city. In addition to his normal pastoral duties, he was engaged in a variety of illegal activities, such as celebrating Masses for partisans in local forests and preparing Jews for baptism. He also worked on behalf of the resistance, installing transmitting devices in his apartment to receive Home Army reports and burying the corpses of fallen Home Army soldiers.[62]

Among the priests most prominent in the underground resistance was Józef Prądziński of Poznań's Collegiate Church of Saint Mary Magdalen. Long an advocate for the nationalist cause and aligned with the right-wing and antisemitic National Party, he was a cofounder in 1939 of the resistance organization "Ojczyzna" ("Fatherland"). One of the largest and most influential resistance groups in the annexed regions of western Poland, "Ojczyzna" maintained steady communication with the government-in-exile and was organized into various "bureaus" dedicated to, for example, social welfare, underground education, finance, or information and documentation, which was responsible for documenting German policy and crimes, and then reporting to the government-in-exile's Delegation (Delegatura) of the Polish underground state.[63] Prądzyński, who operated in the resistance under the pseudonyms "Prałat" ("Prelate") and "Omega," was arrested in May 1941 and imprisoned first in Poznań, and later that year in Fort VII. In September 1941 he was deported to Dachau, where he died on May 20, 1942, the victim of an "invalid transport."[64]

Father Stefan (Julian) Mirochna, guardian (i.e., head or superior) of the Franciscan friary in Kalisz, likewise played a significant role, placing his religious house at the center of underground activity in the southeastern part of the Warthegau. Bearing the pseudonym "Kawa" ("Coffee"), Mirochna was a leader of the political and military resistance group OJN or Organizacja Jedności Narodowej (Organization of National Unity), along with his colleague Stanisław Zaborowicz, priest at the Saint Nicolas parish in Kalisz. A regional leader of the National Party, Mirochna nonetheless advocated, unlike many others in the organization, for coordination of the OJN's activities with resistance organizations outside the right-wing nationalist camp. He also used his cloister as a base for the organization, which would have disastrous results when the resistance group was exposed in 1941. When the Gestapo searched the cloister, they uncovered weapons, ammunition, radio receivers, and a printing press. Four members of the order were arrested, but Mirochna succeeded in escaping and fleeing to the General Government. He would then be arrested in November 1942 in Warsaw and sent to Poznań, where he was imprisoned first in the police prison, and then in Fort VII, where he died the following year.[65] As for Father Zaborowicz, he was arrested in March of 1943 along with the other Kalisz Franciscans and imprisoned in Łódź. Soon after, he was shot along with two hundred other Poles in a public execution in Zgierz (Görnau)—a massacre in retaliation for the murder of two German policemen.[66]

A further example of resistance activity emerging out of the Catholic context, the story of the "Poznańska Piątka" or "Poznań Five," has assumed in the postwar years nearly folkloric status in the region. Czesław Jóźwiak, Edward Kaźmierski, Franciszek Kęsy, Edward Klinik, and Jarogniew Wojciechowski were alumni of the Salesian Oratory of Saint John Bosco, a Poznań boarding school. Ranging in age from seventeen to twenty, and motivated by the bonds of friendship from their high school years, they all became engaged in conspiratorial work following the German invasion in September 1939. Assisted by local clergy, the five young men became part of a resistance cell that met with Salesian priests and others in local churches. Some of their work was cultural and spiritual, while some was political, such as intelligence gathering, reconnaissance work on Wehrmacht installations in the city, and distribution of underground newspapers. Denounced to the German authorities, all five were arrested between October 21 and 23, 1940, all five were incarcerated over nearly two years in the same prisons (Fort VII, Wronki [Wronke], Berlin-Neukölln, Zwickau, and Dresden), and all five were guillotined in Dresden on August 24, 1942.[67]

As stated at the outset of this study, the Reichsgau Wartheland was where persecution, resistance, and the demands for compliance met in complex and even contradictory ways. Persecution of the church and its faithful, as the foregoing chapters have illustrated, took countless forms—some merely inconvenient for Catholic Poles, and others deadly. Compliance with the occupation regime's dictates and demands, whether on the part of church leaders or the laity, was generally born of necessity, and few would accuse the majority of Warthegau Catholics of conforming to Nazi policy out of convenience or consent. Oppositional behavior, refusal to comply with the regime's dictates, protest, or resistance carried great risks. Many among the laity and remaining clergy struggled to maintain a degree of spiritual community and level of pastoral care under extraordinarily difficult circumstances. Others engaged in active conspiracy against the occupation regime. Some even served on behalf of armed resistance organizations. In sum, the behavior of Catholics under such circumstances was complex, and the historian's effort to "categorize" the responses of Polish and Warthegau Catholics to Nazi persecution is no less complex. Individual and collective response to persecution can, of course, take many forms, and need not, as seems to be the reflex, always be located along a collaboration—compliance—resistance range. Moreover, it is usually impossible to determine the extent to which a Warthegau Catholic's responses to Nazi measures were precisely motivated by Catholic tradition, conviction, notions of patriotism, or any combination of these or other factors. Attendance at Sunday Mass may well have been for many a gesture of defiance against the German occupiers, but that does not mean that ceasing to attend Mass was necessarily a gesture of compliance. Often it was, but often not, for in many cases, Polish Catholics simply saw their local churches closed and their priests disappear, and as a result were less likely to participate in public expressions of their faith.

Warthegau Catholics who resisted the Nazi occupation in one way or another undoubtedly found inspiration in a variety of sources: in conscience, in patriotism, in fear and hatred of the occupiers, in the traditions and doctrines of their faith, in the examples of their fellow parishioners, and in the examples of some of their leaders among the clergy and church hierarchy. For many, Pope Pius XII was a symbol of the church and faith they were serving and defending. In their efforts to withstand the occupation, to bear its persecutions, to resist its restrictions and demands, or to respond to the persecution of the Jews in their midst, many Catholics looked to him for authority and leadership, and many would be disappointed.

Notes

1. For a concise discussion of developments in the field through the year 2000, see Kershaw, *Nazi Dictatorship*, 183–217.

2. From Harald Jaeger and Hermann Rumschöttel, "Das Forschungsprojekt 'Widerstand und Verfolgung in Bayern 1933–1945,'" in *Archivalische Zeitschrift* 73, no. 1 (December 1977): 214, quoted and translated in Kershaw, *Nazi Dictatorship*, 192.

3. Doris L. Bergen, *War and Genocide: A Concise History of the Holocaust* (Lanham: Rowman and Littlefield, 2016), 263.

4. Detlev J. K. Peukert, *Inside Nazi Germany: Conformity, Opposition, and Racism in Everyday Life* (New Haven, CT: Yale University Press, 1987), 82–85.

5. On this point see Francis R. Nicosia, "Introduction: Resistance to National Socialism in the Work of Peter Hoffmann," in *Germans against Nazism: Nonconformity, Opposition, and Resistance in the Third Reich: Essays in Honour of Peter Hoffmann*, 2nd ed., ed. Francis R. Nicosia and Lawrence D. Stokes (New York: Berghahn, 2015), 1–2.

6. Hans Mommsen, *From Weimar to Auschwitz*, trans. Philip O'Connor (Princeton, NJ: Princeton University Press, 1991), 216.

7. Aleksandra Pietrowicz, "Die Widerstandsbewegung in den eingegliederten polnischen Gebieten 1939–1945," in *Polen under deutscher und sowjetischer Besatzung 1939–1945*, ed. Jacek Andrzej Młynarczyk, Einzelveröffentlichungen des Deutschen Historischen Instituts Warschau, vol. 20 (Osnabrück: Fibre Verlag, 2009), 429.

8. Epstein, *Model Nazi*, 206–7. On resistance activities in the Reichsgau Wartheland in general, see Woźniak, *Encyklopedia konspiracji*, 17–49; Serwański, *Wielkopolska*, 273–455.

9. Felix Michalski, Ankieta, June 20, 1974, AAP, zespół 133, syg. OK 222, 591/74.

10. Gendarmerie-Posten Schmückert, Lagebericht für den Monat Oktober 1941, October 31, 1941, IPN, GK 736/2, 138.

11. Gendarmerie-Posten Schmückert, Lagebericht für den Monat November 1941, November 30, 1941, IPN, GK 736/2, 144.

12. Lagebericht des Höheren SS- und Polizeiführers beim Reichsstatthalter in Posen im Wehrkreis XXI.-Inspekteur der Sicherheitspolizei und den SD, June 24, 1942, IPN, GK 62/210/CD, 111.

13. The reports are assembled in IPN, GK 71/6.

14. Lagebericht für das III. Vierteljahr 1942, Gendarmerieabteilung Alexandrowo to Gendarmeriekreis Hermannsbad in Alexandrowo, September 23, 1942, IPN, GK 71/6, 237.

15. Breitinger, *Als Deutschenseelsorger*, 39.

16. Dymek memorandum, September 21, 1939, AAP, zespół 133, syg. OK 3.

17. Dymek memorandum, April 26, 1940, AAP, zespół 133, syg. OK 3.

18. Dymek memorandum, September 14, 1939, AAP, zespół 133, syg. OK 3; Sicherheitsdienst des Reichsführers—SS, SD—Leitabschnitt Posen, an das Reichssicherheitshauptamt—Amt II B/32, Berlin, December 10, 1940, USHMM, RG-15.007M, reel 38, 471, 1.

19. Heydrich to Reichsminister für die Kirchliche Angelegenheiten, February 13, 1940, BAB, R 5101/22185, 111–12.

20. Serwański, *Pod niemieckim Jarzmem*, 309.

21. Jastrząb, *Archidiecezja Poznańska*, 58.

22. Władysław Pawełczak, Ankieta, May 20, 1975, AAP, zespół 133, syg. OK 224, 531/75.

23. Fijałkowski, *Kościół*, 263; Serwański, *Wielkopolska*, 419.

24. Jastrząb, *Archidiecezja Poznańska*, 57–58.

25. Dymek and Blericq to Pius XII, September 26, 1941, document 315 Annexe, in *ADSS*, vol. 3, no. 1, 474–76.

26. "Niederschrift über die Besprechung der Leiter der Staatspolizei(leit)stellen Posen, Hohensalza und Litzmannstadt mit dem Sachbearbeiter für kirchliche Fragen beim Reichsstatthalter im Warthegau am 19.11.1942 in Hohensalza," November 19, 1942, IPN,

GK 196/19, 118. See also Jastrząb, *Archidiecezja Poznańska*, 57; Śmigiel, "Die apostolischen Administratoren," 261–62; Śmigiel, *Die katholische Kirche*, 192–93; Serwański, *Wielkopolska*, 419–20.

27. Serwański, *Wielkopolska*, 420.

28. "Die Trauerfeier auf dem Hauptfriedhof," *Ostdeutscher Beobachter*, April 14, 1944, 4; Jastrząb, *Archidiecezja Poznańska*, 59; Olszewski, *Straty*, 226.

29. Jastrząb, *Archidiecezja Poznańska*, 59.

30. Marek Budziarek, "Diecezja łódzka podczas okupacji hitlerowskiej," *Więź* 20, no. 3 (1977), 72; Marek Budziarek, "Zarząd i organizacja," 273.

31. Orsenigo to Maglione, February 21, 1940, doc. 117, in *ADSS*, vol. 3, no. 1, 221–22; Sicherheitspolizei Poznań to Reichsministerium für die Kirchliche Angelegenheiten, April 10, 1940, BAB, R 5101/22185.

32. Reichsstatthalter Posen to Reichsministerium für die Kirchliche Angelegenheiten, February 24, 1940, BAB, R5101/22185; Budziarek, "Zarząd i organizacja," 275, 278, 305.

33. Budziarek attributes the authorities' leniency to Jasiński's influence. See Budziarek, "Zarząd i organizacja," 274, 278.

34. Marek Budziarek, *Katedra przy Adolf Hitlerstrasse: z dziejów Kościoła katolickiego w Łodzi 1939–1945* (Warszawa: Instytut Wydawniczy Pax, 1984), 75, 80, 101.

35. Budziarek, "Zarząd i organizacja," 276. Gradolewski also attempted to intervene directly with Greiser's head of Department I-51 in the Reichsstatthalter's office, Heinrich Meyer: Vermerk, November 10, 1942, IPN, GK 62/180, 62. On Gradolewski's activities and ministry under the occupation, and subsequent treatment in the Polish People's Republic, see Sebastian Ligarski, *W kleszczach totalitaryzmów: Księdza Romana Gradowlewskiego i ojca Jacka Hoszyckiego. Życiorysy Niedopoweidziane* (Warszawa: Instytut Pamięci Narodowej–Komisja Ścigania Zbrodni Przeciwko Narodowi Polskiemu, 2017).

36. Budziarek, "Zarząd i organizacja," 277, and 277n57.

37. Reichsminister für die Kirchlichen Angelegenheiten (Roth) to Reichsstatthalter, February 2, 1940, Schnellbrief, IPN, GK 62/197, 2; Orsenigo to Ribbentrop, August 14, 1941, doc. 291, in *ADSS*, vol. 3, no. 1, 426–28; Orsenigo to Ribbentrop, December 4, 1941, document 340, in *ADSS*, vol. 3, no. 1, 510.

38. Śmigiel, "Die apostolischen Administratoren," 262; Śmigiel, *Die katholische Kirche*, 192–93.

39. Jastrząb, *Archidiecezja Poznańska*, 386.

40. Urteil gegen die katholische Ordensschwester Helene Dabrowska, August 28, 1941, IPN, GK 62/197, 39–46; Jastrząb, *Archidiecezja Poznańska*, 661.

41. Niklewska, *Służebnicki*, 119.

42. See note 25 in the introduction to this book.

43. The standard work on the subject remains Alberti, *Verfolgung*.

44. Along with the numerous articles published in the journal of Warsaw's Centrum Badań nad Zagładą Żydów, *Zagłada Żydów–Studia i Materiały*, see, for example, Joshua D. Zimmerman, ed., *Contested Memories: Poland and Jews During the Holocaust and its Aftermath* (New Brunswick, NJ: Rutgers University Press, 2003); Jan T. Gross, *Neighbors: The Destruction of the Jewish Community of Jedwabne, Poland* (Princeton, NJ: Princeton University Press, 2001); Andrzej Żbikowski, ed., *Polacy i Żydzi pod okupacją niemiecką 1939–1945: studia i materiały* (Warszawa: Instytut Pamięci Narodowej–Komisja Ścigania Zbrodni Przeciwko Narodowi Polskiemu, 2006); Dorota Siepracka, "Die Einstellung der Christlichen

Polen gegenüber der jüdischen Bevölkerung im Wartheland, " in *Der Judenmord in den eingegliederten polnischen Gebieten 1939–1945*, Einzelveröffentlichungen des Deutschen Historischen Instituts Warschau, vol. 21, ed. Jacek Andrzej Młynarczyk and Jochen Böhler (Osnabrück: Fibre Verlag, 2010); Jan Grabowski, *Hunt for the Jews: Betrayal and Murder in German-Occupied Poland* (Bloomington: Indiana University Press, 2013); Barbara Engelking, *Such a Beautiful Sunny Day . . . : Jews Seeking Refuge in the Polish Countryside, 1942–1945* (Jerusalem: Yad Vashem, 2016); and Barbara Engelking and Jan Grabowski, eds., *Dalej jest noc: losy Żydów w wybranych powiatach okupowanej Polski*, 2 vols. (Warszawa: Stowarzyszenie Centrum Badań nad Zagłada Żydów, 2018).

45. Epstein, *Model Nazi*, 343.

46. Loose, "Wartheland," 190; Alberti, *Verfolgung*, 3.

47. Raul Hilberg, *The Destruction of the European Jews*, vol. 3 (New Haven, CT: Yale University Press, 2003), 1320.

48. Kershaw, "Arthur Greiser," 116.

49. Siepracka, 345. According to that author's figures, nearly 60 percent of Warthegau Jews lived in the city of Łódź proper.

50. Alberti, *Verfolgung*, 4.

51. Zygmunt Zieliński, "Activities of Catholic Orders on Behalf of Jews in Nazi-Occupied Poland," in *Judaism and Christianity under the Impact of National Socialism*, ed. Otto Dov Kulka and Paul R. Mendes-Flohr (Jerusalem: The Historical Society of Israel and The Zalman Shazar Center for Jewish History, 1987), 387–91.

52. Ewa Kurek, *Your Life Is Worth Mine: How Polish Nuns Saved Hundreds of Jewish Children in German-Occupied Poland, 1939–1945* (New York: Hippocrene, 1997), 105–6.

53. Jastrząb, *Archidiecezja Poznańska*, 331.

54. Jastrząb, 577.

55. "Wysiedlenie Żydów Poznańskich do powiatu Sochaczew-Błonie," November 1939, YV, M.10—Warsaw Ghetto Underground Archives, 1072.

56. Geschäftsführer des Kreises Turek, Vertreter im Amt (Schlemper), NSDAP Kreisleitung Turek to Gauschulungsamt Wartheland, September 24, 1942, Abschrift, IPN, GK 62/197, 59.

57. Gestapo Litzmannstadt to Reichsstatthalter Abt. I/51, October 30, 1942, IPN, GK 62/197, 64.

58. Henryk Kaliszan, Ankieta, June 18, 1974, AAP, zespół 133, syg. OK 220, 519/74.

59. Tadeusz Malinowski, Ankieta, AAP, zespół 133, syg. OK 222, 401/74.

60. Oświadczenie Edmunda Elantkowskiego, April 22, 1947, IZ, Dok. III-27, 6–7; Jastrząb, *Archidiecezja Poznańska*, 569; Marian Woźniak, "Szklarek-Trzcielski Henryk," in Woźniak, *Encyklopedia konspiracji*, 548.

61. Kazimierz Śmigiel, "Tajne duszpasterstwo w Wielkopolsce," in Woźniak, *Encyklopedia konspiracji*, 572; Wełniak, *Duchowieństwo*, 46–51.

62. Marian Kowalewski, Ankieta, June 26, 1974, AAP, zespół 133, syg. OK 220, 521/74; Jastrząb, *Archidiecezja Poznańska*, 577.

63. On the structure and activities of the organization see Jan Jacek Nikisch, "Ojczyzna," in Woźniak, *Encyklopedia konspiracji*, 399–402; Pietrowicz, "Die Widerstandsbewegung," 435–36.

64. Śmigiel, *Die katholische Kirche*, 189–90; Jastrząb, *Archidiecezja Poznańska*, 537; Jan Jacek Nikisch, "Prądzyński Józef," in Woźniak, *Encyklopedia konspiracji*, 466–67; Serwański, *Wielkopolska*, 300–302.

65. Śmigiel, *Die katholische Kirche*, 190–91; Antoni Kut and Marian Woźniak, "Mirochna Stefan Julian," in Woźniak, *Encyklopedia konspiracji*, 355; Serwański, *Wielkopolska*, 338.

66. Librowski, *Ofiary zbrodni*, 170.

67. On the "Poznańska Piątka" see Jastrząb, *Archidiecezja Poznańska*, 398; Łukasz Kaźmierczak, "Do zobaczenia w niebie," *Przewodnik Katolicki*, August 19, 2007, 33–41; Lubomira Broniarz-Press and Marian Woźniak, "Jóźwiak Czesław," in Woźniak, *Encyklopedia konspiracji*, 237; Marian Woźniak, "Kaźmierski Edward Stanisław," in Woźniak, *Encyklopedia konspiracji*, 254–55; Marian Woźniak, "Kęsy Franciszek," in Woźniak, *Encyklopedia konspiracji*, 257; Marian Woźniak, "Kliński, Edward," in Woźniak, *Encyklopedia konspiracji*, 263; Marian Woźniak, "Wojciechowski Jarogniew," in Woźniak, *Encyklopedia konspiracji*, 641. For the texts of letters written by the Five to their families on the day of their execution, see Teresa Jankowska, *Gotowi na wszystko: poznańska piątka salezjańska* (Warszawa: Fidei, 2010), 79–83.

17

"*ET PAPA TACET*"?

Pius XII and the Church in the Warthegau

THE REACH OF GERMAN ANTI-CATHOLIC POLICY IN THE Reichsgau Wartheland was long, and its execution severe. To this, the church's leadership in Rome was compelled to respond. If the broader history of the Catholic Church in the Warthegau remains relatively uncharted, the story of Pius XII's responses to wartime suffering in the Polish lands has received considerably more scholarly attention in, for example, two monographs on the subject, as well as in numerous biographies of Pius XII, and in broader analyses of his papacy during the Second World War.[1] Published documents addressing the papacy's relations with Poland are also available,[2] most significant among them the Vatican's multivolume *Actes et Documents du Saint Siège Relatifs à la Seconde Guerre Mondiale*, of which some fifteen hundred pages relate to Poland.[3] Augmenting this material with archival documentation and other published primary sources, it is possible to outline some of the challenges and dilemmas faced by the papacy when confronted with Nazi measures in the Warthegau, and to assess the value and costs of the Vatican's responses.[4]

At issue in this chapter are four fundamental themes, easily framed as questions. First, when, and in what ways, did Roman Catholicism's highest authority come to the defense of his church in Poland and in the Warthegau? Second, how great were the opportunities for, and barriers against, overt action on behalf of the Polish church? Third, was the pope's restraint in addressing the crisis understood and respected by Polish Catholics, or was it demoralizing and a source of frustration? Fourth, did the papacy's restraint help to prevent a worsening of the situation for Polish Catholics, or would papal action have worked to their benefit?

Already in the fall of 1939, Pope Pius XII was well informed about German atrocities in Poland, the execution and incarceration of priests, and the closure of churches and Catholic institutions. He also remained informed of developments in Poland throughout the war. Yet despite appeals to forcefully condemn German policy, Pius preferred expressions of sympathy and the avenues of diplomacy over overt protest, condemnation, or calls for resistance. Those who defend Pius's limited actions on behalf of Polish Catholics have generally accepted the argument that papal restraint at the very least prevented a worsening of the situation. His detractors, and among them both wartime critics and those since, have argued that Pius's lack of intervention appeared to many as indifference or sympathy toward the Germans, was demoralizing to Polish Catholics and their leaders, and, in effect, forfeited any opportunity to better the Poles' situation.[5]

The papacy had two basic approaches in response to the crisis in occupied Poland. On the one hand, Pius XII and the Vatican issued public statements, reports, and broadcasts concerning the persecution of the church. On the other, the Vatican was engaged throughout the war in diplomatic activity with the Polish government-in-exile in London, with representatives of various states, and especially with the German Ministry of Foreign Affairs. Statements or publications in support of Poland and its church were made, although not nearly as frequently or as forcefully as critics of Pius would have liked. Diplomatic efforts were much more common. Neither strategy was effective in ameliorating the situation of the church in Poland.

The papacy's efforts on behalf of the Warthegau church remained restrained throughout the war, and that restraint was based on both traditions of diplomacy and concern about further punitive measures that the German authorities could or would impose. Warthegau Catholics, both clergy and laity, were bewildered and even angered by Pius XII's reserve, and it is clear that his restrained approach failed to bring about an improvement in the church's situation. One can, however, only speculate over the effects of a more forceful papal response. It is clear, in any case, that Pius XII was not "silent" with respect to the persecution of the Warthegau church, or the church in Poland more broadly. Failure does not equal inaction. The word *silence* as it is used by some in this context is best understood as a charged synonym for reticence, for the papacy relied in its approach to matters in Poland, as it traditionally had, on vague public statements and, especially, diplomacy.

The pope's reticence was evident already at the point of the September 1939 invasion, which he did not explicitly condemn. Despite calls for a papal denunciation from, for example, the French ambassador to the Vatican François Charles-Roux and the Polish ambassador to the Vatican, Kazimierz Papeé,[6] Pius XII issued no explicit condemnation of Nazi aggression or the atrocities that accompanied the invasion. On September 2, Papeé met with Pius, who expressed sympathy for the Poles but also indicated his unwillingness to issue an explicit condemnation, in part out of concern that he might undermine the possibility of mediating the conflict in the future.[7] The pope's unwillingness to speak out was all the more frustrating for the Poles because the Vatican was quick to condemn the Soviet Union's invasion of eastern Poland. In the words of Neil Pease,

> In marked contrast to its hesitant and muted reaction to the German attack, the Vatican denounced the Russian incursion in no uncertain terms. The differences had to do with matters of conviction and tactics alike. In the eyes of the papacy and the Catholic world, the fall of Polish territory to Germany was a dreadful though potentially remediable misfortune, but the fall of Polish territory to Communist Russia was sheer disaster. The horrors that Nazi rule would bring to its subjugated populations lay in the future: the Soviet yoke, it was assumed, would be far harsher, and the westward advance of the Bolshevik tyranny threatened the further spread of atheistic revolution.[8]

As it turned out, of course, the German occupation was much more than a misfortune, and proved disastrous for the Catholic Church in the Reichsgau Wartheland.

Pius XII was informed about the catastrophic situation in Poland by Polish refugees, by members of the Polish episcopate, and by the reports of witnesses to the persecution who provided information directly to the Vatican or to its diplomatic representatives around Europe. Channels of communication were covert and sometimes unreliable, and information was difficult or impossible to verify, but the documented correspondence with Polish bishops—both in exile and in occupied Poland—makes clear that the pope was well informed of the tragic state of the church. The Polish underground was also continually supplying the government-in-exile (in Angers, France, and later in London) with information about the situation in the various regions of annexed and occupied Poland—information that was then passed on to the Polish ambassador, who conveyed it to Vatican officials or to Pius XII directly.

The pope also received reports from the Polish Primate and Archbishop of Poznań and Gniezno, August Cardinal Hlond, who had fled Poland in

September 1939 at the request of the Polish government.[9] When the German Foreign Ministry refused to allow Hlond to return to occupied Poland,[10] the Vatican was alarmed,[11] and issued numerous protests via its nuncio in Berlin, Cesare Orsenigo. These efforts failed, and Hlond remained in exile throughout the duration of the war, from 1940 until 1944 in France, and thereafter in Germany until his liberation. He continued to function as a conduit of information on the situation in Poland, and in the early weeks of the war, the Holy See allowed him to speak to the people of Poland on Vatican Radio. Hlond's patriotic September 1939 broadcast, addressed to "My martyred Poland," offered the Poles words of comfort, words of resolve to stand firm in the face of destruction, and words of assurance that Poland would rise once again.[12] He issued a similar address on November 2. Neither was looked kindly upon by the German authorities,[13] who then used the cardinal's public speeches as a pretext and justification for the intensified persecution of the church in the Warthegau.[14]

Whether or not Pius was using Hlond as a proxy is not clear; German documents do, however, suggest that some members of the high-level Nazi leadership—especially Reinhard Heydrich, head of the Reich Security Main Office—became convinced of what they believed to be the pope's pro-Polish, anti-German sentiments. According to Heydrich, Pius's words in support of Poland in the first months of the war, his first wartime encyclical *Summi Pontificatus*, his September 1939 audience with Poles living in Rome, and his 1939 Christmas message to the College of Cardinals were all clear evidence of papal opposition to Germany's invasion and occupation policies.[15]

What may have appeared to German authorities as evidence of clear papal support for Poland was interpreted by others as weak, circuitous, and characteristic of Pius's unwillingness to be explicit in addressing the persecution and suffering of the church. In his September 1939 audience with Poles at Castel Gandolfo, Pius XII was eloquent in expressing his sympathy and consolation to the victims of Nazi aggression but remained unwilling to name the Nazi aggressors, as if condemning the sin but remaining unwilling to name the sinner.[16] According to Kazimierz Papée, the pope's speech, which "disappointed even the most modest of hopes," condemned neither the invasions nor the Bolshevik-Nazi alliance.[17] The encyclical *Summi*, issued on October 20, 1939, likewise expressed, in its lofty rhetoric, sympathy, but sympathy alone. In Pius's words, "The blood of countless people, even noncombatants, gives rise to a harrowing funereal lament, especially over Poland, a dearly beloved country. Because of its glorious attainments on behalf of Christian civilization, attainments indelibly inscribed in the annals of history, Poland has a right to the world's human and fraternal sympathy, and confident in the powerful intercession of Mary who is the *auxilium christianorum*, it awaits the hour of its resurrection in justice and peace."[18]

Papal criticisms of German persecution of the Polish church continued, if vaguely and sporadically. In early 1940, Pius directed Vatican Radio to denounce German measures, but when the Nazi government protested and threatened "disagreeable repercussions,"[19] he ordered the broadcasts to cease, for he did not, in his words, "want to impose unnecessary sacrifices on German Catholics" who were facing reprisals.[20] He mentioned the plight of the Poles in speeches in June and November of 1940,[21] and certainly continued to offer blessings and words of encouragement to the Polish bishops with whom he corresponded.

In his 1942 Christmas address, the pope did confront, if obliquely, the problem of wartime genocide in Europe. Although this speech met with the approval of many, it remained insufficiently specific for Poland's exile government, to the extent that the Polish president, Władysław Raczkiewicz, sent a letter to the pope requesting a more precise indictment of German policy and crimes.[22] Frustrated with Raczkiewicz's plea, the pope argued in a conversation a few weeks later with the Polish ambassador that the Germans were only waiting for a pretext for further persecution of Poles. Moreover, the pope reminded Papée that Poland was not the only country in Europe that was suffering, and that it was necessary to acknowledge and understand the papacy's difficult situation. In his report on the conversation, Papée somewhat wistfully concluded that Pius XII sincerely and deeply believed that he had already said clearly and explicitly all that could be said in defense of Poland.[23]

The pope finally met with the exile government's approval in a June 1943 allocution before the College of Cardinals. For the first time in three years, he referred explicitly to Poland's suffering, passed judgment on the perpetrators of that suffering (without specifying which peoples or nations were responsible for it), and emphasized the rights of the oppressed.[24] This would be the last time that Pius XII would speak publicly about Poland until after the liberation of Rome.

Clearly, public protest was not Pius's preferred avenue of intervention in the affairs of the Polish church, and the lack of clear statements criticizing

German occupation policy suggested to many Polish Catholics, from members of the hierarchy to the laity, that the papacy was guilty of inaction, or even indifference. As Robert Ventresca has claimed in his biography of Pius XII, "despite persistent diplomatic efforts to protest German occupation policies in Poland and elsewhere, there was a growing perception that the pope was not doing enough. . . . Even high-ranking churchmen," he continues, "stressed that whether fair or not, the perception that Pius XII had abandoned Catholic Poland to its fate was palpable."[25] That sense of abandonment was evident in a letter from Walenty Dymek to the papal nuncio in Berlin. "The situation of the Catholic Church is grim," the bishop wrote while under house arrest, "and I, myself, will likely not enjoy my freedom [!] much longer. I have come to the conclusion that the Apostolic See either cannot help us or for higher reasons does not wish to help us."[26] In November 1942, Hilarius Breitinger reported to Pius that "the Catholic population of the Warthegau poses again and again the question of whether or not the pope can help, and why he remains silent. They wait longingly for a statement from Your Holiness about our state of religious emergency."[27]

It was also clear that the occupation authorities attempted to exploit Polish discontent with the Holy See, and this to some effect, as reported by the Polish underground to the government-in-exile,[28] as reported in the Polish underground press,[29] and as reported directly to the Vatican by Cardinal August Hlond. In an August 2, 1941, letter to Vatican Cardinal Secretary of State Luigi Maglione, Hlond was explicit in detailing the German propaganda efforts to undermine the pope's reputation among the Polish population. He referred not only to the effectiveness of such propaganda but also to the urgent necessity of a papal statement on behalf of Poland's Catholics. According to Hlond, while "trust and veneration for the bishops and priests increases," there was "diminishing affection for the pope and the Holy See."[30] That discontent with the papacy was also reflected in a secret report of a government-in-exile representative appended to Hlond's letter, which stated, "We hear that the Poles are complaining that the pope does not protest against crimes when the Germans have three thousand Polish priests killed in concentration camps, that he does not speak out in condemnation when hundreds of priests and members of Catholic Action, including papal chamberlains, are shot to death, all exterminated without the slightest offense on their part."[31]

Opposition forces in occupied Poland were also critical of papal inaction. According to a report of the Security Police in Poznań from June 1942, a flyer distributed by a Polish resistance group described in detail the frustration felt by many Poles:

> In the villages one can see a waning of religious life as a result of the indifference of the Vatican toward the fate of the Catholic churches in Poland. The peasants are mystified that not the pope but President Roosevelt was the one who has accused Hitler of antireligious tendencies. The acquiesence and timid behavior of the clergy in no way improves the situation. The inscrutable policies of the Vatican will only contribute to a deepening of this process. The socialists and members of the Peasants' Party have determined, and complain, that the pope is remaining loyal to the Italians.[32]

Elements of the underground Polish press were also severe in their indictments of Pius XII. A July 1942 article in *Głos Pracy* (The worker's voice) asked,

> Where are those authoritative defenders who should have stopped this horrible martyrdom? Are there any authoritative voices left? Yes, there are. One of these authorities is supreme head of the Catholic Church, the Holy Father. But alas, the successor to St. Peter, the greatest leader of Christian souls, has shut himself up in the Vatican Palace and does not bother to defend his own faithful. . . . O supreme Shepherd! The so-called Christian nations are slaughtering defenceless Christians whom Chirst [*sic*] said they should love. Your predecessors hurled anathemas, which you disdain to hurl on the barbarians, just as you even refuse to command the Catholics of the whole world to withhold bread, water and warmth from the bandits. But if even an anathema had no result, You, Shepherd, should leave your noble castle in sign of protest, and the whole world would be moved. The Communists and schismatics are saying maliciously that, just as Leo XIII called on the Poles to pray for and admire the Tsars, so You are telling the Poles to persevere tenaciously in their martyrdom, to pray, and carry out faithfully what the brutal forces of occupation command us to do.[33]

For its part, the Polish government-in-exile also warned the Vatican secretary of state in November 1942 that only a formal and public condemnation of Nazi policy could preserve the Polish people's sympathy for the Holy See.[34] The pope perhaps took these words into account in his Christmas address the following month, but his words on that occasion were, as noted above, met with criticism from the Polish president.

Frustration with the Vatican was perhaps most bitterly expressed by the exiled head of the Warthegau's Włocławek diocese, Bishop Karol Radoński. Living in London, and with a seat on the Polish National Council (a consultative body of the Polish government-in-exile), the bishop had become somewhat of a public figure and involved in exile politics.[35] Moreover, he had assumed the role of an unofficial public advocate for the persecuted Polish church, and emerged as a vocal critic of Pius XII. In September 1942, he complained to Maglione, "The churches are profaned or closed, religion is scorned, worship ceases, bishops are driven [from their sees], hundreds of priests are dead or imprisoned, nuns are in the hands of spoiled depraved thieves, innocent hostages are murdered almost daily before the eyes of children, people are dying of hunger, and the pope keeps silent ["et papa tacet"] as if what happens to his flock doesn't concern him."[36]

Radoński continued his criticisms in the months ahead: in November 1942 he published an article critical of the pope in a Polish emigré newspaper,[37] and in December broadcast a report on the Polish church's struggles on BBC radio.[38] In a letter of January 9, 1943, Maglione responded to Radoński's complaints in rather strident tones, stating, "If you ask why the documents sent by the Pontiff to the Polish bishops have not as yet been made public, know that it is because it seems better in the Vatican to follow the same norms that the bishops themselves observe. As is known, they have not made these documents public so that the sheep confided to their care do not become victims of new and still more fierce persecutions. Isn't this what has to be done? Should the father of Christianity increase the misfortunes suffered by the Poles in their own country?"[39]

Although reprimanded, Radoński sent in February 1943 another letter critical of the pope to the Vatican secretary of state. The bishop had learned that the papal nuncio in France, Valerio Valeri, had publicly told Marshal Philippe Pètain, chief of state of Vichy France, that Pius did not approve of Vichy's anti-Jewish legislation.[40] Attempting to put the pope's relative "silence" on the issue of German occupation policy in the Polish lands in context, Radoński wrote, "Who can wonder, most Eminent Lord, if these Poles, ignorant of the cause of [Pius XII's] silence, would unjustly accuse the Pope. They remember Pius XI, who comforted with strong words Mexican and Hispanic Catholics during their persecution and condemned their torturers. They [the Poles] heard that the Pope [Pius XII], through his nuncio, condemned the persecution of the Jews in France. They have been asking whether we are but more worthless than the Jews." Radoński then continued, "When such crimes cry to heaven for vengeance, the inexplicable silence of the highest teacher in the Church is an occasion of spiritual ruin to those—and their number is legion—who do not know the reason."[41]

Radoński's words suggest anger over the possibility that Pius would speak on behalf of Jews but so little on behalf of Polish Catholics. Intemperate or inappropriate as the bishop's comparison may have been, it does not appear that Radoński was indifferent to the plight of the Jews, for he had severely condemned their persecution in occupied Poland in a BBC radio address in December of the previous year.[42] Michael Phayer, who has examined the relationship between the papacy's responses to Nazi persecution of Polish Catholics and its responses to Nazi persecution of Jews, suggests that the wealth of information on the genocide of Jews flowing into the Vatican in the second half of 1942, and especially the information provided to the government-in-exile by the Polish resistance fighter and courier Jan Karski, had an effect on Pius XII. That Pius did in fact confront genocide in his Christmas address of 1942 would support this claim.[43] In the end, however, Radoński was ineffective in eliciting from the pope a statement clearly describing German crimes against Poles and condemning the perpetrators.

While Polish discontent with the papacy was clear, it is also clear that Poles and their church leaders in the Warthegau were not aware of the extent of the Vatican's diplomatic efforts on their behalf. Such efforts were conducted for the most part via the papal nuncio in Berlin, Cesare Orsenigo. The nuncio's appeals and protests to the Nazi Foreign Ministry were frequent and addressed a wide variety of issues, especially with respect to the church's situation in the Wartheland.[44] Among them were, for example, requests to extend the nuncio's diplomatic jurisdiction to the annexed areas of occupied Poland[45]; protests against the incarceration of bishops and appeals for their release[46]; protests against the treatment of parish priests, monks, and nuns[47]; protests against the subjection of the order of the Grey Sisters to forced labor (presumably in Bojanowo)[48]; protests against the confiscation of church property[49]; requests to visit the Warthegau[50]; protests against the closure of churches[51]; requests to meet personally with Reichsführer-SS Heinrich Himmler[52]; and protests against Greiser's decree of September 13, 1941, which established in the Warthegau a "new" Catholic denomination for Germans but not Poles.[53] Remonstrances such as these were delivered with such frequency that they began to burden Orsenigo's prime audience at the Foreign Ministry, the somewhat sympathetic secretary of state, Ernst von Weizsäcker.[54] Orsenigo is regarded by some as a weak and craven representative of the Holy See in this time of crisis,[55] but his work on behalf of the Polish church, ineffective as it may have been, also appears to have been ambitious.

Ambition aside, the German government remained unresponsive or hostile to requests and protests on behalf of Warthegau Catholics. It had, since 1940, proceeded from the assumption that the incorporated territories were not subject to the terms of the 1933 concordat between the Nazi state and the Vatican,[56] and its rejection of Vatican diplomatic efforts was formalized in June 1942. On June 2, the head of the Reich Chancellery, Hans Lammers, informed Foreign Minister Ribbentrop that Hitler had, in a recent conversation, stated that the Berlin nuncio's competence and jurisdiction were to be limited to the Altreich.[57] In a formal directive of the following week, Hitler ordered that the Nazi government's relations with the Vatican would be maintained only with regard to the church in the Altreich. According to the decree, Rome had allegedly forfeited any jurisdiction over the church in the Reichgau Wartheland or, in the directive's words, "the Vatican, by informing the German Government that it cannot recognize any political changes of territory for the duration of the war, has automatically excluded itself from an official connection with the territories annexed or occupied since September 1939."[58] In light of this order, the papacy was essentially denied any authority to intervene in annexed or occupied Polish territory, or issue protests to the German government.[59] In short, the Warthegau was beyond the diplomatic reach of the Vatican.

In the aftermath of this directive, and having failed to bring about any changes via its proper diplomatic representative, the Vatican then issued to the German Foreign Ministry two letters regarding the situation of the church in the Warthegau. Both came directly from Cardinal Secretary of State Maglione, and both suggested to the Nazi government that consequences would result should Germany fail to respond appropriately. The first of these, a letter of October 8, 1942, sent to the German embassy at the Vatican, recalled the nuncio's failed efforts, even as it described various injustices against the church, which, in the memo's measured tone, gave "cause for very grave and ever increasing anxiety." The urgency of the situation was evident, however, in Maglione's final warning, which had the tone of an observation more than a threat: "If, as is feared, in consequence of new measures by the Lieutenant's Office [i.e., the office of Greiser, the Reichstatthalter], the situation should be still further aggravated, the Holy See, as in duty bound by its office, would find itself compelled to abandon—and it would do so, however unwillingly—the attitude of reserve which it has hitherto maintained."[60]

The German ambassador to the Holy See, Diego von Bergen, communicated his concern over this in a telegram to the Foreign Ministry three days later: "Resentment on the part of the pope increased dramatically. By nature exceptionally sensitive, as supreme head and patron of the church he sees the need, in evaluating undesireable events, to take a considerably more critical stance than at the time of his service as cardinal secretary of state and nuncio in Berlin." According to von Bergen, Pius XII, who had served as Vatican secretary of state and as nuncio in Berlin, regarded the Foreign Ministry's dismissal of Orsenigo's appeals as disrespectful to his person as well as the Holy See. Moreover, the ambassador claimed that the emerging conflict could mean an end "to the relative reserve of the Vatican and result in the transition of the curia to an actively polemical position."[61] The ambassador's concerns notwithstanding, the German Foreign Ministry was not in any way moved to intervene with Greiser, and Ribbentrop, as will be discussed below, subsequently instructed von Bergen to threaten countermeasures against the church.[62]

More detailed and focused on the situation in the Warthegau was Maglione's letter to Reich Foreign Minister von Ribbentrop dated March 2, 1943. Discussed briefly at the beginning of chapter 13, this was a lengthy and comprehensive register of grievances against German measures in the Warthegau and elsewhere, from the execution of priests to restrictions on religious education, from the separation of German and Polish Catholics to the incarceration of nuns and priests, from the confiscation of church property to Greiser's September 1941 decree establishing new religious denominations. Maglione referred in this document as well to the "greatest reserve" thus far maintained by the Holy See with respect to such issues, and appealed to "put an end to such a painful situation created by dispositions which run counter to natural and divine right."[63]

Whether seen as diplomatic entreaties or mild threats, these communications from the secretary of state were entirely ineffective in ameliorating the church's situation in the Warthegau and do not appear to have influenced future Nazi Kirchenpolitik in any way. In fact, Maglione's letters were rejected outright. According to the postwar testimony of Gustav Adolf Steengracht von Moyland, Weizsäcker's successor as secretary of state in the Foreign Ministry, Ribbentrop had presented both of Maglione's letters directly to Hitler, who, according to Steengracht, replied, "They are just one blunt lie. Give these notes back to the Nuncio through the State Secretary in a sharp form, and tell him that you will never again accept such a matter."[64] Accordingly, Ribbentrop ordered Weizsäcker to return the second letter unacknowledged to Orsenigo, on the grounds that the Vatican had no right to intervene in chuch affairs in German-annexed and occupied territories, which were beyond the Church's territorial competence.[65] The Vatican, bound to traditions of careful diplomacy and fearful of greater persecution of Catholics in Poland and beyond, took a stance of "reserve" that proved inadequate to the challenge of Nazi church policy in Poland, especially in the "model Gau," where the Catholic Church was marked for brutal persecution and destruction in the long term.

It is worth considering in detail the above summation and, in so doing, to historicize appropriately Pius XII's papacy when trying to understand its relationship to the Polish church during the occupation. With respect to "traditions of careful diplomacy," it is important to bear in mind that this was a pope and papacy different from those of subsequent decades. A more private man than his successors John XXIII, John Paul II, or Francis, Pius XII was given to lofty orotund language and cultivated an air of authority and omniscience. Moreover, frequent public statements and "taking a stand" on issues of public life and international affairs were not necessarily the norm for the papacy. It was perhaps to be expected that the pope, trained as a diplomat and by nature conciliatory rather than confrontational, chose to pursue traditional and private channels for communicating his concerns, rather than public pronouncements. Diplomacy was the tradition, but the fact remains that Pius XII was entirely capable of "taking a stand" both in private and in public, as he did in condemning the Soviet invation of eastern Poland in 1939.

The pope was also eager to maintain a stance of impartiality (in his own word, *Unparteilichkeit*) in the Vatican's interactions with and among the belligerent powers in the war.[66] It is important to draw a distinction, as Pius himself did, between *impartiality* and *neutrality*, for the latter term suggested indifference on the part of the papacy.[67] Pius wanted to be available for peace negotiations after the war, and this would be possible only if he did not publicly condemn any of the belligerent powers.[68] More broadly, the principle of "impartiality" was intended as a fundamental tenet of Vatican diplomacy among belligerent states in these years and influenced its responses and reticence in the face of wartime atrocities, mass killing, and genocide. Significantly for the situation in occupied Poland, and as the pope himself emphasized, maintaining impartiality was understood as a way to forestall further persecutory measures against Catholics,[69] whether in Nazi-occupied or Soviet-occupied Polish lands.

By mid-1943, however, in the aftermath of Maglione's rejected March letter, it had to have been clear to the Vatican that papal restraint did not restrain the Nazis in the Warthegau. All this of course prompts the question of what would have happened had the pope issued a clear protest. We will never know, and most serious historians are eager to avoid such counterfactual speculation. A better, if still unsatisfactory question, asks if papal reticence did, in fact, prevent a worsening of the church's situation in Poland. On this, too, one can only speculate, but the evidence suggests the following.

As discussed above, relations between the Vatican and the Polish church were strained, as there was discontent with the papacy among members of the hierarchy, clergy, and laity—all of whom were experiencing firsthand the severity of the occupation. There were, to be sure, also voices among the Polish clergy and hierarchy who eventually appeared satisfied with the pope's approach, or were at least respectful of the challenges that he faced. For example, Cardinal Archbishop of Kraków Adam Sapieha, the de facto head of the Polish church in the absence of Cardinal Hlond, eventually expressed in an October 1942 letter his gratitude to the Holy See for offering words of encouragement to the faithful in Poland, and at the same time expressed his regret that he could not publish the pope's letter because he was fearful that the authorities would implement further harsh measures.[70] This support notwithstanding, calls for papal action persisted—from members of the Polish episcopate, from the Catholic laity, and from the government-in-exile and its representatives. Why, then, did the Holy See not comply with these entreaties? One reason—and as the evidence suggests, the primary reason—was that the pope and Vatican diplomats remained ever concerned about possible German retribution, and it is clear that their concerns were based on information provided not only by sources in Poland, including members of the hierarchy, but also on information and threats issued by the German authorities.

Examples abound. Already in the early weeks of the occupation, Pius XII defended himself against accusations of indifference by voicing his anxieties about Nazi retaliatory measures: "You know," he stated, "which side my sympathies lie. But I cannot say so. . . . I could not say more than I did. There are in Germany fifty million Catholics and plenty of Poles, who would suffer . . . for the curses which they asked me to pronounce."[71] When arrested by the Gestapo in October 1939, Bishop Walenty Dymek of Posen was informed that his arrest was in response to Cardinal Hlond's patriotic broadcast on Vatican Radio.[72] In December 1939, the German Foreign Office informed Orsenigo that there was no sense in his offices attempting to gain the release of prisoners or clemency for those condemned to death, as it would only work to their detriment.[73] The following month, Vatican Undersecretary of State[74] Giovanni Montini (later Pope Paul VI) cited German threats of repercussions should Vatican Radio continue its broadcasts concerning the situation in occupied Poland. The broadcasts were, accordingly, stopped.[75] In March of 1940, Secretary of State Maglione noted that public protests against the treatment of the Polish church could only work to the detriment of the Polish people,[76] a sentiment echoed by Vatican Undersecretary of State Tardini's May 1942 defense of the pope's decision to limit overt protest. Protest, according to Tardini, would be "amply exploited by one of the conflicting parties for political ends. Moreover, the German government would see itself as singled out, and would undoubtedly do two things: it would persecute Catholic Poles more harshly, and would prevent the Holy See from having any contact in any way with the Polish bishops and from carrying out the charitable work that it can now carry out, albeit in a less forceful fashion."[77] Two months later, Tardini reiterated these sentiments in response to a further request from the Polish ambassador for a papal statement on Poland.[78] In the aftermath of the pope's 1942 Christmas message, Ribbentrop informed both von Weizsäcker and von Bergen that should the Vatican threaten or undertake "any political or propaganda campaign against Germany, the Government of the Reich would naturally be compelled to react accordingly. For this purpose, the Reich Government would lack neither effective material nor the possibility of taking concrete measures against the Catholic Church."[79] A passive-aggressive tone was not the norm for the Nazi foreign minister, but the message was nonetheless clear.

Harold Tittman, assistant to Myron Taylor, Franklin Roosevelt's envoy to the Holy See, summarized in a September 1942 memorandum the Vatican's arguments "in support of the pope's silence with respect to the condemnation of Nazi atrocities."[80] The American diplomat emphasized the belief in Vatican circles that any condemnation of Nazi measures "would greatly worsen the already precarious situation of the Catholics obliged to reside in those areas. No lives would be saved thereby. On the contrary, many more would be lost." Tittman continued, "The Vatican claims to be better informed on this phase of the matter than the governments-in-exile who keep urging the Holy Father to speak out."[81]

In light of reprisals both threatened and executed, it is not surprising that Pius XII choose reticence and diplomacy as the appropriate avenues for addressing the crisis in Poland. Under the Nazi occupation, and especially in the Wartheland, pastoral care, the availability of the sacraments, and the institutions of the church had all been dramatically restricted, to the extent that they were unavailable to many. According to Catholic doctrine and tradition, the ministries of the church were not only necessary for the maintenance of its power and influence; they were also necessary for the salvation of souls. Thus, when Pius XII wrote to his friend Konrad Preysing, bishop of Berlin, on April 30, 1943, he made clear that his priority in the Warthegau was the preservation of the pastoral care that was still available. In the pope's measured words, "The considerations . . . and in the special case of the Warthegau, above all, the fear of endangering what remains of the church's ministries, have restrained Us from openly raising the issue of the church's circumstances there."[82]

Jacques Kornberg has characterized Pius XII's restrained responses and what he refers to as the pope's "moral failing" during the Nazi era as resulting from "calculated acquiescence."[83] The pope's responses to the situation in Poland were "calculated" because they were based not merely on reflex, instinct, or tradition but on his consideration of the options before him, all of which were highly unsatisfactory. The pope was not paralyzed by his dilemmas, was not supportive of or complicit in Nazi measures, and also did not condemn them. Pius XII's "acquiescence" meant that he accepted Nazi measures with reluctance, and yet also without clear and public protest. This characterization is useful and effectively describes the pope's response to the dilemmas he faced in the Warthegau, but it still renders him too passive and lacking in agency, for in the end, Pius made a reasoned choice not to condemn publically or confront aggressively the Nazi regime over its treatment of the Warthegau church. The choice, based on a tradition of diplomacy, the principle of impartiality, and the conviction that confronting the regime would result in further persecution of the church, did nothing to improve the church's situation. Nor, however, is there evidence that the church's situation worsened as a result. An overly simplistic analysis of the Holy See's options might present any number of false dichotomies, suggesting, hypothetically for example, that "silence" would mean maintenance of the status quo in Poland, while public papal protest would result in reprisals against the Polish church.[84] The alternatives were not so clear, but the history of the Polish church under German occupation suggests that the former scenario was highly unlikely, and the latter was all but guaranteed. In the final analysis, however, the historian cannot rely on speculation but only on evidence and results.

The results were disastrous, and it is important to emphasize that over the course of the occupation, any improvement in the church's situation was the result not of Vatican protests or diplomacy but of political, economic, and military expediency in the waning months of the war. According to papal historian Robert Graham, the Holy See was able to extract only one concession from the German government: the promise that all incarcerated priests would be brought together in one concentration camp, Dachau, where they could celebrate Mass.[85] As it turned out, even this promise remained unfulfilled. The understated claim that the Vatican's stance of "reserve" proved inadequate to the challenge of Nazism's policies toward the church should not suggest that the historian can offer any post hoc prescriptions for what an "adequate" response would have been, or the benefits and costs of that response. It is clear that Vatican diplomacy did not achieve its goals; it is not certain, however, that a different approach would have yielded better results. Vatican diplomacy and the papacy's rare and limited statements on behalf of the Polish church were no match for the Kirchenpolitik of the Nazis. The story of the Warthegau church is a tragic one on many levels, and as this chapter has shown, it remains a stark reminder of the fundamental weakness of Pius XII and the Vatican in response to an adversary that threatened the power, integrity, and ministries of the church and was simulaneously engaged in a broad and murderous project in the Reichsgau Wartheland and Polish lands beyond.

Notes

1. See, for example, Manfred Clauss, *Die Beziehungen des Vatikans zu Polen während des II. Weltkrieges*, Bonner Beiträge zur Kirchengeschichte, vol. 11 (Köln: Böhlau Verlag, 1979); Waszkiewicz, *Polityka Watykanu*; Carlo Falconi, *The Silence of Pius XII* (Boston: Little, Brown, 1970); Michael Phayer, *Catholic Church*; Michael Phayer, *Pius XII*; Jacques Kornberg, *The Pope's Dilemma: Pius XII Faces Atrocities and Genocide in the Second World War* (Toronto: University of Toronto Press, 2015); Robert A. Ventresca, *Soldier of Christ: the Life of Pope Pius XII* (Cambridge, MA: Belknap, 2013); Frank J. Coppa, *The Life and Pontificate of Pope Pius XII: Between History and Controversy* (Washington, DC: Catholic University of America Press, 2013); David Bankier, Dan Michman, and Ieal Nidam-Orvieto, eds., *Pius XII and the Holocaust: Current State of Research* (Jerusalem: Yad Vashem, 2012).

2. See, for example, Kazimierz Papée, *Pius XII a Polska: przemówienia, listy, komentarze* (Rzym: Editrice Studium, 1954); Saul Friedländer, *Pius XII and the Third Reich: A Documentation*, trans. Charles Fullman (New York: Octagon, 1980).

3. Volume 3, nos. 1 and 2, heretofore referred to as *ADSS*, are devoted specifically to the Vatican's responses to the situation in Poland and the Baltic States.

4. As noted in the introduction to this book, the conclusions drawn here, while based on the available evidence, may well be subject to revision in the years ahead after more documentation becomes available in 2020 through the opening of the Vatican's archival holdings related to the pontificate of Pius XII.

5. This line of argument was rigorously pursued already fifty years ago by papal historian Carlo Falconi, who devoted a significant portion of his well-known indictment of Pius' "silence" to the case of German-occupied Poland. See Falconi, *Silence*, 109–256.

6. Pease, *Rome's*, 207.

7. Papée to Ministerstwo Spraw Zagranicznych, September 4, 1939, Polish Institute and Sikorski Museum, London (hereafter PISM), A.44.122-20.

8. Pease, *Rome's*, 208–9.

9. Early reports of August Hlond to Pius XII, as well as other supplementary documents on the situation of the church in Poland, were published in Hlond, *Persecution*. On Hlond's reports, see also Czesław Madajczyk, "Kościół a polityka okupanta na ziemiach polskich," in *Dzieje Polski a współczesność*, ed. Krystyna Sokól (Warszawa: Książka i Wiedza, 1966), 305–6.

10. Ribbentrop to Germanova Rom (German Embassy to the Holy See), October 13, 1939, National Archives, Kew (hereafter NAK), GFM 33/744, Political Department III: Vatican: Relations with Poland, 1936 June–1940 Feb.; Woermannn, telegram to Germanova Rom (German Embassy to the Holy See), October 13, 1939, NAK, GFM 33/744, Political Department III: Vatican: Relations with Poland, 1936 June–1940 Feb.

11. Bergen to German Ministry of Foreign Affairs, October 17, 1939, NAK, GFM 33/744, Political Department III: Vatican: Relations with Poland, 1936 June–1940 Feb; Conway, *Nazi Persecution*, 303.

12. August Cardinal Hlond, address to the Polish people, September 28, 1939, transcript and German translation of October 14, 1939, BAB, R 5101/24038, 12–14.

13. Auswärtiges Amt to Reichsministerium für Kirchliche Angelegenheiten, December 22, 1939, BAB, R 5101/22185, 77.

14. Clauss, *Die Beziehungen*, 45n122; Breitinger, *Als Deutschenseelsorger*, 41, 56, 59.

15. Heydrich to Lammers, Reichskanzlei, August 17, 1940, BAB, R 43 II/178a, 23. On Pius in *Summi*, see Owen Chadwick, *Britain and the Vatican during the Second World War* (Cambridge: Cambridge University Press, 1986), 82–85; Kornberg, *Pope's Dilemma*, 147. On Pius' audience with Poles in Rome, see José M. Sànchez, *Pius XII and the Holocaust: Understanding the Controversy* (Washington, DC: Catholic University Press, 2002), 155.

16. L'Osservatore Romano, October 1, 1939, 1, quoted in document 15, in *ADSS*, vol. 3, no. 1, 82; Pease, *Rome's*, 210.

17. Papée, Telegram nr. 5 to Polmission-Bukarest, September 30, 1939, PISM A.44-53-1, 87.

18. Translated in Pierre Blet, *Pius XII and the Second World War According to the Archives of the Vatican*, trans. L. J. Johnson (New York: Paulist, 1999), 70.

19. Quoted in Blet, 75.

20. Pius XII to Konrad Graf von Preysing, April 22, 1940, document 45, in *ADSS*, vol. 2, 140–41.

21. Kazimierz Papée to Ministerstwo Spraw Zagranicznych, June 23, 1942, PISM, A.44-122/28, tom II, 16.VI.42-31.XII.42.

22. Raczkiewicz to Pius XII, January 2, 1943, PISM, A.44-122/30, 1943.

23. Papée to Ministerstwo Spraw Zagranicznych, January 23, 1943, PISM A.44-122/30, 1943.

24. Papée to Ministerstwo Spraw Zagranicznych, June 5, 1943, AAN, zespół 495, sygn. 82, 3–9.

25. Ventresca, *Soldier*, 173.

26. Dymek to Orsenigo, n.d., document no. 39, in Volk, *Akten deutscher Bischöfe*, vol. 5, 1055. The document is not dated, but its content makes clear that it postdates October 19, 1942.

27. Breitinger to Pius XII, November 23, 1942, document 444, in *ADSS*, vol. 3, no. 2, 683.

28. "Raport Sytuacyjny okupacji niemieckiej za czas od 1.I. do 1.VII.1941 r." in Sprawozdanie sytuacyjne z kraju 1939–1941, vol. 1, 52, PUMST; "Sprawozdania delegata Rządu za czas od 15 sierpnia do 15 listopada 1941 r." in Sprawozdanie sytuacyjne z kraju, vol. 2, Nr. 1–6, 1941–1942, 36, PUMST.

29. Lagebericht des Höheren SS- und Polizeiführers beim Reichsstatthalter in Posen im Wehrkreis XXI.-Inspekteur der Sicherheitspoizei und den SD, June 24, 1942, IPN, GK 62/210/CD, 112–13.

30. Hlond to Maglione, August 2, 1941, document 287, in *ADSS*, vol. 3, no. 1, 419.

31. Relazione segreta del Delegato del Governo in Polonia, February 15, 1941, document 287, in *ADSS*, vol. 3, no. 1, 422, translated in Blet, *Pius XII*, 80.

32. Lagebericht des Höheren SS- und Polizeiführers beim Reichsstatthalter in Posen im Wehrkreis XXI.-Inspekteur der Sicherheitspoizei und den SD, June 24, 1942, IPN, GK 62/210/CD, 112–13.

33. *Głos Pracy*, July 10, 1942, translated in Falconi, *Silence*, 228–29. For similar critiques of Pius XII emerging in the Polish clandestine press see Falconi, *Silence*, 225–35. See also John T. Pawlikowski, "The Nazi Attack on the Polish Nation: Towards a New Understanding," in *Holocaust and Church Struggle: Religion, Power and the Politics of Resistance*, Studies in the Shoah, vol. 16, ed. Hubert G. Locke and Marcia Sachs Littell (Lanham, MD: University Press of America, 1996), 41.

34. Papée to Maglione, November 12, 1942, document 439, in *ADSS*, vol. 3, no. 2, 673.

35. Clauss, *Die Beziehungen*, 183.

36. Radoński to Maglione, September 14, 1942, document 410, in *ADSS*, vol. 3, no. 2, 634–35, translated in Phayer, *Catholic Church*, 23.

37. Karol Radoński, "Papież a Polska," *Wiadomości Polskie*, nr. 46, November 15, 1942.

38. Libionka, "Antisemitism," 246.

39. Maglione to Radoński, January 9, 1943, document 460, in *ADSS*, vol. 3, no. 2, 716, translated in Blet, *Pius XII*, 84.

40. *ADSS*, vol. 3, no. 2, 738n3.

41. Radoński to Maglione, February 15, 1943, document 477, in *ADSS*, vol. 3, no. 2, 738.

42. "Przemówienie radiowe Ks. Biskupa Karola Radońskiego z racji mordowania Żydów w Polsce," ADW, zespół: Archiwum Kurii Diecezjalnej w Włocławku, dział personalny, syg. 280d, 67.

43. Phayer, *Pius XII*, 31.

44. The nuncio's emphasis on the situation in the Reichsgau Wartheland is evident not only in Vatican documents but also in the documents of the German Foreign Ministry. See Broszat, "Verfolgung," 76–77.

45. Memorandum, Ernst von Weizsäcker, December 5, 1941, document no. 547, in United States Department of State, *Documents on German Foreign Policy 1918–1945*, series D, vol. 13 (Washington, DC: United States Government Printing Office, 1962), 959–60.

46. Woermann to Reichsministerium für Kirchliche Angelegenheiten, November 29, 1939, BAB, R 5101/22185, 70; Orsenigo to Ribbentrop, December 4, 1941, document 342, Annexe, in *ADSS*, vol. 3, no. 1, 510; Orsenigo to Ribbentrop, December 12, 1941, document 371, Annexe, in *ADSS*, vol. 3, no. 2, 561–62.

47. Orsenigo to Ribbentrop, August 14, 1941, *ADSS*, III/2, doc. 291, Annexe, 426–28.

48. Broszat, "Verfolgung," 76n1.

49. Orsenigo to Ribbentrop, August 28, 1941, document 301, in *ADSS*, vol. 3, no. 1, 448–50.

50. Memorandum, Ernst von Weizsäcker, December 5, 1941, document no. 547, in United States, Department of State, *Documents on German Foreign Policy 1918–1945*, series D, vol. 13 (Washington, DC: United States Government Printing Office, 1962), 959–60.

51. Aufzeichnung des Leiters der Politischen Abteilung im Auswärtigen Amt, Unterstaatssekretär Ernst Woermann, über die politische Unzweckmäßigkeit von Maßnahmen gegen die Kirche, April 21, 1942, document 238, in Gruber, *Katholische Kirche*, 474.

52. Broszat, *Nationalsozialistische*, 149.

53. On the nuncio's response to the September Decree, see "Memorandum of the Secretariat of State to the German Embassy regarding the religious situation in the 'Warthegau,'" October 8, 1942, re: persecution of the Catholic Church in the Warthegau, document 3263-PS, in IMT, vol. 32, 92–93.

54. Already on January 19, 1940, Weizsäcker had noted, "Seit einiger Zeit kommt der Nuntius beinahe jede Woche einmal zu mir, um ein halbes Dutzend Verbalnoten oder Aufzeichnungen und wohl ebensoviele Erinnerungen an unerledigte Beschwerden vorzubringen. Wegen der schleppenden und vielfach negativen Erledigung dieser Dinge gestalten sich die Gespräche mit dem Nuntius oft wenig ergiebig. Der Hauptsorgenpunkt des Nuntius ist gegenwärtig der Zustand der Kirchenverhältnisse im ehemaligen Polen." Quoted in Broszat, *Nationalsozialistische*, 213n165. See also Ernst von Weizsäcker, *Memoirs of Ernst von Weizsäcker*, trans. John Andrews (London: Victor Gollancz, 1951), 282.

55. On Orsenigo's lack of resolve with respect to the situation in Poland, see Phayer, *Catholic Church*, 27; Phayer, *Pius XII*, 28–29. According to Kornberg, Orsenigo was also guilty of callousness toward the plight of Polish forced laborers in the Altreich, and this behavior elicited an angry response from the Berlin bishop Konrad von Preysing. See Kornberg, *Pope's Dilemma*, 295.

56. Lammers to Kerrl, August 28, 1941, BAB, R 43-II/150a, 98–99.

57. Lammers to Ribbentrop, June 2, 1942, Abschrift, YV, TR.2, NG 4576, JM 2031.

58. Von Weizsäcker to Bergen, telegram, June 22, 1942, in Friedländer, *Pius XII*, 161; Protokoll einer interministeriellen Besprechung im Auswärtigen Amt unter Beteiligung des Chefs der Sicherheitspolizei und des Sicherheitsdienstes der SS sowie des Oberkommandos der Wehrmacht über die Beziehungen des Deutschen Reiches zum Heiligen Stuhl, June 22, 1942, document 239, in Gruber, *Katholische Kirche*, 475.

59. Clauss, *Die Beziehungen*, 88.

60. "Memorandum of the Secretariat of State to the German Embassy regarding the religious situation in the 'Warthegau,'" October 8, 1942, re: persecution of the Catholic Church in the Warthegau, document 3263-PS, in IMT, vol. 32, 92–93.

61. Von Bergen to Auswärtiges Amt, telegram, October 11, 1942, document 241, in Gruber, *Katholische Kirche*, 477.

62. Ribbentrop to von Bergen, January 13, 1943, in Friedländer, *Pius XII*, 167–69; Clauss, *Die Beziehungen*, 83.

63. Maglione to Ribbentrop, March 3, 1943, doc. 3264-PS in IMT, vol. 32, 93–105.

64. Testimony of Gustav Adolf Steengracht von Moyland, March 26, 1946, IMT, vol. 10, 115.

65. Von Weizsäcker, *Memoirs*, 282–83; Broszat, "Verfolgung," 79–80.

66. In his correspondence with the Archbishop of Munich-Freising, Pius stated, "Wir haben Unser Verhalten zu den Kriegsfragen mit dem Ausdruck 'Unparteilichkeit' bezeichnet; nicht mit dem Wort 'Neutralität'. Neutralität könnte im Simme [*sic*] einer passiven Gleichgültigkeit verstanden werden, die dem Oberhaupt der Kirche einem solchen Geschehen gegenüber nicht anstünde. Unparteilichkeit besagt für Uns Beurteilung der Dinge nach Wahrheit und Gerechtigkeit, wobei Wir aber, wenn es sich um öffentliche Kundgebungen Unsererseits handelte, der Lage der Kirche in den einzelnen Ländern alle nur mögliche Rücksicht angedeihen liessen, um den Katholiken dortselbst vermeidbare Schwierigkeiten zu ersparen." Pius XII to Michael Cardinal von Faulhaber, Archbishop of Munich-Freising, January 31, 1943, document 96, in *ADSS*, vol. 2, 293–94.

67. On the theme of the papacy's "impartiality" in the years prior to and during World War II and the Holocaust, see Coppa, *Life and Pontificate*, 124–73. Emphasizing that the policy of impartiality did not originate with Pius XII but emerged during World War I and the papacy of Benedict XV, Coppa writes, "It specified that the pope, as Vicar of Christ, could and should condemn policies that violated principles of the faith, without naming those who violated these principles and thus assuring papal political neutrality. Pius XII adopted it during the course of the Second World War when the Nazi regime committed horrible transgressions that culminated in genocide. Recognizing the need to condemn such abuses, but fearful of antagonizing Hitler, it proved a useful construct." Coppa, *Life and Pontificate*, 154.

68. Clauss, *Die Beziehungen*, 174.

69. Pius XII to Michael Cardinal von Faulhaber, Archbishop of Munich-Freising, January 31, 1943, document 96, in *ADSS*, vol. 2, 294.

70. Kazimierz Papée, memorandum, "Rozmowa z Kardynałem Maglione w dniu 27 Listopada 1942," November 27, 1942, PISM, A44-122/28; Clauss, *Die Beziehungen*, 182–83.

71. Quoted in Chadwick, *Britain*, 81–82. See also Pease, *Rome's*, 210.

72. Breitinger, *Als Deutschenseelsorger*, 56. On German retribution for Vatican Radio broadcasts, see also Harold Tittman, *Inside the Vatican of Pius XII: The Memoir of an American Diplomat During World War II* (New York: Doubleday, 2004), 111.

73. Clauss, *Die Beziehungen*, 175–76.

74. His official title: substitute for ordinary affairs. See Clauss, *Die Beziehungen*, 3.

75. Giovanni Montini, notes, January 27, 1940, document 108, in *ADSS*, vol. 3, no. 1, 208.

76. Maglione notes, March 30, 1941, document 58, in *ADSS*, vol. 8, 155. See also Clauss, *Die Beziehungen*, 106.

77. Domenico Tardini, notes, May 18, 1942, document 378, in *ADSS*, vol. 3, no. 2, 569–70, translated in Sanchez, 158.

78. Tardini notes, July 20, 1942, document 414, in *ADSS*, vol. 5, 615.

79. Ribbentrop to Bergen, January 13, 1943, translated in Friedländer, *Pius XII*, 168. Ribbentrop's cable to Weizsäcker of January 24, 1943, with similar content, is quoted in

Robert M. W. Kempner, letter to the editor, *Commentary* 37, no. 6 (June 1964): 12. Kempner was US deputy chief of counsel at the International Military Tribunal in Nürnberg and served as a prosecutor in the subsequent Nürnberg proceeding commonly known as the "Ministries Trial."

80. Tittman, *Inside the Vatican*, 118.

81. Tittman, 120.

82. Pius XII to Konrad Graf von Preysing, April 30, 1943, doc. 246, in Gruber, *Katholische Kirche*, 487.

83. Kornberg, *Pope's Dilemma*, 8–9, 274, 301.

84. For a discussion of this dichotomy, in somewhat different form, see Clauss, *Die Beziehungen*, 177.

85. Robert A. Graham, *The Pope and Poland in World War Two* (London: Veritas, 1968), 22.

18

KURSWECHSEL

A Change in Course

Dramatic change in the Nazi regime's Kirchenpolitik in the Reichsgau Wartheland would come about not because of Pius XII's intervention but because of Allied intervention. Chapter 14 emphasized consistency in the Gau administration's policy toward the church after 1941, and consistent it would largely remain, until the final weeks of the occupation. Yet as Germany's military situation worsened over the course of 1943 and 1944, the Nazi regime implemented minor yet nonetheless significant changes to its Polenpolitik, and corollary to these, minor changes in its policy toward the churches.

The war was the indirect cause of these changes. As ever more men were conscripted into military service, there were fewer officials, bureaucrats, and policemen available to implement and enforce policy and measures directed against the church. As the Soviet army advanced in the east and the bombing campaigns increased in the west, the number of German refugees and settlers in the Warthegau increased dramatically, and many of these refugees and settlers wanted access to the church and its ministries.[1] As the war economy demanded an effective and cooperative workforce in the Gau, the need for concessions toward the Poles increased. Poles and their Catholicism had always been barriers to the Germanization process, but at the same time, Poles were a necessary labor resource to be exploited and maintained, especially in a time of military and economic crisis.

The tension between the racial-ideological goals of the regime and the economic-pragmatic demands of the wartime economy would affect in countless ways the stability of the Nazi state, its economic productivity, and its annihilationist agenda. As Adam Tooze has succinctly stated, "In relation to the cardinal problem of manpower, it is hard to avoid the impression that the Third Reich faced an unresolvable contradiction between its genocidal racial ideology and the practical imperatives of production."[2] In occupied Polish territory, racial ideology and economic exploitation were often in conflict with one another: the racial transformation meant either *Eindeutschung* (literally, "Germanization") of Poles, or their removal through deportation, incarceration, or murder; economic exploitation required that some Poles be left at home and others sent into forced labor, but that all be provided a minimal material existence. Thus, the application of Volkstumspolitik could range from near total exclusion of the Polish population and withdrawal of their civil rights in the Warthegau, to broad Germanization via the Deutsche Volksliste in East Upper Silesia.[3]

In the optimistic mood of autumn 1941, Arthur Greiser was able to proclaim the primacy of ideology in his Polenpolitik: "The nationality question [*Volkstumsfrage*] is decisive, not the labor question." The Pole, he argued, "must achieve a certain level of labor productivity" but is "nothing more than manpower." As such, the Pole was to be "confronted without sentimentality."[4] Over the course of the following year, however, Greiser appears to have understood that better treatment of the Polish population was necessary for effective war production, and his office therefore instituted a number of changes reflecting a slightly more conciliatory approach, such as improved bread rations, new legal protections for Poles,[5] restrictions on the use of Polish churches for secular purposes,[6] and allowances for additional church services on holidays.[7] Gau officials did, in fact, see a relationship between Polenpolitik and economic production, and therefore Kirchenpolitik and economic production. For example, in October 1942, the Łódź Gestapo recommended against the closure of the Polish Catholic church in Chlebów because such a measure "would call forth significant disquiet among the Poles which, with regard to the Polish labor force essential to the war economy, must be avoided."[8] Greiser's administration even went so far as to establish an "Association of Achieving Poles" (Verband der Leistungspolen), which the Gauleiter announced in December 1942. Loyal and industrious Poles were invited to join the organization, and they were to be rewarded with wages and rations equivalent to those received by Germans.[9] Apparently intended as an incentive for Poles to contribute to the war economy, the organization, Greiser later claimed, also had the purpose of sowing discord in the Polish community by creating a cadre of regime-loyal elites.[10] In this it failed. The association was unable to garner the interest of many Poles, who were understandably suspicious of it, and it was apparently neglected by the German authorities.[11]

By the spring of 1943—that is, following the Wehrmacht's defeat at Stalingrad—there were voices among the Nazi leadership calling for a more substantial shift in the regime's policies in occupied Poland. An increase in passive and active Polish resistance in the General Government led some officials there to conclude that a basic revision of policy was necessary. Methods of intimidation and terror, as well as the effort to destroy the Polish intelligentsia, had, they argued, been misguided and ineffective.[12] In a position paper issued in June 1943, Governor General Hans Frank himself would advocate for a "thorough transformation in the treatment of the Poles."[13] Although a number of minor concessions were made, including the expansion of cultural opportunities for Poles and the reopening of a Catholic seminary, calls for broader change in the regime's Polenpolitik never won Hitler's approval.[14]

While officials in the General Government were contemplating a revision in their approach to the Poles, Arthur Greiser was emphasizing consistency in the separation of the Polish and German populations. In a March 1943 speech, he stressed that the German people and nation, with the declaration of "total war," were experiencing a "test of character." Essential to the current struggle, Greiser maintained, was holding to the clear division between German and Pole. Only under the direction of Germans, he argued, were the Polish people capable of any positive achievement. The current period, he added, was merely a transitional phase in which the Poles were to be exploited to the fullest, in order that they would one day disappear. To that end, the German had to wield an "energetically firm hand" to "extract that which has to be extracted." The Gauleiter was also clear in attacking the Catholic clergy for the power it wielded over the Polish population, using the "gloss and hocus-pocus" of the church in the struggle against Germany. According to Greiser, the Polish intelligentsia—of which the clergy was a part—remained active in the ethno-racial struggle. "As long as an intellectual elite is tolerated," he stated, "we cannot assume that the ethnic danger posed by the Polish population is one hundred percent exorcised."[15]

Greiser's words may seem difficult to reconcile with some of the conciliatory measures implemented by the Gau administration at the time. The apparent contradiction illustrates the ongoing tension between ideological rigor and economic pragmatism discussed above, even as it illustrates what

Catherine Epstein has appropriately described as the Gauleiter's own "torn attitudes" toward Poles. "He wanted to encourage Poles to work harder," she writes, "but he didn't want to undermine his radical anti-Polish schemes."[16] This tension—whether in Greiser's personality or in occupied Poland as a whole—was never resolved, for both Polenpolitik and Kirchenpolitik in the Warthegau remained fraught with contradictions through the end of the occupation.

These contradictions likely contributed to the rumors that were circulating among Warthegau Poles in early 1943. According to an SD report in April of that year, there was widespread speculation that a *Kurswechsel*, or change of course in the regime's policies vis-à-vis the Poles, was in the offing. Pork and fat rations for Poles had recently been increased, the hours in which Poles were permitted to shop were expanded, wages for domestic workers rose, and the authorities loosened restrictions on the use of the Polish language. All these measures were implemented independently by individual offices in the Gau administration, but when viewed as an aggregate, they led to lively speculation about a general, centralized shift in policy, as well as rumors about the regime's church policies. Poles, it was rumored, would soon be allowed to open churches; a portion of the Polish clergy was to be released from Dachau; the Poznań cathedral would soon be reopened and restored to its former purpose; and Bishop Walenty Dymek had been set free.[17] The Polish underground also reported on such rumors and suggested that they had been spread by the German authorities to gain favor among the Poles.[18] All these rumors proved to be false, but it was nonetheless true that in the aftermath of Stalingrad, the Gau administration was working to address not only issues of labor productivity but also the "optics" of antichurch policy, for public perceptions were becoming important. Enemy propaganda could and did exploit German policy toward the churches, Catholic Germans in the Altreich might fear forthcoming aggressive measures, Reichsdeutsche moving into the Gau could resent the restrictions on their religious practices, while Volksdeutsche native to the Warthegau and from elsewhere in Europe might become disillusioned with the regime's aggressively antireligious policies.

Warthegau Poles were, of course, less important than any of these Germans, and the Gau administration's church policy was largely directed at Polish Catholics, their clergy, and their churches. Nazi policy after 1941 was indeed marked by consistency, but the evidence suggests that by 1943, as Germany's military situation became ever more precarious, Greiser's administration and the police appeared ever more hesitant to alienate the Poles, and were willing to make a few minor concessions to them even with respect to their church. This was evident, for example, in March 1943, when the Reichsstatthalter's office issued a memorandum expressing concern over how the use of closed and confiscated churches in the Warthegau was perceived by the public. Nazi propaganda had been emphasizing the danger that the Bolshevik Soviet Union posed for the churches, and it was essential, the author of the memorandum argued, that the Gau administration not "stab this propaganda in the back" through excessive use of Polish churches for profane purposes.[19] Greiser's office had issued in October of the previous year an order restricting the use of vacant churches to the storage of grain and military supplies, and demanding that churches not be damaged in the process.[20] Requests for the use of churches had, however, increased dramatically (leading to the "competition" for churches described in chapter 14), and the Reichsstatthalter's files reveal that German individuals and firms, as well as party and state organizations, had no reservations whatsoever about exploiting these buildings in any variety of ways. Greiser's office thus emerged, ironically, as the "protector" of Polish churches in the face of increasing demand for them over the course of 1943.[21] The churches were certainly not reopened, but keeping them vacant and preventing damage to them could at least hinder further offense to Polish Catholic sensibilities.

Nazi officials took other minor measures to avoid further alienating the Gau's Catholic population, both German and Polish. In January 1943, party officials in the Łódź District were instructed to treat the "church question" with "exceptional reserve," and in a departure from previous policy, in April 1943 the RSHA and Poznań Gestapo issued an order stating that no police action was to be taken should Warthegau churches hold large-scale worship services on Good Friday.[22] Later that year, the Reichsstatthalter's office was pressed to intervene when the Hitler Youth began vandalizing church property—throwing stones at church windows, damaging statues, and the like. Such actions could, according to Herbert Mehlhorn, head of the Reichsstatthalter's Department I (general internal affairs and finance), "give our enemies occasion for inflammatory propaganda against the National Socialist rearing of German youth."[23] Measures such as these were arguably directed as much toward German Catholics in the Warthegau as they were to Poles, but they do nonetheless indicate a small shift in attitude, if not in official policy. One need only consider that in 1939 and 1940, the Gestapo was arresting priests who conducted unauthorized services, and the Nazi authorities were destroying statues, shrines, and church property as a matter of policy. By late 1943, however, German boys throwing stones at church windows elicited condemnation from the Reichsstatthalter's office and the stern demand that such behavior be disciplined.

By March of 1944, it was clear that the "church question" in the Warthegau, once so central to the Germanization process and the region's role as a "model Gau," had receded dramatically in importance. According to a Łódź SD report of that month, it had "now more than ever been overshadowed and pushed into the background by military and political developments." Interestingly, the report also noted that many Germans believed that the antichurch measures of the previous years had been the work of Gauleiter Greiser, and that once the war was over, Hitler would set things straight. "The Gauleiter's policy is not the Führer's policy" and "The Führer has not had the last word when it comes to the church question" were common arguments voiced by devout Germans in the Warthegau. Furthermore, the report addressed an ongoing public relations problem of the Gau administration: reports on church affairs in the Soviet Union were encouraging unfavorable comparisons between the persecution of the church there and the persecution of the church in the Warthegau, adding to the population's already palpable discontent.[24]

Discontent was well founded, for the Reichsgau Wartheland was facing disastrous circumstances in early 1944. Joseph Goebbels arrived for a visit in Poznań on January 26 and reported of his strong impression that Greiser was firmly in control, and that the situation in the Warthegau was "extraordinarily consolidated."[25] Greiser may have nominally been in control, but as Catherine Epstein has pointed out, Goebbels's confidence was at odds with reality. "The Warthegau," she writes, "did not exist in isolation. Nazi Germany was in peril. British and American bombers had devastated cities throughout the Old Reich. The Red Army had retaken many areas of the Soviet Union. Hans Frank was barely able to control Poles in the General Government, unrest that threatened to spill into the Warthegau. For all that Greiser's rule seemed strong, his Gau rested on a shaky basis."[26] Moreover, because of the changing military situation, conscription of able-bodied men, and the influx of refugees from both East and West, the population of the Gau had been transformed in dramatic ways. "In contrast to the Nazi vision of a rural Gau neatly populated by soldiers and sturdy peasants," Epstein continues, "the Warthegau had become a Gau of resettlement camps, military hospitals, and overcrowded farms and cities. Moreover, since virtually all able-bodied men were at the front, the Gau's German population was largely made up of women, children, the wounded, and the elderly."[27]

As the war dragged on, the Nazi authorities revealed both their anxiety over the deteriorating military situation and their willingness to make more, if minor, concessions to the Catholic Church in the Warthegau. In May 1944, the German army requested from the Reichsstatthalter's office permission to requisition a number of Polish Catholic churches for storage. Heinrich Meyer refused this request, however, on the grounds that the churches in question had been designated, in the long term, for Polish Roman Catholic worship.[28] Two months later, Meyer would, in fact, be overruled by Greiser's deputy August Jäger, who granted the Wehrmacht access to vacant Polish churches. It remains significant, however, that the future worship needs of Catholic Poles were, if only temporarily, given priority over the needs of the German military. Moreover, it is also significant that Jäger, in granting the Wehrmacht access to the churches, strictly prohibited any *profanacja* of the church buildings or furnishings, demanding that pews, paintings, and the like be removed and stored with care so that that they could, in the future, be replaced for Polish worshippers.[29]

At the same time, the Nazi government was initiating steps to court the favor of the exiled Cardinal Hlond, the Polish primate. In France since June 1940, the cardinal resided in Lourdes until April 1943, when the French authorities ordered him transferred to an abbey in Hautecombe in the Savoy. He remained there until he was arrested by the Gestapo in February 1944 and subsequently imprisoned in Paris, where the Gestapo had attempted to gain the cardinal's collaboration in the fight against the Soviet Union. Hlond firmly rejected these overtures and was subsequently detained in a cloister in Bar-le-Duc, in northeastern France.[30] In June 1944, however, the Nazi regime appeared to renew its efforts to gain the cardinal's favor by providing a subsidy of fifty thousand francs for his upkeep, and attempting to make amends for the propaganda salvos issued against him in the fall of 1939.[31] What, exactly, the Nazi authorities were attempting to accomplish is unclear. Whether hoping for the cardinal's advocacy in the fight against the Soviet Union or attempting to make amends with Catholics in Poland, Germany, the Vatican, or elsewhere, measures such as these suggested both improvisation and desperation in the waning months of the war.

Simultaneous with these overtures were further ordinances in the Warthegau that were intended to protect "Polish" churches. Some Warthegau

Germans had reportedly been dismantling walls and fences around churches in order to use them for building materials, and in late June, Greiser put a stop to this practice. The "gutting of church property" had certain undesirable political ramifications, the Gauleiter maintained, and the destruction of such enclosures could disturb the "village appearance" and "landscape."[32] It seems perplexing that the Nazi authorities would exhibit such concerns in a time of economic crisis and military disaster, but a memorandum issued by August Jäger in July 1944 indicated that the Gau authorities were, in fact, planning to return Polish churches to their former purpose. When and how many of the churches would be opened remained, however, unspecified.[33]

The following month, Greiser appeared to take a major step toward gaining the favor of the Polish population. An enormous effort was underway in the Warthegau to construct fortifications for the defense of the Gau against the approaching Soviet invasion. Thousands of Poles were engaged in this initiative, and during a visit to Łódź on August 15, 1944, the Gauleiter publicly praised them for their industry and loyalty. He also proclaimed that these Poles were to be rewarded for their efforts with a significant increase in rations, and wages equal to those of Germans. "They will," he stated, "deservedly feel that they are protected members [*Schutzangehöriger*] of the Third Reich."[34] In an exceptional gesture, Greiser also took time to chat with Polish women and girls laboring on the fortifications, and voiced his approval of their work.[35] This unprecedented behavior was not lost on some Gau officials, one of whom maintained that "it is not at all understood why now, in the worst of all possible moments, the Poles are pandered to in this way." "It thus appeared especially inappropriate," the official argued, "that the Gauleiter chatted with Polish female workers at the construction sites. This was extremely conspicuous, and would earlier have been out of the question."[36]

As the summer 1944 turned to fall, the sense of crisis surrounding the regime's Polenpolitik appeared more acute and emerged as a matter of concern at the highest levels of the Nazi government. In an October 1944 letter to Himmler, chief of the RSHA Ernst Kaltenbrunner outlined some of the various directions that German policy vis-à-vis the Poles could take, ranging from the "firm but just" approach that had been maintained in the Warthegau; to the more relaxed approach advocated by some in the General Government that included concessions in cultural, educational, and economic affairs; to the establishment of a free and sovereign Poland with its own armed forces. Kaltenbrunner concluded, however, that a significant change in the Polenpolitik of the Incorporated Territories (the Warthegau included) would be impossible, as these were still intended to remain regions of German settlement. In other words, the regime's racial imperative remained in force, despite the desperate circumstances brought about by the war. Nonetheless, Kaltenbrunner also recommended an end to any public propaganda that included discriminating or defaming anti-Polish content, as well as an end to any measures that the Poles might find unscrupulous or could incite them to acts of resistance.[37]

That same month, a position paper emerging from Department IIIB (Security Service, domestic ethnic relations)[38] of Kaltenbrunner's RSHA considered the past and future trajectory of the regime's Polish policies. Although critical of measures in the past that had alienated the Polish population, the document, like Kaltenbrunner's letter to Himmler, discouraged any significant relaxation in policy for Poland's Incorporated Territories because these regions were to remain destinations for German settlement. As far as occupied Poland as a whole was concerned, the paper argued that any major shift in the regime's Polenpolitik prior to Germany reasserting its military dominance would be a dangerous step, in effect prematurely undermining its clout and squandering its political capital.[39] Both of these documents are remarkable, and in similar ways. They both emerge from the RSHA offices in Berlin, still relatively far from the front, and hold to the unrealistic assumption that Germany still had the opportunity and means to win the war. Moreover, both documents are highly theoretical, and suggest an unfamiliarity with the realities of the situation on the ground in Nazi-occupied Poland, which was in a state of collapse.[40] Finally, both documents hold to the racial imperative that was to guide policy in the Wartheland. Minor concessions had been made there to Poles in the hopes of winning their favor, gaining their cooperation, or at least undermining their tendency toward resistance; at the same time, however, the regime held strictly to a policy of separation between Poles and Germans.

It was this "concessions, yet segregation" approach that characterized the regime's policies toward the Polish Catholic Church in the Warthegau during the final months of the occupation. On October 7, 1944, the Gau administration took a small but unprecedented step: by order of the Reichsstatthalter's office and the Gestapo, the retired priest Franz Jankowski was permitted to assume duties in a Gniezno parish.[41] Later that month, both Greiser and Meyer issued new and strident warnings to local officials demanding that they prevent damage to churches designated for

Poles.[42] In November, the Gestapo ordered Józef Sarniewicz, a priest serving in the Mogilno Subdistrict, to begin serving Our Lady of Sorrows parish in Poznań, which, as one of only two churches open in the city, was desperately in need of pastoral care.[43]

But even as the authorities were taking these somewhat conciliatory measures, Greiser and his staff were maintaining a firm line on their policy of segregating Poles and Germans in both public life and church life. In a November 1944 position paper on National Socialist racial policy, the Gauleiter appeared to be digging in his heels on Volkstumspolitik in the Wartheland. "The separation of ethnicities," he stated in a tone reminiscent of the first weeks of the occupation, "is the necessary precondition for the strengthening of one's own people." "The ethnic struggle," he continued, "cannot become a mere historical memory. It must go on, both on the political field of battle and also the biological field of battle." Moreover, Greiser argued, Catholicism, potentially a "connecting bracket" for Germans and Poles, could pose a grave danger by bringing the two peoples together, despite the "principle of ethnic separation."[44]

Thus, even at this late date, and despite the minor concessions made to Polish Catholics, segregation remained in force. In November 1944, local Nazi authorities were reporting that Poles had begun participating, in ever-increasing numbers, in worship services in "German" churches, especially when Masses were celebrated by military chaplains. Greiser's office responded with threats: should Polish participation not come to an end, the churches would be closed, and appropriate measures would be taken against the German priests who failed to enforce the policy of separation.[45] In a remarkable December incident, the police undertook a thorough *Kontrolle* of worshippers at the abbey church in Krotoszyn. The priest had announced at the beginning of the service that the church was open only to Germans, and a sign on the church made this clear. After the service, those worshippers not wearing a Nazi insignia on their clothing were forced to provide identification. The procedure enabled the police to tap three Polish women for violating the segregation policy.[46] On behalf of the Reichsstatthalter's office, Heinrich Meyer recommended that no legal action be taken against the German priest because the church had been clearly designated "for Germans only." It would suffice, he stated, to arrest the three Polish women.[47]

The rigor with which the authorities continued to uphold the principle of segregation of the Catholic faithful is striking. Three weeks before the commencement of the Red Army's offensive from the Vistula to the Oder, and only four weeks before Soviet forces reached the outskirts of Poznań, the Gau authorities were directing manpower and resources to the arrest of three Polish women attending Mass in the wrong church. It is clear that the sole concern here was racial, for at the same time that officials were continuing to enforce the "nationality principle," the Gau administration was making plans to open hundreds of churches. It is therefore clear that in these final weeks of crisis, anti-Christian and anti-Catholic ideology had receded in importance, and there was no evidence of concern over the church's alleged anti-German, conspiratorial role. But the separation of Poles and Germans—the ethnic struggle of the Volkstumskampf—had to go on, even in the face of the Warthegau's imminent collapse.

The turning point in the regime's policy came far too late to be of any real benefit to Warthegau Catholics and is marked by a lengthy memorandum of December 22, 1944—two days after the Krotoszyn *Kontrolle*—in which Heinrich Meyer outlined how the regime should respond to the burgeoning demand for churches in those tumultuous weeks. According to Meyer, there were in the Gau between 1,200 and 1,300 closed Polish churches and chapels. Approximately 500 of them were currently being used for storage, and some 70 more were being used by German Catholics. Meyer calculated that in the years ahead (he was either assuming German victory in the war, or at least making a pretense of such an assumption), another 150 churches would be needed for German Catholics, and a large number for German Protestants as well. Most significantly, however, Meyer called for opening between 150 and 200 additional churches to Catholic Poles. In all, then, of the 1,200 to 1,300 Polish churches currently inaccessible, as many as 500 were to be restored to their former purpose. As for the hundreds of other Polish churches remaining, these would, according to Meyer, have to be maintained for "political reasons."[48] Apparently, it was feared that tearing them down, or simply leaving them to decay, would alienate the German and Polish populations.

Meyer also noted that he had secured for this plan the support of the Nazi Party Chancellery in Munich, and this is especially significant. It suggests, first, that the impetus for the more liberal policy had its origins in Poznań rather than Munich or Berlin. Second, it points to the ongoing importance of Warthegau Kirchenpolitik for the central party authorities. Why else would Meyer ask for the party's blessing? Like in the Altreich, economic crisis and military collapse in the Warthegau were resulting in a greater concern over public opinion, a more relaxed approach to the churches, and a desire to avoid the appearance of persecution. In 1939, Nazi Kirchenpolitik demanded that Polish churches in the Warthegau be closed and their priests shot or arrested. At the end of 1944, it demanded that churches be opened and priests restored to their parishes.

In the weeks that followed, the churches in the Reichsgau Wartheland opened, many priests still living returned, and parishioners returned to their houses of worship. They did not, however, do so as a result of a dramatic shift in Nazi policy but because the Nazi authorities had been driven out. It is not clear how many churches were opened because of orders from the Reichsstatthalter's office or the police, but given the rapid movement of the Eastern Front westward in January and February 1945, it is likely that the vast majority simply became accessible at some point after the Germans had fled.[49]

The Soviet offensive from the Vistula to the Oder, a "lightning operation"[50] in which "Polish cities fell one after the other,"[51] began on January 12. Within days, the eastern portions of the Reichsgau Wartheland, including most of the Gniezno and Włocławek dioceses, were liberated. Łódź and Kutno fell on January 19, and soon thereafter, the Red Army reached the outskirts of Poznań. Hitler had declared the already fortified Warthegau capital a "stronghold city" (*Festungsstadt*), and although most of it was quickly captured, a remnant of German forces held out in an interior citadel until February 23.[52]

Soviet forces had, however, liberated the Łazarz neighborhood, where Our Lady of Sorrows parish was located, nearly four weeks earlier. To mark the end of Nazi rule, Bishop Walenty Dymek called for a pontifical Mass of thanks on Sunday, February 11.[53] Amid the rubble, and with guns and artillery sounding in the near distance, it was undoubtedly a peculiar scene. When asked after the war if he had received any honors for his service during the occupation, Father Marian Frankiewicz, administrator of the parish, recalled, "I received no military or state decorations. . . . The most beautiful reward for me was to emerge from Gestapo interrogations unscathed, to survive the occupation, and to have the opportunity to preach the first homily in a free Poznań on the occasion of a Mass of gratitude celebrated by Bishop Walenty Dymek in the presence of civilian authorities and Polish and Soviet generals on 11 February 1945."[54]

Notes

1. Śmigiel, *Die katholische Kirche*, 114.

2. Adam Tooze, *The Wages of Destruction: The Making and Breaking of the Nazi Economy* (New York: Penguin, 2006), 520.

3. See Bömelburg and Musial, "Die deutsche Besatzungspolitik," 51–52.

4. "Bericht über die Tagung der Reichstreuhänder der Arbeit der Ostgebiete in Posen," October 9, 1941, IPN, GK 196/37, 48.

5. Epstein, *Model Nazi*, 220.

6. Reichsstatthalter to Landrat des Kreises Lask, March 24, 1942, IPN, GK 62/218/CD, 97; Reichsstatthalter (Jäger) to Herren Landräte und Oberbürgermeister im Reichsgau Wartheland, Staatspolizeistellen Posen, Litzmannstadt, Hohensalza, October 16, 1942, APP, zespół 449, syg. 449/0/2/40, microfilm O-153553; Reichsstatthalter to Herrn Landrat des Kreises Kempen, September 9, 1942, IPN, GK 62/218/CD, 308. In this letter, the Reichsstatthalter's office for church affairs instructed the Kępno Landrat not to use the local Catholic church as a warehouse for the Wehrmacht because such use of the church would alienate the local population. In the event that no other storage space was to be found, the authorities were instructed to use the nearby synagogue.

7. Gestapo Posen (Trenke) to den Herrn Regierungspräsidenten in Posen, die Herren Landräte des Bezirks, die Aussendienststellen des Bezirks, March 21, 1942, IPN, GK 831/177, 154.

8. Gestapo Litzmannstadt to Reichsstatthalter Abteilung I/51, October 30, 1942, IPN, GK 62/197, 64.

9. Epstein, *Model Nazi*, 219–21.

10. Bericht über die Arbeitstagung des Gauamtes für Volkstumspolitik am 20. u. 21.3.1943 in Posen, March 21, 1943, IPN, GK 196/37, 105.

11. Lagebericht, SD-Abschnitt Litzmannstadt, Aussenstelle Kalisch, 28 January 1944, IPN, GK 70/56, 8; Epstein, *Model Nazi*, 221.

12. Broszat, *Nationalsozialistische*, 169.

13. Broszat, 170.

14. Broszat, 168, 171.

15. Bericht, Arbeitstagung des Gauamtes für Volkstumspolitik am 20. u. 21.3.1943 in Posen, March 21, 1943, IPN, GK 196/37, 104.

16. Epstein, *Model Nazi*, 221.

17. Bericht (Müller) über die Gerüchte innerhalb des Polentums hinsichtlich eines vermuteten Kurswechsels in der Volkstumspolitik, April 13, 1943, IPN, GK 62/126, 2–4. The use of the Polish language in public was officially permitted via a direct order from Greiser: Greiser to alle Behörden nachrichtlich an den Gauleiter und Reichsstatthalter, Militärbehörden, körperschaften des öffentlichen Rechts, usw., February 23, 1943, APP, zespół 299, syg. 1174, 180–82.

18. "Raport o sytuacji na Ziemiach Zachodnich Nr. 5 (do 15.V.1943 r.)," in Mazur, Pietrowicz, and Rutowska, *Raporty z ziem*, 101.

19. Vermerk, Reichsstatthalter Abteilung I/51, March 12, 1943, IPN, GK 62/222/CD, 16.

20. Reichsstatthalter (Jäger) to Herren Landräte und Oberbürgermeister im Reichsgau Wartheland, Staatspolizeistellen Posen, Litzmannstadt, Hohensalza, October 16, 1942, APP, zespół 449, syg. 449/0/2/40, microfilm O-153553, 19–22.

21. Reichsstatthalter Abteilung I/51 to Landrat des Kreises Lask, September 4, 1943, IPN, GK 62/222/CD, 80. Files 62/218/CD, 62/219/CD, and 62/223/CD also attest to the Reichsstatthalter's office assuming such a role.

22. Gestapo Posen (Schuster) to den Herrn Landrat im Lissa, April 17, 1943, APP, 53/1023/0/-/12, microfilm O-83184, 10.

23. Mehlhorn to den Führer des Gebietes Wartheland der HJ, Obergebietsführer Kuhnt, October 20, 1943, APP, zespół 299, syg. 1189, 7.

24. Bericht des SD-Abschnitts Litzmannstadt über die Lage auf politisch-konfessionellem Gebiet im Regierunsbezirk Litzmannstadt, March 6, 1944, IPN, GK 62/153, 285–86.

25. Joseph Goebbels, entry of January 26, 1944, in *Die Tagebücher von Joseph Goebbels*, ed. Elke Fröhlich, part II, vol. 8 (München: K. G. Saur, 1993), 175.

26. Epstein, *Model Nazi*, 289.

27. Epstein, 291.

28. Meyer to Heereszeugamt Posen, Abt. Allgem. Verwaltung, May 8, 1944, IPN, GK 62/225, 13.

29. Reichsstatthalter Abt. I/51 (Jäger) to Landräte and Oberbürgermeister im Reichsgau Wartheland, July 18, 1944, APŁ, zespół: Akta Miasta Łodzi, syg. 32473.

30. Vermerk, Hauptamt Sicherheitspolizei IV A 4 a K, June 21, 1944, Polish translation, IPN, BU 01283/1/J, 17; Śmigiel, *Die katholische Kirche*, 119–25; Madajczyk, *Okkupationspolitik*, 363–64.

31. Telegram. Der Befehlshaber der Sicherheitspolizei und des SD im Bereich des Militärbefehlshabers in Frankreich to Befehlshaber der Sicherheitspolizei und des SD Paris, June 1, 1944, BAB R58/7021, 1; Vermerk, Betr. Kardinal Hlond, z.Zt. Bar-le-Duc, June 16, 1944, IPN, BU 01283/1/J, 16.

32. Landrat Kempen to Herren Bürgermeister und Amtskommissare des Kreises, June 26, 1944, APP, zespół 452, syg. 8, 146.

33. RSH I/51 (Jäger) to Landräte und Oberbürgermeister im Reichsgau Wartheland, July 18, 1944, APŁ, zespół Akta Miasta Łodzi, syg. 32473.

34. *Ostdeutscher Beobachter*, August 15, 1944, 1.

35. *Ostdeutscher Beobachter*, August 16, 1944, 3.

36. Lagebericht Kalisch (Lorenz), August 18, 1944, IPN, GK 70/52, 123. On Greiser's visit to Łódź see also Epstein, *Model Nazi*, 292–93.

37. Kaltenbrunner to Himmler, n.d., Abschrift, BAB, R 58/1002, 16–17. Although the transcription of the letter is not dated, its content makes clear that it was written in October 1944.

38. Hilberg, *Destruction*, vol. 1, 284.

39. "Bisherige Polenpolitik im GG und Vorschläge zu ihrer Auflockerung bzw. Neuordnung," Abschrift, October 19, 1944, BAB, R 43 II/172, 18–20.

40. By October 1944, Białystok, Lublin, and Lwów were all in Soviet hands, refugees were streaming westward, and a frantic effort was underway to expand the fortifications begun earlier in the year. See Epstein, *Model Nazi*, 298.

41. Gestapo Gnesen (Wolf) to Landrat des Kreises Gnesen, October 7, 1944, AAG, zespół 0164, syg. 8, 47.

42. Reichsstatthalter (Meyer) to Herrn Bürgermeister der Stadt Brunnstadt, October 27, 1944, IPN, GK 62/225, 54; Reichsstatthalter to Kreisleiter, Landräte and Oberbürgermeister im Reichsgau Wartheland, October 28, 1944, Abschrift, IPN, GK 831/59, 116.

43. Świadectwo Ks. Józefa Sarniewicza, n.d., IPN, GK 196/19, 168; Marian Frankiewicz, Relacja, October 25, 1947, IZ, Dok. II-123, 1.

44. Greiser, "Gedanken zur Nationalsozialistischen Volkstumspolitik," November 1944, YV, TR. 17, file 12309, item 4068282.

45. Reichsstatthalter (Reischauer) to Vorstand der römisch-katholischen Kirche deutscher Nationalität im Reichsgau Wartheland, Abschrift, November 17, 1944, APP, zespół 465, syg. 110, 339; Reichsstatthalter (Reischauer) to Vorstand der römisch-katholischen Kirche deutscher Nationalität im Reichsgau Wartheland, November 17, 1944, AAG, zespół 0164, syg. 8, 50; Reichsstatthalter (Reischauer) to Landräte, Oberbürgermeister, Gestapo Posen and Litzmannstadt, November 17, 1944, APP, zespół 465, syg. 110, 340.

46. Vermerk, Schutzpolizeidienstabteilung Krotoschin, Abschrift, December 3, 1944, IPN, GK 62/211/CD, 21.

47. Meyer, Vermerk ü. Kirchenbesuch von Polen, December 20, 1944, IPN, GK 62/211/CD, 22.

48. Vermerk, Meyer-Eckhardt, IPN, GK 196/19, 58–61.

49. A postwar survey in the Włocławek Diocese revealed that among 111 parish churches, 12 were opened in January 1945, 14 were opened in February, and 4 were opened in March. A small minority of them had remained open for German or Polish use throughout the occupation, and the vast majority were simply listed as having remained closed until the end of the war. These numbers are based on the author's examination of one volume (Tom 1) of the surveys archived—that is, roughly half of the parishes in the diocese: Ankieta Strat Wojennych Diecezji Włocławskiej w l. 1939/45, przeprowadzona przez Archiwariusza Diecezjalnego w r. 1947, Tom 1.

50. Andrzej Paczkowski, *The Spring Will Be Ours: Poland and the Poles from Occupation to Freedom*, trans. Jane Cave (University Park: Pennsylvania State University Press, 2003), 138.

51. Kochanski, *Eagle Unbowed*, 515.

52. Madajczyk, *Okkupationspolitik*, 631; Kochanski, *Eagle Unbowed*, 517.

53. Marian Frankiewicz, Relacja, October 25, 1947, IZ, document II-123, 4.

54. Marian Frankiewicz, Ankieta, January 19, 1974, AAP, zespół 133, syg. OK 217, 517/74.

CONCLUSION

Father Marian Frankiewicz's expression of gratitude as the Nazi occupation drew to a close is, of course, tinged with a certain poignancy when one considers the context of his reflections. Frankiewicz, his parish, and his Catholic Church had survived, but the experience of the past five and half years was arduous, exhausting, and at times even savage. Faced with the task of rebuilding, clergy and laity alike were forced to confront the church's catastrophic losses—human, material, and moral—in the years 1939–1945.

Losses among the clergy were devastating. Over the course of the war and occupation, more than 1,800 Polish Catholic clergymen died. Persecution of the clergy in the Reichsgau Wartheland was considerably more severe than elsewhere in occupied Poland. Of the 2,100 secular and religious clergy in the Warthegau in 1939, 133 were killed in the Gau, 1,523 were arrested, and 1,092 were deported to concentration camps, where 682 died. Statistics broken down according to the four main dioceses in the Warthegau reveal figures even more dramatic. In the Poznań and Gniezno dioceses, both of which were located almost entirely within the Warthegau, losses amounted to 35 and 37 percent of the clergy, respectively. Thirty-eight percent of the priests in the Łódź diocese died during the occupation. The Włocławek diocese lost more than half of its clergymen. Putting these numbers in simpler terms, nearly three-fourths of Catholic clergymen in the Reichsgau Wartheland were at some point arrested and detained in a prison or camp. More than half were in concentration camps. Well more than one-third died during the occupation.[1]

Statistics on the number of clergy incarcerated or killed is, of course, only one measure of the church's experience under Nazi control. Church communities were decimated by military deaths, massacres of civilians, deportations to camps, forced labor in the Altreich or elsewhere in occupied Poland, malnutrition, and disease. Every parish in what had been the Reichsgau Wartheland had its own postwar account of immeasurable human tragedy. The material losses, if not as grievous, were immense as well. Nearly all (some 97 percent) of churches, chapels, and shrines had been closed or destroyed during the occupation.[2] The loss of church property and resources through requisition, confiscation, plunder, and war was incalculable. Countless church institutions—schools, seminaries, publishers, hospitals, orphanages, service agencies for the vulnerable—had been dissolved or destroyed. And combined with this human and material destruction was, of course, the moral and spiritual devastation brought about by the war, occupation, and Holocaust in the Polish lands.

The foregoing analysis has shown how National Socialism's hostility to Christianity was provided a testing ground in occupied Poland in 1939 and how it reached its apex in the Reichsgau Wartheland in the years that followed. The Warthegau was where the regime's basic anticlerical animus met the frontier opportunities associated with the "German East"; where Arthur Greiser's authoritarianism and administrative ambition, backed by the Nazi leadership, found fertile ground for testing radical antichurch policies and measures that some hoped to implement in the Altreich after the war; where the Nazi regime's anxiety over Polish conspiracy and resistance removed from the public arena what for many Poles was their only forum for community association—the Catholic Church; where hostility toward Polish Catholicism met the aggressively transformative priorities of Germanization in the "model Gau"; where cultural Germanization merged with the regime's racial imperatives—imperatives that demanded not only the destruction of Jews but also the displacement of ethnic Poles or, at the very least, their strict segregation from Germans in so many aspects of private and public life, including religious life.

The Reichsgau Wartheland offered opportunity, means, and motive for the implementation of this radical and destructive Kirchenpolitik. First, the opportunities in this "virgin territory" of the "German East" were great. Although only two hundred kilometers from Berlin, it remained a place apart, an experimental field free from many of the strictures of state administration and bureaucracy. With greater freedom from the control of Berlin ministries, the Warthegau could, to a great extent, chart its own course for Germanization. Free from the purview of the German episcopate and the Vatican, and bound to neither the concordat with Poland nor with Nazi Germany, Greiser and his staff could pursue their agenda without fear of significant or effective resistance from the church hierarchy. And in a Warthegau overwhelmingly populated by Poles, they could enact policies relatively free from concern about German public opinion or adverse reactions on the part of German Catholics.

Second, the Wartheland provided the means for aggressive implementation of measures against the Polish church. An administrator both cruel and ambitious, Arthur Greiser was intent on waging the Volkstumskampf with vigor and brutality. The merger of the dual roles of Gauleiter and Reichsstatthalter only brought him closer to this goal, and under his leadership, ideological, executive, and administrative authority were centralized in his single office. Greiser enjoyed good relations with members of the Nazi elite and strong party support for his measures against the church, and at the same time, had at his disposal an extensive administration, bureaucracy, and police apparatus. Often ideologically committed and aggressively anti-Polish, many of the Warthegau's Reichsdeutsche and Volksdeutsche proved willing and efficient executors of the Gauleiter's policies.

Third, with respect to motives, it is clear that from the start the Mustergau Wartheland was intended to showcase any variety of innovative initiatives, the most pressing and destructive of which was the broad program of Germanization, which was particularly challenging in a region that was overwhelmingly Polish. Kirchenpolitik was a constituent aspect of that program, especially as it was directed against the Catholic Church. As a religious faith and institution, Roman Catholicism was international, interethnic, and intercultural. In the Reichsgau Wartheland it was Polish, which made it intolerable to the National Socialists. They persecuted it on many levels, and of all the diverse aspects of Warthegau Kirchenpolitik, segregation of Poles and Germans remained essential to the regime's anti-Polish and antichurch agenda and was consistently enforced through the end of the occupation. The Gau authorities eventually permitted what they regarded as a vestige of the institutional "Polish" church, and some even saw value in maintaining it for a time, but that church was to remain separate and distinct from the vestigial "German" Roman Catholic "religious association" established in the fall of 1941. As the Red Army approached from the east, Greiser's office made more church buildings available, but there was no question of letting Germans and Poles share those spaces for worship or any other confessional activities. "The separation of the peoples is the prerequisite for the strengthening of one's own people,"[3] the Gauleiter stated in a November 1944 article. Reminiscent of the ideological rigor and aggressive optimism of 1939, Greiser's words were published only weeks before he and his administration would flee Poznań before advancing Soviet forces.

Ideological rigor prevailed when it came to the segregation policy, but other aspects of Nazi church policy varied over space and time. Application and enforcement of measures in the Warthegau, although often brutal, varied according to region, district, municipality and, not least, according to the sentiments and disposition of German bureaucrats, officials, and police. Arguably at its most violent in the first weeks and months of the occupation, persecution of the church culminated in the mass arrests of Catholic priests and closure of churches in the fall of 1941. For the next three years, the Gau authorities were consistent in their treatment of the remnant of the church that remained. In the waning months of the occupation, the regime showed a degree of flexibility—albeit a flexibility born of desperation—as it began to open churches and attempted, in vain, to court the favor and support of the Poznań auxiliary bishop and the exiled Polish primate.

The motives behind Nazi policy also changed over time. The regime's basic antagonism toward Catholicism was clear, but it was not the primary and decisive factor in developing and executing church policy in the Wartheland. The axiom that the Polish church was a mainstay of Polish national sentiment, agitation, and resistance was a pillar of the regime's policy throughout most of the occupation. As the tides of war and needs of the German economy changed, however, church policy in the Warthegau was increasingly determined by political and economic expediency, revealing that there were limits to what the Gau administration could, or chose, to accomplish. Despite the severity of their antichurch measures, there were some among the Nazi authorities who feared that too aggressive a stance vis-à-vis the church could alienate Catholics in the Altreich or elsewhere in Nazi-occupied Europe, or perhaps lead the papacy to abandon its stance of reserve toward the Third Reich's policies and crimes in occupied Poland. This prompts the question of what "too aggressive" might have meant, given that the National Socialists sent more than half of all Warthegau priests to concentration camps and closed 97 percent of all Catholic Churches designated as "Polish." And as it turned out, both the papacy and the Catholic hierarchy in the Altreich revealed a rather high tolerance for persecution of the Warthegau church, for neither explicitly, forcefully, and publicly condemned the Nazi regime or its actions.

Because of their reticence in the face of Nazi aggression and crimes, the German church and the papacy emerged from the Second World War as institutions compromised. Such was not the case for the Catholic Church in Poland, which had survived more than five years of Nazi occupation and emerged in 1945 an institution with significant moral capital and, in the eyes of some, an institution morally and spiritually stronger and more prepared for the challenges it would face ahead. As stated in the introduction, the purpose of this study has not been to ennoble the Warthegau church or to extol its endurance or fortitude—or that of its adherents—in the face of persecution. It is, however, appropriate to consider at a basic level the extent to which National Socialism succeeded or failed in its goals and policies, how the church and its adherents responded, and how their responses may have provided certain lessons and models for the future.

In occupied Poland, the Nazi regime set out to destroy Roman Catholic institutions—religious orders, organizations, social service agencies, schools, and the like. While this may have been a short-term success—all such organizations were, in fact, dissolved in the Reichsgau Wartheland—in the long term, the policy failed. After the war, most Catholic institutions would be restored, only to suffer again under communism, but most institutional structures and organizations of the church would prosper in the long run, whether despite or because of the strictures imposed by the communist government of the Polish People's Republic.

Greiser's administration was also committed to neutralizing the Warthegau clergy in their roles as spiritual guides and standard-bearers of national identity. This was largely accomplished by deporting and incarcerating priests and by killing them, and the statistics cited above attest to the effectiveness of this policy in the short term. Again, however, the church would reopen its seminaries and theological faculties after the war, and a new generation of clergymen would take the place of those lost during the occupation. Encumbered by the policies of the Polish People's Republic, that process would, however, take decades.

National Socialism also proved unsuccessful in its goal of undermining Polish nationalism via measures against the Catholic Church. German officials sometimes claimed that the removal of priests and closing of churches had rendered the Poles docile and passive, but evidence for this is anecdotal at best. There is also little evidence that the Catholic Church as an institution was a clear motive force or catalyst for anti-Nazi resistance in the conventional sense, but it certainly did function as a locus of identity, solidarity, and defiance, if at times only in implicit ways. One might not associate attendance at Mass, participation in a burial service, or partaking of the sacraments with anti-Nazi resistance, but these were nonetheless gestures that were social and, although legal, in their own way also clearly opposed to the secular, exploitive, and racialized anti-Polish ideologies of the occupation regime and its program of Germanization.

The regime also failed in its goal of developing a model for the postwar Reich. Legal and administrative measures imposed on the church in the Reichsgau Wartheland were never applied in the Altreich, and the German clergy as a whole never suffered the persecution and brutalities of their counterparts in the Warthegau. The secular authority of National Socialism had aimed to develop in the Mustergau Wartheland a template for the dissolution and demise of the churches in the Third Reich of the future. Instead, the experience of the years 1939–1945 may have provided the Polish church with a template of its own for perseverance and even prosperity in the challenging decades that followed, as it drew on not only its theological and structural traditions but also on impulses that emerged under the German occupation—the church's patriotic disposition, lay activism, oppositional inclinations, or, more broadly, what many regarded as the church's moral authority over temporal power.

Notes

1. The statistics here are provided in Kłoczowski, Müllerowa, and Skarbek, *Zarys dziejów*, 357–58, and Śmigiel, "Duchowieństwo Polskie," 140.
2. Kłoczowski, Müllerowa, and Skarbek, *Zarys dziejów*, 350.
3. Arthur Greiser, "Gedanken zur nationalsozialistischen Volkstumspolitik," n.d., YV, TR.17-12309, 4068282, 663. The article is not dated but is marked as having been received by the Wolsztyn (Wollstein) local commissioner on December 9, 1944, and is described as a reprint of an article from November of that year.

BIBLIOGRAPHY

Archival Collections

Archiwum Akt Nowych, Warsaw (AAN)

Zespół 493/Konsulat Gen.-Nowy York.
Zespół 495.
Zespół 497.

Archiwum Archidiecezjalne w Gnieźnie, Gniezno (AAG)

Zespół 0131, AKM I.
Zespół 0164.
Zespół 2177, AKM I.

Archiwum Archidiecezjalne w Poznaniu, Poznań (AAP)

Zespół 133, OK 3.
OK 117.
OK 121.
OK 122.
OK 128.
OK 133.
OK 214.
OK 215.
OK 216.
OK 217.
OK 218.
OK 220.
OK 221.
OK 222.
OK 224.
OK 235.
OK 237.

Archiwum Diecezjalne we Włocławku, Włocławek (ADW)

Ankieta Strat Wojennych Diecezji Włocławskiej w l. 1939/45, przeprowadzona przez Archiwariusza Diecezjalnego w r. 1947, tom 1, tom 2.
Archiwum Kurii Diecezjalnej w Włocławku, Dział Personalny.

Archiwum Państwowe w Łodzi, Łódź

Zespół Akta Miasta Łodzi 32473.

Archiwum Panstwowe w Poznaniu, Poznań (APP)

Zespół 53/299/0/1.30/1186.
" 53/299/0/1.39/1832.
" 53/465/0/2/105.
" 53/1023/0/-/12.
" 53/1023/0/-/13.
" 299/0/1.39/1832.
" 299/1174.
" 299/1176/42.
" 299/1176/82.
" 299/1181.
" 299/1187.
" 299/1189.
" 299/1191.
" 301/273.
" 301/284.
" 301/285.
" 449.
" 452.
" 465.

Archiwum Zgromadzenia Sióstr Służebniczek Niepokalanego Poczęcia Najświętszej Maryi Panny, Luboń (AZSS)

M. Petronela Dyderska, manuscript, photocopy.
S. M. Loyola Sommerfeld sł. M., "Wspomnienia z Bojanowa," Manuscript, September 1, 1946.
Wspomnienia z obozu—Schmückert, n.d.
Wstęp—introduction to memoir collection.

Archiwum Zgromadzenia Sióstr Wspólnej Pracy od Niepokolanej Maryi, Włocławek (AZW)

Anna Zalewska to Naczelny Sąd Administracyjny, Ośrodek Zamiejscowy Wydz. II w Łodzi, May 22, 2001.
Oświadczenie Teresy Jakubka, October 5, 1980.
Oświadczenie Bernardy Sobańskiej, September 24, 1980.
Oświadczenie Jozefiny Styśkiej, September 25, 1980.
Zaświadczenie, Urząd Miasta i Gminy Bojanowo, August 26, 1999.
Życiorys Siostry Hilarii Bojakowskiej, December 12, 1999.
Życiorys Siostry Anny Agaty Zalewskiej, 2006.

Bundesarchiv Berlin (BAB)

R 43-II/150a.
R 43-II/170.
R 43 II/172.
R 43-II/178a.
R 58/1002.
R 58/7021.
R 58/7216.
R 58/7468.
R 58/7470.
R 58/7578.
R 58/7581.
R 70-Polen/252.
R 70/36.
R 70/83.
R 5101/22181.
R 5101/22185.
R 5101/22437.
R 5101/24038.

Institut für Zeitgeschichte, Munich (IfZ)

Broszat, Martin. "Verfolgung polnischer katholischer Geistlicher 1939–1945." Gutachten des Instituts für Zeitgeschichte, September 1959.
Fa 199/51.
Fb 53.
Fb 95/39.
Fb 125.
MA 544.
NO-1653.

Instytut Pamięci Narodowej–Komisja Ścigania Zbrodni przeciwko Narodowi Polskiemu, Łódź (IPN-Ł)

9/104.
11/255.

Instytut Pamięci Narodowej–Komisja Ścigania Zbrodni przeciwko Narodowi Polskiemu, Warsaw (IPN)

831/177.
BU 01283/1/J.
GK 62/19.
GK 62/126.
GK 62/153.

GK 62/166/CD.
GK 62/170.
GK 62/176/CD.
GK 62/180.
GK 62/182/CD.
GK 62/186/CD.
GK 62/187/CD.
GK 62/196/CD.
GK 62/197.
GK 62/200.
GK 62/202.
GK 62/208.
GK 62/210/CD.
GK 62/211/CD.
GK 62/214/CD.
GK 62/215/CD.
GK 62/218/CD.
GK 62/219/CD.
GK 62/222/CD.
GK 62/223/CD.
GK 62/225.
GK 70/36.
GK 70/44.
GK 70/48.
GK 70/52.
GK 70/56.
GK 70/73.
GK 71/6.
GK 162/55.
GK 162/468.
GK 162/558.
GK 174/30.
GK 196/11/CD.
GK 196/12/CD.
GK 196/13/CD.
GK 196/16/CD.
GK 196/19.
Gk 196/20.
GK 196/28.
GK 196/30.
GK 196/31/CD.
GK 196/34.
GK 196/37.
GK 196/38/CD 1.
GK 713/9.
GK 736/2.
GK 755/129.

GK 831/59.
GK 831/169.
GK 831/177.

Instytut Zachodni, Poznań (IZ)

Dokumenty I-129.
I-445.
I-903.
II-94.
II-123.
III-1.
III-27.
III-147.
Dział IV–Fotografie z lat 1939–1945.

National Archives, Kew (NAK)

GFM 33/744, Political Department III: Vatican: Relations with Poland, June 1936–February 1940.

Polish Institute and Sikorski Museum, London (PISM)

A.44.53-1.
A.44.122-20.
A.44.122-28, tom II.
A.44.122-30, 1943.

Polish Underground Movement Study Trust, London (PUMST)

Sprawozdanie sytuacyjne z kraju 1939–1941, tom 1.
Sprawozdanie sytuacyjne z kraju, tom II, Nr. 1–6, 1941–1942.

United States Holocaust Memorial Museum, Washington (USHMM)

RG 15.007M, Reel 15.
RG 15.007M, Reel 21.
RG 15.007M, Reel 38.
RG 15.007M, Reel 47.

Yad Vashem. World Holocaust Remembrance Center, International Institute for Holocaust Research, Jerusalem (YV)

M.10—Warsaw Ghetto Underground Archives.
M.49-ZIH.
TR.2, NG 4576, JM 2031.
TR.17.

Published Documents

Austria. *Gesetzblatt für das Land Österreich*. Wien: Staatsdruckerei Wien, 1939.

Beckmann, Joachim, ed. *Kirchliches Jahrbuch für die Evangelische Kirche in Deutschland, 1933–1944*. Gütersloh: C. Bertelsmann, 1948.

Friedländer, Saul. *Pius XII and the Third Reich: A Documentation*. Translated by Charles Fullman. New York: Octagon, 1980.

Germany, Auswärtiges Amt. *Dokumente zur Vorgeschichte des Krieges*, 1939, no. 2. Berlin: Reichsdruckerei, 1939.

Germany, Gauamt für Volkstumsfragen. *Wir und die Polen: Was jeder Einheitenführer vom Zusammenleben der Deutschen und Polen aus der Geschichte unseres Gaues wissen muß*. Posen: Führerdienst Gebiet Wartheland, 1943.

Gruber, Hubert, ed. *Katholische Kirche und Nationalsozialismus 1930–1945: ein Bericht in Quellen*. Paderborn: Ferdinand Schöningh, 2006.

Grünzinger, Gertraud, ed. *Dokumente zur Kirchenpolitik des Dritten Reiches: die Kirchenpolitik in den ein- und angegliederten Gebieten (März 1938–März 1945)*. Vol. 6, nos. 1–2, 1938–1945. Gütersloh: Gütersloher Verlagshaus, 2017.

Harvard Law School. Nuremberg Trials Project. Testimony of Leo Michalowski. December 21, 1946. Accessed February 11, 2018, via Harvard Law School, Nuremberg Trials Project. http://nuremberg.law.harvard.edu/transcripts/1-transcript-for-nmt-1-medical-case?seq=889&q=miochalowski.

Hlond, August. *The Persecution of the Catholic Church in German-Occupied Poland. Reports Presented by H. E. Cardinal Hlond, Vatican Broadcasts and Other Reliable Evidence*. New York: Longmans Green, 1941.

International Military Tribunal (IMT). *Trial of the Major War Criminals before the International Military Tribunal. Nuremberg 14 November 1945–1 October 1946*. 42 vols. Nuremberg: International Military Tribunal, 1945–1947.

Lehnstaedt, Stephan, and Jochen Böhler, eds. *Die Berichte der Einsatzgruppen aus Polen 1939*. Berlin: Metropol, 2013.

Łuczak, Czesław, ed. *Dyskryminacja Polaków w Wielkopolsce w okresie okupacji hitlerowskiej: wybór źródeł*. Poznań: Wydawnictwo Poznańskie, 1966.

———, ed. *Położenie ludności polskiej w tzw. Kraju Warty w okresie hitlerowskiej okupacji*. Vol. 13, Documenta Occupationis. Poznań: Instytut Zachodni, 1990.

Mallmann, Klaus-Michael, Jochen Böhler, and Jürgen Matthäus, eds. *Einsatzgruppen in Polen: Darstellung und Dokumentation*. Darmstadt: Wissenschaftliche Buchgesellschaft, 2008.

Mazur, Zbigniew, Aleksandra Pietrowicz, and Maria Rutowska, eds. *Raporty z ziem wcielonych do III Rzeszy (1942–1944)*. Vol. 20, Biblioteka Przeglądu Zachodniego. Poznań: Instytut Zachodni, 2004.

Nuernberg Military Tribunals (NMT). *Trials of War Criminals before the Nuernberg Military Tribunals under Control Council Law No. 10. Nuernberg, October 1946–April 1949*. 15 vols. Washington, DC: United States Government Printing Office, 1951.

Papée, Kazimierz. *Pius XII a Polska: Przemówienia, listy, komentarze*. Rzym: Editrice Studium, 1954.

Pospieszalski, Karol Marian, ed. *Hitlerowskie "prawo" okupacyjne w Polsc. Wybór dokumentów i próba syntezy*. Vol. 5, no. 1, Documenta Occupationis. Poznań: Instytut Zachodni, 1952.

Röhr, Werner, and Elke Heckert, eds. *Die faschistische Okkupationspolitik in Polen (1939–1945)*. Köln: Pahl-Rugenstein, 1989.

Schnabel, Reimund, ed. *Macht ohne Moral: eine Dokumentation über die SS*. Frankfurt am Main: Röderbergverlag, 1957.

Secrétairerie D'État de Sa Sainteté. *Le Saint Siège et la Situation religieuse en Pologne et dans les Pays Baltes 1939–1945*. Vol. 3, nos. 1 and 2, Actes et Documents du Saint-Siège Relatifs à la Seconde Guerre Mondiale. Città del Vaticano: Librera Editrice Vaticana, 1967.

United States Department of State. *Documents on German Foreign Policy 1918–1945*. Series D, vols. 12–13. Washington, DC: United States Government Printing Office, 1962.

Volk, Ludwig, ed. *Akten deutscher Bischöfe über die Lage der Kirche 1933–1945*. Vols. 5–6. Veröffentlichungen der Kommission für Zeitgeschichte. Series A, no. 34. Mainz: Matthias-Grünewald-Verlag, 1983.

Wietrzykowski, Albin. *Zbrodnie niemieckie w Żabikowe: zeznania-dokumenty*. Poznań: Nakładem Księgarni Wydawniczej w Poznaniu, 1946.

Newspapers, Magazines, and Serial Publications

Atheneum Kapłańskie
Biuletyn Głównej Komisji Badania Zbrodni Hitlerowskich w Polsce
Biuletyn Instytutu Pamięci Narodowej
Bulletin für Faschismus- und Weltkriegsforschung
Central European History
Chrześcijanin w Świecie
Commentary
Contemporary European History
Dachau Review
Dachauer Hefte
Gesetzblatt für das Land Österreich
Głos Pracy
Homo Dei
Journal of Contemporary History
Kronika Diecezji Włocławskiej
Kronika Miasta Poznania
L'Osservatore Romano
Miscellanea Historiae Ecclesiasticae
Nurt: Miesięcznik Społeczno-Kulturalny
Ostdeutscher Beobachter
The Polish Review
Posener Tageblatt
Przegląd Zachodni
Przewodnik Katolicki
Das Reich
Reichsgesetzblatt
Roczniki Historii Kościoła
Der Schulungsbrief
Seminare

Slavic Review
Studia Historiae Oeconomicae
Studia Historyczne
Studia nad Totalitaryzmami i Wiekeim XX-Totalitarian and 20th Century Studies
Studia Włocławskie
Verordnungsblatt des Reichsstatthalters im Warthegau
Vierteljahrshefte für Zeitgeschichte
Wartheland: Zeitschrift für Aufbau und Kultur im deutschen Osten
Wiadomości Polskie
Więź
Zagłada Żydów–Studia i Materiały
Die Zeit
Zeitschrift für Ostmitteleuropa-Forschung
Zeitschrift für Sozialgeschichte des 20. und 21. Jahrhunderts

Memoirs and Diaries

Bielerzewski, Ludwik. *Ksiądz nie zostaje sam. Wspomnienia*. Poznań, Poland: Księgarnia Św. Wojciecha, 1976.

Breitinger, Hilarius. *Als Deutschenseelsorger in Posen und im Warthegau 1934–1945: Erinnerungen*. Series A, vol. 36, Veröffentlichung der Kommission für Zeitgeschichte. Mainz: Mahttias-Grünewald-Verlag, 1984.

Fidelis, S. M. "Wspomnienie z obozu w Bojanowie." *Homo Dei* 18, no. 3–4 (1949): 460–62.

Goebbels, Joseph. *Die Tagebücher von Joseph Goebbels*. Edited by Elke Fröhlich. 32 vols. München: K. G. Saur, 1993–2008.

Groscurth, Helmuth. *Tagebücher eines Abwehroffiziers 1938–1940. Mit weiteren Documenten zur Militäropposition gegen Hitler*. Edited by Helmut Krausnick, Harold C. Deutsch, and Hildegard von Kotze. Vol. 19, Quellen und Darstellungen zur Zeitgeschichte. Stuttgart: Deutsche Verlags-Anstalt, 1970.

Halder, Franz. *The Halder War Diary, 1939–1942*. Edited by Charles Burdick and Hans-Adolf Jacobsen. Novato, CA: Presidio, 1988.

Hitler, Adolf. *Hitler's Table Talk 1941–1944: His Private Conversations*. Translated by Norman Cameron and R. H. Stevens. New York: Enigma, 2008.

Hohenstein, Alexander [Franz Heinrich Bock], *Wartheländisches Tagebuch aus den Jahren 1941/42*. Vol. 8, Veröffentlichungen des Instituts für Zeitgeschichte, Quellen und Darstellungen zur Zeitgeschichte. Stuttgart: Deutsche Verlags-Anstalt, 1961.

Katolicki Ośrodek Wydawniczy Veritas, ed. *Cudem ocaleni: wspomnienia z kacetów. Praca zbiorowa*. London: Katolicki Ośrodek Wydawniczy Veritas, 1981.

Levi, Primo. *The Drowned and the Saved*. New York: Summit, 1980.

Nawrowski, Ewaryst. *W szponach gestapo: Urywki z moich przeżyć w obozie Fort VII (Übergangslager S. S. Posen)*. Poznań: Muzeum Martyrologiczne w Żabikowie, 2008.

Rapalski, Stanisław. *Byłem w piekle: wspomnienia z Radogoszcza*. Łódź: Wydawnictwo Łódzkie, 1963.

Rosenberg, Alfred. *Das politische Tagebuch Alfred Rosenbergs, 1934/35 und 1939/40*. München: Deutscher Taschenbuch, 1964.

Rost, Nico. *Goethe in Dachau*. Berlin: Volk und Welt, 1999.

——. *Goethe in Dachau: Literatuur en Werkelijkheid*, Amsterdam: L. J. Veen's Uitgeversmaatschappij N.V., 1948.

Siegmund, Harry. *Rückblick: Erinnerungen eines Staatsdieners in bewegter Zeit*. Raisdorf: Ostsee, 1999.

Tittman, Harold. *Inside the Vatican of Pius XII: The Memoir of an American Diplomat During World War II*. New York: Doubleday, 2004.

Weizsäcker, Ernst von. *Memoirs of Ernst von Weizsäcker*. Translated by John Andrews. London: Victor Gollancz, Ltd., 1951.

Zámečník, Stanislav. *That Was Dachau 1933–1945*. Paris: Fondation internationale de Dachau/le cherche midi, 2004.

Books, Book Chapters, and Articles

Abramczuk, Olga. "Magdalenki." In *Życie religijne w Polsce pod okupacją hitlerowską 1939–1945*, edited by Zygmunt Zieliński, 858–80. Warszawa: Ośrodek Dokumentacji i Studiów Społecznych, 1982.

Adamska, Jolanta. *Reżimy totalitarne wobec duchownych kościołów chrześcijańskich okupowanej Polski 1939–1945*. Warszawa: Rada Ochrony Pamięci Walk i Męczeństwa, 2008.

Adamska, Jolanta and Jan Sziling. *Man to Man . . . : Destruction of the Polish Intelligentsia in the Years 1939–1945. Mauthausen/Gusen*. Warszawa: Rada Ochrony Pamięci Walk i Męczeństwa, 2009.

——. *Polscy księża w niemieckich obozach koncentracyjnych: transport 527 duchownych 13 grudnia 1940 r. z Sachsenhausen do Dachau*. Warszawa: Rada Ochrony Pamięci Walk i Męczeństwa, 2007.

Alberti, Michael. *Die Verfolgung und Vernichtung der Juden im Reichsgau Wartheland 1939–1945*. Vol. 17, Deutsches Historisches Institut Warschau, Quellen und Studien. Wiesbaden: Harrassowitz, 2006.

——. "'Exerzierplatz des Nationalsozialismus': Der Reichsgau Wartheland 1939–1941." In *Genesis des Genozids: Polen 1939–1941*, edited by Klaus-Michael Mallmann and Bogdan Musial, 111–26. Darmstadt: Wissenschaftliche Buchgesellschaft, 2004.

Alvis, Robert E. *Religion and the Rise of Nationalism: A Profile of an East-Central European City*. Syracuse, NY: Syracuse University Press, 2005.

——. *White Eagle, Black Madonna: One Thousand Years of the Polish Catholic Tradition*. New York: Fordham University Press, 2016.

Arani, Miriam Y. *Fotografische Selbst- und Fremdbilder von Deutschen und Polen im Reichsgau Wartheland 1939–1945, Unter besonderer Berücksichtigung der Region Wielkopolska*, 2 vols. Hamburg: Dr. Kovac, 2008.

Bajohr, Frank. "Gauleiter in Hamburg: Zur Person und Tätigkeit Karl Kaufmanns." *Vierteljahrshefte für Zeitgeschichte* 43, no. 2 (April 1995): 267–95.

Bankier, David, Dan Michman, and Ieal Nidam-Orvieto, eds. *Pius XII and the Holocaust: Current State of Research*. Jerusalem: Yad Vashem, 2012.

Bartoń, Władysław. "Życie lądzkich więźniów (wspomnienia ks. W. Bartonia SDB)." In Jarosław Wąsowicz. *Lądzcy męczennicy: obóz dla duchowieństwa w Lądzie n/Wartą styczeń 1940–październik 1941*, 52–61. Ląd: WSD Towarzystwa Salezjańskiego w Lądzie, 2013.

Bejze, Bohdan, and Antoni Galiński, eds. *Martyrologia duchowieństwa polskiego 1939–1956*. Lódź: Archidiecezjalne Wydawnictwo Łódzkie, 1993.

Berben, Paul. *Dachau 1933–1945: The Official History.* London: Comité International de Dachau, 1980.

Bergen, Doris L. *Twisted Cross: The German Christian Movement in the Third Reich.* Chapel Hill: University of North Carolina Press, 1996.

———. *War and Genocide: A Concise History of the Holocaust.* Lanham, MD: Rowman and Littlefield, 2016.

Bernacki, Zbigniew, ed. *Święty Wojciech 997–1947: księga pamiątkowa.* Gniezno: Wydawnictwo Kurii Metropolitalnej w Gnieźnie, 1947.

Biskupski, M. B. *The History of Poland.* Westport, CT: Greenwood, 2000.

Biskupski, Stefan. *Księża polscy w niemieckich obozach koncentracynych.* London: F. Mildner and Sons, 1946.

———. "Męczeńskie biskupstwo księdza Michała Kozala." *Atheneum Kapłańskie* 45, nos. 1–2 (August–September 1946): 42–66.

Bjork, James E. *Neither German nor Pole: Catholicism and National Indifference in a Central European Borderland.* Ann Arbor: University of Michigan Press, 2008.

Blet, Pierre. *Pius XII and the Second World War According to the Archives of the Vatican.* Translated by L. J. Johnson. New York: Paulist, 1999.

Blobaum, Robert, ed. *Antisemitism and Its Opponents in Modern Poland.* Ithaca, NY: Cornell University Press, 2005.

Böhler, Jochen. *Auftakt zum Vernichtungskrieg: die Wehrmacht in Polen 1939.* Frankfurt am Main: Fischer Taschenbuch, 2006.

Bömelburg, Hans-Jürgen, and Bogdan Musial. "Die deutsche Besatzungspolitik in Polen 1939–1945." In *Deutsch-polnische Beziehungen 1939–1945–1949: eine Einführung*, edited by Włodzimierz Borodziej and Klaus Ziemer, 43–111. Vol. 5, Einzelveröffentlichungen des Deutschen Historischen Instituts Warschau. Osnabrück: Fibre, 2000.

Borodziej, Włodimierz, and Klaus Ziemer, eds. *Deutsch-polnische Beziehungen 1939–1945–1949: eine Einführung.* Vol. 5, Einzelveröffentlichungen des Deutschen Historischen Instituts Warschau. Osnabrück: Fibre, 2000.

Braun, Hannelore, and Gertraud Grünzinger. *Personenlexikon zum deutschen Protestantismus.* Göttingen: Vandenhoeck und Ruprecht, 2006.

Brechenmacher, Thomas, and Harry Oelke. *Die Kirchen und die Verbrechen im nationalsozialistischen Staat.* Vol. 11, Dachauer Symposien zur Zeitgeschichte. Göttingen: Wallstein, 2011.

Breitman, Richard. *The Architect of Genocide: Himmler and the Final Solution.* New York: Knopf, 1991.

Brewing, Daniel. *Im Schatten von Auschwitz: deutsche Massaker an polnischen Zivilisten 1939–1945.* Vol. 29, Veröffentlichungen der Forschungsstelle Ludwigsburg der Universität Stuttgart. Darmstadt: Wissenschaftliche Buchgesellschaft, 2016.

Broniarz-Press, Lubomira, and Marian Woźniak. "Jóźwiak Czesław." In *Encyklopedia konspiracji Wielkopolskiej 1939–1945*, edited by Marian Woźniak, 237. Poznań: Instytut Zachodni, 1998.

Broszat, Martin. *Nationalsozialistische Polenpolitik.* Frankfurt am Main: Fischer Bücherei, 1961.

———. *Zweihundert Jahre deutsche Polenpolitik.* Frankfurt am Main: Suhrkamp, 1972.

Browning, Christopher R. *Nazi Policy, Jewish Workers, German Killers.* Cambridge: Cambridge University Press, 2000.

———. *Remembering Survival: Inside a Nazi Slave-Labor Camp*. New York: W. W. Norton, 2011.

Browning, Christopher R., and Jürgen Matthäus. *The Origins of the Final Solution: The Evolution of Nazi Jewish Policy, September 1939–March 1942*. Lincoln: University of Nebraska Press, 2004.

Bryant, Chad. *Prague in Black: Nazi Rule and Czech Nationalism*. Cambridge, MA: Harvard University Press, 2007.

Budziarek, Marek. "Diecezja łódzka podczas okupacji hitlerowskiej." *Więź* 20, no. 3 (1977): 64–75.

———. "Geneza, przebieg i następstwa masowych aresztowań duchownych katolickich 5–7 października 1941 roku (ze szczególnym uwzględnieniem diecezji łódzkiej)." In *Martyrologia duchowieństwa polskiego 1939–1956*, edited by Bohdan Bejze and Antoni Galiński, 34–57. Lódź: Archidiecezjalne Wydawnictwo Łódzkie, 1993.

———. *Katedra przy Adolfhitlerstrasse: z dziejów Kościoła katolickiego w Łodzi 1939–1945*. Warszawa: Instytut Wydawniczy Pax, 1984.

———. "Zarząd i organizacja diecezji Łódzkiej 1939–1945." In *Kościół katolicki na ziemiach Polski w czasie II Wojny Światowej: Materiały i Studia*, vol. 7, no. 3, edited by Franciszek Stopniak, 266–322. Warszawa: Akademia Teologii Katolickiej, 1978.

Burleigh, Michael. *Germany Turns Eastward: A Study of* Ostforschung *in the Third Reich*. Cambridge: Cambridge University Press, 1988.

———. *The Third Reich: A New History*. New York: Hill and Wang, 2001.

Caplan, Jane, and Nikolaus Wachsmann, eds. *Concentration Camps in Nazi Germany: The New Histories*. London: Routledge, 2010.

Chadwick, Owen. *Britain and the Vatican during the Second World War*. Cambridge: Cambridge University Press, 1986.

Chruścielski, Piotr, and Marcin Owsiński, eds. *Konferencja: "Od Westerplatte do Norymbergi. Druga wojna światowa we współczesnej historiografii, muzealnictwie i edukacji" w Muzeum Stutthof (2–5 września 2009 r.)*. Sztutowo, Poland: Muzeum Stutthof, 2009.

Cienciała, Anna M. "The Foreign Policy of Józef Piłsudski and Józef Beck: Misconceptions and Misinterpretations." *The Polish Review* 56, no. 1–2 (2011): 111–51.

Clauss, Manfred. *Die Beziehungen des Vatikans zu Polen während des II. Weltkrieges*. Vol. 11, Bonner Beiträge zur Kirchengeschichte. Köln: Böhlau, 1979.

Conway, John S. *The Nazi Persecution of the Churches, 1933–1945*. London: Weidenfeld and Nicholson, 1968.

Conway, Martin. *Catholic Politics in Europe 1918–1945*. New York: Routledge, 1997.

Coppa, Frank J. *The Life and Pontificate of Pope Pius XII: Between History and Controversy*. Washington, DC: Catholic University of America Press, 2013.

Datner, Szymon. *Crimes Committed by the Wehrmacht during the September Campaign and the Period of Military Government*. Poznań: Instytut Zachodni, 1962.

Davies, Norman. *God's Playground: A History of Poland*. 2 vols. New York: Columbia University Press, 1982.

Dembski, Krzysztof. "Adamski Stanisław." In *Wielkopolski słownik biograficzny*, edited by Antoni Gąsiorowski and Jerzy Topolski, 19–20. Poznań: Państwowe Wydawnictwo Naukowe, 1981.

Dębowska, Krystyna. "Les congrégations féminines religieuses en Pologne au cours des années 1939–1945 (données statistiques fondamentales)." *Miscellanea Historiae*

Ecclesiasticae 9, Bibliothèque de la revue d'histoire ecclésiastique, no. 70. Bruxelles: Nauwelaerts, 1984: 370–72.

Dierker, Wolfgang. *Himmlers Glaubenskrieger: der Sicherheitsdienst der SS und seine Religionspolitik, 1933–1941*. Series B, vol. 92, Veröffentlichungen der Kommisssion für Zeitgeschichte. Paderborn: Ferdinand Schöningh, 2003.

"Discussion Forum: Richard Steigmann-Gall's 'The Holy Reich.'" *Journal of Contemporary History* 42, no. 1 (January 2007): 5–78.

Domagała, Jan. *Ci, którzy przeszli przez Dachau: duchowni w Dachau*. Warszawa: Pax, 1957.

Duda, Henryk. *Nonnenlager Schmückert. Obóz sióstr zakonnych w Bojanowie*. Vol. 1, Skice Bojanowskie. Bojanowo: Urząd Miasta i Gminy w Bojanowie, 1999.

Ebbinghaus, Angelika, and Karl Heinz Roth. "Vorläufer des Generalplans Ost. Eine Dokumentation über Theodor Schieders Polendenkschrift vom 7. Oktober 1939." *Zeitschrift für Sozialgeschichte des 20. und 21. Jahrhunderts* 7, no. 1 (1999): 62–94.

Eckert, Eike. "Gotthold Rhode." In *Handbuch der völkischen Wissenschaften: Personen, Institutionen, Forschungsprogramme, Stiftungen*, edited by Ingo Haar and Michael Fahlbusch, 589–92. München: K. G. Saur, 2008.

Engelking, Barbara. *Such a Beautiful Sunny Day . . . : Jews Seeking Refuge in the Polish Countryside, 1942–1945*. Jerusalem: Yad Vashem, 2016.

Engelking, Barbara, and Jan Grabowski, eds. *Dalej jest noc: losy Żydów w wybranych powiatach okupowanej Polski*, 2 vols. Warszawa: Stowarzyszenie Centrum Badań nad Zagłada Żydów, 2018.

Epstein, Catherine. *Model Nazi: Arthur Greiser and the Occupation of Western Poland*. Oxford: Oxford University Press, 2010.

Ericksen, Robert P. *Complicity in the Holocaust: Churches and Universities in Nazi Germany*. Cambridge: Cambridge University Press, 2012.

———. *Theologians under Hitler*. New Haven, CT: Yale University Press, 1985.

Ericksen, Robert P., and Susannah Heschel, eds. *Betrayal: German Churches and the Holocaust*. Minneapolis: Fortress, 1999.

Evans, Richard. "Nazism, Christianity and Political Religion: A Debate," *Journal of Contemporary History* 42, no. 1 (2007): 5–7.

———. *The Third Reich in Power*. New York: Penguin, 2005.

Falconi, Carlo. *The Silence of Pius XII*. Boston: Little, Brown, 1970.

Fijałkowski, Zenon. *Kościół katolicki na ziemiach polskich w latach okupacji hitlerowskiej*. Warszawa: Książka i Wiedza, 1983.

Frącek, Teresa. "Franciszkanki Rodziny Maryi." In *Życie religijne w Polsce pod okupacją hitlerowską 1939–1945*, edited by Zygmunt Zieliński, 821–57. Warszawa: Ośrodek Dokumentacji i Studiów Społecznych, 1982.

Frątczak, Wojciech. *Biskup Michał Kozal: życie-męczeństwo-kult*. Włocławek: Wydawnictwo Duszpasterstwa Rolników, 2009.

———. *Diecezja włocławskiej w okresie II wojny światowej*. Włocławek: Wydawnictwo Duszpasterstwa Rolników, 2013.

———. "Listy obozowe biskupa Michała Kozała." *Atheneum Kapłańskie* 472 (1987): 532–38.

Friedlander, Henry. *The Origins of Nazi Genocide: From Euthanasia to the Final Solution*. Chapel Hill: University of North Carolina Press, 1995.

Friedrich, Klaus-Peter. "Collaboration in a 'Land without a Quisling': Patterns of Cooperation with the Nazi German Occupation Regime in Poland during World War II." *Slavic Review* 64, no. 4 (winter 2005): 711–46.

Frieling, Christian. *Priester aus dem Bistum Münster im KZ: 38 Biographien*. Münster: Aschendorff, 1992.

Gailus, Manfred. *Protestantismus und Nationalsozialismus: Studien zur nationalsozialistischen Durchdringung des protestantischen Sozialmilieus in Berlin*. Köln: Böhlau, 2001.

Galiński, Antoni, and Marek Budziarek, eds. *Akcje okupanta hitlerowskiego wobec Kościoła katolickiego w Kraju Warty*. Łódź: Okregowa Komisja Badania Zbrodni Przeciwko Narodowi Polskiemu w Łodzi–Instytut Pamięci Narodowej/Muzeum Historii Miasta Łodzi, 1997.

"Die Gaugebiete des Reiches: Fläche und Bevölkerungsziffer des Reichsgaues Wartheland." *Ostdeutscher Beobachter*, March 23, 1941, 4.

Gąsiorowski, Antoni, and Jerzy Topolski, eds. *Wielkopolski słownik biograficzny*. Poznań: Państwowe Wydawnictwo Naukowe, 1981.

Glemp, Józef. "Zabłocki Mateusz." In *Wielkopolski słownik biograficzny*, edited by Antoni Gąsiorowski and Jerzy Topolski, 855. Poznań: Państwowe Wydawnictwo Naukowe, 1981.

Główna Komisja Badania Zbrodni Hitlerowskich w Polsce–Rada Ochrony Pomników Walki i Męczeństwa. *Obozy hitlerowskie na ziemiach polskich 1939–1945—Informator encyklopedyczny*. Edited by Czesław Pilichowski, Jolanta Adamska, Józef Frieske, Magdalena Kunicka-Wyrzykowska, Jan Laskowski, Kazimierz Lesczyński, Halina Maj-Popek, Maria Motyl, and Zofia Tokarz. Warszawa: Państwowe Wydawnictwo Naukowe, 1979.

Goebbels, Joseph. "Der kulturelle Aufbau im Osten wird vom Gesamtreich getragen-Ansprache zur Eröffnung des Reichsgautheaters Posen, gehalten im Großen Haus am 18. März 1941." *Wartheland: Zeitschrift für Aufbau und Kultur im deutschen Osten* 1, no. 4 (April 1941): 1–3.

Gołos, Jerzy, Agnieszka Kasprzak-Miler, Tomasz Łuczak, and Przemysław Nadolski. *Straty wojenne: Zabytkowe dzwony utracone w latach 1939–1945 w granicach Polski po 1945 roku (z wyłączeniem ziem należących przed 1939 rokiem do Rzeszy Niemieckiej)*. Vol. 2 (woj. poznańskie). *Wartime Losses: Historic Bells Lost between 1939–1945 within Post 1945 Borders of Poland (Except Those from Regions beyond the Pre-1939 Polish-German Border)*. Vol. 2 (The Poznań Voivodship). Polskie Dziedzictwo Kulturalne, Seria A. Straty kultury polskiej. Polish Cultural Heritage, Series A, Losses of Polish Culture. Poznań: Ministerstwo Kultury i Dziedziectwa Narodowego, Departament do spraw Polskiego Dziedzictwa Kulturowego za Granicą, 2006.

Grabowski, Jan. *Hunt for the Jews: Betrayal and Murder in German-Occupied Poland*. Bloomington: Indiana University Press, 2013.

Graham, Robert A. *The Pope and Poland in World War Two*. London: Veritas, 1968.

Greiser, Arthur. "Der Aufbau im Warthegau," *Der Schulungsbrief* 8, no. 5/6 (1941): 68–73.

———. *Der Aufbau im Osten*. Jena: Gustav Fischer, 1942.

———. "Schmelztiegel Warthegau: Wege der Neubesiedlung im Osten," *Das Reich* 22 (October 20, 1940): 10.

Gross, Jan Tomasz. *Neighbors: The Destruction of the Jewish Community of Jedwabne, Poland*. Princeton, NJ: Princeton University Press, 2001.

Gruner, Wolf, and Jörg Osterloh, eds. *The Greater German Reich and the Jews: Nazi Persecution Policies in the Annexed Territories 1935–1945*. Translated by Bernard Heise. New York: Berghahn, 2015.

Gürtler, Paul. *Nationalsozialismus und evangelische Kirchen im Warthegau: Trennung von Staat und Kirche im nationalsozialistischen Weltanschauungsstaat*. Göttingen: Vandenhoeck und Ruprecht, 1958.

Haar, Ingo. *Historiker im Nationalsozialismus: Deutsche Geschichtswissenschaft und der 'Volkstumskampf' im Osten*. Vol. 143, Kritische Studien zur Geschichtswissenschaft. Göttingen: Vandenhoeck und Ruprecht, 2000.

———. "German *Ostforschung* and Anti-Semitism." In *German Scholars and Ethnic Cleansing 1919–1945*, edited by Ingo Haar and Michael Fahlbusch, 1–27. New York: Berghahn, 2005.

Haar, Ingo, and Michael Fahlbusch, eds. *Handbuch der völkischen Wissenschaften: Personen, Institutionen, Forschungsprogramme, Stiftungen*. München: K.G. Saur, 2008.

Hagen, William W. *Germans, Poles, and Jews: The Nationality Conflict in the Prussian East, 1772–1914*. Chicago: University of Chicago Press, 1980.

Harvey, Elizabeth. *Women and the Nazi East: Agents and Witnesses of Germanization*. New Haven, CT: Yale University Press, 2003.

Herbert, Ulrich, Karin Orth, and Christoph Dieckmann, eds. *Die nationalsozialistischen Konzentrationslager–Entwicklung und Struktur.* Vol. 2. Göttingen: Wallstein, 1998.

Heschel, Susannah. *The Aryan Jesus: Christian Theologians and the Bible in Nazi Germany*. Princeton, NJ: Princeton University Press, 2008.

Hilberg, Raul. *The Destruction of the European Jews*. Vol. 3. New Haven, CT: Yale University Press, 2003.

Hildebrandt, Klaus. *The Foreign Policy of the Third Reich*. Translated by Anthony Fothergill. Berkeley: University of California Press, 1973.

Hinkel, Sascha. "'Vielleicht werden Kirchenhistoriker in hundert Jahren über mich auch so urteilen; dabei habe ich nur das Beste gewollt'. Adolf Kardinal Bertram im Spiegel neuer Forchsungsergebnisse." In *Die Kirchen und die Verbrechen im nationalsozialistischen Staat*, edited by Thomas Brechenmacher and Harry Oelke, 201–18. Vol. 11, Dachauer Symposien zur Zeitgeschichte. Göttingen: Wallstein, 2011.

Hirschfeld, Gerhard, ed. *The Policies of Genocide: Jews and Soviet Prisoners of War in Nazi Germany*. London: Allen and Unwin, 1986.

Hlond, August. *The Persecution of the Catholic Church in German-Occupied Poland. Reports Presented by H. E. Cardinal Hlond, Vatican Broadcasts and Other Reliable Evidence*. New York: Longmans Green, 1941.

Hoffmann, Bedrich. *And Who Will Kill You: The Chronicle of the Life and Sufferings of Priests in the Concentration Camps*. Poznań: Pallottinum, 1994.

Huener, Jonathan. *Auschwitz, Poland, and the Politics of Commemoration, 1945–1979*. Athens: Ohio University Press, 2003.

———. "Nazi *Kirchenpolitik* and Polish Catholicism in the Reichsgau Wartheland, 1939–1941." *Central European History* 47 (2014): 105–37.

———. "Polityka Niemiec wobec Kościoła i polskiego Kościoła katolickiego w diecezji Kraju Warty i łódzkiej." In *Łódź pod okupacją 1939–1945: Studia i szkice*, edited by Tomasz Toborek and Michał Trębacz, 311–40. Vol. 45, Biblioteka Oddziału Instytutu Pamięci Narodowej w Łodzi. Łódź: Instytut Pamięci Narodowej, 2018.

Iwanicki, Ryszard, Grażyna Janaszek, and Andrzej Rukowiecki. *A Book of Łódź Martyrdom: A Guide to Radogoszcz and Sites of National Remembrance*. Łódź: Museum of the Independence Traditions in Łódź, 2005.

Jacewicz, Wiktor, and Jan Woś, eds. *Martyrologium polskiego duchowieństwa rzymskokatolickiego pod okupacją hitlerowską w latach 1939–1945*. 5 vols. Warszawa: Akademia Teologii Katolickiej, 1977–1981.

———, eds. *Martyrologium polskiego duchowieństwa rzymskokatolickiego pod okupacją hitlerowską w latach 1939–1945, Straty osobowe*. Vol. 2, no. 1, Kościół katolicki na ziemiach Polski w czasie II Wojny Światowej. Warszawa: Akademia Teologii Katolickiej, 1977.

Jaeger, Harald, and Hermann Rumschöttel. "Das Forschungsprojekt 'Widerstand und Verfolgung in Bayern 1933–1945.'"*Archivalische Zeitschrift* 73, no. 1 (December 1977): 209–20.

Jankowska, Teresa. *Gotowi na wszystko: poznańska piątka salezjańska*. Warszawa: Fidei, 2010.

Jastrząb, Łukasz. *Archidiecezja Poznańska w latach okupacji hitlerowskiej 1939–1945*. Poznań: Uniwersytet im. Adama Mickiewicza w Poznaniu, Wydział Teologiczny, 2012.

Jędraś, Stanisław. *Miasto i Gmina Bojanowo*. Leszno: Nakładem Gminy Bojanowo, 2005.

Jędrzejczak, Maria. "Siostry Wspólnej Pracy." In *Życie religijne w Polsce pod okupacją hitlerowską 1939–1945*, edited by Zygmunt Zieliński, 893–904. Warszawa: Ośrodek Dokumentacji i Studiów Społecznych, 1982.

John, Jürgen, Horst Möller, and Thomas Schaarschmidt, eds. *Die NS-Gaue: regionale Mittelinstanzen im zentralistischen "Führerstaat."* München: R. Oldenbourg, 2007.

Kaczmarek, Ryszard. "Zwischen Altreich und Grenzgebiet: der Gau Oberschlesien 1939/41–1945." In *Die NS-Gaue: regionale Mittelinstanzen im zentralistischen "Führerstaat,"* edited by Jürgen John, Horst Möller, and Thomas Schaarschmidt, 348–60. München: R. Oldenbourg, 2007.

Karp, Hans-Jürgen, and Joachim Köhler, eds. *Katholische Kirche unter nationalsozialistischer und kommunistischer Diktatur: Deutschland und Polen 1939–1989*. Köln: Böhlau, 2001.

Kaźmierczak. Łukasz. "Do zobaczenia w niebie." *Przewodnik Katolicki*, August 19, 2007: 33–41.

Kempner, Benedicta Maria. *Nonnen unter dem Hakenkreuz*. Würzburg: Johann Wilhelm Naumannn, 1979.

Kepplinger, Brigitte, Gerhart Marckhgott, and Hartmut Reese, eds. *Tötungsanstalt Hartheim*. Vol. 3, Oberösterreich in der Zeit des Nationalsozialismus. Linz: Oberösterreichischen Landesarchiv/Lern- und Gedenkort Schloss Hartheim, 2008.

Kershaw, Ian. "Arthur Greiser–ein Motor der 'Endlösung.'" In *Die Braune Elite II. 21 weitere biographische Skizzen*, edited by Ronald M. Smelser and Rainer Zitelmann, 116–27. Darmstadt: Wissenschaftliche Buchgesellschaft, 1993.

———. *The Nazi Dictatorship: Problems and Perspectives of Interpretation*. New York: Oxford University Press, 2000.

———. "'Working towards the Führer.' Reflections on the Nature of the Hitler Dictatorship." *Contemporary European History* 2, no. 2 (July 1993): 103–18.

Kęszka, Sławomir. "Posługa polskich księży w KL Dachau i jej upamiętnienie." *Biuletyn Instytutu Pamięci Narodowej*, no. 146–47 (January–February 2018): 49–59.

Klee, Ernst. *Das Personenlexikon zum Dritten Reich: Wer war was vor und nach 1945*. Frankfurt am Main: Fischer Taschenbuch, 2003.

———. *Die SA Jesu Christi: Die Kirchen im Banne Hitlers*. Frankfurt-am-Main: Fischer Taschenbuch, 1989.

Kłoczowski, Jerzy. *A History of Polish Christianity*. Cambridge: Cambridge University Press, 2000.

Kłoczowski, Jerzy, Lidia Müllerowa, and Jan Skarbek, eds. *Zarys dziejów Kościoła katolickiego w Polsce*. Kraków: Wydawnictwo Znak, 1986.

Kochanski, Halik. *The Eagle Unbowed: Poland and the Poles in the Second World War*. Cambridge, MA: Harvard University Press, 2012.

Kogon, Eugen. *Der SS-Staat: das System der deutschen Konzentrationslager*. München: Kindler, 1997.

Kornberg, Jacques. *The Pope's Dilemma: Pius XII Faces Atrocities and Genocide in the Second World War*. Toronto: University of Toronto Press, 2015.

Korszyński, Franciszek. *Jasne promienie w Dachau*. Poznań: Pallotinum, 1957.

Kosmala, Beate. "Polnische Häftlinge im Konzentrationslager Dachau 1939–1945." *Dachauer Hefte* 21 (November 2005): 94–113.

Kowalski, Nikodem. "Cofta Czesław." In *Encyklopedia konspiracji Wielkopolskiej 1939–1945*, edited by Marian Woźniak, 124–25. Poznań: Instytut Zachodni, 1998.

———. "Jankowski Alfons." In *Encyklopedia konspiracji Wielkopolskiej 1939–1945*, edited by Marian Woźniak, 227. Poznań: Instytut Zachodni, 1998.

Köhler, Joachim. "Adolf Kardinal Bertram (1859–1945). Sein Umgang mit dem totalitären System des Nationalsozialismus." In *Katholische Kirche unter nationalsozialistischer und kommunistischer Diktatur. Deutschland und Polen 1939–1945*, edited by Hans-Jürgen Karp and Joachim Köhler, 175–93. Köln: Böhlau, 2001.

Kranz, Alexander. *Reichsstatthalter Arthur Greiser und die "Zivilverwaltung" im Wartheland 1939/1940: Die Bevölkerungspolitik in der ersten Phase der deutschen Besatzungsherrschaft in Polen*. Potsdam: Militärgeschichtliches Forschungsamt, 2010.

Krausnick, Helmut. "Denkschrift Himmlers über die Behandlung der Fremdvölkischen im Osten (Mai 1940)." *Vierteljahrshefte für Zeitgeschichte* 5, no. 2 (April 1957): 194–98.

Krausnick, Helmut, and Hans-Heinrich Wilhelm. *Die Truppe des Weltanschauungskrieges: Die Einsatzgruppen der Sicherheitspolizei und des SD 1938–1942*. Quellen und Darstellungen zur Zeitgeschichte 22. Stuttgart: Deutsche Verlags-Anstalt, 1981.

Król, Eugeniusz Cezary. *Propaganda i indoktrynacja narodowego socjalizmu w Niemczech 1919–1945: Studium organizacji, treści, metod i technik masowego oddziaływania*. Warszawa: Oficyna Wydawnicza Rytm, 1999.

Kundrus, Birthe. "Regime der Differenz: Volkstumspolitische Inklusionen und Exklusionen im Warthegau und im Generalgouvernement 1939–1944." In *Volksgemeinschaft: Neue Forschungen zur Gesellschaft des Nationalsozialismus*, edited by Frank Bajohr and Michael Wildt, 105–23. Frankfurt am Main: Fischer Taschenbuch, 2009.

Kulka, Otto Dov, and Paul R. Mendes-Flohr, eds. *Judaism and Christianity under the Impact of National Socialism*. Jerusalem: The Historical Society of Israel and The Zalman Shazar Center for Jewish History, 1987.

Kurek, Ewa. *Your Life Is Worth Mine: How Polish Nuns Saved Hundreds of Jewish Children in German-Occupied Poland, 1939–1945*. New York: Hippocrene, 1997.

Kut, Antoni, and Marian Woźniak. "Mirochna Stefan Julian." In *Encyklopedia konspiracji Wielkopolskiej 1939–1945*, edited by Marian Woźniak, 355. Poznań: Instytut Zachodni, 1998.

"Ląd–niemiecki obóz przejściowy dla duchowieństwa." *Kronika diecezji włocławskiej* 50, no. 6–10 (June–October 1967): 235–36.

Lehnstaedt, Stephan, and Jochen Böhler. "Einführung." In *Die Berichte der Einsatzgruppen in Polen 1939*, edited by Stephan Lehnstaedt and Jochen Böhler, 7–17. Berlin: Metropol, 2013.

Leszczyński, Kazimierz. "Działalność Einsatzgruppen Policji Bezpieczeństwa na Ziemiach Polskich w 1939r. w świetle Dokumentów." *Biuletyn Głównej Komisji Badania Zbrodni Hitlerowskich w Polsce* 22 (1971): 7–290.

Lewicki, Stanisław. *Radogoszcz*. Warszawa: Książka i Wiedza, 1971.

Libionka, Dariusz. "Antisemitism, Anti-Judaism, and the Polish Catholic Clergy during the Second World War, 1939–1945." In *Antisemitism and its Opponents in Modern Poland*, edited by Robert Blobaum, 233–64. Ithaca, NY: Cornell University Press, 2005.

———. "The Catholic Church in Poland and the Holocaust, 1939–1945." In *The Holocaust in the Christian World: Reflections on the Past, Challenges for the Future*, edited by Carol Rittner, Stephen D. Smith, and Irena Steinfeldt, 74–78. New York: Continuum, 2000.

———. "Duchowieństwo diecezji łomżyńskiej wobec antysemityzmu i zagłady Żydów." In *Wokół Jedwabnego*, edited by Paweł Machcewicz and Krzysztof Persak, vol. 1, 63–82. Warszawa: Instytut Pamięci Narodowej, 2002.

———. "Die Kirche in Polen und der Mord an den Juden im Licht der polnischen Publizistik und Historiographie nach 1945." *Zeitschrift für Ostmitteleuropa-Forschung* 51, no. 2 (2002): 188–215.

Librowski, Stanisław. *Ofiary zbrodni niemieckiej spośród duchowieństwa diecezji włocławskiej 1939–1945*. Włocławek: Księgarnia Powszechna i Drukarnia Diecezjalna, 1947.

Ligarski, Sebastian. *W kleszczach totalitaryzmów: Księdza Romana Gradowlewskiego i Ojca Jacka Hoszyckiego. Życiorysy niedopoweidziane*. Warszawa: Instytut Pamięci Narodowej–Komisja Ścigania Zbrodni Przeciwko Narodowi Polskiemu, 2017.

"Listy biskupa Michała Kozala z obozu koncentracyjnego w Dachau." *Studia włocławskie* 17 (2015): 539–61.

Loose, Ingo. "Wartheland." In *The Greater German Reich and the Jews: Nazi Persecution Policies in the Annexed Territories 1935–1945*, edited by Wolf Gruner and Jörg Osterloh, translated by Bernard Heise, 189–218. New York: Berghahn, 2015.

Lubicz, Jerzy, and Józef Woliński. "Polityka okupanta hitlerowskiego wobec wyznań religijnych w polsce w latach 1939–1945." *Biuletyn Głównej Komisji Badania Zbrodni Hitlerowskich w Polsce* 9 (1957): 71–111.

Lukas, Richard. *The Forgotten Holocaust: The Poles under German Occupation 1939–1945*. New York: Hippocrene, 1997.

Łuczak, Agnieszka. "Eksterminacja elit narodu polskiego w Wielkopolsce w 1939r." In *Konferencja: "Od Westerplatte do Norymbergi. Druga wojna światowa we współczesnej historiografii, muzealnictwie i edukacji" w Muzeum Stutthof (2–5 września 2009 r.)*, edited by Piotr Chruścielski and Marcin Owsiński, 57–65. Sztutowo, Poland: Muzeum Stutthof, 2009.

Łuczak, Agnieszka, and Aleksandra Pietrowicz. *Polityczne oczyszczanie gruntu: zagłada polskich elit w Wielkopolsce (1939–1941). Politische Flurbereinigung: die Vernichtung der polnischen Eliten in Großpolen (1939–1941)*. Poznań: Instytut Pamięci Narodowej, 2009.

Łuczak, Czesław. *Arthur Greiser: hitlerowski władza w Wolnym Mieście Gdańsku i w Kraju Warty*. Poznań, Poland: PSO, 1997.

———. "Das deutsche Okkupationssystem im unterworfenen Polen während des zweiten Weltkrieges." *Studia Historiae Oeconomicae* 22 (1997): 41–52.

———. *Pod niemieckim jarzmen (Kraj Warty 1939–1945)*. Poznań: Pracownie serwisu Oprogramowania, 1996.

Machcewicz, Paweł, and Krzysztof Persak, eds. *Wokół Jedwabnego*. Vol. 1. Warszawa: Instytut Pamięci Narodowej, 2002.

Madajczyk, Czesław. "Kościół a polityka okupanta na ziemiach polskich." In *Dzieje Polski a współczesność*, edited by Krystyna Sokól, 286–311. Warszawa: Książka i Wiedza, 1966.

———. *Die Okkupationspolitik Nazideutschlands in Polen 1939–1945*. Köln: Pahl-Rügenstein-Verlag, 1988.

———. *Politika III Rzeszy w okupowanej Polsce*, 2 vols. Warszawa: Państwowe Wydawnictwo Naukowe, 1970.

Malak, Henryk Maria. *Shavelings in Death Camps: A Polish Priest's Memoir of Imprisonment by the Nazis, 1939–1945*. Jefferson, NC: McFarland, 2012.

Mallmann, Klaus-Michael, and Bogdan Musial, eds. *Genesis des Genozids: Polen 1939–1941*. Darmstadt: Wissenschaftliche Buchgesellschaft, 2004.

Mazower, Mark. *Hitler's Empire: How the Nazis Ruled Europe*. New York: Penguin, 2008.

Messerschmidt, Manfred. *"Größte Härte . . .": Verbrechen der Wehrmacht in Polen September/Oktober 1939*. Vortrag bei der Eröffnung der gleichnamigen Ausstellung am 2. September 2005 in der Friedrich-Ebert-Stiftung Bonn. Vol. 63, Gesprächskreis Geschichte. Bonn: Historisches Forschungszentrum der Friedrich-Ebert-Stiftung, 2005.

Mistecka, Maria Lucyna. "Zakony żeńskie w życiu religijnym okupowanej Polski." In *Życie religijne w Polsce pod okupacją hitlerowską 1939–1945*, edited by Zygmunt Zieliński, 795–811. Warszawa: Ośrodek Dokumentacji i Studiów Społecznych, 1982.

Młynarczyk, Jacek Andrzej, ed. *Polen unter deutscher und sowjetischer Besatzung 1939–1945*. Vol. 20, Einzelveröffentlichungn des Deutschen Historischen Instituts Warschau. Osnabrück: Fibre, 2009.

Młynarczyk, Jacek Andrzej, and Jochen Böhler, eds. *Der Judenmord in den eingegliederten polnischen Gebieten 1939–1945*. Vol. 21, Einzelveröffentlichungen des Deutschen Historischen Instituts Warschau. Osnabrück: Fibre, 2010.

Modras, Ronald. *The Catholic Church and Antisemitism: Poland, 1933–1939*. Amsterdam: Harwood Academic Publishers, 2000.

Moll, Martin. "Der Reichsgau Steiermark 1938–1945." In *Die NS-Gaue: regionale Mittelinstanzen im zentralistischen "Führerstaat,"* edited by Jürgen John, Horst Möller, and Thomas Schaarschmidt, 364–77. München: R. Oldenbourg, 2007.

Mommsen, Hans. *From Weimar to Auschwitz*. Translated by Philip O'Connor. Princeton, NJ: Princeton University Press, 1991.

———. "Der Nationalsozialismus: kumulative Radikalisierung und Selbstzerstörung des Regimes." In *Meyers Enzyklopädisches Lexikon* 16, 785–90. Mannheim: Bibliographisches Institut, 1976.

———. "The Realization of the Unthinkable: The 'Final Solution of the Jewish Question' in the Third Reich." In *The Policies of Genocide: Jews and Soviet Prisoners of War in Nazi Germany*, edited by Gerhard Hirschfeld, 97–144. London: Allen and Unwin, 1986.

Montague, Patrick. *Chelmno and the Holocaust: The History of Hitler's First Death Camp*. Chapel Hill: University of North Carolina Press, 2012.

Müller, Klaus-Jürgen. *Das Heer und Hitler: Armee und nationalsozialistisches Regime 1933–1940*. Stuttgart: Deutsche Verlags-Anstalt, 1969.

Nawrocki, Stanisław. *Policja hitlerowska w tzw. Kraju Warty w latach 1939–1945*. Vol. 10, Badania nad okupacja niemiecką w Polsce. Poznań, Poland: Institut Zachodni, 1970.

Neuhäusler, Johannes. *What Was It like in the Concentration Camp at Dachau? An Attempt to Come Closer to the Truth*. München: Trustees for the Monument of Atonement in the Concentration Camp at Dachau, 1973.

Nicosia, Francis R. "Introduction: Resistance to National Socialism in the Work of Peter Hoffmann." In *Germans against Nazism: Nonconformity, Opposition, and Resistance in the Third Reich: Essays in Honour of Peter Hoffmann*, 2nd ed., edited by Francis R. Nicosia and Lawrence D. Stokes, 1–2. New York: Berghahn, 2015.

Nicosia, Francis R., and Lawrence D. Stokes, eds. *Germans against Nazism: Nonconformity, Opposition, and Resistance in the Third Reich: Essays in Honour of Peter Hoffmann*. 2nd ed. New York: Berghahn, 2015.

Nikisch, Jan Jacek. "Ojczyzna." In *Encyklopedia konspiracji w Wielkopolsce 1939–1945*, edited by Marian Woźniak, 399–402. Poznań: Instytut Zachodni, 1998.

———. "Prądzyński Józef." In *Encyklopedia konspiracji Wielkoplskiej 1939–1945*, edited by Marian Woźniak, 466–67. Poznań: Instytut Zachodni, 1998.

Niklewska, Waleria Syksta. *Służebnicki Niepokalanego Poczęcia Najświętszej Maryi Panny (Pleszew)*. Vol. 3, Żeńskie zgromadzenia zakonne w Polsce 1939–1947. Lublin: Redakcja Wydawnictw Katolickiego Uniwersytetu Lubelskiego, 1985.

Nitecki, Piotr. *Biskupi kościoła w Polsce: słownik biograficzny*. Warszawa: Ośrodek Dokumentacji i Studiów Społecznych, 1992.

Olszewski, Marian. *Fort VII w Poznaniu*. Poznań, Poland: Wydawnictwo Poznańskie, 1974.

———. *Straty i martyrologia ludności polskiej w Poznaniu 1939–1945*. Poznań: Wydawnictwo Poznańskie, 1973.

Paczkowski, Andrzej. *The Spring Will Be Ours: Poland and the Poles from Occupation to Freedom*. Translated by Jane Cave. University Park: Pennsylvania State University Press, 2003.

Pawlikowski, John T. "The Nazi Attack on the Polish Nation: Towards a New Understanding." In *Holocaust and Church Struggle: Religion, Power and the Politics of Resistance*, edited by Hubert G. Locke and Marcia Sachs Littell, 33–44. Vol. 16, Studies in the Shoah. Lanham, MD: University Press of America, 1996.

Pease, Neil. *Rome's Most Faithful Daughter: The Catholic Church and Independent Poland, 1914–1939*. Athens: Ohio University Press, 2009.

Peukert, Detlev J. K. *Inside Nazi Germany: Conformity, Opposition, and Racism in Everyday Life*. New Haven, CT: Yale University Press, 1987.

Phayer, Michael. *The Catholic Church and the Holocaust, 1930–1965*. Bloomington: Indiana University Press, 2000.

———. *Pius XII, the Holocaust, and the Cold War*. Bloomington: Indiana University Press, 2008.

Pieniężna, Izabela. "Zakonnice i zakonnicy w niemieckich więzieniach i obozach zbiorczych w Kraju Warty 1939–1945." In *Konferencja "Od Westerplatte do Norymbergi. Druga wojna światowa we współczesnej historiografii, muzealnictwie i edukacji w Muzeum Stutthof (2–5 września 2009 r.),"* edited by Piotr Chruścielski and Marcin Owsiński, 242–55. Sztutowo, Poland: Muzeum Stutthof, 2009.

Pietrowicz, Aleksandra. "Die Widerstandsbewegung in den eingegliederten polnischen Gebieten 1939–1945." In *Polen unter deutscher und sowjetischer Besatzung 1939–1945*, edited by Jacek Andrzej Młynarczyk, 427–51. Vol. 20, Einzelveröffentlichungen des Deutschen Historischen Instituts Warschau. Osnabrück: Fibre, 2009.

Pietrzak, Jerzy. "Dymek Walenty." In *Wielkopolski słownik biograficzny*, edited by Antoni Gąsiorowski and Jerzy Topolski, 165–66. Poznań: Państwowe Wydawnictwo Naukowe, 1981.

Pohl, Dieter. "Die Reichsgaue Danzig-Westpreußen und Wartheland: Koloniale Verwaltung oder Modell für die zukünftige Gauverwaltung?" In *Die NS-Gaue: regionale Mittelinstanzen im zentralistischen "Führerstaat,"* edited by Jürgen John, Horst Möller, and Thomas Schaarschmidt, 395–405. München: R. Oldenbourg, 2007.

Pollmann, Viktoria. *Untermieter im christlichen Haus: die Kirche und die 'jüdische Frage' in Polen anhand der Bistumspresse der Metropolie Krakau 1926–1939*. Wiesbaden: Harrassowitz, 2001.

Porter-Szűcs, Brian. *Faith and Fatherland: Catholicism, Modernity, and Poland*. New York: Oxford University Press, 2011.

Porzycki, Wiesław. *Posłudzni aż do śmierci (niemieccy urzędnicy w Kraju Warty 1939–1945)*. Vol. 3, Dzieje Gospodarcze Wielkopolski. Poznań: PSO, 1997.

Powidzki, Janusz. "Losy katedry gneiźnieńskiej podczas okupacji 1939–1945." In *Święty Wojciech 997–1947: księga pamiątkowa*, edited by Zbigniew Bernacki, 293–318. Gniezno: Wydawnictwo Kurii Metropolitalnej w Gnieźnie, 1947.

Prawdzić, Alicja. "Hitlerowska obóz dla sióstr zakonnych w Bojanowie 1941–1943." *Chrześcijanin w świecie* 10 (1978): 21–40.

Radoński, Karol. "Papież a Polska." *Wiadomości Polskie*, November 15, 1942.

Rahe, Thomas. "Die Bedeutung von Religion und Religiosität in den KZs." In *Die nationalsozialistischen Konzentrationslager-Entwicklung und Struktur*, vol. 2, edited by Ulrich Herbert, Karin Orth, and Christoph Dieckmann, 1006–22. Göttingen: Wallstein, 1998.

Ramet, Sabrina P. *The Catholic Church in Polish History: From 966 to the Present*. New York: Palgrave Macmillan, 2017.

Rogall, Joachim, ed. *Die Räumung des "Reichsgaus Wartheland" vom 16. bis 26. January 1945 im Spiegel amtlicher Berichte*. Sigmaringen, Ger.: Jan Thorbecke, 1993.

Romanowski, Zdiszław. "Poprzez Gdańsk do Poznania." *Nurt: miesięcznik społeczno-kulturalny* 5, no. 13 (May 1966): 8–11.

Rossino, Alexander B. *Hitler Strikes Poland: Blitzkrieg, Ideology, and Atrocity*. Lawrence: University Press of Kansas, 2003.

Röhr, Werner. "'Reichsgau Wartheland' 1939–1945: vom 'Exerzierplatz des praktischen Nationalsozialismus' zum 'Mustergau'?" *Bulletin für Faschismus- und Weltkriegsforschung* 18 (2002): 29–54.

Rudnicki, Szymon. "Anti-Jewish Legislation in Interwar Poland." In *Antisemitism and its Opponents in Modern Poland*, edited by Robert Blobaum, 148–70. Ithaca, NY: Cornell University Press, 2005.

Rutherford, Phillip. *Prelude to the Final Solution: The Nazi Program for Deporting Ethnic Poles, 1939–1941*. Lawrence: University Press of Kansas, 2007.

Rutowska, Maria. *Lager Glowna: niemiecki obóz przesiedleńczy na Głównej w Poznaniu dla ludności polskiej (1939–1940)*. Vol. 16, Documenta Occupationis. Poznań: Instytut Zachodni, 2008.

———. "NS-Verfolgungsmaßnahmen in den eingegliderten Gebieten." In *Polen unter deutscher und sowjetischer Besatzung 1939–1945*, edited by Jacek Andrzej Młynarczyk,

197–216. Vol. 20, Einzelveröffentlichungen des Deutschen Historischen Instituts Warschau. Osnabrück: Fibre, 2009.

———. *Wysiedlenia ludności polskiej z Kraju Warty do Generalnego Gubernatorstwa 1939–1941*. Vol. 71, Prace Instytutu Zachodniego. Poznań, Poland: Instytut Zachodni, 2003.

Sadkowski, Konrad. "Clerical Nationalism and Antisemitism: Catholic Priests, Jews, and Orthodox Christians in the Lublin Region, 1918–1939." In *Antisemitism and its Opponents in Modern Poland*, edited by Robert Blobaum, 171–88. Ithaca, NY: Cornell University Press, 2005.

Sànchez, José M. *Pius XII and the Holocaust: Understanding the Controversy*. Washington, DC: Catholic University Press, 2002.

Schleunes, Karl. *The Twisted Road to Auschwitz: Nazi Policy toward German Jews, 1933–1939*. Urbana: University of Illinois Press, 1979.

Schnabel, Reimund. *Die Frommen in der Hölle: Geistliche in Dachau*. Frankfurt am Main: Röderberg, 1966.

Schwanninger, Florian. "The Murders of Priests at Hartheim Castle under 'Sonderbehandlung 14f13.'" *Studia nad Totalitaryzmami i Wiekiem XX—Totalitarian and 20th Century Studies* 2 (2018): 158–69.

———. "'Wenn Du nicht arbeiten kannst, schicken wir Dich zum Vergasen.': Die 'Sonderbehandlung 14f13' im Schloss Hartheim 1941–1944." In *Tötungsanstalt Hartheim*, edited by Brigitte Kepplinger, Gerhart Marckhgott, and Hartmut Reese, 155–208. Vol. 3, Oberösterreich in der Zeit des Nationalsozialismus. Linz: Oberösterreichischen Landesarchiv/Lern- und Gedenkort Schloss Hartheim, 2008.

Serwański, Edward. "Materiały do sprawy eksterminacji w tzw. Kraju Warty, Powiaty: Wieluń–woj. Łódzkie, Gostynin–woj. Warszawskie." *Przegląd Zachodni* 12 (1955): 616–21.

———. *Wielkopolska w cieniu swastiki*. Warszawa: Instytut Wydawniczy "Pax," 1970.

Siepracka, Dorota. "Die Einstellung der Christlichen Polen gegenüber der jüdischen Bevölkerung im Wartheland." In *Der Judenmord in den eingegliederten polnischen Gebieten 1939–1945*, edited by Jacek Andrzej Młynarczyk und Jochen Böhler, 345–68. Vol. 21, Einzelveröffentlichungen des Deutschen Historischen Instituts Warschau. Osnabrück: Fibre, 2010.

Sigel, Robert. "The Cultivation of Medicinal Herbs in the Concentration Camp: The Plantation at Dachau." *Dachau Review* 2 (1990): 78–86.

Sipowicz, Kasper. *Prześladowania religijne w Kraju Warty: represje wobec Polaków i duchowieństwa polskiego a polityka wyznaniowa rządu III Rzeszy 1939–1945*. Łódź: Księży Młyn Dom Wydawniczy, 2016.

Smelser, Ronald M., and Rainer Zitelmann, eds. *Die Braune Elite II. 21 weitere biographische Skizzen*. Darmstadt, Ger.: Wissenschaftliche Buchgesellschaft, 1993.

Sokól, Krystyna, ed. *Dzieje Polski a współczesność*. Warszawa: Książka i Wiedza, 1966.

Sołomieniuk, Michał. "Katedra gnieźnieńska: polsko-niemieckie zmagania o symbole w czasie zaborów, dwudziestolecia międzywojennego i okupacji hitlerowskiej." *Seminare* 39, no. 3 (2018): 169–81.

Spicer, Kevin P. *Hitler's Priests: Catholic Clergy and National Socialism*. DeKalb: Northern Illinois University Press, 2008.

Stasiewski, Bernhard. "Die Kirchenpolitik der Nationalsozialisten im Warthegau 1939–1945," *Vierteljahrshefte für Zeitgeschichte* 7, no. 1 (1959): 46–74.

Stehle, Hansjakob. "Ein Eiferer in der Gesellschaft von Mördern," *Die Zeit*, October 7, 1983, 12.

Steigmann-Gall, Richard. "Christianity and the Nazi Movement: A Response." *Journal of Contemporary History* 42, no. 2 (April 2007): 185–211.

———. *The Holy Reich: Nazi Conceptions of Christianity, 1919–1945*. Cambridge: Cambridge University Press, 2003.

Stopniak, Franciszek, ed. *Kościół katolicki na ziemiach Polski w czasie II Wojny Światowej: Materiały i Studia*, vol. 7, no. 3. Warszawa: Akademia Teologii Katolickiej, 1978.

Strobel, Georg W. "Die Kirche Polens, das gesellschaftliche Deutschensyndrom und beider Rolle bei der Sowjetisierung Polens." In *Katholische Kirche unter nationalsozialistischer und kommunistischer Diktatur: Deutschland und Polen 1939–1989*, edited by Hans-Jürgen Karp und Joachim Köhler, 103–31. Köln: Böhlau, 2001.

Sziling, Jan. "Hitlerowska polityka eksterminacji duchowieństwa katolickiego w Kraju Warty." In *Akcje okupanta hitlerowskiego wobec Kościoła katolickiego w Kraju Warty*, edited by Antoni Galiński and Marek Budziarek, 13–23. Łódź: Okręgowa Komisja Badania Zbrodni Przeciwko Narodowi Polskiemu w Łodzi–Instytutu Pamięci Narodowej/Muzeum Historii Łodzi, 1997.

———. "Die Kirchen im Generalgouvernement." *Miscellanea Historiae Ecclesiasticae* 9 (1984): 277–88.

———. *Polityka okupanta hitlerowskiego wobec Kościoła katolickiego 1939–1945: tzw. okręgi Rzeszy: Gdańsk-Prusy Zachodnie, kraj Warty i regencja Katowicka*. Vol. 11, Badania nad okupacją niemiecką w Polsce. Poznań: Instytut Zachodni, 1970.

Śmigiel, Kazimierz. "Die apostolischen Administratoren Walenty Dymek und Hilarius Breitinger." In *Katholische Kirche unter nationalsozialistischer und kommunistischer Diktatur: Deutschland und Polen 1939–1989*, edited by Hans-Jürgen Karp and Joachim Köhler, 259–64. Vol. 32, Forschungen und Quellen zur Kirchen- und Kulturgeschichte Ostdeutschlands. Köln: Böhlau, 2001.

———. *Die katholische Kirche im Reichsgau Wartheland*. Series A, vol. 40, Veröffentlichungen der Forschungsstelle Ostmitteleuropa an der Universität Dortmund. Dortmund: Forschungsstelle Ostmitteleuropa, 1984.

———. *Kościół katolicki w tzw. Okręgu Warty 1939–1945*. Lublin: Katolicki Uniwersytet Lubelski, 1979.

———. "Losy Kościoła katolickiego w okupowanym Poznaniu," *Kronika miasta Poznania* 77, no. 3 (2009): 63–78.

———. "Tajne duszpasterstwo w Wielkopolsce." In *Encyklopedia konspiracji Wielkopolskiej 1939–1945*, edited by Marian Woźniak, 572–73. Poznań: Instytut Zachodni, 1998.

———. "Walka władz hitlerowskich z katolickim kultem religijnym na terenie archidiecezji gnieźnieńskiej w latach 1939–1945." In *Studia Historyczne*, vol. 2, Towarzystwo Naukowe Katolickiego Uniwersytetu Lubelskiego–Rozprawy Wydziału Historyczno-Filologicznego, no. 34, 251–387. Lublin: Towarzystwo Naukowe Katolickiego Uniwersytetu Lubelskiego, 1968.

———. "Życie religijne w 'Kraju Warty.'" In *Życie religijne w Polsce pod okupacją hitlerowską 1939–1945*, edited by Zygmunt Zieliński, 57–75. Warszawa: Ośrodek Dokumentacji i Studiów Społecznych, 1982.

Świniarski, Józef. "Ląd–niedawny etap męczeństwa." *Kronika diecezji włocławskiej* 50, no. 6–10 (June–October 1967): 225–35.

Thoma, Emil. *Die Geistlichen in Dachau sowie in anderen Konzentrationslager und Gefängnissen*. Mödling, Austria: Missionsdruckerei St. Gabriel, 1971.

Toborek, Tomasz, and Michał Trębacz, eds. *Łódź pod okupacją 1939–1945: Studia i szkice*. Vol. 45, Biblioteka Oddziału Instytutu Pamięci Narodowej w Łodzi. Łódź: Instytut Pamięci Narodowej, 2018.

Tooze, Adam. *The Wages of Destruction: The Making and Breaking of the Nazi Economy*. New York: Penguin, 2006.

"Die Trauerfeier auf dem Hauptfriedhof." *Ostdeutscher Beobachter*, April 14, 1944, 4.

United States National Catholic Welfare Conference. *The Nazi War against the Catholic Church*. Washington, DC: National Catholic Welfare Conference, 1943.

Ventresca, Robert A. *Soldier of Christ: The Life of Pope Pius XII*. Cambridge, MA: Belknap, 2013.

Wachsmann, Nikolaus. *KL: A History of the Nazi Concentration Camps*. New York: Farrar, Straus and Giroux, 2015.

Wagner, Jens-Christian. "Work and Extermination in the Concentration Camps." In *Concentration Camps in Nazi Germany: The New Histories*, edited by Jane Caplan and Nikolaus Wachsmann, 127–48. London: Routledge, 2010.

Walkusz, Jan. "Kontakty polonijnego duszpasterza ks. Wawrzyńca Wnuka z Polską." *Roczniki Historii Kościoła* 1, no. 3 (58) (2011): 133–46.

Wardzyńska, Maria. *Był rok 1939: operacja niemieckiej policji bezpieczeństwa w Polsce. Intelligenzaktion*. Warszawa: Instytut Pamięci Narodowej-Komisja Ścigania Zbrodni Przeciwko Narodowi Polskiemu, 2009.

Waszkiewicz, Zofia. *Polityka Watykanu wobec Polski 1939–1945*. Warszawa: Państwowe Wydawnictwo Naukowe, 1980.

Wąsowicz, Jarosław. *Lądzcy męczennicy: obóz dla duchowieństwa w Lądzie n/Wartą styczeń 1940–październik 1941*. Ląd: WSD Towarzystwa Salezjańskiego w Lądzie, 2013.

Weinberg, Gerhard L. *Germany, Hitler, and World War II: Essays in Modern German and World History*. Cambridge: Cambridge University Press, 1996.

Weitbrecht, Dorothee. "Ermächtigung zur Vernichtung: die Einsatzgruppen in Polen im Herbst 1939." In *Genesis des Genozids: Polen 1939–1941*, edited by Klaus-Michael Mallmann and Bogdan Musial, 57–70. Darmstadt: Wissenschaftliche Buchgesellschaft, 2004.

Wełniak, Renata. *Duchowieństwo w obozie żabikowskim (1943–1945)*. Żabikowo, Poland: Muzeum Martyrologiczne, 2010.

Wietrzykowski, Albin. *Powrót Arthura Greisera*. Poznań: Pomóc, 1946.

Winnicka Krystyna. "Camp pour les religieuses organisé par les Allemands à Bojanowo." *Miscellanea Historiae Ecclesiasticae* 9. Vol. 70, Bibliothèque de la revue d'histoire ecclésiastique, fascicule. Bruxelles: Éditions Nauwelaerts, 1984, 434.

Woźniak, Marian, ed. *Encyklopedia konspiracji Wielkopolskiej 1939–1945*. Poznań: Instytut Zachodni, 1998.

———. "Kaźmierski Edward Stanisław." In *Encyklopedia konspiracji Wielkopolskiej 1939–1945*, edited by Marian Woźniak, 254–55. Poznań: Instytut Zachodni, 1998.

———. "Kęsy Franciszek." In *Encyklopedia konspiracji Wielkopolskiej 1939–1945*, edited by Marian Woźniak, 257. Poznań: Instytut Zachodni, 1998.

———. "Kliński, Edward." In *Encyklopedia konspiracji Wielkopolskiej 1939–1945*, edited by Marian Woźniak, 263. Poznań: Instytut Zachodni, 1998.

———. "Szklarek-Trzcielski Henryk." In *Encyklopedia konspiracji Wielkopolskiej 1939–1945*, edited by Marian Woźniak, 548. Poznań: Instytut Zachodni, 1998.

———. "Wojciechowski Jarogniew." In *Encyklopedia konspiracji Wielkopolskiej 1939–1945*, edited by Marian Woźniak, 641. Poznań: Instytut Zachodni, 1998.

Wrońska, Małgorzata Wirgilia. "Służebniczki Maryi (pleszewskie)." In *Życie religijne w Polsce pod okupacją hitlerowską 1939–1945*, edited by Zygmunt Zieliński, 905–30. Warszawa: Ośrodek Dokumentacji i Studiów Społecznych, 1982.

"Wstęp." In *Położenie ludności polskiej w tzw. Kraju Warty w okresie hitlerowskiej okupacji*, edited by Marian Olszewski, V–XVI. Vol. 13, Documenta Occupationis. Poznań: Instytut Zachodni, 1990.

Ziegler, Armin. *Wer kennt schon Zabikowo . . . : Ein Bericht über das "Polizeigefängnis der Sicherheitspolizei und SS-Arbeitserziehungslager Posen-Lenzingen."* Schönaich, Ger.: Armin Ziegler, 1994.

Zieliński, Zygmunt. "Activities of Catholic Orders on Behalf of Jews in Nazi-Occupied Poland." In *Judaism and Christianity under the Impact of National Socialism*, edited by Otto Dov Kulka and Paul R. Mendes-Flohr, 381–94. Jerusalem: The Historical Society of Israel and the Zalman Shazar Center for Jewish History, 1987.

———. *Życie religijne w Polsce pod okupacją hitlerowską 1939–1945*. Warszawa: Ośrodek Dokumentacji i Studiów Społecznych, 1982.

Zimmerman, Joshua D., ed. *Contested Memories: Poles and Jews During the Holocaust and its Aftermath*. New Brunswick: Rutgers University Press, 2003.

Zipfel, Friedrich. *Kirchenkampf in Deutschland 1933–1945: Religionsverfolgung und Selbstbehauptung der Kirchen in der nationalsozialistischen Zeit*. Vol. 11, Veröffentlichungen der Historischen Kommission zu Berlin beim Friedrich-Meinecke-Institut der Freien Universität Berlin. Vol. 1, Publikationen der Forschungsgruppe Berliner Widerstand beim Senator für Inneres von Berlin. Berlin: Walter de Gruyter, 1965.

Żbikowski, Andrzej, ed. *Polacy i Żydzi pod okupacją niemiecką 1939–1945: studia i materiały*. Warszawa: Instytut Pamięci Narodowej–Komisja Ścigania Zbrodni Przeciwko Narodowi Polskiemu, 2006.

INDEX

JONATHAN HUENER is Associate Professor of History at the University of Vermont and author of *Auschwitz, Poland, and the Politics of Commemoration, 1945–1979*.

Lightning Source UK Ltd.
Milton Keynes UK
UKHW040643131021
391805UK00012B/238

9 780253 054043